The English Short Story
in Canada

The English Short Story in Canada
From the Dawn of Modernism to the 2013 Nobel Prize

REINGARD M. NISCHIK

McFarland & Company, Inc., Publishers
Jefferson, North Carolina

LIBRARY OF CONGRESS CATALOGUING-IN-PUBLICATION DATA

Names: Nischik, Reingard M., author.
Title: The English short story in Canada : from the dawn of modernism to the 2013 Nobel Prize / Reingard M. Nischik.
Description: Jefferson, North Carolina : McFarland & Company, Inc., Publishers, 2017. | Includes bibliographical references and index.
Identifiers: LCCN 2017008648 | ISBN 9781476668598 (softcover : acid free paper) ∞
Subjects: LCSH: Short stories, Canadian—History and criticism. | Canadian fiction—History and criticism.
Classification: LCC PR9192.52 .N576 2017 | DDC 813/.0109971—dc23
LC record available at https://lccn.loc.gov/2017008648

BRITISH LIBRARY CATALOGUING DATA ARE AVAILABLE

ISBN (print) 978-1-4766-6859-8
ISBN (ebook) 978-1-4766-2807-3

© 2017 Reingard M. Nischik. All rights reserved

No part of this book may be reproduced or transmitted in any form or by any means, electronic or mechanical, including photocopying or recording, or by any information storage and retrieval system, without permission in writing from the publisher.

Front cover image © 2017 iStock

Printed in the United States of America

McFarland & Company, Inc., Publishers
  Box 611, Jefferson, North Carolina 28640
  www.mcfarlandpub.com

Acknowledgments

Surveying a century's worth of rich material provided by the Canadian short story, this book has of necessity required many years to take shape. Accordingly, various student assistants of mine have been helpful with the intensive research in connection with the present study, and I thank all of them collectively here. I would, however, like to express special thanks to the most recent student assistants who have been involved with this book. Katrin Schmitt always retained her good spirits while tackling numerous bibliographical checks and solved all the bibliographical riddles conscientiously and reliably. She and Bettina Mack, MA, were also very helpful with the research for the most recent chapter I wrote for this book, on the motif of aging in the Canadian short story. The best thing that can happen in such a collaboration between professor and student assistants is that the latter, too, develop a strong interest in the topic, and that happened here. Srdjan Perko very patiently read the complete manuscript twice and was very helpful with polishing the text further. In addition to me, he also did the proofreading before print. Dr. Emily Petermann read the introduction and Chapters 5 and 8 and made very useful suggestions. As always, I could count on Christine Schneider's expertise and reliability for the technical formatting of the manuscript. Elvira Weimann and Katrin Schmitt meticulously prepared the index.

With such rich and extensive material and so long a gestation period as with the book at hand, it seems apt that many chapters are based on earlier separate publications of mine, which I had, however, always envisioned as eventually coming together in a monograph on the Canadian short story. Other chapters appear here for the first time. The chapters with topics I published on earlier have all been revised (updated, partly rewritten, shortened or extended, integratively linked to one another) for this book's publication. Against this background, I acknowledge the publication of earlier versions of the following, and I thank all the publishers concerned for their permission to make use of the texts for the present book: chapters 1 and 3 in Reingard M. Nischik, ed., *History of Literature in Canada* (Rochester: Camden House, 2008);

chapters 2 and 9 in Reingard M. Nischik, *Comparative North American Studies: Transnational Approaches to American and Canadian Literature and Culture* (New York: Palgrave Macmillan, 2016); Chapter 4 in *Études Canadiennes/Canadian Studies* (2014); Chapter 6 in Martin Kuester and Charlotte Sturgess, eds., *Reading/s from a Distance: European Perspectives on Canadian Women's Writing* (Augsburg: Wißner, 2008); Chapter 7 in J. Brooks Bouson, ed., *Margaret Atwood: Critical Insights* (Ipswich, MA: Salem Press, 2013); Chapter 10 in Jutta Ernst and Brigitte Glaser, eds., *The Canadian Mosaic in the Age of Transnationalism* (Heidelberg: Winter, 2010); chapters 11 and 12 and a part of Chapter 6 in Reingard M. Nischik, ed., *The Canadian Short Story: Interpretations* (Rochester: Camden House, 2007); Chapter 13 in Eva Gruber, ed., *Thomas King: Works and Impact* (Rochester: Camden House, 2012); and Chapter 14 in *Margaret Atwood Studies* (2011).

Finally, some personal remarks seem to be in order. Although it was unplanned in this particular constellation, this book has turned out to be a precious anniversary book for me in several respects. It is my thirtieth book, and so I am particularly aware of what it signifies for my scholarly work. Both Canadian literature and the short story have been lasting interests throughout my career, so it seems appropriate that it should be this book that brings together both interests. In this particular combination, my scholarly pursuits have been on-going for more than 30 years now (my first publication on the Canadian short story dates back to 1982). As such an enduring devotion and fascination would indicate, this book also includes, along with innumerable other writers of the Canadian short story, treatments of two of my long-time favorite writers, one of whom ranks among Canada's top short story writers, next to her numerous other achievements, while the other is a pure short story writer: Margaret Atwood and Alice Munro.

The number "30" is of other, still more personal, significance for me. The year this book is published marks the thirtieth anniversary of the two by far most important strands of my adult life: It was in my *annus mirabilis* 1987 that I met my beloved partner, and only two months later in the same year, at the age of 34, that I was first appointed professor, then at the University of Mainz—which at the time, by truly miraculous and fateful coincidence, brought my private and professional lives geographically close together. So, finally, not having thanked my precious partner in a book since 1991, here is, for the second and for all times, a deeply heart-felt, extremely grateful *Thank You* for making life so beautiful, and for, highly empathetically, having borne so long with my other, time-consuming love relationship with literature and scholarship.

Table of Contents

Acknowledgments   v
A Note on Terminology   ix
Introduction   1

Part One: History

1. The Modernist Canadian Short Story: Forging a Tradition   15
2. The Modernist Canadian and American Short Story: A Comparative Approach   28
3. The Canadian Short Story Since 1967: Between (Post)Modernism and (Neo)Realism   48
4. The Noble Genre: Alice Munro Brings the Nobel Prize in Literature to Canada   71

Part Two: Approaches

5. "Pen Photographs": On Short Story Poetics and the Canadian Short Story Cycle   85
6. Multiple Challenges: The Canadian Artist Story and Gender   95
7. Gender and Genre: Margaret Atwood's Short Stories and Short Fictions   106
8. Multiple Liminality: Aging in the Canadian Short Story   118
9. Liminal Spaces, Liminal States: Crossing the Canada–U.S. Border in Canadian Border Stories   135

10. Cultural Locations of Ethnicity: Vancouver Short Fiction
by First Nations and Chinese Canadian Writers
in English 150

Part Three: Analyses

11. (Un-)Doing Gender: Alice Munro, "Boys and Girls" 165
12. Canadian Artist Stories: John Metcalf, "The Strange
Aberration of Mr. Ken Smythe" 176
13. Blending Indigenous and Western Traditions
of Storytelling: Thomas King's Short Fiction 189
14. Crossing Generic Borders: Margaret Atwood's
Short Prose Collection *The Tent* 203

Chapter Notes 211
Works Cited 225
Index 243

A Note on Terminology

In accordance with common usage in Canadian Studies and Quebec Studies, formulations such as "the Canadian short story" or "Canadian literature" throughout this book refer exclusively to Canadian literary texts written in English. Literature in Canada written in French in the province of Quebec is commonly referred to as "Quebecois literature" (on such fundamental, also terminological, issues in Canada see Nischik 2008b, especially 4-7; on the relationship between English Canada and French Canada/Quebec see Nischik 2008a as well as Nischik 2014, especially chs. 1, 7, and 12). As the title indicates, this book, then, deals with the Canadian short story written in English. The Quebecois *conte* or *nouvelle* forms a different tradition of storytelling that is beyond the scope of this work (and is dealt with, for instance, in Eibl 2008a and 2008b).

For "A Note on the Works Cited and the Index" see the end of the Introduction.

Introduction

The Canadian short story is a relatively recent literary phenomenon, spanning not much more than a hundred years to date in its main course of development. With the emergence of the short story as a national genre in Canada toward the end of the nineteenth century, the genre became established in Canada some 70 years after the beginnings of the American short story around 1820. Canadian short stories of the late nineteenth century (written by Isabella Valancy Crawford, Susan Frances Harrison, Ernest Thompson Seton, and Charles G. D. Roberts), to say nothing of even earlier stories from around the middle of the nineteenth century, could not live up to the excellence and impact of American short story writers of the American Renaissance (around the middle of the nineteenth century), such as Nathaniel Hawthorne, Edgar Allan Poe, and Herman Melville. It was only with Raymond Knister and Morley Callaghan's development of the modernist Canadian short story in the 1920s that the genre came into its own in Canada in the twentieth century. The crucial ascent of the short story in Canada, however, began in the 1960s (see also Nischik 1987), raising the quality, diversity, and prominence of the genre in Canada to new heights, and reached a climax in the bestowal of the Nobel Prize in Literature to Canadian short story writer Alice Munro in 2013.

The short story in Canada is a particularly productive and vital genre today. Its continuing success is reflected, first of all, in the fact that major Canadian writers have almost without exception devoted considerable effort to the form, and have succeeded in producing internationally acknowledged collections of short stories. Second, several Canadian short story writers undoubtedly rank among the world's best—and best-known—contemporary writers of short fiction, in particular Alice Munro and Margaret Atwood. Not only have these authors had devoted readerships at home and abroad, they have also gained international recognition from critics and scholars alike, as well as major international literary prizes for their works. Several Canadian writers have first published their short stories in *The New Yorker*, the genre's foremost international forum. Even leaving international achievements aside, the contemporary Canadian short story is highly productive. For more than 30 years now, one in three Governor General's Awards (here: for Fiction), Canada's top literary prize, have been given to short story collections rather than novels. Furthermore, the number of anthologies of Canadian short stories published in Canada has been remarkably high.

In contrast to this, literary theory and criticism have hardly engaged with the Canadian short story. The relatively few existing contributions can be broken up into the categories of historical, generic or subgeneric, literary-sociological, narratological, regional, and didactic approaches (see also "Further Reading" in Nischik 2007, 387–88). Historical approaches are more common, yet only few relatively systematic and wide-ranging historical surveys (outside the literary histories) of the Canadian short story have been undertaken so far (Gadpaille 1988 and 2001; Nischik 2007). Students and scholars thus often lack the necessary generic context when studying the Canadian short story or individual stories. The present project contributes to filling this gap. It does so by honoring the fact that the crucial development of the Canadian short story began in the 1920s, that is, in the period of modernism. Thus, after a short contextualizing look at the short story in Canada *before* modernism in the introduction, this book sets out to trace major developments and qualitative highlights of the Canadian short story since modernism throughout the twentieth and into the twenty-first century, up to the point when Alice Munro, in 2013, received the Nobel Prize in Literature explicitly for her short story oeuvre.

The tripartite structure of the book at hand approaches its vast and rich material via a mainly historical approach in Part One (chapters 1–4), then features important approaches to Canadian short fiction in Part Two (chapters 5–10), before finally zooming in on individual short stories, a story collection, and a single author's oeuvre in Part Three (chapters 11–14). The three historical survey chapters of Part One respectively deal with the modernist Canadian short story, subsequently with a comparative angle on the development of the modernist Canadian and American short story, and finally with the Canadian short story since 1967. Chapter 4 then zooms in on the defining moment when the short story, through the works of Alice Munro, was awarded its first Nobel Prize in Literature, as well as the first for Canada. The chapters of Part Two (chapters 5–10) respectively present a focus on the Canadian short story cycle, the Canadian artist story, the combination of gender and genre in short fiction, Canadian border narratives, and cultural locations of ethnicity in short fiction by First Nations and Chinese Canadian writers. Part Three (chapters 11–14) contains chapters that center on individual short stories (by Alice Munro and by John Metcalf, respectively), on one short story collection (Margaret Atwood's later short prose collection *The Tent*), and on a complete short story oeuvre (by First Nations writer Thomas King). These concluding chapters link up to the focus on approaches in the preceding part by means of textual examples dealing with gender, with the figure of the artist, and with ethnicity as crucial motifs in Canadian short fiction. The final chapter considers the genre-bending aspects of Canada's most varied short story oeuvre with an analysis of Atwood's *The Tent* that suggests the short story's "limitless possibilities" (Matthews 1994, 48).

Early Canadian Short Prose

> At the time of Confederation in 1867, short fiction already filled the magazines of the new country. These early stories, however, differed from the modern short story, often being closer in form and content to other prose genres such as the sketch, anecdote, editorial, and essay.... Today's definitions of short fiction must be relaxed when one surveys fiction of these earlier times...; much that was then considered excellent writing, appears nauseatingly sweet to the twentieth-century reader.

Thus begins Michelle Gadpaille's short survey of "Canadian Short Fiction" (2001, 2898). Indeed, numerous short stories had been written and published by the middle of the nineteenth century in Canada, though they have been largely ignored by processes of canon formation and have had less of an influence on the development of the short story genre in Canada. These texts include sketches of pioneer life by authors such as Susanna Moodie and Catharine Parr Traill, popular sentimental fiction by May Agnes Fleming, and pieces of social critique by Harriet Vaughan Cheney and others (for a collection of women's fiction of the early to mid-nineteenth century, see McMullen and Campbell 1993).

Gadpaille indicates parallels and divergences between early Canadian and early American short fiction, American short fiction having been more of a model for the developing genre in Canada than British short fiction. Among the parallels are the role of the sketch and the anecdote as significant antecedents of the short story; the fact that many writers of short fiction worked in journalism as well, which bears on the structure and style of their fiction; and the presence of strong local color traditions in both literatures in the last decades of the nineteenth century, which resulted in the genre moving toward naturalism and realism. Among the divergences between early Canadian and American short fiction, Gadpaille mentions the French Canadian development[1]; the relative lack of an African Canadian tradition of storytelling in Canada, in contrast to African American works such as those of Charles W. Chesnutt; the lesser importance of the tall tale, as represented by Mark Twain in the United States; and the lack of "the detective, supernatural, or scientifically speculative tale" (Gadpaille 2001, 2899) in Canada in the tradition of Edgar Allan Poe. One should add the significant difference that the American short story of the nineteenth century contributed many of the classic representatives of the genre to world literature, whereas in Canada, nineteenth-century short prose rather laid the groundwork for the short story proper, which, with its taut structure, would not fully emerge until the early twentieth century in the period of modernism.

In a local color context, Thomas McCulloch and Thomas Chandler Haliburton introduced the humorous tradition to Canadian short prose, which would later be picked up and further improved at the beginning of the twentieth century by the Canadian master of humorous prose, Stephen Leacock. McCulloch's *Letters of Mephibosheth Stepsure* first appeared in the *Acadian Recorder* in 1821 and 1822 (1862 in book form), Haliburton's Sam Slick stories in *The Novascotian* between 1835 and 1836 (in book form in 1836 as *The Clockmaker; or, The Sayings and Doings of Samuel Slick of Slickville*). Both texts were originally published as a series of short stories and hence were precursors of what later developed into the short story cycle, still a popular form in Canada (see Chapter 5). Both texts make use of local color, character sketches, anecdotes, irony, and national stereotyping for their humorous effects.

Other notable Canadian writers of short prose in the nineteenth century include Rosanna Leprohon, Isabella Valancy Crawford, Susan Frances Harrison, Gilbert Parker, and Edward William Thomson. Today they are mainly known for a few of their less formulaic stories reprinted in anthologies of Canadian short fiction. Nevertheless, even these stories tend to draw skeptical comments from today's critical perspective[2]: in nineteenth-century Canadian fiction, sentimental romances, plot-driven adventure tales, and formula writing were the order of the day.

The two major original nineteenth century contributions to Canadian short fiction were the Canadian animal story and Duncan Campbell Scott's story collection *In the Village of Viger*. Ernest Thompson Seton and Charles G. D. Roberts are the main representatives of the animal story. Roberts "invented" the genre in 1892 with "Do Seek Their Meat from God" (in *Earth's Enigmas*), the first of some two hundred animal stories that were to follow from his pen and that proved very successful at the time—also with an international readership, not least because the stories fit the prevalent image of Canada as a country of wilderness. Animal stories for a time came to stand for the Canadian short story as such, and they were translated into many languages. The subgenre brought radical innovation to the time-honored representation of animals in world literature, resulting in the naturalistic or realistic wild animal story. This new type of story was informed by scientific research such as Darwin's evolutionary theory and offered unsentimental, psychological insight into the struggle for survival from the animals' perspective. The difference between Roberts, who was the more sophisticated storyteller, and Seton, who regarded himself foremost as a naturalist and a painter, was summarized by Alec Lucas: "For Roberts it was art first; for Seton it was science" (1958, vi). With its accurate representation of the Canadian wilderness and wildlife, the animal story took Canadian fiction a decisive step further in the direction of realism.

Duncan Campbell Scott's story collection *In the Village of Viger* (1896) can be seen as a turning point in the development of Canadian short fiction, foreshadowing modernism. Set in Quebec, his stories provide a largely realistic depiction of character and of complex psychological states in the context of a village community. Sara Jeannette Duncan, influenced by the American realists William Dean Howells and in particular Henry James, had formulated the Canadian realist credo: "Life should be represented as it is and not as we would like it to be" (*Montreal Star*, January 17, 1888). Though she only authored one collection of short fiction (*The Pool in the Desert*, 1903), Duncan's sophisticated writing style and treatment of theme ushered in the new century—which was to bring tremendous changes to Canadian short fiction, traced in this book.

The Canadian Short Story Since Modernism

Chapter 1 on the modernist Canadian short story begins by stressing the significance of Raymond Knister for the development of a modernist esthetics and for the modernist short story in Canada, in his capacities as a literary critic, theorist, editor, anthologist, and writer of short fiction. Early on, Knister also wanted to see the Canadian short story set off against the American short story, much as he appreciated the latter's unrivaled excellence at the time. Frederick Philip Grove, who published his first short story in 1926, is a transitional figure who worked in the period of modernism, but in a—somewhat belated—realist and partly naturalist manner explored the Canadian prairie region through his short stories. Morley Callaghan also published his first short story in 1926, and he developed into the first Canadian short story writer to catch up, to some extent, with the American short story. Callaghan, who initially published primarily in the United States, was also the first Canadian author to see his short prose printed in collected form during his lifetime (both in Canada and the United States), and he introduced the big city as setting and motif to the Canadian short story. Sinclair Ross was the first Canadian short story writer who did not (have to) look abroad to see his texts published, but whose stories were mainly printed in Canadian magazines in the 1930s and 1940s. Ross's best-known stories, set in the

Depression era, further established the Canadian realist prairie short story. Ethel Wilson, in turn, further developed the Canadian city story, with her special treatment of Canada's westernmost metropolis, Vancouver, combining both its urban identity and its unique natural iconography. Joyce Marshall and, particularly, Sheila Watson prepared the Canadian short story for a postmodernist style of writing, and Watson's texts of the 1950s, in their intricate intertextuality and complex opacity, partly already point to the subsequent period in Canadian literature as of the 1960s. The modernist period in Canada thus saw the first Canadian theorist of the short story and the first anthology of Canadian short stories (Knister), as well as the establishment of the prairie (Grove, Ross) and of the city (Callaghan, Wilson) as important settings and motifs of the short story; moreover, the period saw Canada's first internationalist (Callaghan) and important female writers (Wilson, Marshall, Watson), whose work within the genre was especially innovative.

Chapter 2 approaches the Canadian modernist short story from a comparative perspective by closely comparing its development with the American short story of the time. Against the backdrop of very different preconditions of the genre in the modernist period in the two countries, the chapter compares the short story oeuvres, and a representative story example, of Raymond Knister and Sherwood Anderson, as well as Morley Callaghan and Ernest Hemingway. Anderson and Knister were the decisive modernist innovators of the short story genre in their respective countries, while Hemingway and Callaghan can be called successful internationalists of their literary craft. It is demonstrated that in both countries the modernist esthetics in the genre developed at nearly the same time: in the United States around 1915, with short stories published by Anderson, and in Canada in the early 1920s, with Knister's short stories. Nevertheless, through a detailed comparison of the stories "I Want to Know Why" (Anderson) and "The First Day of Spring" (Knister), as well as of "Cat in the Rain" (Hemingway) and "The Shining Red Apple" (Callaghan), it becomes clear that in the two American short stories the modernist writing agenda is implemented to a greater extent, more decisively, and more successfully. Indeed, the direction of influence in the two North American literatures in the period of modernism was largely one-sided, with Canadian writers very much aware of American writing, while Americans paid hardly any attention to Canadian developments in the genre—Knister and Callaghan, names then known in the United States, were clearly exceptions.

This imbalance was to change in the following literary period, after Canada's centennial in 1967, sometimes called the "Canadian Renaissance." Chapter 3 sketches the torrent of Canadian short story production between modernist and postmodernist and realist and neorealist writing styles. It considers the considerable expansion of the literary infrastructure (such as publication forums) at the time, as well as the crucial role of mentors of the short story, such as Robert Weaver, Geoff Hancock, and John Metcalf, the latter with, among other contributions, some 40 edited anthologies of Canadian short fiction to his credit. The chapter then approaches the wealth of short fiction of the period by focusing on specific relevant groups of short story writers and their achievements. The so-called Montreal Story Tellers of the 1970s (Clark Blaise, Hugh Hood, John Metcalf, Ray Smith, Raymond Fraser) were all male. The three leading authors of the genre in Canada are all female (Alice Munro, Margaret Atwood, and the late Mavis Gallant). Regionalism is highly significant for the genre, with a vast regional spread from West Coast short fiction (Audrey Thomas, Jack Hodgins, Jane Rule) via Prairie short fiction (Margaret Laurence, Rudy Wiebe, Guy Vanderhaeghe) as well as the big cities in the East (Hugh Hood, Margaret Atwood, Austin Clarke), to the Atlantic provinces/Maritime short fiction (Alden Nowlan, Alistair MacLeod, David Adams Richards). A further subsection focuses on female short story writers between compliance, innovation, and rebellion, starting with Margaret Laurence's *A Bird in the House* (1970) and also dealing with Marian Engel, Jane Rule, Audrey Thomas, and Carol Shields, as well as with younger writers such as Sandra Birdsell, Isabel Huggan, Katherine Govier, and Diane Schoemperlen. The chapter also addresses the remarkable multicultural variety in the contemporary Canadian short story and can only hint at how the genre owes its impressive diversity to its numerous multicultural voices as well: Indigenous (Thomas King, Lee Maracle), Caribbean Canadian (Austin Clarke, Dionne Brand, Neil Bissoondath), Asian Canadian (Rohinton Mistry), as well as the many writers with European backgrounds, such as Icelandic (Kristjana Gunnars, W. D. Valgardson) and Ukrainian (Janice Kulyk Keefer). Taking a wide view at the development of the Canadian short story since the 1960s, it becomes apparent that practically all well-known Canadian writers have made important contributions to the short story, that there is a strikingly high proportion of short story cycles (see also Chapter 5), and that, in contrast to the American short story of the same period, the modernist-realist tradition of storytelling has retained its primacy in the contemporary Canadian short story. The final subsection of the chapter, however, also points out the strand of nonrealist (surreal, metafictional, postmodernist) writing in Canadian short fiction of the period, in the hands of writers such as Leon Rooke, George Bowering, Matt Cohen, and Dave Godfrey. Particularly since the 1980s, a style of writing has been practiced (for instance, by Carol Shields and Alice Munro) that can be called "crossover fiction" (David Lodge), a kind of neorealist fiction that shows a consciousness both of the modernist-realist and the hyperrealist, surreal, or metafictional style of writing in one and the same text.

Alice Munro's art of the short story brought Canada the first Nobel Prize in Literature, a momentous event in the history of the Canadian short story that Chapter 4 focuses on, thereby concluding the historical examination of Part 1. After pinpointing the magnitude of Munro's achievement, the chapter sketches how Munro went from Canadian small-town life to global literary renown, delineates her short story poetics and the art of her writing, and, finally, analyzes her story "Fiction" (2007) in detail, demonstrating the utter finesse of her writing. With several critics having claimed, particularly in the later decades of the twentieth century, that the short story is Canada's national art form (for a survey see Nischik 1987), it seems no coincidence that it is this genre that finally brought Canada its first, long-awaited Nobel Prize in Literature.

The second part of the book (chapters 5–10), dealing with varied approaches to the Canadian short story, opens with a chapter exploring the poetics of the short story cycle, as well as the reasons for its striking prominence in Canadian literature. To delineate the development and prominence of the short story cycle in Canada, it is necessary to revisit the very beginnings of literature in Canada in colonial times. In the eighteenth and nineteenth centuries, due to the low population size and density, that is, mainly due to the lack of potential readers, the book market in Canada (particularly compared to that of Great Britain and the United States) struggled to develop, the repercussions of which can still be seen today. Instead of book publication, regional newspapers became the primary outlet for literature in Canada in the second half of the eighteenth century (gradually replaced by literary magazines in the course of the nineteenth century). Numerous newspapers reserved their front pages exclusively for literary texts. The origin of the short story cycle in Canada was in the often partly fictional "letters to the editor," usually sequenced into a series of texts. With an often descriptive, even documentary bent in a large country, these historical origins of the short story cycle explain its often regional orientation. The chapter connects these historical and formational findings with the still pertinent fundamental aspects of the genre, such as the dichotomy between the autonomy and integration of individual texts as well as the opportunity for multiple publication and repeated remuneration. Canada's proximity to the United States as well as both countries' early focus on short forms, in contrast to the former mother country Britain, and the regional orientation of the works are further concerns. In a next step, the distinctive poetological characteristics of the short story cycle are described, taking as a case study Alice Munro's *Lives of Girls and Women* (1971), which, at her publisher's request, she tried very hard to form into a novel, yet which eventually came out as a short story cycle. The form is shown to be ideally compatible with Munro's outlook, where synchronic concentration and seemingly disconnected, sometimes even contradictory experiences displace the focus on a diachronic development that the novel form suggests.

Chapter 6 focuses on the Canadian artist story and combines it with a gender-based approach, underscoring the "double eccentricity" of being an artist *and* a female artist. The artist story is a relatively recent literary format in Canadian literature (especially from the 1960s onward), which is significant for its sheer quantity, overall quality, and, moreover, varied treatment of gender issues, particularly by female authors in Canada. The chapter analyzes three artist stories by Alice Munro and Margaret Atwood ("Dulse" and "The Office" by the former and "Significant Moments in the Life of My Mother" by the latter) and differentiates between artist stories that predominantly feature gender-affliction, gender-consciousness, and gender-affirmation. It becomes clear how both writers take a decisive step toward raising an awareness of the *female* tradition in writing and thereby toward an affirmative view of female gender within an overall metafictional set-up. Even when considering artist stories by the same writer, the impressive variability in thematic orientation and narrative technique of the contemporary Canadian artist story becomes apparent.

Chapter 7 continues the involvement with gender issues by focusing on Margaret Atwood's short stories and short fictions, with regard to their development of the motif of gender over the decades and within several subgenres of short prose in her works, such as prose poetry, "short fictions," and "essay-fictions" (see also Chapter 14). It can be argued that Atwood is at her most experimental in her short prose, and this is also apparent in her treatment of gender, especially in her early and middle creative periods, so that in her short fiction oeuvre the "arbitrariness and undecidability of generic boundaries" (Delville 1997, 57) are coupled with a foregrounding of the, to some extent, arbitrariness and undecidability of *gender* boundaries, à la Judith Butler. As the chronologically structured assessment of Atwood's short fiction oeuvre demonstrates, her works emphasize that genre and gender should not be taken for granted, in an essentialist manner, but are subject to change, since both are responsive to social, ideological, and cultural developments. This is shown, for instance, by Atwood's intertextual involvement with popular text formats such as women's magazines as well as with world literature, as in her revisionist rewriting of Charles Baudelaire's prose poetry, notorious for its misogynist and sexualized reification of women. Atwood, with her typical injections of playful and comic elements, cleverly subverts Baudelaire's masculinist themes and evaluations and uses full-fledged inversion techniques, not least to show gender to be a construct.

Chapters 8 and 9 are both based on the concept of liminality in connection with short fiction. Chapter 8 first deals briefly with the concept of liminality as such and demonstrates to what extent the short story in general, both concerning its preferred themes and techniques, has strong affinities with liminality, more precisely, with liminal states and liminal locations. This is then exemplified by focusing on the period of "old/er age" (Nischik) as a liminal period of life. After briefly discussing Age Studies, Aging, and Old/er Age in more general terms, the chapter elaborates on a researched text corpus of some 40 Canadian short stories dealing with aging, classifying the text material into four discrete perspectives on aging in these stories: Aging as a Journey, Liminal States of Consciousness and Aging, Liminal Locations of Aging, and Aging and Death as Liminal Periods. One textual representative of each story group is dealt with in greater detail (by Mavis Gallant, Alice Munro, Audrey Thomas, and Margaret Atwood), demonstrating the centrality of liminal states and liminal locations in Canadian stories of aging.

Whereas Chapter 8 stresses the temporal underpinning of liminality, Chapter 9 emphasizes liminality's spatial axis. The latter chapter turns to a particular subspecies of the Canadian short story that in its theme also implies a comparative impetus, namely the border story, which, in this study, features a border crossing between Canada and the United States as well as the different imagological views of both countries that tend to accompany such border crossings in literature. Similar to the motif of old/er age, the motif of crossing a physical, and often also mental, border seems specifically appropriate for the genre of the short story, with its poetics of the significant moment, of initiation, transition, being on the threshold, indeed, of crossing the border between two "states." I thematically differentiate between stories where the border is crossed for political reasons (Thomas King), where the border is experienced as a liminal space and threshold, if in hindsight (Miriam Waddington), and where it is associated with (national) dreams and (national) nightmares, both before and after 9/11 (Alice Munro, Laurie Gough). These border narratives are what Herb Wyile, in a similar context, called a "literalization of liminality," thus literalizing Arnold van Gennep and Victor Turner's concept of liminality as a transitional phase and/or space that exists at the intersection between, but at the same time outside of, two "states" (in more than one sense here) or locations. The genre of the short story, with its restricted size and relatively tight structure, seems ideally suited to this kind of liminality.

Chapter 10, which rounds off the approaches part of the book, also deals with (liminal) spaces, in that it examines cultural locations of ethnicity in short fiction set in one of Canada's most multicultural cities, Vancouver, from its beginnings in the twentieth century until today. The two ethnic groups focused on are those most frequently represented in Vancouver short fiction, namely Chinese Canadian and First Nations. It is stressed how Vancouver short fiction by First Nations and Chinese Canadian writers has incorporated specific ethnically defined spaces—such as neighborhood bars and community centers—and boundaries, but also border crossings and border dissolutions into the representations of the big city. The First Nations stories exhibit a chronological development from a retrograde turn to the pre-contact past of First Nations' history in Vancouver (Pauline Johnson), followed by a presentation from a white point of view, which, though sympathetic to Native life, emphasizes its poverty, tragic hopelessness, and clash with a white lifestyle (Emily Carr), and finally to a strongly segregated view of Native and white city lives in the most recent story of my text corpus (Lee Maracle). The Chinese Canadian Vancouver short stories deal with the diaspora situation, the tensions between present and past and between various family generations, as well as the more or less successful integration of first- and second-generation Chinese into Vancouver/Canadian society (Sky Lee, Madeleine Thien). This chapter also foregrounds how the Canadian short story, which for long stretches of the twentieth century was largely committed to the small town as a setting, has in recent decades come to embrace the big city as its locale.

The final section of the book, the analyses part, focuses in four chapters on individual short stories (chapters 11 and 12), on a complete short story oeuvre (Chapter 13), and on the genre-crossing characteristics of a later collection of Canada's most versatile short story writer (Chapter 14). Chapter 11 first deals with an early Munro story from her first short story collection and demonstrates Munro's involvement with gender from her earliest work on. Her story "Boys and Girls," first published in 1964 during the Second Wave of the women's movement, prototypically and ingeniously renders, in fictional, "personalized" terms, the constructivist aspect of gender identity. The female gender role that the young female protagonist in the story is to be socialized into is shown to be an utterly restrictive one, with the concept of "girl" appearing as a "conflictual site" (Derrida qtd. in Heble 1994, 38) in the story. The traditional female gender role imposed upon the adolescent girl by a closed rural society is presented as clearly working against the interests of women by drastically reducing their options for leading a fulfilling life according to their individual—and not predominantly categorical, gender-related—characteristics and desires. The story, narrating a painful initiation into a gendered conception of life, features a strongly differential view of the sexes and their separate spheres and developments. At the same time, by describing restrictive gender roles from the experiential perspective of the girl (a budding writer), Munro's story calls into question a strictly essentializing view of gender. The complexity and density of even this early Munro story show how a short prose text, in the hands of a world-class writer like Munro, may in fact surpass the novel in terms of incisive intensity.

Chapter 12 turns to an exemplary analysis of an artist story, John Metcalf's "The Strange Aberration of Mr. Ken Smythe" (1973), the most dismal in outlook of Metcalf's many artist stories. As surveyed at the beginning of the chapter, Metcalf was a crucial mentor of the short story in Canada, with an elitist, demanding view of literature, and the chapter traces his concern with art and the artist in Canada in his own fiction. The story selected for close analysis is read as a telling allegory about the precarious status of the artist in Canadian society and popular culture, and what true art is all about—in the face of the audience's ignorance, intolerance, prejudice, or even downright hostility toward the uncompromising artist dedicated solely to their art, rather than to what such an audience finds palatable.

Chapter 13 surveys the short story oeuvre of Canada's best-known First Nations writer, Thomas King. It is demonstrated how essential aspects of his writing style are better suited to short fiction than to longer prose, such as the oral tradition of Native storytelling and King's leaning toward parabolic and satirical styles of narration. His 30 collected stories are classified into four different groups, with one selected text sample of each group analyzed in detail: Creation Stories/(Bible) Parodies, Trickster Stories/(Re-)Creating History, Fantastic Stories/Parables, and Family Stories. King effectively combines elements of the (originally white) North American written tradition of the short story with those of Native storytelling (oral narration, "written orality," a "participatory" tradition of narrative transmission, the foregrounding of storytelling practices). His short fiction is characterized as a specific kind of magic realism in that his writing combines realist with surreal (fantastic, mysterious, or mythical) elements. King's engaging, speech-oriented, often humorous writing, mixing comic and tragic elements, is just one example of how ethnically foregrounded short prose thematically and technically increases the range, versatility, and abundance of contemporary Canadian short fiction.

The final chapter of the book is reserved for the author I regard as Canada's most versatile and altogether most experimental (short story) writer, Margaret Atwood. The chapter deals with generic border crossings, typical for Atwood's art of writing, and thereby stresses the variability of the short prose form. Atwood's short prose, as already suggested above, may be divided into short stories proper and "short fictions," "prose-poems," and "essay-fictions," among other hybrid classifications. Her recent collection *The Tent* comprises 35 texts that the back cover shrewdly describes in general terms as "fictional pieces": these include short dialogues that verge on drama, texts close to poetry, fables, and episodic rewritings of previous literary texts such as *Hamlet* ("Horatio's Version"). Although several of these texts have a pronounced narrative impulse, the dominant impression the volume as a whole conveys is rather a reflective than a narrative one, not least because most of these "fictional pieces" belong to a hybrid text form that can be called "essay-fictions." These texts, often written in the first-person form, show a mind at work that ponders some state of affairs or some problem, rather than recounting a sequence of events. Yet these "mini-musings" are not passed off as coming straightforwardly from the author's pondering mind, as in a traditional essay, but are clothed in fictional, narrative, literary frameworks. Their narrative impulse, however, is toned down in favor of metaphorical, symbolic, and parabolic, rather than referential, meaning. This generic hybridization of the short prose form innovatively played through by Atwood is demonstrated by an analysis of the texts "Encouraging the Young," "Voice," and "The Tent." In Atwood's bending, twisting, crossing, and transcending of accepted genre boundaries, not least of those of the short story, Canada's leading writer proves an experimental if not avant-garde practitioner of a genre that already Brander Matthews, one of the earliest (American) critics of the short story, had hyperbolically characterized as having "limitless possibilities" (1994, 48).

A Note on the Works Cited and the Index

The Works Cited list was composed in a pragmatic manner, with optimal usefulness for the reader in mind. Secondary literature quoted from or referred to in the text is listed in the Works Cited (with very few exceptions of texts that are less relevant for the project at hand; in these rare latter cases, the secondary literature is documented in footnotes rather than incorporated in the Works Cited). Literary texts dealt with, the majority of which are innumerable individual short stories and short story collections, required a different procedure to keep the Works Cited list manageable. All original collections of short stories mentioned in the present book are listed in the Works Cited. Individual short stories mentioned in the text are not included in the Works Cited unless quoted from. If not quoted from, the sources of these individual stories are always, however, broadly documented in the text with the title of the respective author's collection the story was published in. In this manner, all of the numerous individual stories I refer to are easily retrievable via the titles of the pertinent story collections added in the text and listed in the Works Cited. Books of selected stories or volumes of complete stories of a writer that are mentioned but not quoted from are omitted from the Works Cited. The same applies to the few novels and poems referred to in the text if not also quoted from.

The more inclusive Index includes all the titles of the story collections as well as of the individual short stories mentioned in the book.

PART ONE: HISTORY

1

The Modernist Canadian Short Story
Forging a Tradition

The short story in Canada began to coalesce as a national genre in the 1890s, with writers such as Isabella Valancy Crawford, Susan Frances Harrison, Ernest Thompson Seton, and Charles G. D. Roberts (see also Chapter 2 note 3). Yet the gap between pre-modernist and modernist writing in Canadian short fiction could hardly be more evident, with the Canadian short story fully emerging as a distinct literary genre only with the advent of the modernist short story in the 1920s. This is indeed the period when Canadian short fiction correlates with our modern-day definition of the short story, as described by Misao Dean (see in greater detail Chapter 2):

> The fast pace of "modern" life and the demand for intense experiences seemed to suggest a correspondingly short and intense prose form, leading to the conventional and highly formalized generic definition of the short story as a "fragment of life": a story unified in place, action and time, whose dramatization of a revelatory and emotionally intense moment manages to suggest the outcome of a complete "life story" in a concentrated form [2000, xvi].

The modernist development of the Canadian short story is closely connected to the life and works of Raymond Knister (1899–1932). Knister was crucial in the genre's early stage, as well as for the development of Canadian literary modernism in general. His importance with regard to the Canadian short story stems from his contributions to the poetics of the Canadian brand of the genre, his early attempts—as editor of Canada's first anthology of Canadian short stories—to create a canon of the genre, and his own short story output.

In "Democracy and the Short Story" (written in 1920, first published in 1975), Knister emphasizes the unrivaled excellence of the contemporary American short story and relates its significance to the large number of short stories published in the United States and their distribution in widely-circulating popular magazines. Concomitantly, he denounces the "Americanization" of the genre, against which he would like the Canadian short story to take a stand. Knister understands "Americanization" to mean the commercialization of short story writing, fostered by the success of correspondence schools with their stereotypical plot and formula stories that leave no room for innovation. Instead, Knister promotes—as did T. S. Eliot in his seminal essay "Tradition and the Individual Talent" (1919)—individuality and originality as well as a pronounced consciousness of technique and form in order to achieve technical versatility and variation, often in an indirect, concealed manner ("The great art is that which is concealed," Knister 1975c, 392). Though not using the term explicitly, he thus advocates a "new form" (391), the modernist short story. For Knister (whose equally noteworthy lyrical oeuvre is, significantly, indebted to the imagist movement), short fiction is linked to precise observation, narrative economy, stylistic succinctness, as well as concise, "objectifying" images to indirectly convey feelings and emotions (see Eliot's "objective correlative"). Knister's sparsely plotted stories open up to a new, realist dimension, as opposed to the schematically structured plot story: "If his [the new writer's] eye be true and his emotions universal and directed, he will be one of the artists for which Canada has awaited to heighten the consciousness of portions of her life. And it may be that a time will come at which he can find a publisher awaiting him in his own country" (ibid.).

Knister's influential role in the development of Canadian literature in general and the Canadian short story in particular manifests itself in his editorship of *Canadian Short Stories* (Toronto: Macmillan, 1928), the first anthology of Canadian short stories and Knister's first published book. Seven months of intense research and twelve years of extensive reading resulted in a pioneering work. Knister himself wrote some hundred short stories, 50 of which are available in print today. Among his best-known stories are his farm stories (for example, "The First Day of Spring," "Mist-Green Oats," "The Strawstack," "The Loading," all in Knister 1976a), set in southwestern Ontario and mainly focusing on male protagonists and their experiences of initiation (such as first love), disillusion, guilt and innocence, tensions between family members—in particular between father and son—and death. The vague, hardly realistic hopes and tentative attempts of the protagonists to overcome their sense of confinement on the farm often pivot on their imaginative identification with and spiritualization of nature in all its mythic beauty—in stark contrast to the numbing chores of a monotonous farm life. In his farm stories, Knister introduces the reader to his characters' inner worlds with distinctively modernist narrative techniques such as subjective narrative focalization, allusion, ellipsis, epiphany, and the indirect, symbolic rendering of information. His "state-of-mind stories" (for instance "Elaine," "The Fate of Mrs. Lucier," both in Knister 1976a) reduce the external plot even more than his farm stories, ultimately minimizing it to the function of merely intimating an awareness of their female protagonists' states of consciousness. A third group of stories draws on Knister's brief work experience in the United States: his "Chicago stories" or "crime stories" (for instance, "Hackman's Night," "Innocent Man," both in Knister 1976a).

Knister's stories smoothed the way for the modernist short story in Canada. They deal with a wide range of themes and employ a variety of narrative styles, demonstrating a general competence in the use of narrative strategies. Once in a while, however, the author's narrative techniques and his use of language betray some of his texts as "beginner's stories," which would have benefited from revisions at a more mature artistic stage (which he did not experience due to his early death at 33). "Elaine," for instance (Knister's fifth story), overuses modernist strategies such as ambiguity, allusion, ellipsis, and the portrayal of consciousness to the point of excessive obscurity, as does "The Loading." Stylistic inconsistencies such as unclear pronoun referents, clumsy sentence rhythms, and awkward expressions occasionally disturb the quality of Knister's innovative stories.

Frederick Philip Grove (1879–1948), a friend of Knister's and 20 years his senior, had his first short stories published in 1926. Grove is primarily known as the first significant prairie novelist in Canada to write in a realist or naturalist manner. Further, he is the author of semi-autobiographical novels in which the deliberate mingling of fact and fiction anticipates later postmodernist strategies. Ever since 1972, when Douglas O. Spettigue exposed Grove's spectacular autobiographical lie (unmasking Grove as the German writer and translator Felix Paul Greve, who had faked suicide in Germany and established a new identity as Frederick Philip Grove in Canada), the interest in Grove's fascinating persona has tended to eclipse the study of his work. But the 1970s also saw the belated rediscovery of Grove as an author of short stories. Like Knister, Grove managed to publish some pieces during his lifetime (mainly in the *Winnipeg Tribune Magazine* in 1926 and 1927), but did not live to see a collection of his stories in print. *Tales from the Margin: The Selected Stories of Frederick Philip Grove* was not published until 1971, introducing the readership to a multifaceted short story oeuvre that is at least on a par with the author's novels. Until then, knowledge of Grove's short stories had been by and large confined to the frequently anthologized story "Snow" (1932, in *Tales from the Margin*; published in an earlier version under the title "Lost" in 1926), which, in a naturalist manner, reflects key elements of Grove's novelistic oeuvre: the setting in an inhospitable prairie landscape, in the depths of winter; the overpowering, inevitable influence of the natural or social environment on taciturn characters whose fate appears to be preordained; the detailed, realistic portrayal of setting (particularly the natural surroundings), characters, and plot; the depiction of hardship and deprivation in the lives of the pioneers, who do not so much act but react—even to the point of downright fatalism at the end of the story. The symbolically coded *in medias res* beginning of "Snow" reveals how vividly Grove's writing used the Canadian prairie as a formative setting for the modernist Canadian short story—a pioneering achievement indeed, which would soon inspire writers such as Sinclair Ross and, later in the twentieth century, W. O. Mitchell, Margaret Laurence, and Rudy Wiebe.

Although Grove's classification as a prairie writer builds on a central aspect of his work, a full appraisal of his short story oeuvre has to acknowledge a greater variety than is usually done. His settings, for instance, embrace a diversity of Canadian landscapes and cities, as well as the coastal region of northern France in the important story "The Boat," and the indeterminate, allegorical "far-away-country" in the anagrammatically titled story "In Search of Acirema" (that is, "America"; all stories mentioned in this paragraph are in *Tales from the Margin*). Grove's protagonists, despite appearing and feeling insignificant in the face of a seemingly omnipotent nature, are far from one-dimensional or repetitive. Stories such as "Saturday Night at the Crossroads" present an array of succinctly crafted individuals, such as the penny-pinching Jewish merchant Kalad and his wife as well as friendly farmer Sunny Sam. Grove also commands a broad range of narrative tones, which surpasses what might be expected to accompany the unmitigated tragedy he is usually associated with in light of his best-known story "Snow"; he employs irony (for instance, in "The Sale"), life-affirming optimism (see the ending of "Lazybones"), and even humor (in "The Extra Man").

Grove is thus a writer whose literary work remains as hard to pin down as his biography, with critics labeling his style as an example of realism (psychological, social, or regional), naturalism, symbolism, and even existentialism. A correlation with "modernism" is missing in this context—and rightly so. Grove clearly stands between tradition and modernity. As the first important English Canadian writer of realist or naturalist stories, publishing about thirty years after Duncan Campbell Scott's and Sara Jeannette Duncan's short story collections, Grove wrote in the vein of American authors of the last decades of the nineteenth century, such as Bret Harte, Mark Twain, Ambrose Bierce, Stephen Crane, and Jack London. Notwithstanding the importance of Grove's efforts to establish the postromantic, realist short story in Canada, his narrative style in the late 1920s lagged behind the avant-garde modernist writings of Canadian contemporaries such as Raymond Knister and Morley Callaghan.

With Morley Callaghan (1903–1990), the Canadian short story in the late 1920s to some extent caught up with the American short story. Callaghan's productive period ranges over almost seven decades, until his death in 1990.

His first short story, "A Girl with Ambition," appeared in the Paris journal *This Quarter* in 1926 (in *Morley Callaghan's Stories*), and his main phase of short story writing stretches from the late 1920s to the early 1950s. Although Callaghan, like Knister and Grove, initially suffered from the still underdeveloped literary infrastructure in Canada at the time, he was already successful in his younger years, especially in the United States and in Europe. In fact, Callaghan was "Canada's first great internationalist" (Boire 1992, 208), and he soon saw his short prose published in collected form. His first short story collection, *A Native Argosy*, appeared in 1929, published by Scribner in New York and Macmillan in Toronto. Not counting his novellas, Callaghan wrote more than one hundred short stories. Often first published in *The New Yorker* or *Scribner's Magazine*, they later appeared in four collections: *A Native Argosy*, comprising the early work; *Now That April's Here and Other Stories* (1936), featuring the stories of the 1930s, arguably his prime creative phase; *Morley Callaghan's Stories* (1959), his most representative collection, which combines a selection from the earlier collections with twelve new stories; and finally *The Lost and Found Stories of Morley Callaghan* (1985), presenting stories that had hitherto not been collected.

Callaghan charted the big city for the Canadian short story. Most of his stories are set in his hometown Toronto, but some—particularly in the later collections—are set in New York or Montreal. At the same time, his stories also feature small-town or rural settings, especially of southern Ontario. In his first collection in particular—still heavily influenced by the naturalist tradition—Callaghan shows a preference for characters at the margins of society, isolated outsiders in constant struggle with themselves and with their social environment, whom the author, although displaying an implicitly moralistic tone, nonetheless depicts in their individuality and dignity. In his later stories, too, Callaghan portrays lower-middle-class characters, dealing with their problems in private relationships and questions of social acceptance. The moral-didactic bent of his early texts with regard to the "human condition" (Callaghan) explains their similarity to the genre of the parable, their interlocking of realist and symbolist narrative levels; exaggerating his case, Milton Wilson in 1962 spoke of Callaghan's "uneasy mixture of parable and case-history, of hagiology and sociology" (1975, 81).

Callaghan's contribution to the further development of the modernist style of writing in the short story is irrefutable. Like Knister, he de-emphasizes plot in favor of fragmentary reflections on his characters' inner worlds and points out the significant in the everyday. Further trademarks of his narrative style are the ironic narrative voice, the ambiguity of plot and language, and, above all, the sometimes laconic diction, which has time and again given rise to comparisons with Ernest Hemingway (for a detailed comparison of both authors' style of short story writing, see Chapter 2). Callaghan summarizes his modernist credo as follows: "Tell the truth cleanly.... Strip the language, and make the style, the method, all the psychological ramifications, the ambiance of the relationships, all the one thing" (Callaghan 1979 [1963], 20, 148), which suggests modernist techniques such as the objective correlative, epiphany, and imagism. Particularly in his early work, Callaghan's vocabulary and syntax create a deceptively simple and direct, deliberately repetitive, unadorned style. The combination of narrative techniques that objectify and document while engaging the reader was inspired to a large extent by Callaghan's side job as a journalist for the *Toronto Daily Star* (where he also met Hemingway). Hemingway and Fitzgerald, in particular, recommended young Callaghan to editors and publishers in Paris and New York and thereby helped him to achieve early and lasting international success (see Chapter 2). Beginning in 1928 and for the ensuing 14 years, Callaghan's short stories were included in the annual volumes *Best (American) Short Stories*. As Callaghan remarked: "I was the only guy I knew of in America somehow selling my non-commercial stories in the great commercial market and staying alive" (Barry Callaghan in Callaghan 2003b, 305). Indeed, the prolific Callaghan afforded the Canadian short story not only international standing and praise, he was also the first Canadian writer to prove the genre could be profitable on the literary market.

Sinclair Ross (1908–1996), on the other hand, who was discovered as a remarkable author only in the 1970s, could not make a living of his writing; he supported himself as a bank clerk. Compared to Callaghan, Ross's was a fairly small oeuvre, which owes its considerable reputation mostly to his early work, his first novel *As for Me and My House* (published 1941 in New York) and his short stories published primarily in the 1930s and 1940s. Ross was the first modern Canadian short story writer whose stories were mainly published in Canadian magazines, mostly in the Canadian scholarly journal *Queen's Quarterly*. Against the cultural background of the 1930s in Canada, the Canadian literary magazines' acceptance of Ross's, that is, a Canadian writer's, works at the time may be due to his less experimental style in comparison to Knister and Callaghan, a style that in regard to form and narrative technique is rather conventional. His preferred setting, in the early stories in particular, of the Canadian prairie during the Depression era may also have contributed to his early approval in Canada. Form, setting, and theme link Ross to his predecessor Grove. The first collection of his short stories, *The Lamp at Noon*, consists almost exclusively of pieces from this geographical and historical context, thereby introducing Ross as the first native-born prairie writer, who re-creates the Saskatchewan prairie not only as a documentary setting, but as a region of the mind, opening up to the reader the psychological world of the characters. Following the example of the immigrant Grove, Ross turned against the earlier romance-like if not sentimental representation of the prairie (for instance, in the works of bestselling author Ralph Connor, 1860–1937), and in the process firmly established the Canadian realist prairie short story.

Among the idiosyncrasies of narrative representation in Ross's prairie stories are the close connection between humans and their natural environment, with the prairie farmer repeatedly pitted against an extreme climate and struggling for physical and mental survival in the face of what seems to be an overpowering and indifferently cruel nature; the isolation and alienation of the individual in that environment; the spatial and psychological isolation between husband and wife; and the imminence of death. In a modernist fashion, Ross's narrative economy transforms external incidents and images into symbolic, indirect expressions of the characters' inner states (for instance, the "lamp at noon" burning in defiance of the surrounding darkness of the sandstorm). In Ross's classic stories, the desolate conditions in the prairie region in the 1930s, when economic depression and years of drought went hand in hand, are often narrowed down to the emotional and communicative deficits in hopeless relationships between man and woman. Both sexes display a conventionally gendered behavior, outdated from today's point of view: the emotionally repressive, outward-oriented male, who finds his self-esteem by successfully managing his daily work, in particular the subjugation of nature, versus the lonely housewife confined to the domestic sphere, who feels neglected both emotionally and sexually and strives in vain to alter her frustrating existence. The continual thwarting of hopes and dreams in these depressing stories frequently occurs in the context of parent-child relations, when parents, especially mothers, struggle to help their children to overcome the local and mental restrictions they themselves must submit to. Ross repeatedly writes from a child's point of view and thereby also produced initiation stories (for example, "Cornet at Night," "The Outlaw," "The Runaway," "Circus in Town," "One's a Heifer," all in *Lamp at Noon*; "The Flowers That Killed Him" and "A Day with Pegasus," both in *Race*). As Laurence Ricou commented on Ross's "puritan" prairie fiction: "An empty, unproductive, and oppressive existence in an empty, unproductive, and oppressive landscape makes an intense fictional impact" (1973, 94). The manner in which Ross—despite his predominant portrayal of extreme deprivation and human limitations—nevertheless finds meaning in existence and human dignity in his characters enhances the significance of his stories of the 1930s and 1940s far beyond their temporal and regional frame. That his short stories cannot be reduced to this immediate context is particularly apparent in his later pieces, such as "Spike" and "The Flowers That Killed Him" (both in *Race*) which explore the criminal mind and the motivation for the crime. Ross's short prose further features urban settings (though only in "Saturday Night," in *Race*), deals with the lives of soldiers (for example, "Jug and Bottle," in

Race), and even displays a comical streak (for instance, "No Other Way," "Saturday Night," "The Race," all in *Race;* and "The Outlaw," in *Lamp*).

Ethel Wilson (1888–1980), whose short stories first appeared between 1937 and 1987 (about one-third of them posthumously), took the short story all the way to the Far West of Canada: More than half of Wilson's nearly thirty published stories (the best of which were collected in *Mrs. Golightly and Other Stories* in 1961) are at least partly set in Vancouver, various others in the rural interior regions of British Columbia, Canada's westernmost province. Even stories with locations outside British Columbia frequently feature Vancouverites as protagonists, for instance, "Haply the Soul of My Grandmother" and "We Have to Sit Opposite" (all stories mentioned in this paragraph are in *Mrs. Golightly*). Although Wilson thus more than any other writer put Vancouver, her place of residence for many decades (1898–1980), on the literary map, she is not a "city writer" like her contemporaries Morley Callaghan and Hugh Garner (see below). For even in the stories set in Canada's westernmost metropolis, Wilson underscores the contrast between Vancouver's urban identity on the one hand and the more natural, more rural aspects of both the city itself and the wider region on the other. She thereby often divests the picturesquely situated city of all typically metropolitan characteristics (thus preserving the image of Vancouver as a frontier town, a vestige of an earlier phase in the city's history, which Wilson herself experienced after emigrating to Vancouver from England in 1898 at the age of ten). Wilson frequently portrays Vancouver as a liminal space, a space of transition and even escape, but also as the awaited sanctuary from disappointing if not dangerous human relationships (symbolized by the repeatedly described "flying birds"), for instance in "The Window" and "Till Death Us Do Part." Echoes of an arcadian contextualization of the big city are continually undercut by the depiction of threats arising from urban and adjoining areas, ranging from juvenile delinquency (in "Fog") to murderous intentions and homicide (in "The Window" and "Hurry, Hurry"). Pastoral yearnings are not satisfied by natural settings either. The short story "On Nimpish Lake" (1942), for instance, presents flora and fauna, and especially birds, as admirable "protagonists." The three fishermen have hardly more than walk-on parts, and the American tourist in particular appears downright out of place in the natural idyll: "'I'm just crazy about this lake. I'm just crazy about Nature anyway. I thought I'd like to stay here a week but I think I'd get kinder [*sic*] restless'" (*Mrs. Golightly*, 39). And yet, the story's symbolically fashioned ending—which can be said to cite the romantic heightened awareness of man toward nature—concludes this example of Wilson's "nature writing," despite its epiphanic pathos, on an antipastoral, melancholy note: "He [the lame man] felt a queer exaltation, a sudden flash that was deepest envy of the wild geese, strongly flying and crying together on their known way, a most secret pain" (ibid.) In stories like "Hurry, Hurry" and "The Birds," even an encroachment of horror upon the beauties of nature can be found. Human existence in both the city and in natural settings in Wilson's stories turns out to be precarious, if not dangerous ground for the protagonists, who are often depicted as lonely and alienated. Not without reason does the epigraph to *Mrs. Golightly* by Edwin Muir state: "life '…is a difficult country, and our home.'"

With regard to theme, characters, and narrative technique, Wilson's stories are very diverse. Among the best-known are "Mrs. Golightly and the First Convention" and "We Have to Sit Opposite" (both 1945, both in *Mrs. Golightly*), which are set, respectively, in the United States and in Europe—two texts interspersed with irony and comedy, yet conveying a grim level of meaning. The latter story stages the intercultural confrontation between two cultured Canadian ladies and a lower-class German family in a train compartment *en route* to Munich in the 1930s. The story not only parades common national stereotypes of both countries, but also deals, in retrospect, with the then-impending international threat of Nazi Germany. As these texts demonstrate, the polishing of preferably simple words and sentences to a highly concise and elegant style had become Ethel Wilson's trademark. Her contemporary, the poet Dorothy Livesay wrote in a review: "What F. P. Grove struggled for and did not attain, what Ethel Wilson found and perfected, and what Knister grasped at, was the need for a wholly original way of handling language" (1974, 82).

Wilson has even been likened by some critics to her contemporaries Virginia Woolf and Katherine Mansfield, and it is a paradox only at first sight that she has nevertheless received relatively little critical attention. The reason why this talented writer ultimately did not achieve a standing in world literature comparable to that of Woolf's or Mansfield's partly stems from the precarious literary constellations in Canada at the time. It is also a result of Wilson's modest and conscious contentment with being a wife in the first place and a writer only secondarily (if she identified with the latter role at all) and, accordingly, of her very slow artistic development, in particular the relatively short creative phase in which she actually published—she had her first short story printed at the age of 49, her first novel when she was 59, and she stopped writing after her husband's death in 1966. Her slim oeuvre still made her English Canada's most important female modernist writer (Eric Nicol in a review in 1956 hailed her as the "First Lady of Letters in Canada"), who would later inspire even more eminent writers such as Margaret Laurence (1926–1987) and Nobel laureate Alice Munro (1931–). It was Munro who stated of Ethel Wilson: "I *was enormously* excited by her work because the style was such an enormous pleasure in itself.… It was important to me that a Canadian writer was using so elegant a style … that a point of view so complex and ironic was possible in Canadian literature" (in Struthers 1983, 18; original emphasis).

With the prolific Hugh Garner (1913–1979), who published short stories from 1938 through a creative period of four decades, the Canadian short story became a popular genre in a wider sense. Garner wrote a hundred stories, which were often first published in Canadian popular magazines such as *Chatelaine, Canadian Home Journal,* and *National Home Monthly* and were reprinted in five collections during the author's lifetime: *The Yellow Sweater,* 1952; *Hugh Garner's Best Stories,* 1963; *Men and Women,* 1966; *Violation of the Virgins,* 1971; and *The Legs of the Lame,* 1976. Particularly until the early 1960s, Garner professed his interest in reaching a large audience (in 1951 alone, he sold 17 stories to Canadian magazines). Garner's artistic credo could be said to pander to the reader: "I believe, along with W. Somerset Maugham, that the first duty of a writer of fiction is to entertain" (Garner 1952, n.p.). This approach, together with Garner's undeniably great narrative talent, probably made him the most widely read short story author in Canada in the 1950s. For the same reason, though, literary critics have often remained skeptical, mistrusting Garner's popular success and the style that he cultivated to achieve it (for instance, his stock repertoire of drastic plot elements). His frequent anti-intellectual statements and his candidness—for instance, in his autobiography *One Damn Thing After Another* (1973), in which he discussed his often hasty creative process under the pressure of deadlines—did not help him with the critics either. Consequently, and also due to some clichéd or formulaic, too "well-made" qualities of some of his most popular stories, Garner is still a disputed and barely studied author among literary scholars. One can agree with Paul Stuewe's classification of Garner as a "lowbrow," "middlebrow," and "highbrow" writer all in one (Stuewe 1985, 112). Garner is today particularly known for his short story oeuvre, not least thanks to the frequent anthologization of some of his classic stories (including "One-Two-Three Little Indians" and "The Yellow Sweater," both in *Yellow Sweater;* and "The Legs of the Lame," in *Legs*). In such pieces, particularly from his early phase, Garner proves his narrative expertise in the tradition of Ernest Hemingway and displays a sure command over the genre's form.

Like Callaghan, Garner is basically a city writer, with a strongly developed sense of place. Most of his stories are set, more or less discernibly, in Toronto (see also his paramount novel on Toronto's *Cabbagetown,* 1950), but sometimes also in Montreal or elsewhere in Quebec. Garner adheres to a social-realist agenda. What sets him apart from the American realists he took as examples (such as Theodore Dreiser), however, is the moralistic, even sentimental dimension of some of his stories. In his settings and themes, Garner is a genuinely Canadian writer; in his preface to *The Yellow Sweater* he remarks: "These are Canadian stories; the people in them are all Canadian; the locale is Canada ... and they were written in Toronto and ... Quebec" (Garner 1952, n.p.). Characteristic aspects of Garner's writing can be traced, for instance, in his most frequently anthologized story, "One-Two-Three Little Indians" (1950). The story relates the tragic impact of racism on an Indigenous family, thereby illustrating the grim situation of Native Canadians trapped between their economic dependence on tourism on the one hand and miserable living conditions on the other.

Joyce Marshall (1913–2005) has received even less critical attention than Garner, and unjustly so. She published her first story in 1936, and many of her more than 30 stories were first read on CBC Radio. Her three collections *A Private Place* (1975), *Any Time at All and Other Stories* (1993), and *Blood and Bone/En chair et en os* (bilingual edition, 1995) document her most creative phase, from 1952 through 1995, and explore in various ways the effects of modernity on human consciousness in an often urban setting (Toronto, Montreal). Faced with a world that seems alien and inscrutable to them, Marshall's characters struggle for a sense of identity by projecting their own aspirations and speculations onto their surroundings, thus repeatedly substituting ersatz images for authentic contact with their environment. In a process of extensive self-reflection, Marshall's almost exclusively female protagonists (who are of all ages) oscillate between feelings of alienation and the insignificance of existence on the one hand and the search for insight on the other. In none of Marshall's texts is the unbridgeable gap between human beings highlighted as symbolically as in "The Old Woman" (1952, in *Any Time*), her most anthologized story. The secluded setting in northern Quebec and the isolation of the English protagonist Molly, who after three years of separation has joined her Canadian husband Toddy there, mirror the characters' inner worlds and the impossible love between them: Years of loneliness in the Canadian wilderness have left Toddy utterly transfixed by nature and hence incapable of human interaction. The electrical power station where he is employed and which he personifies as "The Old Woman" becomes a substitute for his wife—the end of the story sees him succumbing to complete isolation, in fact to madness, with his wife left to cope with this gruesome situation.

Among Marshall's modernist stylistic techniques are *in medias res* beginnings, allusions, and experimental narrative forms. A good example is "The Heights" (1993) from *Any Time at All*. Featuring young Martha, who spends her childhood as an anglophone in Quebec, the story establishes an internal discourse on Martha's different stages of development right at the beginning of the story by introducing a second narrative consciousness, a "ghost" from the past, to comment in retrospect: "All through this story … you'll have to imagine the occasional presence of another person, watching, weighing, adding things up…. The strange thing is that I don't remember her … though she must often have been in the same place at the same time, since she saw many of the same things. Or so she says" (Marshall 1993, 34). Marshall's stories probe the mental worlds of characters in twentieth-century Canada who find themselves in an acute phase of uncertainty but do not completely lose track of their aim to better understand themselves and their environment. In the course of her career, Marshall's narrative style increasingly developed postmodernist traits, as structural and thematic aspects of her third collection *Blood and Bone/En chair et en os* clearly show. The story "Kat," for instance—consisting predominantly of a conversation—denies the reader a spatial reference system any more specific than a "room" in the "city," emphasizing the universality of the story's thoughts and implications, which seem to speak and stand for themselves. According to Marshall, this self-reflexivity may hint at the constructedness of literary texts, but at the same time also at their enduring connection to reality.

Yet it is Sheila Watson (1909–1998) who definitively marks the transition from modernist to postmodernist paradigms in Canadian literature and in the Canadian short story. Her significance for Canadian literature is larger than her slim oeuvre would suggest (two novels, only five short stories, some essays in literary criticism). Her literary work stems almost exclusively from the 1950s, although some texts were published much later, for instance, the story "And the Four Animals" (1980, in *Five Stories*). Watson's long literary silence, which extended from around 1958 to her death in 1998, that is, for about 40 years after her most creative decade, remains an enigma in Canadian literary history. Under the title *Five Stories*, Watson's short stories were collected only in 1984, after they had previously appeared as *Four Stories* in 1979 (before the publication of "And the Four Animals").

Watson was particularly interested in narrative esthetics and its renewal through a turn away from the realist and regional paradigms that had dominated Canadian fiction until then. She expands the suggestive ambiguity of modernist texts toward a hermetic and abstract system of multiple meanings, producing texts of intricate intertextuality and complex intransparency, which are primarily geared toward an academically educated audience. Her allegorical compositions often draw on ancient mythology (four of her five short stories refer to Oedipus; she also mentions, for instance, Antigone, Ismene, Atlas, and Daedalus), but also on more recent European mythology and literature, for instance, the Bible, Shakespeare, James Joyce, Gertrude Stein, Freud, and Jung. These extremely dense, impersonal allegories feature fragmentary plots, in which splinters of meaning from the realm of mythology and literature are superimposed, in a collage-like fashion, on aspects of Canada in the twentieth century, creating an abstract, seemingly unreal level of meaning. Watson's texts use a stripped-down plot as well as imagery, symbols, allusions, and associations to construct an open, complex framework of meaning, which—in a self-referential and postmodernist manner—engenders literature on literature and emphasizes the text's level of discourse (rather than its plot). Watson's elaborate language links her fiction to prose poetry,

1. The Modernist Canadian Short Story 27

for instance, in "And the Four Animals," the earliest text in *Five Stories* and the shortest, at only three pages. Shirley Neuman argues convincingly for an interpretation of this story as "one of the most concise histories of mankind's journey from Creation to Apocalypse ever told" (Neuman 1982, 48). Watson's most frequently anthologized story, "Antigone" (1959, in *Five Stories*), still presents a roughly comprehensible plot, namely the story of Antigone's cousin, in love with Antigone rather than with her sister Ismene. Antigone, outspoken and individualistic, revolts against her father's system of order and discipline by burying a bird on the premises of the mental asylum (Watson grew up in such a place, as the director's daughter). As Shirley Neuman summarizes the story:

> The Provincial Mental Hospital of Watson's childhood and its inmates are transformed and undercut by their allegorical conflation with characters from Greek tragedy. Watson's Antigone is no princess burying a dead brother in the six feet of soil due to him ... Creon no longer rules Thebes but a land where Atlas eats dirt, Helen walks naked and all is but a demented inversion of Greek myths and Greek tragedies.... This modern parable provides no moral resolution of its dualities [Neuman 1982, 48].

Stephen Scobie has argued that Watson's fundamental combination of conflicting elements might in itself be considered either modernist, a form of duality, or postmodernist, a form of duplicity (1985, 270)—a position that once again emphasizes Watson's watershed function (pointed out by George Bowering in 1982) in contemporary Canadian fiction. As a female writer, Watson's position on the threshold between different literary paradigms confirms Barbara Godard's thesis that women's social eccentricity predisposes them to the role of innovators in literary history: "Women have long been pioneers in new subjects, new forms, new modes of discourse" (qtd. in Legge 1992, 45). The development from Ethel Wilson to Joyce Marshall to Sheila Watson, as it has been traced here, thus anticipates the explosion of female creativity in Canadian writing as of the 1960s, not least in the genre of the short story (see Chapter 3).

2

The Modernist Canadian and American Short Story
A Comparative Approach

While Chapter 1 presents a survey of the modernist Canadian short story and its most important contributors, this chapter zooms into the early development of the modernist Canadian short story and compares it with the early development of the modernist American short story. "Modernism" is understood as a periodizing concept within the arts, in the present context a literary period of international significance that was characterized by a network of interrelated historical, technological, intellectual, and esthetic developments, and resulted in innovative forms and styles of expression in the arts and literature. Since this fundamental transformation was a multinational phenomenon that involved increased traffic of all kinds (including intellectual and artistic) across regional boundaries, questions of similarities, commonalities, and differences between different cultural regions arise. After assessing the different states of development and the status of the short story in both North American countries at the beginning of the modernist period, I focus upon two Canadian and two American short story writers essential for the development of the modernist short story in their respective countries: in each of two comparative analyses I examine a Canadian and an American writer and their works, Raymond Knister and Sherwood Anderson, followed by Morley Callaghan and Ernest Hemingway. The results of these correlative investigations and text analyses lead to a general comparative evaluation of the modernist Canadian and American short story, the genre that has so far been neglected in studies of American and Canadian modernism.[1]

The short story genre in the modernist period developed under completely different preconditions in its literary-historical contexts in the United States and Canada. In the United States, the beginnings of this genre go back to Washington Irving in the 1820s. In the period of the American Renaissance around the middle of the nineteenth century, the American short story saw a first peak, with outstanding writers such as Edgar Allan Poe, Nathaniel Hawthorne, and Herman Melville, leading critics to claim the short story to be a particularly American genre. Before the period of modernism, the American short story had flourished again in the period of realism and naturalism in the later part of the nineteenth and partly in the beginning of the twentieth century, with writers such as Ambrose Bierce, Mark Twain, Stephen Crane, Henry James, Edith Wharton, Theodore Dreiser, and Willa Cather. The first decade of the twentieth century in the United States saw short story collections by writers such as Edith Wharton, Henry James, Willa Cather, O. Henry, and Theodore Dreiser. In other words, the genre was already in full swing in nineteenth-century America and started vigorously in the twentieth century, boasting many writers who have achieved canonical status. The healthy state of the American short story was supported by its infrastructure with a wide range of possibilities, and indeed a demand, for magazine publication of individual stories: "The beginning of the twentieth century saw a huge growth in the popularity and sales of the short story.... In 1885 there were around 3,300 magazines in the United States which published short stories. By 1905 this figure had risen to 10,800."[2]

The situation was quite different in Canada, where writers, especially avant-garde writers with a modernist writing style, had to look for publication venues outside their country, turning to European and American magazines. Ken Norris states that "it was not until the 1960s that avant-garde literary magazines began to appear in Canada, some fifty years after the outburst of radical European Modernism" (1984, 9). It comes as no surprise, then, that the Canadian short story was still closer to its beginnings in the modernist period, and it could be argued that this genre in Canada came into its own at this time (see Chapter 1).[3]

The Decisive Innovators: Sherwood Anderson and Raymond Knister

Sherwood Anderson (1876–1941) counts among the most important writers of the American short story. Although he also published seven novels, his main literary achievements, also by his own estimation, were in the short story.[4] The publication of his short story cycle *Winesburg, Ohio* (1919) revolutionized short story writing, and Anderson, himself influenced by Ivan Turgenev[5] and Gertrude Stein,[6] became an influential model for many contemporary and later short story writers such as Ernest Hemingway, William Faulkner, Flannery O'Connor, Eudora Welty, J. D. Salinger, and Raymond Carver.[7] Anderson published more than 70 short stories, most of them reprinted or first published in his four short story collections: *Winesburg, Ohio* (1919), *The Triumph of the Egg* (1921), *Horses and Men* (1923), and *Death in the Woods* (1933). Anderson's short story oeuvre clusters around the 1920s, when he was at the peak of his creativity in this genre.

Born in Ohio, a largely self-educated man and a voracious reader without a college degree, Anderson brought a new esthetics to the short story. A lifelong opponent of the commercialized magazine or plot stories, written for effect and to please the masses, Anderson worked against what he saw as calculated, artificial, and unrealistic plot stories: "There are no plot short stories in life.... To take the lives of ... people and bend or twist them to suit the needs of some cleverly thought out plot to give your readers a false emotion is as mean and ignoble as to sell out living men or women" (Anderson 1925, 23, 39). Anderson coined the phrase "The Poison Plot" (1968 [1924], 255) to characterize what he detested, namely the overemphasis on plot in stories. He instead sought that ever-elusive "large, loose sense of life" (qtd. in Curry 1976, 100). In *A Story Teller's Story*, he elaborated:

> There was a notion that ran through all story telling in America, that stories must be built about a plot and that absurd Anglo-Saxon notion that they must point a moral, uplift the people, make better citizens, etc., etc. The magazines were filled with these plot stories ... "The Poison Plot" I called it ... as the plot notion did seem to me to poison all story telling. What was wanted I thought was form, not plot, an altogether more elusive and difficult thing to come at [ibid.].

Anderson thus sought the kind of narrative that suited, and indeed conditioned, his material; a narrative that seemed natural to the story, posing questions rather than giving answers and solutions.

In his numerous essays, notebooks, autobiographical writings (diaries, memoirs), and letters, Anderson also, if diffusely, delineated a kind of poetics of the short story. In contrast to the then still influential plot-oriented short story poetics, he favored an anti-constructivist, intuitive, moment-oriented, and "organic" view of short story writing. In *The Writer's Book*, he states: "The short story is the result of a sudden passionate interest. It is an idea grasped whole as one would pick an apple in an orchard."[8] Anderson associated the conception of a short story with "moments that bring glory into the life of the writer" (qtd. in Curry 1975, 91), implying how highly he esteemed short fiction. Indeed, the short story's form correlates with his view that the "true history of life is but a history of moments. It is only at rare moments that we live" (qtd. in Papinchak 1992, 3).

Anderson wrote the first 15 of the 22 stories collected in *Winesburg, Ohio* (1919) between fall 1915 and fall 1916.[9] Eleven, exactly half of the *Winesburg* stories, were first published in the little magazines *Masses* (New York), *The Little Review* (Chicago/New York), and *The Seven Arts* (New York) between

2. The Modernist Canadian and American Short Story 31

1915 and 1918 before they were collected in *Winesburg, Ohio*. The modernist short story, it follows, was created in the United States as of 1915, simultaneously with modernist American poetry. Anderson's best-known stories outside the *Winesburg* cycle were first published in 1919 ("I Want to Know Why"), 1920 ("The Egg," both in *Triumph*), 1923 ("The Man Who Became a Woman," in *Horses*), and 1926 ("Death in the Woods," in *Death*). Around 1920, then, the modernist short story had been established by Sherwood Anderson in the United States. Ernest Hemingway and F. Scott Fitzgerald, who were both also from the Midwest—the focus area of the modernist American short story in the 1920s before the shift to writers from the American South in the 1930s, 1940s, and 1950s—followed in Anderson's footsteps, themselves publishing important short story collections in the 1920s.

The Canadian Raymond Knister (1899–1932)—like Anderson a writer of short stories, poetry, novels, and literary and cultural criticism—started to publish his innovative short stories just a few years after Anderson. His earliest stories ("The One Thing," "Mist-Green Oats," and "The Loading"; all stories mentioned in this paragraph are in Knister 1976a) appeared in the American avant-garde literary magazine *The Midland* in Iowa in 1922 and 1924 as well as in the Paris avant-garde magazine *This Quarter*[10] ("Elaine" and "The Fate of Mrs. Lucier") in 1925. In his own country, Knister published but one story, "The Strawstack," in *The Canadian Forum* (1923), a few stories in the Canadian popular magazines *MacLean's Magazine* (as it was called at the time) and *Chatelaine*, and a series of sketches in the *Toronto Star Weekly*, all in the 1920s. In his lifetime (Knister died by drowning at the age of 33) Knister saw only 27 of his altogether some hundred written short stories published; another 20 of his stories were printed posthumously. Also, Knister never saw a collection of his stories published in his lifetime.[11] The reasons for this, apart from Knister's early demise, were the poor opportunities for publishing fiction, to say nothing of innovative short stories, in Canada at the time: Canadian publishers and literary magazines were few and far between and they were not keen on modernist experiments—in fact, not keen on Canadian literature in general. Knister did not get tired of complaining about the situation of serious writers in Canada at the time: "A most significant circumstance in the development of the Canadian short story has been the dearth of editors to encourage and discover writers of value.... Of our better writers ... practically all have been obliged to adjust their contributions to foreign markets" (1971a [1928], xvii).[12]

At the same time, Knister worked to alleviate the situation. He wrote perceptive essays in which he expressed general poetological statements that are reminiscent of those of T. S. Eliot (whose seminal essays "Tradition and the Individual Talent" and "Hamlet and His Problems" were published in 1919). Similar to Anderson, Knister made a point of communicating with

Canadian and international writers of the time who were also involved in the modernist project (see his extensive correspondence). He worked very hard to make a living as a creative writer in Canada, against all odds, supporting himself by freelancing for several (mainly American) newspapers, writing numerous reviews and several important essays. At the time of his early death, Knister had innovated the Canadian short story, published imagist poetry and two novels (a third was published posthumously in 2006), and was hopeful for a budding Canadian literature.

Like with Anderson, Knister's lasting contributions (in addition to his poetry) mainly constitute themselves in the short story and in an innovative poetics. He was very much aware of contemporary literature (he had read, for instance, Sherwood Anderson) and he was far from believing that an awareness of international literary developments might hamper the further development of Canadian literature. At the same time, Knister was involved in Canadian canon formation, especially concerning the short story. His first published book was an anthology titled *Canadian Short Stories* (Toronto: Macmillan, 1928), for which he—after a long time of reading all the Canadian short stories he could unearth—selected 17 short stories to show the first examples of a national history in the genre (he modestly left out his own stories). The book also includes an important introduction ("The Canadian Short Story"), a useful list of Canadian short stories hitherto printed in magazines (comprising 280 titles), and a list of books of short stories by Canadian authors (comprising 91 titles).[13] Knister opens the introduction to his anthology with a statement that illustrates his awareness of being on a cultural threshold and that uses imagery reminiscent of his involvement with farm life[14]: "At the outset of a new era there is opportunity to look back upon the old; and in nothing have we more clearly passed an epoch than in the short story, here in Canada. Literature as a whole is changing, new fields are being broken, new crops are being raised in them, and the changes apparent in other countries show counterparts in our development" (1971a [1928], xi). Just like Anderson, Knister criticizes the commercialization of short story writing: "The general materialism had imposed a false aesthetics, on this continent" (ibid., xiii). He denounces the "Americanization" (that is, the commercialization) of short story writing, against which he would like the Canadian short story to take a stand (Knister 1976b [1923]). At the same time, Knister recognizes the unrivaled excellence of the contemporary American short story and in part relates its significance to the large number of short stories published in the United States and their distribution in widely circulating popular magazines (see Knister 1975b).

Although both Anderson and Knister also wrote stories set in the city (see, for instance, their texts set in Chicago), they are mainly known for their stories in rural or small-town settings: Anderson with reference mainly to the Midwest and, to a lesser extent, the South (Anderson published some seven stories set in the South), and Knister likely with reference to southwestern Ontario (mostly unspecified). Both writers were born and raised in a rural context, and although they also traveled or stayed abroad for some time, they both remained faithful to their country of origin and did not emigrate or become expatriate writers (for a while), as so many of their colleagues did at the time. Both Anderson and Knister were largely self-educated,[15] and both were voracious readers.[16] It is known that Knister was acquainted with Anderson's stories and admired them.[17] In contrast, there is no evidence that Anderson had read any of Knister's few published stories, although this cannot be ruled out (see especially Knister's publications in *The Midland*).

Significant parallels as well as differences concerning Anderson's and Knister's short stories become apparent in a direct comparison of their narratives. I will analyze two of their best and best-known stories, written in the space of five years, with a similar theme, similar motifs, and some comparable narrative techniques: Sherwood Anderson's "I Want to Know Why" (1919) and Raymond Knister's "The First Day of Spring" (1976c; written in 1924–25). As to the production, publication, and reception of these stories, Anderson's "I Want to Know Why" (set in Kentucky and in upstate New York) was composed in August 1919 and was first printed only three months later in H. L. Mencken's magazine *Smart Set*. The story was then included in Anderson's second short story volume *The Triumph of the Egg* in 1921 and went on to become one of his canonical stories, often reprinted, taught, and analyzed. Raymond Knister wrote "The First Day of Spring" (set in a rural, otherwise unspecified area) in 1924–25, but although it is a competent story, it was not printed until 1976 when Peter Stevens made it the title story of his collection of Knister's stories and other prose, rescuing those texts from oblivion half a century after their conception. Accordingly, in the still scant Knister criticism, there is practically no detailed treatment of this story, apart from one fairly recent, excellent reading (Breitbach 2007). In other words, whereas Anderson's "I Want to Know Why" is recognized as a classic of the American short story, Knister's "The First Day of Spring" is still being established as an important early step in the development of the Canadian short story.

Both "I Want to Know Why" and "The First Day of Spring" deal with growing up and are initiation stories—to be precise, "uncompleted initiation stories" in Mordecai Marcus's terminology (Marcus 1960–61), in the sense that the process of coming to grips with a new level of awareness of the self and the world is a painfully ongoing process at the end of the stories. Both texts deal with the awakening of sexuality and the turbulent, diffuse emotions of their teenage male protagonists. The main characters' initiation into the adult world is coupled with excruciating disillusionment and a gnawing lack of understanding on their part. Both stories also make use of elements of their authors' lives: on the one hand the farm life Knister experienced when growing up and working as a farmhand on his German father's farm in southwestern Ontario; on the other hand, the racetrack for horses which was Anderson's passion especially as a boy.[18] In both stories, animals play a crucial role in the protagonists' development, by means of the modernist device of symbolic displacement. In Anderson's story, the boy narrator sees his beloved racehorses as exuding a covert sexuality. The animals are later linked to a prostitute ("the one that was lean and hard-mouthed and looked a little like the gelding Middlestride but not clean like him," 12) and particularly to the horse trainer Jerry Tillford. The boy briefly feels love for Tillford during their nonverbal communication about the racehorses, before his affection turns to hate when he sees Jerry with a prostitute, engaged in the same rapport as he had earlier been with the boy about the fabulous stallion Sunstreak. A similar displacement of human beings and animals is at play in Knister's description of the horse Cherry as a "long-haired bay mare with trim legs," holding "her head high" (3). At the epiphanic end of this text, the boy strokes "the warm nose of a colt" while whispering to the animal: "You're going to be broken in" (8). This instance also marks an oblique reference to the boy's own distressing initiation into the adult world—which has just taken place due to a painful event brought to the narrator's attention by his father: the schoolgirl the boy had been longing for had become pregnant by and got married to another boy, and then most probably killed her baby in a pig trough (7).

Whereas the striking similarities between both stories thus mainly concern theme and motif, the significant differences between them mainly concern their style and technique or, to put it differently, the extent to which an innovative modernist writing agenda is implemented in each of these texts. For one, Anderson is the better stylist. He is known to have been a heavy reviser—he claimed that rather than revising portions of a text, he would throw away an entire manuscript and write it from scratch until he was satisfied. In this way, he had spent ten years working on his other well-known initiation story, "Death in the Woods" (1926) (see Curry 1976, 102–05). Anderson was about 45 years old when he wrote "I Want to Know Why," while Knister was 20 years his junior and had not yet developed such a meticulous approach to writing. Many of the stories from the beginning of his career were still unpublished at the time of his early death; had he lived longer, they would surely have benefited from later revisions.

Although both stories are told by youthful first-person narrators, Anderson's verbal style is much more authentic and gripping, more "modern." The narrative has a convincing oral and vernacular touch not least because of Anderson's intense study of Mark Twain's *The Adventures of Huckleberry Finn*. In contrast, Knister's story is written in a more formal, indeed partly poetic style, which comes across as much more conservative than Anderson's; for instance, Knister writes: "The blue of the sky softens, the air lifts, and it is as though the lightness of a life above the earth were being made ready, an entering spirit to pervade the uncoloured and frost-clogged flesh of the world; or perhaps it is as though this flesh had suddenly sighed in its sleep, an exhalation intoxicating to men and beasts" (3). Compare this with Anderson, whose style is reminiscent of J. D. Salinger (or rather Holden Caulfield) some 30 years later: "Well, I must tell you about what we did and let you in on what I'm talking about. Four of us boys from Beckersville … made up our minds we were going to the races, not just to Lexington or Louisville, I don't mean, but to the big Eastern track we were always hearing our Beckersville men talk about, to Saratoga. We were all pretty young then" (6).

Both passages are taken from close to the beginning of the stories, and they also demonstrate another difference between the two texts: Whereas Anderson uses an *in medias res* beginning that was innovative at the time (see, for instance, the non-referential sequence signal in the form of the pronoun at the very beginning: "We got up at four in the morning, that first day in the East," 5), Knister opts for a conventional exposition in an omniscient narrative voice:

> It had been a mild winter, and yet when March came, and days in which wheels threw the snow like mud in stretches of road where snow still lay, the world was changed.
> This change was more than seeming. Who misses the first day of spring? Snow may linger on the ground and return, but the new smell is there, more potent perhaps than it is ever to be in lush days of blossoms [3].

After these opening paragraphs in the omniscient voice, the Knister story shifts, rather abruptly, to a first-person perspective.

Such differences in structure and in the narrative process significantly influence the reader's reception of both stories. Anderson's "I Want to Know Why" with its many digressions, apparent "formlessness," disorderliness, and fragmentation, as well as the open question posed by the story's title—all meant to reflect the confused narrator's state of mind—integrates modernist tenets into the narrative process more decisively and successfully than Knister does in his story.[19]

The Successful Internationalists: Ernest Hemingway and Morley Callaghan

Ernest Hemingway and Morley Callaghan provide a vantage point for the second comparison for several reasons. First of all, they were born just four years apart, Hemingway in 1899 (committing suicide in 1961) and Callaghan four years later in 1903 (surviving Hemingway by some 30 years, until 1990). Both started writing at around the same time, with Hemingway's first published work, *Three Stories & Ten Poems*, published in 1923,[20] and Callaghan's only three years later, in 1926 ("A Girl with Ambition" in the Paris journal *This Quarter*; in *Morley Callaghan's Stories*). Both authors wrote numerous short stories: Hemingway published nearly 60 stories during his lifetime, and is known to have written over 80 stories in total; Callaghan wrote about 150 stories and had 115 of them published. Both authors published their modernist experimental short fiction internationally, in avant-garde magazines in both Europe and the United States (as did Raymond Knister). Hemingway's first collection of short stories, *Three Stories & Ten Poems*, was published with a French publisher (Paris: Contact Publishing), and *in our time*, too, was published in Paris (Three Mountains Press). The book was soon expanded and reissued as *In Our Time* by Boni & Liveright in New York in 1925.[21] Callaghan's first collection of short stories, *A Native Argosy*, was published six years later in 1929, simultaneously by Scribner in New York and Macmillan in Toronto. Both writers left their countries for a while (especially Hemingway, repeatedly)—see, for instance, Morley Callaghan's memoir *That Summer in Paris* (1963), in which he relates his "Memories of Tangled Friendships with Hemingway, Fitzgerald, and Some Others" (thus the book's subtitle), particularly of the legendary summer those writers spent together in Paris in 1929—the "last months of glory, before the great Depression descended and sent the Americans [sic] scurrying back home" (Woodcock 1993, 15). Hemingway became one of the best-known and most influential short story writers not only of North American literature but also of world literature, eventually winning the Nobel Prize in Literature in 1954; Callaghan, in turn, is regarded as "Canada's first great internationalist" (Boire 1992, 208), to whom the Canadian short story (and novel) is indebted for catching up with American literature in the late 1920s. Both authors, in fact, even had the same publisher—after his breakthrough with *In Our Time*, five of Hemingway's eight collections of short stories[22] were first published by Scribner in New York; Callaghan published his first short story collection (of altogether four)[23] with that publisher, in addition to his four earlier novels as well as nine of his short stories in *Scribner's Magazine* (all in the 1920s and 1930s).

Moreover, the two writers knew each other quite well, and in fact became friends in their early twenties. Both writers started out as journalists and worked for the *Toronto Star* in the early 1920s (Hemingway from 1920 to 1924 and Callaghan in the summer of 1923 and afterward part-time throughout the 1920s). Callaghan's memoir *That Summer in Paris* is devoted to a large extent to his relationship with Hemingway, and he relates in vivid detail how the two budding writers met in Toronto at the *Star*. According to this account, it was Callaghan who had first shown some of his early writing to Hemingway, at the latter's request (not the other way round—see Callaghan's account of this in Callaghan 1979, 27–33, and the "follower" issue below). Hemingway was highly appreciative and supportive of Callaghan and his writing, soon opening the publishing doors for him in Paris and in the United States (as Fitzgerald did with Scribner in New York). In fact, Hemingway and Callaghan thought highly of each other and of each other's writing, and Callaghan stressed Hemingway's essential support for his development into a writer (similar to how Sherwood Anderson had helped Hemingway), calling Hemingway "my only reader and booster" in 1923 and 1924, who "would keep on passing the word around about me"—"my confidence had become tremendous" (Callaghan 1979, 60, 38, 51; see also Callaghan 2008c [1964], 24). By the time of "That Summer in Paris" in 1929, it seems to have been mainly their regular boxing sessions that cemented their friendship—and at the same time eventually brought them apart because of the legendary boxing fight between Hemingway and Callaghan in which Fitzgerald miscounted the time and Callaghan knocked Hemingway down—an event later even making it to the *New York Herald Tribune*, alienating the three writers from each other,[24] although Callaghan eventually finishes his memoir in harmonious terms, significantly with Hemingway as the topic of its final sentence: "But I was glad to hear that in the last year of his [Hemingway's] life out in Sun Valley, he talked to the photographer so affectionately about those days in Paris with Scott [Fitzgerald] and me, and sent me at last his warm regards" (Callaghan 1979, 255). One reason for Callaghan having been regarded, unjustly, as a follower or even imitator of Hemingway is the fact that Hemingway had had a start of a few years in his publication history, as shown above, and also that Scribner in New York used the better-known Hemingway as a model of comparison for Callaghan when marketing Callaghan's first novel *Strange Fugitive* (1928). Callaghan was never happy about this and wanted to be judged on his own terms (see Callaghan 1979, 63–64 and 93–94).

Yet both writers had some similarities in their writing styles or, rather, their writing credo. Hemingway was a master of omission and suggestion, of the use of indirect reference and objective correlative (cf. William Carlos Williams: "no ideas but in things"). His seemingly simple, concise, and yet highly elaborate, artfully repetitive, and engaging writing style was groping toward that "fourth and fifth dimension of prose" (Hemingway 1935, 33), which is also involved in his well-known "iceberg theory": "If a writer of prose knows enough about what he is writing about he may omit things that he knows and the reader, if the writer is writing truly enough, will have a feeling of those things as strongly as though the writer had stated them. The dignity of movement of an iceberg is due to only one-eighth of it being above water."[25] Like Hemingway, Callaghan de-emphasizes plot in favor of fragmentary reflections of his characters' inner world rather than extraordinary external events, and points out the significant in the everyday. Callaghan, too, uses ambiguity of events and language and, above all, a laconic style that has often evoked associations with Hemingway. Callaghan summarizes his modernist credo as follows: "Tell the truth cleanly.... Strip the language, and make the style, the method, all the psychological ramifications, the ambience of the relationships, all the one thing" (Callaghan 1979, 20, 148), which equally suggests modernist techniques such as objective correlative, epiphany, and imagism. Callaghan's vocabulary and syntax, too, particularly in his early work, create a deceptively simple and direct, deliberately repetitive, unadorned style. Both writers' combination of narrative techniques that objectify and "document" while engaging the reader may also be connected to their journalistic training and work.

With Callaghan's writerly ties to Hemingway, Fitzgerald, and Anderson, among other international writers, it is not surprising that Callaghan strongly regarded himself as a North American rather than a Canadian writer (he once even called himself an "American" writer), downplaying his nationality even though most of his stories are set in Toronto or, later, occasionally also in Montreal (and New York). Many of his stories were first published in prestigious U.S. journals such as *Atlantic Monthly*, *Scribner's Magazine*, and *The New Yorker*. Beginning in 1928 and for the ensuing 14 years, Callaghan's short stories received the mark of excellence by being included in the annual selective series *Best (American) Short Stories*. Callaghan's memoir *That Summer in Paris* reveals his very international orientation, whereas his Canadianness is hardly an issue. There are just a few hints and (indirect) references to the literary climate in Canada at the time, as when Hemingway tells Callaghan that he will go to Paris because he just cannot write literature in Toronto— "He had come to Toronto with good expectations, and now he seemed to feel smothered" (Callaghan 1979, 27)—or when Callaghan states: "It never occurred to me that the local poets had anything to do with me.[26] Physically ... I was wonderfully at home in my native city, and yet intellectually, spiritually, the part that had to do with my wanting to be a writer was utterly, but splendidly and happily, alien" (Callaghan 1979, 22). Callaghan, even more so than Raymond Knister, practically *lived* the consequences for this state of affairs through his international outlook and orientation—at a time some hundred years ago when "Toronto, the Good" (see Rosenthal 2011, 179 *passim*) was still a far cry from the buzzing "world in a city" that is Toronto's self-characterization today. George Woodcock summarizes the seemingly paradoxical situation as follows: "So from 1929 onwards Callaghan became a writer working in Canada, seeing himself as within the American tradition, but writing books about Canadians in Canadian settings that were published in New York. There was little mutual understanding or respect between him and the inhabitants of the barren ground that passed for a Canadian literary world during the years between the two great wars" (1993, 15–16). With Callaghan's productive period ranging over almost seven decades, this prolific writer in his main phase of short story writing (the 1920s to 1950s) brought the Canadian short story international praise and standing, and he was also the first Canadian short story writer to prove this genre profitable on the literary market, while Knister had paved the way for later successful Canadian practitioners of the genre. Woodcock points out that when by the 1960s Callaghan's work had finally been accepted by the Canadian reading public as modern Canadian classics, he had largely lost his American readership: "We see him inevitably in a double image: as the survivor of the 1920s revolution in American writing whose leaders (his friends) he portrayed so vividly in *That Summer in Paris*, and as one of the leaders (a half-witting one) of the other revolution which in the years after World War II resulted in what we now see as a Canadian literature" (Woodcock 1993, 17).

For a direct comparison of these two writers' stories, I have selected two texts from their early creative phases, which are somewhat similar in motif and, to some extent, narrative technique: "Cat in the Rain" (1925, in *Men*) by Hemingway and "The Shining Red Apple" (1935) by Callaghan. What unites the two selected stories, along with the motifs of longing and frustration, is mainly their central use of the objective correlative.

Hemingway's "Cat in the Rain" is a compact and highly suggestive text, which, with its 1,148 words, can be called a short short story. Everything in this seemingly simple, yet at closer analysis skillfully composed text—figures, setting, atmosphere, dialogue, action—is found to point to the unsatisfactory relationship between the married couple (on holiday in an Italian resort) and particularly the "American wife's" resulting frustration. This state of affairs is shown more or less indirectly, thus engaging the reader to fill in the hermeneutic gaps the discourse provides (David Lodge in 1980 calls the story "indexical"). Critics of this frequently analyzed story have long discussed the possible reasons for the wife's frustration, which are subtly and variously indicated in the text. These are mainly her wish to have a baby, denied to her by one of the partners' lack of fertility or, more likely, by the husband's rejection of this wish of hers, and, connected to this, a performed or impending abortion (see also Hemingway's story "Hills Like White Elephants" of 1927 with a similar topic). Her husband George's insensitivity and his lack of understanding for her, as well as her lack of, and longing for, a well-off, comfortable bourgeois domesticity may be further potential reasons for the woman's apparent frustration.

Hemingway gives support to such readings mainly through the use of symbolism and the objective correlative. The setting, for one, is highly symbolic, and despite the brevity of the story, it is often referred to. As for spatial symbolism, the information pertaining to the inside setting of the hotel in the first two sentences shows the couple in isolation right from the start. The empty square in front of the hotel, too, may be regarded as pointing to the lack of vitality and of events in the couple's apparently empty and sterile marital life. The wife's repeated looking out of the window (four references) could point to her feeling trapped and longing for a change in her dismal situation and for some meaningful perspective for her future. Another issue contributing to the story's dreary atmosphere is the frequent reference to the rain: seven direct references and 22 indirect references to it symbolize the ubiquity of the misery the woman feels envelops her. As to temporal symbolism, the war monument referred to three times at the beginning of the text situates the story in a post-war (World War I) setting. Toward the end of the story, the time of day is referred to as many as three times: The increasing darkness mirrors the woman's growing gloominess in her attempt at getting her desperation across to her husband, who is constantly reading, thus driving a cultural wedge between his wife's spontaneous as well as deep-rooted wishes and his own self-oriented preferences:

> "I want to pull my hair back tight and smooth and make a big knot at the back that I can feel," she said. "I want to have a kitty to sit on my lap and purr when I stroke her."
> "Yeah?" George said from the bed.
> "And I want to eat at a table with my own silver and I want candles. And I want it to be spring and I want to brush my hair out in front of a mirror and I want a kitty and I want some new clothes."
> "Oh, shut up and get something to read," George said. He was reading again.
> His wife was looking out of the window. It was quite dark now and still raining in the palm trees ["Cat in the Rain," 325].

We see how the setting contributes considerably to the atmosphere in the story and symbolically comments on the events or, rather, state of affairs.

The cat in the rain—there are as many as 33 references to a cat in this short short story—is perhaps the best-known example of an objective correlative in American literature, keeping in mind T. S. Eliot's definition of "objective correlatives" as "a set of objects, a situation, a chain of events which shall be the formula of that particular emotion; such that when the external facts, which must terminate in sensory experience, are given, the emotion is immediately evoked" (qtd. in Baker 1963, 56). The cat can be understood as an objective correlative for a wanted child, or at least for someone the American woman may love and take care of, with her husband retreating from and showing no genuine interest in her. The typically open ending is also connected to the/a cat and has been much discussed, in particular the question of whether the cat that the maid brings to the American woman is the same as the one outside in the rain that the woman had longed for earlier. Carlos

Baker (1963) says yes, while most other critics of the story say no, for various reasons. It is indeed probable that the "big tortoiseshell cat" (326) at the end is not the same as the animal referred to as "poor kitty" (323) by the American woman earlier in the story. In any case the hotel owner's gift points to the woman's misery once again: if the tortoiseshell cat is the same cat, it is nevertheless a poor substitute for what the woman actually desires. If the big cat is a different cat, this would even exacerbate the sadness of the ending: this cat, which is so big that it swings down against the maid's body, is then another instance of the hotel owner's merely professional attentiveness to her, derived from his endeavor to accommodate his clients. The hotel owner, like her husband, is far from understanding her true needs—the tortoiseshell cat, or any cat, will not fill the emptiness she feels within. This ending also shows how deluded the woman is in expecting the (old) hotel owner to take a personal interest in her. Desperate for affection, she had previously attached her sympathies to him, simply because he is polite to his client, thereby serving as a foil to her indifferent husband:

> The wife liked him [the hotel owner]. She liked the deadly serious way he received any complaints. She liked his dignity. She liked the way he wanted to serve her. She liked the way he felt about being a hotel-keeper. She liked his old, heavy face and big hands.
> Liking him she opened the door and looked out. It was raining harder [324].

This passage is also an instance of Hemingway's art of repetition; in fact, the passage may be regarded as Hemingway's imitation of Gertrude Stein, one of the most formative influences on his style.[27] There are other important repetitions in the story apart from the ones already mentioned above (rain and the woman's window view): We are told five times that George, her husband, is reading, and the expression "I want" occurs 16 times in the story, always in connection with the woman. Such instances of repetition emphasize the very action or state they describe and also mirror the repetitiveness of the couple's life. They *show* the reader cumulatively and insistently what is not *told* directly and they symbolically emphasize essential aspects of the situation. Thus the childlike cascade of "I want" (see above), which bursts out of the woman as her husband remains uninvolved, drastically shows her desperation about the situation. The repeated reference to George's reading shows him almost continuously involved in a lonely activity, frustrated by the nagging, if not the mere presence, of his wife.

In lieu of a more detailed analysis of assorted further aspects of this short short story, as demonstration of how each and every feature of this text contributes in a carefully orchestrated manner to its overall design and impact, only a few references to further aspects of the story must suffice—such as the function of the Italian maid ("Have you lost something?"[28]), the man in the rubber cape on the empty square (who has been read by scholars, as in Joyce's *Ulysses*, as a harbinger of sterility, of dearth, and the death of love), the waiter across the square in the doorway of the café looking out at the empty square (another atmospheric symbol of stagnation and lifelessness), the symbolic orchestration of light, artificial light, and eventual darkness, or suggestive linguistic subtleties like the variation in referring to the female protagonist as "woman," "wife," or "girl"—for instance, the narrator switches over to referring to the American wife as "girl" immediately after she realizes that the cat has gone, has been "lost," as the Italian maid had, unknowingly, formulated it before. It is almost as if—in the story's perspective—the woman is robbed of some of her adult femininity by not having a creature to care for. The diminutive term of address "girl" is then used four times within a few lines (324). After the hotel owner has made her feel "very small and tight inside" (324) and "really important" (325) (possibly suggestive of pregnancy), the narrator significantly reverts to referring to her as "wife." We thus see how Hemingway's short short story, in spite of its at first sight simple vocabulary and sentence structures, is a highly integrative, resonating, complex modernist short story that, mainly through its use of symbolism, the objective correlative, and repetition, is a skillful illustration of Hemingway's narratological credo of the iceberg principle.

Whereas Hemingway's "Cat in the Rain" has been frequently analyzed, there are apparently no analyses of Callaghan's story "The Shining Red Apple," even more significant considering that the story was first published some 80 years ago, in *The New Yorker* in 1935. As in the Hemingway story, the central objective correlative has titular prominence—here the object of craving is a "shining red apple," polished for display and seduction by the fruits and vegetables dealer Joe Cosentino. In the Callaghan story, it is a hungry, skinny, probably poor boy ("he must have been very hungry," 156) who dearly longs for an object. The story is told, as in the Hemingway story, by an external narrator, here clearly focusing on one figure, the storekeeper and his thoughts, rather than presenting an "objective" external view of the situation, as the Hemingway text tends to do. We thus get a more subjectively filtered and "narrated" rather than scenically presented view of a situation of deprivation and longing, here about the existential state of hunger and, presumably, poverty.

The story—encompassing 1,546 words, and thus 398 words more than the more complex Hemingway text—presents a kind of serious "game"[29] between the storekeeper and the boy, with the boy apparently trying to get in a position to steal an apple out of sheer hunger, and the storekeeper, for the longer part of the story, trying to undermine the boy's intention by popping into his sight whenever the boy seems ready to snatch an apple. Whereas the boy is simply characterized as longing for the apple and trying to get at

2. The Modernist Canadian and American Short Story   43

it by not being seen, thus aware of the fact that he would be stealing yet intending to do so out of an existential despair, the storekeeper is presented in a more varied and more complex manner. His store is not as prosperous as it used to be (the story was published in the postdepression era, after all), so he cannot tolerate theft of his goods even for this reason. Yet for a while he seems to get some satisfaction from the fact that the hungry boy seems to be in a worse situation than his own. Then, too, the boy's lurking intention and his maneuvering himself into the right position brings some change and "event" into the storekeeper's apparently monotonous life, with few—or hardly any—customers showing up in his store. The storekeeper is first shown as aware of the boy's intention to steal an apple, then as clever enough to keep the boy from doing so by showing up at the right moment, then as developing some kind of malicious pleasure in the boy's dismal state of hunger, and then even with a sort of sadistic joy in the boy's plight: "So, doing a thing he hardly ever did, he went out onto the street, and, paying no attention to the kid, who had jumped away nervously, he ... lazily picked up one of the apples from the top of the pile, as though all such luxuries of the world were within his reach. He munched it slowly with great relish.... The kid must have been very hungry, for his mouth dropped open helplessly, and his blue eyes were innocent and hopeless" (156).

After the first part of the story, which sets the conflict, a second, shorter part is interspersed, providing a glimpse of Joe's family life. His wife, "wide-hipped and slow-moving now, with tired brown eyes" (156), enters the store from a room at the back. In their brief dialogue it becomes clear that their baby daughter has been ill and Joe's wife feels so tired that she soon retreats again, not without admonishing Joe to "watch the kid" (157) and the apples. Part three of the story follows, in which the storekeeper, now more aware of his own deplorable situation, becomes more lenient toward the boy and eventually seems to see a parallel between their fates: "Joe grew restless and unhappy, and he looked helplessly around the untidy store, as if looking upon his own fate" (157). In fact, he now even *wants* the boy to take an apple ("really hoping it would happen," 157), just as he would like his own fate to brighten up. The shining apple[30] becomes here an objective correlative for any improvement in one's fate—a small yet "shining," colorful, positive, concrete hope for the future (see also the parallel to the Hemingway story in Joe's habitually looking out of the window, 154). The boy, by now so frightened of a watchful storekeeper protecting his store against youthful thieves, may not realize Joe's change of mind and runs away terrified of him, without the longed-for apple. Yet the boy's focused and existential desire for an apple seems to have been diffusely, as a *pars pro toto*, transferred to Joe at the end of the story, also pointing back to his own gloomy situation, yet apparently without much hope for either of their futures: "Joe followed a few steps, but the kid wouldn't look back. Joe stood on the sidewalk, an awful eagerness growing in him as he stared at the shining red apple and wondered what would happen to the kid he was sure he would never see again" (158).

Although there are several parallels between the two stories by Hemingway and Callaghan, on the thematic/motivic level and concerning their central use of the objective correlative, it has to be stated that the Hemingway text is the more skillful and technically and stylistically more advanced piece of writing. Whereas Hemingway *shows* the monotony and repetitiveness in his protagonist's life scenically, Callaghan *tells* it: "Joe was sitting on his high stool at the end of the counter where he sat every afternoon looking out of the window" (154). Whereas Hemingway *suggests* his characters' dissatisfaction and longing, Callaghan *tells* about it, even at the very beginning of his story: "It was the look of longing on the boy's face" (154); "always staring, wanting the apple more and more" (156). Whereas we have to *infer* the American wife's dissatisfaction and deterioration from her speech and from objective correlatives as analyzed above, in the Callaghan story the author *tells* us about such issues more directly: "There wasn't much business, there seemed to be a little less every day, and sitting there week after week, he grew a little fatter and a little slower.... The store was untidy" (155). The implied author rather obviously even steers the reader's attention to the parallels between the storekeeper's and the boy's situation ("as if looking upon his own fate," 157). In stark contrast to Hemingway's scenic presentation and his frequent use of dialogue to indirectly characterize the figures and their situation, there is little dialogue in the Callaghan story but predominantly narration by an omniscient, commenting, and evaluating narrator ("feeling powerful because he knew so surely just what would happen," 155). What gives the story an even old-fashioned touch is Callaghan's heavy and rather pedestrian use of the narrative technique of direct thought (quoted monologue),[31] which used in this manner belongs more to a nineteenth-century and earlier narrative inventory and does not constitute a modernist narrative technique, for instance:

"Ah, it goes just like a clock. I know just what he'll do," Joe thought. "He wants it, but he doesn't know how to take it because he's scared. Soon he wants it so much he'll have to take it. Then I catch him. That's the way it goes," and he grinned [156].

"Now for sure he'll grab one. He won't wait now. He can't." Yet to tantalize him, he didn't go right into the store [156].

"Look at the face on you. Look out, kid, you'll start and cry in a minute," he said to himself [157].

Such passages, which were far from innovative at the time and which we today regard as a clumsy technique, weaken the Callaghan text. The story nevertheless manages to provide a resonating glimpse of postdepression life by means of an inventive, interesting character constellation and correlation as well as effective character revelation. The further locale of the store is left unspecified: "Callaghan's work is marked by a strong sense of place despite his refusal to identify Toronto until late in his publishing career" [Morley 1978, 11].

We can thus conclude that the fact that Hemingway and Callaghan knew each other and their work quite well should not distract from the fact that their writing style is rather different, to a greater extent than the (technical and esthetic) difference between Sherwood Anderson and Raymond Knister as analyzed above. Paul Goetsch, too, states: "Because he esteemed Hemingway highly and quoted some of Hemingway's statements about art approvingly in *That Summer in Paris*, some critics have exaggerated Hemingway's importance for Callaghan's development (see Sutherland 1972). Callaghan lacks Hemingway's sophistication and sense of style, and where Hemingway is economical, allusive, and suggestive, Callaghan is rather simple and chatty" (2007, 96).[32] The very kind of usage of their modernist and, in the case of Callaghan, partly outdated narrative techniques shows the esthetic distance between the two writers—although Callaghan's story was published 10 years later than Hemingway's and although Hemingway was only 25 when he published "Cat in the Rain." Callaghan, who was influenced by Sherwood Anderson just as much, if not more than by Hemingway,[33] always had the grace to acknowledge Hemingway's superior mastership. In 1926 Callaghan stated in an article published in *Saturday Night*: "I believe Hemingway is writing the best short stories coming from an American today" (2008d, 42); and some 40 years later Callaghan wrote about the 1920s and Hemingway's style: "Having given up newspaper work, he was committed to writing and was turning out a kind of story that was so suggestive, so stripped, so objective, so effective in capturing pure sensation that it became a unique kind of poetry" (2008c, 25). In fact, Hemingway did reach that "fourth or fifth dimension of prose" which Morley Callaghan did not quite master.

Conclusion

Drawing conclusions at the end of this comparative assessment of the early stages of the modernist short story in the United States and Canada, it should first be stressed that both in Canada *and* in the United States the cultural climate was felt to be backward and little inspiring by North American avant-garde writers at the beginning of the period. For this reason, American modernist writers such as Gertrude Stein, Ezra Pound, Ernest Hemingway, F. Scott Fitzgerald, and T. S. Eliot felt it necessary to depart their country for Europe as the focus-point of cultural and literary innovations at the time. The "lost generation" of American writers were to quite some extent expatriate writers, with some of them (Stein, Eliot, Pound) eventually deciding to stay in Europe for good.

Both in the United States and in Canada, modernism developed at the beginning of the twentieth century. Whereas in the United States as of ca. 1905 new impulses were seen as originating from Europe (especially Paris and London), in Canada the cultural modernist "awakening" began more haltingly and about a decade later, and it took longer to gain traction on a larger scale. Apart from Europe, the neighboring United States became the main source of cultural inspiration for Canadian writers. As Dorothy Livesay put it, "At that time the United States represented for Canadians ... a place to breathe in" (1977, 130). The lack of a supportive cultural infrastructure in Canada led to a partial "brain drain" mainly to the United States (although Callaghan and Knister repeatedly went to and published in the United States, they never left Canada for good). Expatriation was thus another parallel between the two countries in this period—though, significantly so, with movements in largely different directions: Europe for American writers and the United States for Canadian writers.[34] Hence, in Canada modernism also became linked to continentalism, while in the United States, the pull was largely transatlantic.

Also, owing to the still strong political and cultural ties of Canada with its former mother country—in contrast to the United States, which since the American Renaissance had not regarded itself as a "postcolonial" country and culture—the cultural forces of tradition working against the modernist literary innovations were stronger in Canada than in the United States. This also explains why modernism on a larger scale had become established in Canada only at a time when the United States was already about to enter the postmodern age.[35] Finally, while in the United States modernism was largely seen as an enrichment of a national literature, in Canada, which achieved political independence almost a century later than the United States, an internationally oriented Canadian writer such as Morley Callaghan was long seen as a threat endangering the further development of a genuinely Canadian tradition in literature. No wonder, then, that at the beginning of the twenty-first century, research on Canadian modernism, in spite of its expansion, has still also been occupied with taking stock—for instance, with the discovery and addition of new, particularly female authors who do not fit in the established narrative of a "dominant, elitist, masculinist ... and exclusionary Canadian modernism."[36]

My comparative investigation of the beginnings and early phase of the modernist short story in Canada and the United States has shown that the modernist short story started to develop at roughly the same time in both countries. This happened in a completely different generic literary-historical context, however: The American modernist short story was an important innovation of a literary genre "invented" in the United States and flowering there since the 1820s, whereas the Canadian short story was still closer to its beginnings at the time, after starts around the middle of the nineteenth century. While the innovative short stories by American writers—although also published in Europe—were able to find American venues for publication, Canadian modernist writers had practically no publication options in their own country: "The plight of fiction and literary magazines in Canada in the 1920s and 30s has been documented by Callaghan and others…. Canada was dominated by American and British branch-plant publishers. A complex of economic, political, and historic conditions, including a relatively tiny anglophone population, precluded large-circulation magazines…. It was inevitable that he [Callaghan] should aim at the large American market" (Morley 1978, 8).

Not least for such infrastructural reasons, the modernist American short story was altogether more accomplished and successful than the Canadian short story of the period, which was clearly not as technically advanced and influential (not even in Canada) as its U.S. counterpart. Whereas the American modernist short story developed rather quickly as of the later 1910s, in Canada this evolution was much slower and more halting.[37] As a consequence, the direction of influence was largely one-sided at the time, with Canadian writers very much aware of American writing, while Americans paid hardly any heed to Canadian developments in the genre—Raymond Knister and, particularly, Morley Callaghan were clearly exceptions, as writers who were known in the United States at the time.

The colonial time lag between the countries of some one hundred years, among other factors, is thus also evident in the development of the North American modernist short story. Canadian literature had to wait until the 1960s before producing first-rate short stories that were also globally read and appreciated, for instance, with the work of writers such as Alice Munro and Margaret Atwood. Yet as has been shown above, the Canadian modernist branch of the genre did start to develop at about the same time as that of the United States, if haltingly and more modestly so, and the explosion of short story writing in Canada as of the 1960s would hardly have been possible if the early practitioners of Canadian short story writing during this period had not paved the way (in particular Knister, Callaghan, Sinclair Ross, and Ethel Wilson; see Chapter 1 and Nischik 2007).

Comparing the American and Canadian short story since the 1960s would yield quite different results, culminating in the Nobel Prize in Literature of 2013 being awarded to Canadian short story writer Alice Munro (see Chapter 4)—but that is a different story.

3

The Canadian Short Story Since 1967

Between (Post)Modernism and (Neo)Realism

The Canadian short story got off to a hesitant start in the twentieth century. As shown in Chapters 1 and 2, this was due, to a considerable extent, to the lack of appreciation that Canadian literature had to grapple with in its own country and, consequently, the limited publication facilities in Canada at the time. Early short story writers such as Raymond Knister, Frederick Philip Grove, and Morley Callaghan were thus forced to find their way into print mainly outside the country. The collected stories of all the major modernist writers, except for Callaghan and Hugh Garner, appeared decades after their conception, in the 1960s, the period sometimes called the "Canadian Renaissance."

The Short Story After 1967

The explosive development of Canadian literature starting in the 1960s, partly boosted by new supportive cultural policies, had a crucial impact on the short story. Owing to the fact that short stories typically enjoy multiple publications—a first printing in a magazine, followed by publication in later collections by a single author and/or in anthologies—the genre relies particularly heavily on a flourishing print industry. Indeed, the period finally saw the growth of the kind of literary infrastructure that is necessary for a vital national literature. Publishing houses specializing in Canadian literature were founded, such as House of Anansi Press, Coach House Press, Talonbooks, and Oberon Press. Several literary magazines were inaugurated as

3. The Canadian Short Story Since 1967

well (*University of Windsor Review*, est. 1965; *Wascana Review*, 1966–2012; *Malahat Review*, est. 1967; *Lakehead Review*, 1968–1977), providing an essential forum for short story writing. These periodicals, which had a low circulation and are often referred to as "little magazines," were and to some degree continue to be sustained by government subsidies: Even in the late 1990s, the Canada Council granted a total of $400,000 annually to some 30 English-language literary magazines in Canada. Despite the odd voice of protest, such as John Metcalf's (see below), these cultural measures did much to promote a diverse, competitive literature, including short story writing. Norman Levine (1923–2005), known primarily as an author of short stories (eight collections between 1961 and 2000), memorialized literary debuts and the importance of the little magazines in his story "We All Begin in a Little Magazine" (1972, in *Frozen River*).

Another underwriter of Canadian short story writing was the public Canadian Broadcasting Corporation (CBC) with its various radio programs featuring the reading of Canadian short stories, sometimes by the authors themselves. The internationally unique program *Anthology*, initiated and produced for more than 20 years by Robert Weaver (1921–2008), is of particular interest here, as it broadcast weekly readings of Canadian literature for over 30 years (1953–1985). While *The New Yorker* is considered to be the most prestigious U.S. venue for short story publication, Weaver's *Anthology* was for a long time its Canadian counterpart. Every year, approximately 40 stories by well-known and lesser-known Canadian writers were broadcast to an average audience of 55,000 listeners per week. Not only did Weaver recognize the affinities between radio and the short story genre, he also edited important anthologies of Canadian short stories. With Oxford University Press he launched the *Canadian Short Stories* series in 1960, which comprised five volumes by 1991 and documents the evolution of the Canadian short story in one of its most important phases. Moreover, Weaver together with Margaret Atwood edited *The Oxford Book of Canadian Short Stories in English* in 1986 and *The New Oxford Book of Canadian Short Stories in English* in 1995, both of which have become standard works.

Only John Metcalf (1938–) matches Weaver's indefatigable support of the Canadian short story. A productive and acknowledged writer of short stories, novellas, novels, and literary and cultural criticism, Metcalf has contributed significantly to the short story genre not only through his creative work, but also by editing countless anthologies and book series (see Chapter 12 and Nischik 1987). In his somewhat controversial, sometimes aggressive critical style, Metcalf argues in favor of the traditional realist-modernist strain of the short story, whose representatives are included in his approximately 40 anthologies, many of them written for the classroom (for instance, *Sixteen by Twelve: Short Stories by Canadian Writers*, 1970; *Making It New:*

Contemporary Canadian Stories, 1982). In addition, he has figured in almost all of the strikingly numerous book series of Canadian short story anthologies, for instance, *Best Canadian Short Stories* and *New Canadian Stories*. In *Best Canadian Stories* he repeatedly gave newcomers the chance to publish in an established forum, and thus greatly stimulated up-and-coming generations of writers.

While Weaver and Metcalf have preferred the more conventional narrative forms of the Canadian short story, Geoff Hancock, editor of *Canadian Fiction Magazine* between 1975 and 1998, supported experimental, postmodernist short fiction in particular. In various articles and edited anthologies (for instance, *Illusion One/Illusion Two: Fables, Fantasies and Metafiction,* 1983; *Moving Off the Map: From 'Story' to 'Fiction,'* 1986), he encouraged the rejection of the realist-modernist tradition in fiction. As he wrote in the introduction to *Illusion*, with an overstated sideswipe at prairie realist Sinclair Ross: "Gone at last are those boring fictional depictions of the prairie depression.... The illusionists are filling in those blank spaces on the literary map of Canada by uncovering the fantastic." He even states: "Canadian Literature begins again" (Hancock 1983, 9, 8). Hancock's partiality for postrealist narratives also explains his fondness for French Canadian short fiction, which he tried to make accessible to an English-speaking audience in articles as well as book editions (for instance *Invisible Fictions*, 1987). However, despite such influential and zealous defenders as Hancock, the postrealist short story did not flourish in English Canada to the extent that it did in the United States (or, for that matter, in French Canadian literature), not even during postmodernism's heyday in the 1960s and 1970s. Although partly experimental, deconstructive, and self-referential, the Canadian short story was less committed to these features in and of themselves than its American counterpart and more often combined them with the traditional Canadian interest in realist representation. Robert Kroetsch's well-known dictum that Canadian literature skipped the modernist phase and after nineteenth-century Victorianism advanced directly to postmodernism is therefore questionable in the case of the short story genre, too (see chapters 1 and 2): To this day, the Canadian short story is marked by a clear predominance of modernist and neorealist narratives over outright antirealist, postmodernist styles.

In the past decades an impressive number of collections, book series, and anthologies of Canadian short stories have appeared at an unusual rate even by international standards, which testifies to the prominent position of the short story on the Canadian literary scene (and also to the continued state support of literature in Canada). The stories are collected and grouped according to various criteria in these books: author, quality and representativeness, region, era, ethnicity, gender, etc. At the beginning of the 1980s, the late German critic Helmut Bonheim proposed that "the short story has been the most active ambassador of Canadian literature abroad" (Bonheim 1980–81, 659), while Canadian critic David Arnason similarly stated that "the short story has always been a popular literary genre in Canada, and it is the form of Canadian writing that has traditionally had the largest appeal to international audiences" (Arnason 1983, 159). The Canadian editor of a short story anthology at the turn of the millennium even described the contemporary Canadian short story as "the literary equivalent of a national display of fireworks" (J. Thomas 1999, vii). The high standing of the short story in Canada is further reflected in its popularity with literary prize juries: Since 1978, about one third of the books awarded the most prestigious literary prize in Canada—the Governor General's Award—have been short story collections, among others by Alice Munro (three times), Mavis Gallant, Guy Vanderhaeghe, and Diane Schoemperlen. The Canadian Giller Prize, in existence since 1994, has also been repeatedly awarded for short story collections. And, to top it all, the first-ever Nobel Prize in Literature for Canadian literature was awarded in 2013 to Alice Munro for her short story oeuvre. Furthermore, demanding stories by prominent Canadian authors such as Alice Munro, Margaret Atwood, Mavis Gallant, Alistair MacLeod, and W. D. Valgardson, to name but a few, were often first printed in Canadian magazines with large circulation, such as *Saturday Night*, or in U.S. magazines such as *The New Yorker*, *The Atlantic Review*, and *The Saturday Evening Post*. What Raymond Knister had claimed in the 1920s with regard to the contemporary American short story—that strength in the number of short stories written and published helped to raise the genre's general quality (see Chapter 1)—also proved true in Canada half a century later.

The Montreal Story Tellers

The so-called Montreal Story Tellers made a decisive contribution to the success story of short fiction in Canada. This group of writers, living in Montreal at the time, was founded by John Metcalf in 1970 and included Clark Blaise, Hugh Hood, Ray Smith, and Raymond Fraser. With the exception of the lesser known Fraser (1941–), all members remained active in the short story genre even after the group's dissolution in 1976. Their official title, the Montreal Story Teller Fiction Performance Group, points to their distinctiveness: Metcalf and company wanted to show that perhaps even more than poetry, the short story also lends itself to public reading. The readings, as the group members sometimes self-ironically recall in their memoirs (published in Struthers 1985), were intended to be performance events and took place in front of audiences of up to 150 listeners, mostly at universities or colleges, but also in schools and bookstores, especially in the Montreal area.

Metcalf was not only the founder but the most important member of this relatively short-lived group. Over the years he developed into an even more active anthologist of Canadian short fiction than Weaver, but also into an acid-tongued, uncompromising critic of the Canadian literary scene. While nationalism and thematic criticism held sway over literary Canada, Metcalf raised his voice against subsidizing mediocre literature, irrespective of its themes, its focus on content related to Canada, or other aspects that he considered ancillary. For him, the only acceptable yardstick of a then still-budding national literature was literary excellence (see, among others, Metcalf's controversial works *Kicking Against the Pricks*, 1982a; *The Bumper Book*, 1986; *Freedom from Culture: Selected Essays 1982–92*, 1994; as well as his memoirs, *An Aesthetic Underground*, 1996).

Besides his other merits, Metcalf has to be counted among Canada's best short story writers and was dubbed "one of Canada's best-kept literary secrets" by the American magazine *Harper's Bazaar*. He has published four short story collections (among them *The Teeth of My Father*, 1975; *Adult Entertainment*, 1986) plus three volumes of selected stories (among them *Selected Stories*, 1982c; *Standing Stones: The Best Stories of John Metcalf*, 2004). Some of his longer prose narratives are best described as novellas ("Polly Ongle," "Travelling Northward," "Private Parts: A Memoir," "Girl in Gingham," "The Lady Who Sold Furniture"), as is one of his more recent publications, *Forde Abroad: A Novella* (2003). Metcalf the critic once referred to his own narrative style as experimental. But in his literary work he relies on the modernist narrative tradition rather than on postmodernist innovation, which he once dismissed as a frequent excuse for poor, sloppy writing. A good example of Metcalf's style is "Gentle as Flowers Make the Stones" (1982d [1975]). The story describes the struggles of poet and translator Jim Haine, above all in relation to his creative writing, and his attempts at gaining public recognition in a social context that proves hostile to art. Events such as Haine's poetry reading or the ensuing sex scene with a woman from the audience are recounted from Haine's perspective, with Metcalf embracing Joycean stream of consciousness and simultaneity in his narrative technique. The story is a satirical turn on the exclusive demand that art makes on a writer's life—Haine reveals himself to be committed to his literary work only.

Considering Metcalf's critical take on Canadian culture and its politics, his particular interest in the satirical artist story comes as no surprise (see also "The Teeth of My Father," "The Years in Exile," and "The Strange Aberration of Mr. Ken Smythe," all in *Selected Stories*; see Chapter 12). A further subcategory of the short story that Metcalf masters in equal measure is the initiation story (see, for instance, "Early Morning Rabbits," in *Lady*; "Keys and Watercress," in *Selected Stories*).

Clark Blaise (1940–) has published eight short story collections to date,

3. The Canadian Short Story Since 1967   53

as well as three novels and five partly autobiographical nonfiction works. The thematic content of his story collections is hinted at in their titles: *A North American Education* (1973), *Resident Alien* (1986), and *Man and His World* (1992). Beginning in 2000, Porcupine's Quill Press (for which John Metcalf was editorial advisor for some time) began publishing a four-volume project, *The Selected Stories of Clark Blaise*, that combines selected, already published stories with some of Blaise's more recent ones, structuring the individual volumes according to the cultural geographies they cover: volume 1, *Southern Stories*, 2000; volume 2, *Pittsburgh Stories*, 2001; volume 3, *Montreal Stories*, 2003; volume 4, *World Body*, 2006. This project testifies to Blaise's cosmopolitanism and cultural mobility, which is traceable to his childhood: Born in 1940 in North Dakota (his first citizenship being American) to an English Canadian mother and a French Canadian father, he changed schools 25 times owing to his parents' nomadic lifestyle, so that even as a child he would travel between Canada and the United States. Together with his Calcutta-born wife, and fellow writer Bharati Mukherjee, he settled in Montreal from 1966 to 1978, which left its mark on his early work in particular ("I've always thought of myself as a French Canadian, but.... I was writing in English, not in French," Blaise in Wahl 1997, 51). In 1973, Blaise was granted Canadian citizenship; he regards himself as Canadian but today lives in the United States. Blaise's fiction has also been referred to as a sequential fictional "autobiography," centering on a socially estranged male protagonist whose identity is permanently under threat. This predicament may be considered the epitome of the "North American condition" concerning "rootlessness, homelessness ... dislocating contrasts to be found among juxtaposing groups within North American culture" (Davey 1976, 73).

Blaise's frequently anthologized short story "A Class of New Canadians" (1984 [1970]; collected in *A North American Education*) is representative of his vast short story oeuvre. Eighteen months before the story opens, protagonist Norman Dyer has left the United States upon receiving his PhD and has come to Montreal, which has made him think of himself as a "semi-permanent, semipolitical exile" (4). He works as a lecturer in English literature at McGill University and teaches a colorful group of new immigrants from all over the world. His arrogant, self-absorbed attitude toward his students encapsulates the fragility of the idealized concept of multiculturalism known as the Canadian Mosaic (according to which Canadian society is made up of diverse ethnic groups with equal rights and opportunities). Dyer's positive image of Canada not only seems artificial, it also fails to win over the immigrants (some of whom regard Canada merely as a stepping stone to the United States), thus uncovering the frequently precarious identities of Blaise's protagonists. The story's final scene shows Dyer as an insecure and fearful "resident alien." Other exceptional short stories by Clark Blaise include "A North

American Education," "Eyes," "Going to India," and "Notes beyond a History" (all in *North American Education*), "I'm Dreaming of Rocket Richard" and "How I Became a Jew" (both in *Tribal Justice*), and "North" and "Identity" (both in *Resident Alien*).

The thematic and stylistic heterogeneity of the Montreal Story Tellers also shows in the works of Hugh Hood and Ray Smith. Hood (1928–2000) prided himself above all on his novelistic work, especially his *roman-fleuve*, the novel series The New Age/Le nouveau siècle, published at regular intervals beginning in 1975 and with 12 planned volumes, the last of which appeared on schedule in 2000, shortly before Hood's death. Hood's intention in this ambitious project was to delineate a fictional panorama of contemporary Canadian culture. Set against the vastness of his complete works, Hood's reception by critics and audiences alike seems quite moderate. He is appreciated above all as a writer of short stories. His collected stories, published over 40 years between 1962 (*Flying a Red Kite: Stories*) and 2003 (*After All! The Collected Stories V*), comprise ten original book publications plus several volumes of reprinted stories, making Hood one of the most prolific Canadian short story writers. Most of his stories are located in eastern metropolises (Toronto, Montreal); a bilingual, Hood was the only one of the Montreal Story Tellers who lived in this city throughout his writing life. His second collection, *Around the Mountain: Scenes from Montreal Life* (1967), deliberately published at the time of the EXPO World's Fair in Montreal in 1967, conveys an almost documentary attention to detail—Hood's style has in fact often been described as journalistic. A self-professed Catholic and a professor at the University of Montreal for over 30 years, Hood is regarded as one of Canada's most intellectual writers. In his apparently accessible and, to use his own phrase, "super-realistic" and often allegorical writing style, he combines realistic elements with supernatural, transcendental aspects, uncovering philosophical and religious questions in the mundane patterns of daily life. Some representative examples of his highly polished stories include "Flying a Red Kite" and "Three Halves of a House" (from *Flying a Red Kite*, 1962), "Going Out as a Ghost" (from *Dark Glasses*, 1976), as well as "Getting to Williamstown" (from *The Fruit Man, The Meat Man and The Manager*, 1971). Despite some formal innovations (such as the comatose first-person narrator in "Getting to Williamstown," who supplies the central perspective and thereby lends the plot a dreamlike, surreal touch), Hood's narrative style remains largely traditional.

Ray Smith (1941–) is the most experimental of the Montreal Story Tellers. The fact that he published three short story collections between 1969 and 1986, and two novels as late as the 1990s, is evidence of his initial predilections in matters of genre, although clear genre boundaries are difficult to establish with this postmodernist author. His best-known stories include "The

Princess, the Boeing, and the Hot Pastrami Sandwich" (from his short story cycle *Lord Nelson Tavern*, 1974) and "Cape Breton Is the Thought-Control Centre of Canada," from his eponymous first story collection (1969). "Cape Breton" unmistakably belongs to the 1960s, an age that questioned conventions also in literary terms. As the text self-referentially proclaims, we are dealing with "compiled fiction," a piecemeal, fragmentary collection of dialogues, reflections, aphorisms, and miniature stories, 31 fragments in all. Insofar as thematic threads are still discernible, these fragments deal with the precarious national identity of postcolonial Canada at the time of the Canadian Renaissance—especially in connection with the economic and cultural threat posed by the United States at the time—with writing and art, and with relationships and love. The text also rejects any "sense of an ending," to use Frank Kermode's term, and closes instead with the following anti-American paragraph: "For Centennial Year, send President Johnson a gift: an American tourist's ear in a matchbox. Even better, don't bother with the postage" (35).

The Three Leading Authors of the Canadian Short Story: Alice Munro, Mavis Gallant and Margaret Atwood

While the Montreal Story Tellers, who were so instrumental in the development of the short story as a genre, were all male, the three most highly regarded and also the best-known short story writers in Canada today are female. The first of these is Alice Munro (1931–), who in 2013 received the Nobel Prize in Literature for her short fiction oeuvre, a fact in which literary critics all over the world rejoiced (see Chapter 4). Munro wrote[1] exclusively short stories, and thereby represents the very rare case of a writer committed to a single literary genre. Between 1968 and 2012, she published 14 collections of short stories as well as seven volumes of selected stories, although *Lives of Girls and Women* (1971) and *Who Do You Think You Are?* (1978; published as *The Beggar Maid* in the United States and Great Britain) can be described as short story cycles because of the unifying interconnectedness of the individual stories (see Chapter 5). Munro often addresses specifically gendered themes, often from a female perspective, such as restrictive gender roles in rural and small-town milieus (for instance, "Boys and Girls" from *Dance of the Happy Shades*, 1968; see Chapter 11), complex and difficult mother-daughter relationships ("The Peace of Utrecht" from *Dance*), gender-related professional issues ("The Office" from *Dance* or "The Ottawa Valley" from *Something I've Been Meaning to Tell You*, 1974), emotional enslavement in love relations ("Dulse" from *The Moons of Jupiter*, 1982), and problems of aging ("The Moons of Jupiter" from

Moons or "The Bear Came Over the Mountain" from *Hateship, Friendship, Courtship, Loveship, Marriage*, 2001). One of Munro's trademarks is her elaborate style, which not only fulfills high esthetic demands but also attains an unusually complex expressiveness, for instance, in the idiosyncratic combining of seemingly paradoxical adjectives ("People's lives, in Jubilee and elsewhere, were dull, simple, amazing, and unfathomable—deep caves paved with kitchen linoleum," "Epilogue: The Photographer," *Lives*, 249). Munro's stories also achieve her self-proclaimed purpose of emotionally affecting her readers.

Her writing has had a considerable impact on the literary world. For instance, *Time Magazine* counted her among the 100 most influential living personalities at the beginning of the twenty-first century, a rare honor for a writer of fiction. Her first short story collection, *Dance of the Happy Shades*, was awarded the Governor General's Award for fiction in 1968, a coveted prize that she has twice been awarded since then. Since the publication of *Lives of Girls and Women*, that is, since the early 1970s, her new books have regularly topped bestseller lists. The first appearance of many of her stories in *The New Yorker* testifies to the international dimension of her work. Munro is also the most frequently anthologized author of short stories in Canada. As with Atwood, Munro demonstrates her skill in a narrative and linguistic style that never lacks complexity or fails to challenge the reader, yet her stories are also popular with a large readership. Munro is also a "writer's writer," who often interweaves poetological questions into her texts (for instance, in "Fiction" from *Too Much Happiness*, 2009, see Chapter 4; and "Material" from *Something*), deftly switches between traditional and nonlinear, digressive narratives ("Dulse" and "White Dump" from *The Progress of Love*, 1986), celebrates multiple narrative perspectives ("Fits" from *Progress*, or "The Albanian Virgin" from *Open Secrets*, 1994) and Joycean epiphany ("Simon's Luck" from *Who*, 1978), and subtly blends the mundane with the extraordinary ("Dear Life" from *Dear Life*, 2012). The short story form itself serves one of Munro's central arguments concerning the impenetrability and fragmentariness of the human condition and the episodic, fleeting nature of experience that never coagulates into a consecutive, cumulative sequence (for which the novel form would seem more appropriate; see Chapter 5): "And what happened, I asked myself, to Marion? … Such questions persist, in spite of novels" ("Epilogue: The Photographer," *Lives*, 247; for a more detailed treatment of Munro's art of the short story see chapters 4 and 11).

Mavis Gallant (1922–2014), at the beginning of the twenty-first century the second most anthologized short story writer in Canada, grew up bilingually in Montreal, moved to Europe in 1950 at the age of 27, and traveled extensively. As of 1960 and until her recent death, she lived in Paris as the best-known expatriate author of Canadian origin writing in English. Unlike

Munro, Gallant has tried her hand at other genres as well, having published two novels (in 1959 and 1970) and various journalistic essays, but the short story was closest to her, for poetological reasons similar to Munro's. With her emigration to France as well as her frequently European settings, characters, and themes, Gallant for a long time was among Canada's lesser-known writers, at least with her early collections (*The Other Paris*, 1956; *My Heart Is Broken*, 1964), although she always thought of herself as a Canadian (Gallant once referred to this as "the national sense of self"). Her books were first published in the United States and England for a long time; the first to appear in Canada was *The End of the World and Other Stories* (1974). It was only with the publication of *From the Fifteenth District* (1979) that Canadian critics and scholars, somewhat belatedly, acknowledged Gallant to be one of the best Canadian short story writers.

Having found brief employment as a journalist, her international literary career began in the early 1950s when she submitted one of her stories to *The New Yorker*. Her second submission in 1951 made it into print: "Madeline's Birthday" (in *Cost of Living*), the first of altogether 116 short stories by Gallant published in this distinguished magazine. In 1964 *The New Yorker* negotiated a first-option contract with Gallant, so that most of Gallant's stories were first published with that magazine, which, however, proved a hindrance to Gallant's reception in Canada from the 1950s up to the 1970s.

Gallant's situation as an emigrant has had a lasting effect on her work from a thematic and narrative point of view. Time and again, she writes about immigration and exile, outsiders, psychological rootlessness in place and time, socially estranged foreigners in Europe and North America, cultural conflicts and failed communication, multi- and transculturalism (often against the historical background of World War II and the postwar period), about political and social rifts reflected in individual destinies and mentalities. The setting of several of her short story collections is predominantly or even exclusively Paris, her adopted home (see, for instance, *Overhead in a Balloon: Stories of Paris*, 1985). *The Pegnitz Junction* (1973) deals with Germany and the Germans. *Home Truths: Selected Canadian Stories* (1981), the collection for which she received the Governor General's Award for fiction in Canada, provides Canadian readers with critical views of their homeland and of themselves. The breadth and variety of her settings, characters, and themes made Gallant one of the most flexible, cosmopolitan authors in Canada. Her typically distanced, apparently uninvolved narrative voice has been attributed by scholars to her own personal situation as an immigrant and could partly be responsible for her modest readership compared to Munro's or Atwood's. Although her detached narrative voice may be a subject for debate ("There is something rather chilling in Gallant," Rooke 1986, 267), what particularly commands respect is her nuanced, polished style, often drenched in wry humor, understatement, or more or less subtle satire.

The thematic and technical breadth and complexity of her narrative art, which also comprises novellas (for instance, "The Pegnitz Junction"), is reflected in some of the most frequently anthologized of her short stories, such as "The Ice Wagon Going Down the Street," "Acceptance of Their Ways," and "My Heart Is Broken" (from *My Heart Is Broken*), "The Moslem Wife," "The Latehomecomer," and "From the Fifteenth District" (from *From the Fifteenth District*), as well as in "In Youth Is Pleasure" (from *Home Truths*). Although herself nationally "dislocated, perhaps forever"—like her character Lottie Benz in "Virus X" (204) from *Home Truths*, a young Canadian of German ancestry whose visit to Strasbourg in 1953 unsettles her formerly secure sense of home and belonging—Gallant, with her 14 short story collections published over half a century (including *The Selected Stories of Mavis Gallant*, 1996, which comprises 52 of her stories), remains an international flagship figure of the Canadian short story, and honors the multicultural, cosmopolitan inclination of contemporary Canadian letters (for an analysis of her story "In Transit" see Chapter 8).

Margaret Atwood (1939–) has placed less emphasis on the short story genre than Munro and Gallant, yet only relatively speaking. The acknowledged figurehead of Canadian literature—not only for the exceptional quality of her writing but also because of the volume and versatility of her creative output—Atwood has published somewhat more novels and books of poetry than collections of short fiction. However, she has published a considerable body of short stories over the decades (see Chapter 7), too, which in quality and quantity make her one of the leading Canadian short story writers, on a par with Munro. Atwood is on the whole more experimental than either Gallant or Munro as far as genre conventions are concerned, extending and blending them, for instance, with those of poetry and the prose poem. Her collections *Dancing Girls* (1977), *Bluebeard's Egg* (1983), and *Wilderness Tips* (1991) as well as her short story cycle *Moral Disorder* (2006) contain stories that are in formal terms relatively conventional and are anchored in the tradition of psychological realism. Even her very first collection, *Dancing Girls*, gives a glimpse into the thematic resourcefulness of the author: "The Man from Mars" and "Dancing Girls" shed a critical light on Canada's national dream of multiculturalism; "Giving Birth" creates a metapoetical parallel between the human act of conception and creative writing; "A Travel Piece," "Under Glass," and "Polarities" outline psychological problems and pathological developments, in the case of "Polarities" set against the background of an uneven power struggle between Canada and the United States. "A Travel Piece," "The Resplendent Quetzal," "The Grave of the Famous Poet," "Hair Jewellery," and "Lives of the Poets" employ travel motifs in various contexts, while a central theme of the collection is relationship crises that result in identity conflicts, mostly on a personal, but occasionally also on a national level.

Indeed, Atwood places her stories in a specifically Canadian context, even more so than Munro, which, for instance, is obvious in stories from *Wilderness Tips* such as "Hairball," "Death by Landscape," "The Age of Lead," and "Wilderness Tips," as they take up Canadian settings (the "wilderness," but also the metropolis of Toronto), Canadian history (the Franklin expedition in search of the Northwest Passage), Canadian national challenges (ecological issues, the proximity to and difference from the United States, Canadian identity, multiculturalism), and Canadian myths (Sir John Franklin, the Canadian Mosaic). In addition, and to a greater extent than Gallant and even Munro, Atwood confronts the differences between the sexes and the difficulties of gender relations, not only in her formally more conventional stories (for instance, "Uglypuss" and "Bluebeard's Egg" from *Bluebeard's Egg*), but especially in the experimental short texts in *Murder in the Dark: Short Fictions and Prose Poems* (1983), for instance "Worship," "Iconography," "Liking Men," and "Women's Novels" (see Chapter 7). Atwood's later short prose collection *Good Bones* (1992) takes on gender aspects from an even more critical perspective, with the remarkably well-read Atwood making intertextual use of classic works of world literature and also of popular culture texts. Her short dramatic monologue "Gertrude Talks Back" rewrites Shakespeare's *Hamlet*, the quasi-prose poem "Men at Sea" references Charles Baudelaire's poem "L'homme et la mer," while "The Little Red Hen Tells All" takes up an English children's story, and the delightful "Making a Man" alludes to certain types of texts in women's magazines, especially the recipe format (see Chapter 7). Atwood's short fiction also reveals her extraordinary talent of lending a humorous if not comical twist to even the most serious matters, while preserving their intellectual seriousness and complexity. As a storyteller, Atwood experiments with narrative structure in her short stories (exemplified by the alternating point of view in "The War in the Bathroom" [in *Dancing Girls*], the montage-like composition in "The Age of Lead," and the dense intertextuality in "Bluebeard's Egg"). Last but not least, Atwood the stylist (and poet) is revealed in the linguistic brilliance of many of her stories (for a more detailed treatment of Atwood's short fiction oeuvre see chapters 7 and 14).

Regionalism and the Short Story

In its initial stage of development in such a vast country, the modern Canadian short story was closely linked to regional themes and to mainly rural backgrounds. In contemporary Canadian literature, an increasing cosmopolitanism is noticeable, which is often reflected in a much wider and more varied choice of setting (see, for instance, Clark Blaise's fictional geographies). But even in connection with the contemporary short story, one can still distinguish significant regions spanning literary Canada from coast to coast. There are the large cities in the East (Toronto, Montreal, Ottawa), which serve as backdrops for stories, for instance, by the Montreal Story Tellers, Atwood, and Austin Clarke. Vancouver, the western metropolis, is often the chosen setting of writers like Audrey Thomas and Jane Rule. And there are the more rural regions, including southwestern Ontario, the prairies, the Pacific coast, and the Atlantic provinces.

The prairie writers W. O. Mitchell, Margaret Laurence, Rudy Wiebe, and Guy Vanderhaeghe, though treading in the footsteps of their forerunners, the prairie realists Frederick Philip Grove and Sinclair Ross (see Chapter 1), adapt and renew this tradition in various ways. Mitchell (1914–1998) was one of the most successful screenwriters in Canada, also a playwright, yet is today mainly known for his novels, such as *Who Has Seen the Wind* (1947). Mitchell's short story collections *Jake and the Kid* (1961) and *According to Jake and the Kid: A Collection of New Stories* (1989) became bestsellers in Canada—partly because the stories, which began to appear in 1942 in both Canadian and American magazines, were rewritten by Mitchell for a radio format (and aired over about 250 CBC programs between 1950 and 1956)—and were finally adapted for television. It was only after they had acquired this media publicity that the texts were released in book form as short story cycles. Mitchell's writing invests the prairie story with a more cheerful, humorous streak. With their coarse humor, which draws from the oral tradition and that of tall tales, their emphasis on small-town local color, and their child protagonist and his relationship to a fatherly mentor, Mitchell's texts gave the prairie short story new impulses and twice won him the Stephen Leacock Award for Humour. Their sentimental, leveling, roughly moralizing aspects led Margaret Laurence to conclude in her review of *Jake and the Kid* in 1962 that these stories particularly addressed a younger audience (70).

Margaret Laurence (1926–1987) herself delivered one of the best Canadian short story cycles with *A Bird in the House* (1970) as part of her exceptional Manawaka fiction series, which is for the most part set on the prairie. Written over a span of eight years and, according to Laurence, the only semi-autobiographical piece of fiction she ever wrote, *A Bird in the House* recounts the making of an artist in a cycle of eight stories. The writer-to-be Vanessa MacLeod grows up in the 1930s in Manawaka, a fictional small town on the prairie, modeled upon the author's own home town Neepawa in Manitoba. The events are described from the perspective of a grown-up, 40-year-old Vanessa, but the focus is nevertheless on the experiences of the maturing child. Through her writing, among other things, Vanessa tries to break out of the constricting family and gender roles that are imposed upon her by a patriarchal small-town community. Her purpose is to escape the stifling life based around family life that her mother had to resign herself to. The text delivers a realistic evocation of small-town life and social structures in the Canadian prairie, subtle character sketches, and a gradual thematic buildup in the manner of a bildungsroman. Another essential feature is the accessible style and the balanced, consistent tension between the experiencing and the reminiscing Vanessa, the latter learning to reconsider, as a "professional observer," the judgments of her younger self.

Casting off chains of limitation is a central theme for Laurence, which her prairie works mostly address in connection with the empowerment of female characters. Her African stories, inspired by her years in Africa between 1950 and 1957, have been read as a thematic preparation for this, yet most of them were written later than her prairie stories. Collected in *The Tomorrow-Tamer* (1963), these stories—including "The Rain Child," "A Gourdful of Glory," "Godman's Master," and "The Tomorrow-Tamer"—are set against the African struggles for independence and revolve around the topic of freedom, its chances and challenges, from the political to the personal.

Rudy Wiebe (1934–) grew up in the prairie provinces Saskatchewan and Alberta, where he still lives. A Mennonite, he is a member of a religious minority; his parents had been persecuted on religious grounds and emigrated from the Soviet Union to Canada. Wiebe is mainly known as an author of novels in which he recounts the experiences of the Mennonites in the New World, but he also directs his attention toward other minorities such as the First Nations, the Inuit, and the Métis, particularly in the Canadian West. Many of his works recreate landmarks and figures of Canadian history, yet his pronounced authorial voice takes sides with the minorities and reconsiders official historiography. From 1970 onward Wiebe edited various short story anthologies, and between 1974 and 2010 he published four collections of his own stories: *Where Is the Voice Coming From?* (1974), *The Angel of the Tar Sands and Other Stories* (1982), *River of Stones: Fictions and Memories* (1995), and *Collected Stories: 1955–2010* (2010). The opening sentence of Wiebe's best-known and most complex story, "Where Is the Voice Coming From?," already points to one of his central themes, namely the difficulties of writing and rewriting history on the one hand and the complexity of perspective and form in fictional representation on the other, both aspects often being correlated. Although Wiebe's writing leaves behind the limitations of realistic storytelling from a narrative as well as thematic point of view (see, for instance, "The Angel of the Tar Sands") and shares characteristics with a postmodernist style, Wiebe still believes in the meaningfulness of language and existence. He struggles for a better understanding of their complex nature in his highly experimental works, despite occasionally leaning a little too much toward the didactic and the moral. Stories such as "Where Is the Voice

Coming From?" and "The Naming of Albert Johnson" (both based on historical facts) make it clear that Wiebe accords a higher level of veracity to fiction than to official historiography, not least because the former gives voice to Indigenous, that is, marginal aspects in Canadian cultural history. Such epistemological problems trickle down into the narrative form, especially in "Where Is the Voice Coming From?" In this metafictional story that exposes both literature and history as artificial constructs, the narrator becomes ever more aware of the difficulty of story construction while trying to piece together the story of Almighty Voice, a young Cree Indian, who was tracked down and killed for his various crimes in the nineteenth century by the Canadian Mounted Police. The narrator realizes in the course of a disillusioning narrative process that the numerous but fragmentary historical "facts" are contradictory, and that a coherent picture of the events, also taking into account the Indigenous perspective, is thus impossible to achieve. Language itself also threatens to hinder rather than ensure access to the truth. Almighty Voice's death cries remain incomprehensible to the storyteller, encoded as they are by intercultural difference—a "wordless cry" that nevertheless reaches beyond the narrative at hand, not least because of the homophony between "Cree" and the French "cri" (cry): "I say 'wordless cry' because that is the way it sounds to me. I could be more accurate if I had a reliable interpreter who would make a reliable interpretation. For I do not, of course, understand the Cree myself" (143).

Belonging to a later generation of prairie writers, Guy Vanderhaeghe (1951–) is, next to Wiebe, sometimes referred to as a "man's writer," as he describes the Canadian prairie primarily from a male perspective. Vanderhaeghe received the Governor General's Award for fiction for his first book, *Man Descending: Selected Stories* (1982). Especially with this first collection, Vanderhaeghe developed the tradition of the Canadian prairie story. There followed *The Trouble with Heroes: And Other Stories* (1983) and *Things As They Are? Short Stories* (1992). These titles are programmatic in that Vanderhaeghe's male protagonists, mentally drained antiheroes, have become ill at ease with conventional male codes of behavior and face up to their weaknesses and their failure to come to terms with life (see especially "Man Descending" and "Cages"). Some of his stories deal with younger protagonists ("Reunion," "The Watcher," "Drummer"; all mentioned stories are in *Man Descending*).

One of the best-known male writers of the Canadian west coast is Jack Hodgins (1938–). Deeply rooted on Vancouver Island all his life, Hodgins has immortalized this western region of Canada in various novels, but also in his two short story cycles, *Spit Delaney's Island* (1976) and *The Barclay Family Theatre* (1981). His works characteristically feature hopelessly entwined family relations (the latter volume portrays seven sisters and their extended families), eccentric characters, fantastic burlesque twists and turns, and a hyperbolic style. They convey a sense of place in connection with living on an island, the boundaries it creates and those it dissolves. Hodgins regards "the line between water and land as a kind of separation between one kind of reality and another" (in Hancock 1979–80, 55). His stories also highlight the beauties of nature of the Canadian Pacific Northwest.

Alden Nowlan, who died at the age of 50 in 1983, and David Adams Richards (1950–) are known above all as poets and novelists of the Maritimes, though they also published short story collections in the tradition of hard realism that delineate what Janice Kulyk Keefer has called an "anatomy of poverty" (1987b, 167) of the rural inhabitants of the Atlantic provinces (Nowlan, *Miracle at Indian River*, 1968, and *Will Ye Let the Mummers In?*, 1984; Richards, *Dancers at Night*, 1978). This also applies to the main representative of the short story of the Maritimes, Alistair MacLeod (1936–2014), who published an internationally successful and award-winning novel entitled *No Great Mischief* (1999). His high reputation in Canada and beyond is mainly based on the 16 stories that appeared in his two short story collections, *The Lost Salt Gift of Blood* (1976) and *As Birds Bring Forth the Sun and Other Stories* (1986), as well as in his collected stories (*Island: The Collected Stories*, 2000). Even before his stories had been collected, some of his texts were selected for *Best American Stories*, which considers stories first published in American magazines during the year prior to selection ("The Boat," 1968, and "The Lost Salt Gift of Blood," 1975; both collected in *Lost Salt*). Other excellent stories by MacLeod include "The Road to Rankin's Point" (1976, in *Lost Salt*), "The Closing Down of Summer" (1976), "As Birds Bring Forth the Sun" (1985), and "Vision" (1986, all in *As Birds*). MacLeod's conventionally structured, highly polished stories describe in an elegiac, occasionally lyrical style his semi-autobiographical narrator's departures from and returns to Cape Breton (MacLeod himself split his time between Windsor, Ontario, and Cape Breton) and the loss, but also the maelstrom of local and family bonds. His first-person narratives render an almost palpable impression of the region, with their precise descriptions of ruggedly beautiful landscapes, the hardships of physical work, and the poor economic conditions in the Maritimes. His most frequently anthologized story is "The Boat" (1968), a vivid text that is representative of MacLeod's style and proves once again how so-called regional stories can still convey universal meanings.

Female Writers Between Compliance, Innovation and Rebellion

The roughly equal representation of well-known female and male authors that characterizes Canadian literature also applies to the short story.

Not only do the three leading writers of the Canadian short story happen to be female (see the chapter section above), but such a large number of female authors have written in the genre that this even gender distribution seems self-evident today. It is noteworthy, however, that this state of affairs has partly resulted in a gender-sensitive and gender-oriented writing style in Canadian short fiction and in Canadian literature in general.

Margaret Laurence is a pioneer of gender-conscious writing from a female perspective in Canada. Her works delineate the psychological, emotional, and intellectual development of female characters in a man's world, her short story collection *A Bird in the House* (1970) being paradigmatic in this respect (Laurence: "I was dealing with a lot of the stuff Women's Lib is talking about right now.... My generation of women came to a lot of the same conclusions, but they did it in isolation; you weren't supposed to say those things out loud"; in Atwood 1993 [1974], 386). Marian Engel, Jane Rule, Audrey Thomas, and Carol Shields—all born within five to nine years after Laurence (who was born in 1926)—pursued these approaches in various forms. Despite the fact that Marian Engel (1933–1985) mainly thought of herself as a novelist (her best-known novel being *Bear*, 1976), she published two remarkable short story collections, *Inside the Easter Egg* (1975) and *The Tattooed Woman* (1985). In these stories, most of whose protagonists are middle-aged women, Engel addresses typically "female" issues, such as the socialization of girls and women to define Self in relation to the Other, the consequences of aging, illness, and surgery for women, and the female body ("The Tattooed Woman," "The Confession Tree," both in *Tattooed Woman*). A good example is the title story "The Tattooed Woman," first published in 1975. An unnamed 42-year-old woman, a housewife, hears her husband's confession about his affair with a 21-year-old colleague. The shocked protagonist responds to this disclosure by carving signs, such as houses, trees, and stars, into her skin. Through this form of "writing" she fashions her body, which has been "discarded" by her husband, into a work of art. Ironically, this act makes her visible and confident again: "I am an artist, now, she thought, a true artist. My body is my canvas.... I am Somebody ... and at the same time beautiful and new" (8). Toward the end of her life, Engel gradually shifted from a realistic writing style to a fantastic, surreal, postmodernist style, before her early death in 1985.

Jane Rule (1931–2007), born in the United States, settled in Vancouver in 1956. In 1976 she moved to Galiano Island, one of the Gulf Islands situated between the mainland and Vancouver Island. Early in her career, she became a prominent mouthpiece of the gay rights movement after the success of her debut novel *Desert of the Heart* (1964), which describes a homoerotic relationship between two women and was later made into a successful film (*Desert Hearts*, 1985). In her numerous novels and essays, Rule repeatedly

3. The Canadian Short Story Since 1967

addressed the topic of (mostly female) homoeroticism. Timothy Findley (1930–2002), who sometimes dealt with male homosexuality in his three collections of short stories and more often touched on the broader theme of gender in relation to masculinity, insisted that the significance of his work goes beyond his sexual orientation. The same applies to Rule, who once stated that the problem is not homosexuality but homophobia. In an accessible, structurally conventional manner, her stories tackle unconventional gender issues in an undogmatic, open-minded, and compassionate way, although in particular her earlier texts do not ignore the difficulties that may come along with Otherness. Examples of this are her collections *Theme for Diverse Instruments* (1975) and especially *Outlander: Short Stories and Essays* (1981), with its stories "Lilian" and "Outlander." A representative example of her even more liberal later work is "Slogans" from *Inland Passage and Other Stories* (1985). In this story, three women take turns retelling their life stories to each other at their 25th anniversary class reunion. The long-term couple Nancy and Ann radiate supreme contentment, whereas Jessica, divorced and suffering from cancer, talks of nothing but broken marriages, her own and those of many former classmates. The title story "Inland Passage" is exemplary of the strong regional component of Rule's work, which makes use of the local color and picturesque landscapes of western Canada. Her better-known stories also include "Brother and Sister" and "My Father's House" (both in *Theme*), "Lilian" (in *Outlander*), "The End of Summer," "Joy," and "Puzzle" (all in *Inland Passage*), which deal with childhood and family issues as well as with the past and present lives—and love lives—of elderly female protagonists. Some 15 years before her death, Rule retired from writing after a career of three decades ("I have written what I wanted," Rule in Crean 1991, 11).

Like Jane Rule, Audrey Thomas (1935–) and Carol Shields (1935–2003) were also born in the United States and later received Canadian citizenship (both in the 1970s). The work of the prolific Thomas, who has been described as a "B.C. writer" (by Jean Barman and Carolyn Heiman[2]) has an especially strong regional component. After her move to Canada in 1958 she settled down in British Columbia, for the first 11 years in Vancouver, then, like Rule, on Galiano Island. Thomas has published almost as many short story collections (seven) as novels and has contributed to the development of the Canadian short story for over 30 years, both technically and thematically. Her first short story collection, *Ten Green Bottles*, published in 1967, three years ahead of Laurence's *A Bird in the House*, initiated the portrayal of uniquely female modes of experience in a radically new, authentic, and strongly autobiographical way in Canadian literature. For instance, her earliest story, "If One Green Bottle" (first published in *The Atlantic Monthly* in 1965, collected in *Ten Green Bottles*), deals with miscarriage. Using a consistent stream-of-consciousness technique, the story places Thomas among the formally flexible, experimental, postmodernist writers of short fiction in Canada. She foregrounds the discourse level (for instance, by transcribing lexicon entries and using intertextual references) and self-referentially addresses the topic of writing itself, which she often describes as a liberating act, particularly for female characters. Her strong, playful interest in language sometimes even informs her choice of titles, as in "Initram" ("Martini" spelled backwards; in *Ladies and Escorts*). In "The Man with Clam Eyes" from *Goodbye Harold, Good Luck* (1986), the title is based on an unintentional misspelling ("clam" for "calm"), and the self-referential aspect of language and its conditioning of reality, which permeate the entire story, are also reflected in the plot. Like Laurence, Thomas spent some years in Africa, which functioned as a catalyst for her writing and left traces that went beyond her early work (see, for instance, "Xanadu" [in *Ten Green Bottles*], "Rapunzel" [in *Ladies and Escorts*], "Two in the Bush" [in *Two in the Bush*], and "Out in the Midday Sun" [in *Real Mothers*]). Other stories focus on mother-daughter relationships and family bonds in general (see her collection *Real Mothers*, 1981), the critique of the relationship between the sexes, and the reappraisal of female gender roles (see her 1971 Vancouver story "Aquarius," in *Ladies and Escorts*, 1977). Thomas also confronts themes such as the liminal space between sanity and madness or, in more general terms, between dreams and reality (as an example, see my analysis of Thomas's story "Salon des Refusés" in Chapter 8).

Carol Shields had a remarkable writing career, begun only in her forties, after having raised five children. Particularly well-known are her prize-winning novels *Swann: A Mystery* (1987) and *The Stone Diaries* (1993). But it is particularly in her short story collections *Various Miracles* (1985), *The Orange Fish* (1989), and *Dressing Up for the Carnival* (2000) that Shields proves to be not only a realist-modernist writer, but also open to postmodernist experimentation. Her focus on the female experience of a home environment, for which she was initially reproached by male critics, was gradually reevaluated and eventually came to be celebrated as her trademark (this artistic creed of hers is spelled out particularly clearly in her later story "Soup du Jour," in *Dressing Up*). Her writing may indeed record exceptional, even miraculous aspects of everyday life, but the author never shrinks away from the greater or lesser tragedies of human existence. Placing great emphasis on family in her personal life, Shields's stories often deal with family issues, such as marriage, mother-daughter relationships, and love, as well as the experience of aging (for example, in "Love so Fleeting, Love so Fine" and "Flitting Behaviour," both in *Various Miracles*; "The Orange Fish," "Chemistry," and "Milk Bread Beer Ice," all in *Orange Fish*; "Death of an Artist" and "Edith-Esther," both in *Dressing Up*). Her characters belong to the upper middle class. As a result of her long career as a university lecturer and her marriage to a Canadian professor, she also often deals with the academic world, in an ironic or even parodic tone, as in "The Metaphor Is Dead—Pass It On" and "Mrs. Turner Cutting the Grass" (both in *Various Miracles*). The latter story sets the eventful life of a simple woman in the outskirts of Winnipeg against episodes from the life of an unappealing professor at a Massachusetts college. A satirical take on academic life is taken in stories like "Our Men and Women," "Ilk," and "A Scarf" (all in *Dressing Up*). Shields's works nevertheless often display a joyful, optimistic attitude. Examples of this are stories such as "Pardon" (which hyperrealistically and humorously transforms personal relations into gestures of apology) and "Various Miracles" (both in *Various Miracles*) and "Absence" (in *Dressing Up*).

Among the later generation of female writers born in the 1940s and 1950s are Sandra Birdsell, Isabel Huggan, Katherine Govier, and Diane Schoemperlen. Birdsell (1942–) has resided in Manitoba and Saskatchewan all her life, and the prairie environment and milieu of these provinces have had an impact on the settings and choice of characters in her works (various immigrant groups, but also Mennonites and Métis). Birdsell's first two short story collections, *Night Travellers* (1982) and *Ladies of the House* (1984), were republished in one volume under the title *Agassiz Stories* in 1987. If slightly misleading, the subtitle of the American edition, *A Novel in Stories*, rightfully points to the cyclical nature of Birdsell's short fiction. Agassiz is the name of the fictional place in Manitoba that serves as a setting for the saga of the Lafreniere clan (with a Métis father and a Mennonite mother) over three generations, with an emphasis on its female family members. The partly self-inflicted marginality and dependence of women as well as the situation of the working-class and ethnic minorities prompt Birdsell to describe larger structures of exclusion, isolation, repression, and discrimination; the possibility of change is regarded largely pessimistically in these texts, particularly in connection with the plight of women. Her better-known stories include "Flowers for Weddings and Funerals," "Judgement," and "Night Travellers" (all in *Night Travellers*), "Keepsakes" (in *Ladies of the House*), and "The Man from Mars" (from her fourth collection, *The Two-Headed Calf*).

Multicultural Diversity and the Short Story

The contemporary Canadian short story owes its diversity not least to its numerous multicultural voices. The many contributions to the genre from writers of different ethnic backgrounds can only be hinted at here.

The most important representatives of Native short fiction are Thomas King (1943–), with two short story collections (see, for instance, his stories "Borders" and "One Good Story, That One," both in *One Good Story*; on King see Chapter 13), and Lee Maracle (1950–), also with two collections (see her stories

"Yin Chin" and "Bertha," both in *Sojourner's Truth*; for an analysis of her story "Polka Partners, Uptown Indians and White Folks" see Chapter 10). The best-known and most prolific representative of Caribbean Canadian literature is Barbados native Austin Clarke (1934–2016), who published nine collections of short stories between 1965 and 2013 (see, for instance, *Choosing His Coffin: The Best Stories of Austin Clarke*, 2003). Dionne Brand (1953–; *Sans Souci and Other Stories*, 1988, see especially "Sans Souci" and "Photograph") and Neil Bissoondath (1955–; *Digging Up the Mountains*, 1986; *On the Eve of Uncertain Tomorrows*, 1990) are writers from Trinidad. The foremost proponent of the Asian Canadian short story is Rohinton Mistry, born in Bombay in 1952, who mostly writes about his former home country India, for instance, in his 1987 collection *Tales from Firozsha Baag* (see "Condolence Visit" and "Swimming Lessons").

Not only the so-called ethnic minority writers, but also writers with European backgrounds often deal with problems of migration and diaspora, the history and culture of their native countries, and intercultural themes of immigration and assimilation in multicultural Canada. A representative of Icelandic Canadian literature is Kristjana Gunnars (1948–), who emigrated from Iceland in 1968 (*The Axe's Edge*, 1983; *The Guest House and Other Stories*, 1992; and *Any Day But This*, 2005). Another writer with an Icelandic background is Canadian-born W. D. Valgardson (1939–), whose work was shaped by his upbringing in Icelandic enclaves in Canada (see his stories "Bloodflowers," in *Bloodflowers*; "A Matter of Balance," in *What Can't*). Besides radio and television scripts, Valgardson published six short story collections between *Bloodflowers: Ten Stories* (1973) and *The Divorced Kids Club: And Other Stories* (1999). The versatile Janice Kulyk Keefer (1952–), also active in the field of literary criticism as a professor at the University of Guelph, reveals a high awareness of her Ukrainian cultural background in her work, which on a literary level reflects her theoretical concept of "transculturalism." Keefer has published three short story collections (*The Paris–Napoli Express*, 1986; *Transfigurations*, 1987; and *Travelling Ladies*, 1990).

The Contemporary Canadian Short Story and the Challenges of Modernism, Realism, Postmodernism and Neorealism

Taking a panoramic view of the Canadian short story since the 1960s, several things stand out: first, the diversity and vitality of the genre, partly deriving from the fact that almost all major writers in the fascinating "postnational" literature that is Canadian literature have made contributions to the short story; second, the relatively high number of short story cycles in Canada (see Chapter 5), with a structural tendency that brings this genre closer to the novel without relinquishing the unity of the individual short story—above-mentioned works by Munro, Gallant, Laurence, Hodgins, Hood, Birdsell, Clarke, Smith, Mitchell, and Mistry, as well as Mordecai Richler (*The Street*, 1969) testify to this phenomenon; and finally the primacy of the modernist-realist tradition of storytelling in the Canadian short story.

Having established themselves as short story writers, some authors—such as the aforementioned Smith, Thomas, Wiebe, and Engel, as well as some who have not yet been dealt with here, such as Leon Rooke, George Bowering, Matt Cohen, and Dave Godfrey—have turned away from or outgrown the genre conventions of the realist-modernist short story, redirecting the genre onto an antirealist, surreal, metafictional, postmodernist path (although all of these writers continued to produce stories in the realist-modernist vein—see Bowering's "Apples" (in *Flycatcher*) or Matt Cohen's "Keeping Fit" (in *Columbus*)—and never fully abandoned this writing style). The most prolific and most anthologized among these authors is Leon Rooke (1934–), who has published 12 short story collections and four volumes of selected stories (most recently *Hitting the Charts: Selected Stories*, 2006, including "The Woman Who Talked to Horses," "Wintering in Victoria," and "Art"). George Bowering (1935–), retired literature professor at the Simon Fraser University in Burnaby, British Columbia, and editor of postmodernist stories as well as author of critical articles, has published seven short story collections. Best known is his programmatic "A Short Story" (in *A Place to Die*), a metafictional text that emphasizes the artificiality of writing by giving the individual subsections generic, self-referential titles such as "Setting," "Characters," and "Point of View." Matt Cohen (see his story "The Sins of Tomas Benares," in *Café Le Dog*) had published six short story collections by the time he died in 1999, as well as a volume of collected stories and *Lives of the Mind Slaves: Selected Stories* (1994). It was only at the peak of postmodernism in the 1960s and 1970s that Dave Godfrey (1938–2015) made his contribution to fiction in two short story collections, among them *Death Goes Better with Coca-Cola* (1967; see his stories "River Two Blind Jacks" and "A New Year's Morning on Bloor Street").

Since the 1980s, another writing style has developed in the short story alongside the more prominent modernist-realist tradition, one enriched with hyperrealist, surreal elements, indebted to both realist and postmodernist conventions and fully aware of this double heritage. The vast oeuvre of such authors as Munro and Atwood displays realist, but also metafictional, postmodernist characteristics in one and the same text, sometimes to such an extent that the new, "neorealist" variety of the contemporary Canadian short story suggests new labels such as "crossover fiction" (David Lodge 1997, 9).

Time will tell whether more recent talents in short story writing such as Madeleine Thien (1974–; one collection of short stories to date), Annabel Lyon (1971–; one collection plus one collection of three novellas), and Caroline Adderson (1963–; two collections) will eventually make it into the canon of Canadian short story writing. In any case, their stories, too, may serve to demonstrate the impressive development and range of the Canadian short story in the twentieth and early twenty-first century, particularly since the 1960s.

4

The Noble Genre
Alice Munro Brings the Nobel Prize in Literature to Canada

The previous chapters have traced how the short story came into its own as a literary genre in the period of Canadian modernism of the early twentieth century (chapters 1 and 2) and how the genre has been particularly productive from the 1960s onward (Chapter 3). It took some hundred years for the highest accolade in literature to finally go to a Canadian writer, and, significantly so, to a writer of short stories.

Alice Munro and the Nobel Prize in Literature

On October 10, 2013, it was announced that the Nobel Prize in Literature would be awarded to Canadian short story writer Alice Munro, a decision German literature critic Denis Scheck favorably called a "sensational choice" (perhaps because the prize thereby went to a Canadian, and to a short story writer?), which other experts, however, had considered probable, since it was more than deserved. Recordings of the immediate, on-site reaction of the convened journalists to the announcement of the Permanent Secretary of the Swedish Academy convey jubilant cries of approval. The spontaneous and very positive reception of the laureate on the part of the assembled journalists was sustained in the ensuing international reaction to the committee's selection. The Austrian journalist and author Eva Menasse, for instance, comes to the following conclusion in her homage to Alice Munro in the German national weekly newspaper *Die Zeit*: "The news that Alice Munro is the recipient of the Nobel Prize in Literature for 2013 has filled more authors in the world with deep, honest joy and approval than most of the announcements of past years" (Menasse 2013; my translation from the German original). What, then, is distinctive or even exceptional about this particular choice, which has evoked almost universal approval, indeed enthusiastic reactions of moving praise for this author? I will summarize the multiple reasons in five points.

For one, for the first time in the over one hundred years of its existence, this highest literary distinction has gone to Canada, which had been considered to be long overdue and thrilled not only Canadians but Canadianists worldwide. It had become increasingly inexplicable that a country with such internationally renowned literary luminaries as Margaret Atwood, Alice Munro, and Michael Ondaatje had not yet received the Nobel Prize. Douglas Gibson, Munro's longstanding publisher in Canada—a postcolonial country that has only "found" itself culturally since the 1960s and has since enjoyed a cultural heyday—stated with exultation: "All of Canada is just delighted by this news … it's as if all of Canada has won the award" (*CBC News* 2013) and "It's a great day for all of us, every Canadian should be walking a little taller" (Leung 2013).

A second reason for the momentous appreciation of this decision was that, of the 110 Nobel Prizes in Literature awarded at the time, Munro was only the thirteenth female writer to win this coveted prize. Considering that creative writing is not a field of which one could say that male writers are nine times better (or better at all) than female writers, the decade-long disregard of female writers, with a gender ratio of 1:9 in terms of Nobel prizes won, appears, to put it mildly, inappropriate. At any rate, the fact that seven of the awards from 1990 through 2013, that is, a third of the prizes, had gone to female writers (after only six went to women in the 90 years before) is an indication that the committee may have begun considering and judging nominations with both eyes in the meantime, not only with one—healthily so.

From the perspective of literary studies, it is also remarkable that with Alice Munro a writer has been distinguished who has worked almost exclusively within the short story form. This had never happened before and internationally constitutes an important symbolic appreciation of the short story, which has long stood in the shadow of the novel—not so, however, in Canada: The short story has repeatedly been called Canada's preeminent literary form, and already at the beginning of the 1980s, Munro's short story collection *The Moons of Jupiter* (1982) was the narrative prose text (that is, including novels) for which Penguin had paid the highest advance for the publishing rights of a paperback edition of Canadian literature at the time.

Fourth, it is notable that the prize went to a writer known for her altogether withdrawn lifestyle, who—apart from her literary works—does not participate in public (for instance, political) discourse, unlike her writer colleague and friend Margaret Atwood, who has been in the spotlight for decades. Munro, on the contrary, seems to have only been interested in writing as such, along with her family, for the past six decades, and barely or not at all in the publicity that comes with success. In fact, Munro has appeared to be wary of such publicity; public appearances such as readings have been rare—and so it was not surprising that she did not personally accept the Nobel Prize in Stockholm (because of health concerns). In the 1980s, Munro summarized the two main interests of her life as follows: "All I want is find time to write—what with my husband and my children—well, they're grown up now ... but still."[1] A variation of this statement, which initially appears to be amusing, but is in essence discriminatory from today's perspective, appears in the headline of a 1961 newspaper article on Munro in *The Vancouver Sun*: "Housewife Finds Time to Write Short Stories."

Nevertheless, the domestic work context should not be underestimated since it does not provide the worst conditions for the writer's tasks—as demonstrated paradigmatically in Munro's life work. This leads to the fifth and essentially most important aspect of this honor, which has not always been a matter of course with the Nobel Prize in Literature: Alice Munro is a grandiose writer who masters her craft with virtuosity and whose writing serves as a model for many other writers—with good reason, she has repeatedly been called a "writer's writer."[2] In her case, this has not precluded her success with a general readership: For decades, Munro has been a bestselling author in Canada, the United States, and Great Britain, and not least through translations of her works into other languages, she has also had an established readership in other countries, well before winning the Nobel Prize.[3] Not only her sales success and her resonance in international literary studies, but also the prizes she has received for her writing were indicative of what was to come: Already for her very first short story collection (*Dance of the Happy Shades*, 1968), she received Canada's most illustrious prize for literature, the Governor General's Award for Fiction—two further prizes in this category would follow (in 1978 for *Who Do You Think You Are?* and in 1986 for *The Progress of Love*). Among many other distinctions, she twice received Canada's best-endowed award, the Giller Prize (in 1998 for *The Love of a Good Woman* and in 2004 for *Runaway*), the Ontario Trillium Award three times (in 1990, 1999, and 2013), the Commonwealth Writers' Prize twice (in 1991 und 2004), as well as the U.S. National Book Critics Circle Award (in 1998 for *The Love of a Good Woman*). When in 2009 she also won the distinguished Man Booker International Prize[4] for her life's work, many rightly assumed that it would likely not remain her highest distinction.

Short Biography: From Canadian Small-Town Life to Global Literary Renown

Who is this extraordinary talent who won the first Nobel Prize in Literature both for Canada and for the short story? A basic survey of Munro's biography shows diverse parallels between her life and work. Alice Laidlaw was born in 1931 on a farm on the outskirts of the small town of Wingham, Ontario, in Huron County, the rural area east of Lake Huron in Canada. Alice was the oldest of three children of a former teacher and a farmer—Munro dealt with growing up on such a farm in the context of traditional gender roles in her excellent early story "Boys and Girls" in 1964 (see Chapter 11). While studying English Literature at the University of Western Ontario (today Western University) in London, Ontario, Alice met James Munro, a fellow student whom she married at age 20 in 1951, having dropped out of university after two years due to a lack of financial means. The couple moved to Canada's west coast, first to Vancouver and in the 1960s even further west, to Victoria on Vancouver Island. In Victoria, they opened a bookstore, "Munro's Books" (which still exists). Alice Munro's stories set on Canada's west coast go back to these years, in which Munro also gave birth to three daughters, a familial background reflected in her stories. Alice's own mother was diagnosed with Parkinson's disease when Alice was only 11 years old, and died when Alice was 28, a life-changing experience she gave literary expression to during that same summer in "The Peace of Utrecht" (1960, in *Dance*) and later in "The Ottawa Valley" (1974, in *Something*) and "Friend of My Youth" (1990, in *Friend*). After giving birth to her first daughter, Alice Munro sold her first short story in 1953, at the age of 22, to a Canadian magazine, and became known to a national audience in part through Robert Weaver's *CBC Anthology*, a long-lived Canadian radio program that featured short stories, often read out by the authors themselves. After the birth of her second daughter, Munro regularly wrote short stories and first published them only in Canadian magazines such as the *Tamarack Review* or *Chatelaine*. After 17 such magazine publications, Munro accomplished her national debut in 1968 with her first short story collection, the award-winning *Dance of the Happy Shades*. Her second short story collection, marketed as a "novel," *Lives of Girls and Women* (1971), paved the way for her international breakthrough in the 1970s with *Who Do You Think You Are?* (1978; also published as *The Beggar Maid* in 1979). After 22 years, her first marriage to Jim Munro failed, and after two decades on Canada's west coast in British Columbia, she moved back to her native Ontario. She lived there as of 1975 with her second husband, Gerald Fremlin (who passed away in April 2013), in his parents' home in Clinton, Ontario. Munro would spend the next 40 years in Clinton, back in her beloved southwestern Ontario, a mere 30 kilometers from her birthplace Wingham. Remarkably, for most of her career as a writer, she did not have a room of her own for writing—an experience she dealt with in literary form in "The Office" (1962, in *Dance*). In their house in Clinton, her husband, a geographer, had an office, while she wrote on a small table in the dining room with a view of the driveway. This state of affairs was, however, not detrimental to her writing: 1977 marked the beginning of her decades-long association with the U.S. monthly magazine *The New Yorker*, internationally the top address for the first publication of short stories. Significantly, this magazine, which contributed greatly to making Munro's work known in the United States, secured the first reading right for her short stories.[5]

Alice Munro's Art of the Short Story: Oeuvre, Characteristics, Poetics

Munro oeuvre spans half a century and encompasses 14 short story collections published between 1968 and 2012 (for a listing, see the beginning of Chapter 11). According to her personal statement, the latest volume with the resonant title *Dear Life* was her last, as she can no longer muster the energy that writing demands. A July 2013 *New York Times* report on Munro's (already second) announcement of her resolution to retire is entitled "Alice Munro Puts Down Her Pen to Let the World In" and quotes Munro as stating: "There will be no more books after *Dear Life*.... I don't have the energy anymore ... it's very hard, and you get very tired.... I feel a bit tired now—pleasantly tired.... I feel that I've done what I wanted to do, and that makes me feel fairly content" (McGrath 2013, 1, 2, 3). In other words, Munro had retired from writing before becoming a Nobel laureate, and consequently we can now survey Munro's completed life work (barring possible later posthumous publications).

What exactly are, then, the characteristics of Munro's short stories, what are their poetological conditions and finesses? First of all, Munro is among the authors who have placed a particular region and its inhabitants on the map of world literature, thus immortalizing it: in her case, southwestern Ontario, especially Huron County around London, Ontario. From her early texts (for instance, "Walker Brothers Cowboy," in *Dance*, 1968) to her late work (for instance, "Dear Life," 2011, in *Dear Life*, 2012), this region has been evoked and recreated in her literary work. Although some of her short stories also have other, in part international settings, such as Western Canada or Scotland (where her ancestors originate from), Australia, or Albania, by far most of her short stories are set in the small-town context of southwestern Ontario. As many authors do, Munro dismisses generalizing attributions and differentiates her classification as a regional author as follows: "A lot of people think I'm a regional writer. And I use the region where I grew up a lot. But I don't have any idea of writing to show the kind of things that happen in a certain place. These things happen and the place is part of it. But in a way, it's incidental" (Munro in Hancock 1987, 200). In other words, Munro does not primarily have a documentary interest when selecting settings, although the description of regional idiosyncrasies certainly informs her writing; rather, she is interested in the overarching topics of the human condition, not bound to the region depicted. Instead of recreating the known or recognizable in her settings, in her attempt to grasp what she once metaphorically called "deep caves paved with kitchen linoleum" (*Lives*, 249) she focuses on the puzzling, the unseen, the surprising, and the alienating of the region she is so familiar with. This approach is indicative of the influence of female writers of the American South on Munro's work, such as Flannery O'Connor, Carson McCullers, and especially Eudora Welty, so that Munro's texts have been called "Ontario Gothic" (see Berndt 2010). As Munro once remarked on southwestern Ontario: "The part of the country I come from is absolutely Gothic. You can't get it all down" (Munro in Gibson 1973, 248).

Apart from Munro's preferred regional settings, which, for instance, may result in a realistic use of place names, a second characteristic is that her stories often have female protagonists, are written from a female perspective, and emphasize the corresponding themes: mother-daughter relationships, daughter-father relationships, sister-brother and sister-sister relationships; restrictive gender roles, gender-related professional problems, often also in artistic or writing contexts; love relationships and relationship problems, the wonder of and the wonderful about love, along with its failure and its transience; or problems of growing older and of aging—such thematic emphases are generally rendered from female perspectives that, additionally, refer back to Munro's own life.

Indeed, the evident regional origins and the gender-specific accentuation of her topics point to a third main characteristic of Munro's writing: the strongly autobiographic, or, as Munro herself put it, "personal" roots and dimensions of her work (Munro in Struthers 1983, 17). It can thus be argued that Munro has a tendency to write in line with her own life experiences, largely focused on processing her childhood and adolescence at the beginning of her career, then on career and partnership experiences, and finally on the aging process. Indeed, Munro's stories not only have a propensity to become lengthier, her protagonists also become progressively older[6]—until Munro announced she would rest her pen, as cited above. In a sense, Munro's work can thus be seen as a long, discontinuous, and wide-ranging narration parallel to her own experiences. It is not without reason, for instance, that in the last story of her eponymous last collection of 2012, "Dear Life" (2011), there is a reminiscence of her mother, and that a highly complex, incomplete mother-daughter relationship is a substantial motif in many of Munro's stories. This moving last passage of the story "Dear Life" is not only the last in this collection, but, by her own account, the final chord of her writing career: "I did not go home for my mother's last illness or for her funeral. I had two small children and nobody in Vancouver to leave them with. We could barely have afforded the trip, and my husband had a contempt for formal behavior, but why blame it on him? I felt the same. We say of some things that they can't be forgiven, or that we will never forgive ourselves. But we do—we do it all the time" (*Dear Life*, 319).

What many scholars and readers are fascinated by in Munro's texts—a fourth and perhaps the foremost characteristic of her work—is less the "what" than the "how" of her stories, less the content than the form, or rather, the content in combination with the form: style, narrative technique, the manner of narrative transmission. It is distinctive of Munro's texts that main statements and narrative form elaborately intertwine, resulting in a refined yet comprehensible, indeed readable narrative art that can only be marveled at on a complex level of reception. Munro broadens the boundaries of the short story, experimenting with the genre form in her non-linear, expansive, seemingly digressive, and often montage-like style (for instance, "Dulse," 1980, in *Moons*), or with a multi-perspectival, epiphanic manner of narration (for instance, "Lichen," 1985, in *Progress*), conveying the exceptional, the amazing, but also the threatening in everyday life. Often, her texts reflect on creative writing as such, the relationship between reality and fiction, thus integrating poetological problems into the stories (see also Chapter 6 on Canadian artist stories): "And what happened, I asked myself, to Marion? ... Such questions persist, in spite of novels. It is a shock, when you have dealt so cunningly, powerfully, with reality, to come back and find it still there" ("Epilogue: The Photographer," in *Lives*, 247).

In such passages, Munro repeatedly emphasizes the fragmented, incomplete, and unfathomable of the human experience, as well as the ultimate inability of literary texts to definitively grasp the entire scope of even an individual life. Of the attempts to approach and explain life, the one of which we can be most certain is the focus on the momentary, the fleeting, itself but only nearly a "still point of the turning world," as T. S. Eliot once put it.[7] Consequently, Munro's is an esthetics of the moment, her texts a series of episodes, between which the connection gaps tend to be more evident than explanatory bridges. The result of such a porous view of human experience *and* literature are texts with explanation gaps that contrast various interpretations and different perceptions of the same situation, also of the same character, often at different times: setting the past and the present next to each other connotes parallel rather than sequential plot lines through montage-like renderings, "worlds alongside," as Munro formulated it in *Lives*.[8] In her texts, the structural principle of parallel supplementation and extension is preferred to linear sequencing; there are hardly discernible shifts in perspective and a constant postponing, indeed a withholding of fixed meanings, underlining the fluidity, variability, ambiguity, and ultimate unfathomability of life. As is said with metafictional significance in Munro's story "The Ottawa Valley" (1974; in

Something): "I wanted to find out more, remember more. I wanted to bring back all I could. Now I look at what I have done and it is like a series of snapshots" (197).

The format of the short story most congenially unites Munro's literary views by privileging snippet-like views of the flow of life, episodic and condensed time structure, fragmented presentation, and open endings. With Munro being enamored with linguistic style, the shorter prose form also indulges her penchant for manifold, laborious revisions of her writing. Even in her earlier two books in which Munro dabbled in the novel form, mostly at the request of her publisher at the time,[9] and despite the author's desperate integration attempts as late as in the galleys stage, the underpinnings of the short story are incontrovertible—consequently, I would call the results (namely *Lives* and *Who*) short story cycles, not novels.[10] As Munro herself emphasized in the 1980s: "I think the most attractive kind of writing of all is just the single short story. It satisfies me the way nothing else does.... It took me a long time to reconcile myself to being a short-story writer" (Munro in Hancock 1987, 190). And although her stories tend to be longer in her later collections, Munro has been faithful to her preferred genre, expanding it according to her literary needs.

What Coral Ann Howells calls "indeterminacy" (Howells 1990) in Munro's stories, which Munro masterfully uses for her purposes, influences both her narrative and her linguistic style (especially starting with *The Moons of Jupiter*, 1982) and lends itself to literary compositions rich in resonance that activate her readers. Consider the expressiveness of this one sentence from *Lives of Girls and Women* (249): "People's lives, in Jubilee as elsewhere, were dull, simple, amazing, and unfathomable—deep caves paved with kitchen linoleum." This sentence alone demonstrates a transcending, generalizing extension of meaning beyond the local or regional, as well as an oxymoronic, that is, self-contradictory, ambiguity: If lives are "dull," they can hardly also be "amazing"; if they are "simple," how can they also be "unfathomable"—and yet, through this adolescent writer's view in *Lives*, they are all of these attributes simultaneously. They become interesting in numerous ways through the multidimensional perception the writer aims at, looking behind the façade of the commonplace, the kitchen linoleum, challenged by the "deep caves" of all things human beneath the surface of the mundane. In this manner, the quoted sentence also has metafictional value. The principle of indeterminacy and its semantic surplus noticeable here in but one, and relatively short, sentence of Munro's early writing period especially widens the stories of her middle and late career. The texts create spaces of resonance in which various different possibilities of meaning and interpretation circulate, resisting definitive plot developments and interpretations. The narrative techniques described above interrupt clear plot lines, resulting in multidimensional stories that address both the intellect and the emotions. With their affective and cognitive force, the stories resonate with the readers and incite them to continue deciphering the text. Munro's formulation in a narrative context at the end of her story "Simon's Luck" (1978) may also self-reflexively apply to her own narrative art. At the end of that story, the protagonist Rose, having agonizingly belatedly learned of the death of her new, much-desired lover Simon, contemplates "those shifts of emphasis that throw the story line open to question, the disarrangements which demand new judgments and solutions, and throw the windows open on ... unforgettable scenery" (*Who Do You Think You Are?/The Beggar Maid*, 177).

Exemplary Text Analysis: Alice Munro, "Fiction" (2007)

Of the countless stories that could be paradigmatically analyzed here—in her 14 original collections, Munro has published some 150 short stories—I have chosen one of her later narratives, "Fiction" from *Too Much Happiness* (2009). The story contains all the characteristics of Munro's art of the short story I have described, with the exception of her preferred setting of southwestern Ontario.

The 29-page text is split in two sections, set off by the Roman numerals I and II. Part I is set in a forested area behind the boundaries of the fictional town Rough River on Canada's west coast. A house or trailer is situated every 400 meters of the woodland, with inhabitants who maintain alternative lifestyles dedicated to nature, among whom the protagonist Joyce and her husband Jon have settled in a simple, self-renovated house. Joyce is a music teacher and comes home from her day at work at the Rough River Schools. She is happy to come home, also to her husband Jon, a dedicated carpenter who works at home.

The beginning of the story evokes the scenic setting of Canada's west coast, emphasizing as early as in the second sentence, seemingly parenthetically, how close integral differences can be in everyday life: "The best thing in winter was driving home, after her day teaching music in the Rough River schools. It would already be dark, and on the upper streets of the town snow might be falling, while rain lashed the car on the coastal highway" (32). The second paragraph then turns to Joyce's delight at her return home in the evening and her fascination with patio doors illuminated by the light from within, in homes that radiate the smug safety and comfort of living inside with the glimpses they offer from outside: "These [patio doors] were usually left uncurtained, and ... seemed to be a sign or pledge of comfort, of safety and replenishment ... they displayed the haven of home so artlessly" (32–33).

The (seeming) domestic coziness and security, both important for Joyce, as seen in this passage, are countered by two contrary aspects in the very same short paragraph (supplementarity principle): First, Joyce is aware—in a further variation of Munro's façade motif—that what seems comfortably attractive from the outside can be entirely different from within ("scenes that beguiled her, even if she knew things would not be so special inside," 33)—it all depends on the perspective. Second, the central motif of intrusion and of the intruder into private comfort zones is evoked from the outset by her peering into lit houses through unshielded terrace doors.

A kind of exposition follows, with highly condensed retrospective views of Joyce and Jon's school days, when they met, and how they both dropped out of college after their first year and traveled the North American continent living a bohemian lifestyle before settling for a year along the U.S. Oregon coast, then deciding to study and lead calmer lives, thus eventually landing near Rough River on Canada's west coast. At Joyce's suggestion ("she believed they had an obligation to society," 35), Jon hires a female apprentice, Edie, in the context of a government program. What follows is, in turn, masterful storytelling: In the couple's few conversations about Edie and their exchanges with her, Edie is characterized as a self-assertive, confident, direct, even apodictic, and physically strong woman—ideal for the job of a carpenter; at the same time, the couple's initially belittling, distanced attitude toward Edie is revealed: "They would laugh about something Edie had said. But not in a disparaging way—Edie was like a pet, Joyce sometimes thought. Or like a child" (35).

This condescending opinion toward Edie, held by Joyce in particular, soon turns out to be deceptive narrative irony: Through highly condensed narration, it becomes clear on the next page that a) Jon has fallen in love with Edie and that b), as a consequence, the couple's relationship is about to end. Hardly noticeable at first, this turn of events is revealed by Jon's account of Edie, a now-sober ex-alcoholic unable to bear the sight of the couple's open wine bottles on their kitchen table. The ensuing conversation between Jon and Joyce marks the devastating changes in their lives, first indirectly, and then—evidently from a retrospective view (Part I is written in the past tense; Part II in present tense)—epiphanically pinpointing:

> Also, she thought Jon and Joyce—well, really Joyce—should not leave wine bottles with wine in them right out in sight on the kitchen table.
> "That's her business?" said Joyce.
> "Apparently she thinks so."
> "When does she get to examine our kitchen table?"
> "She has to go through to the toilet. She can't be expected to piss in the bush."
> "I really don't see what business—"
> "And sometimes she comes in and makes a couple of sandwiches for us—"

"So? It's my kitchen. Ours."
"It's just that she feels so threatened by the booze. She's still pretty fragile. It's a thing you and I can't understand."
Threatened. Booze. Fragile.
What words were these for Jon to use?
She should have understood, and at that moment, even if he himself was nowhere close to knowing. He was falling in love [37].

Joyce then ponders the implications of the literal meaning of this particular, for her completely inexplicable "falling in love," interpreted by her as being negative in this case: "No way this could be seen as probable or possible, unless you think of a blow between the eyes, a sudden calamity. The stroke of fate that leaves a man a cripple, the wicked joke that turns clear eyes into blind stones" (37–38). Joyce's subsequent, at first optimistic attempt to save the marriage ("'We will ride this out,' she said"), fails in the smallest narrative space—with but four words Jon utters: "'There is no "we,"' he said" (38).

Several scenes follow that show Joyce's lack of understanding and in particular her desperation: "Her life gone. A commonplace calamity" (40). She moves from their house into an apartment in town, hoping in vain that Jon might come back to her—instead, Edie moves in with him, together with her daughter Christine. Joyce is now exceptionally active in her job as a music teacher and, moreover, tries to appeal to everyone, especially men—yet all her actions, as her focalizing perspective betrays, are geared toward Jon, whom she tries to impress in this manner, lacking alternatives: "She had some idea that Jon would hear about how pretty she looked, how sexy and happy, how she was simply bowling over all the men. As soon as she went out of the apartment she was on stage, and Jon was the essential, if second-hand, spectator" (40–41). Even though Edie's daughter Christine is Joyce's student and a participant in the recital at the end of the school year, this time prepared with special zeal—Joyce hopes Jon and Edie will attend the concert—the two do not appear, probably steering clear of Joyce.

The story's second part begins with an abrupt leap in time and place, to a party hosted by Joyce and Matt, Joyce's second husband, with whom she lives in a big house in North Vancouver. In the meantime, Joyce has become a professional musician, a now grey-haired cellist whose 65-year-old husband, who is married for the third time, is a neurology professor. The life of the culturally interested couple is eventful and fulfilling, full of familial and other social contacts, and Matt and Joyce are both successful in their respective professions. They seem to lead a happy marriage; their togetherness in bed seems to consist of their reading and discussing their reading material with one another. It is mentioned that Joyce had also invited Jon—who is also in his third marriage, after his second marriage to Edie—to Joyce and Matt's birthday party. Jon, however, had to decline due to another familial obligation, the baptism of a grandchild. Joyce seems to have moved on from the previous chapter of her life with Jon; both of them have apparently found new happiness, and Joyce will likely have felt consoled by the fact that Jon's marriage with Edie did not last either.

In spite of the superficially content and indeed happy current state, the past intervenes, at first unbeknownst both to Joyce and the readers. When at the party Joyce approaches a group of younger people standing around her stepson Tommy and makes brief yet witty small talk with them, a young woman called Christie distances herself from the group—to smoke a cigarette in the bushes, as she declares when asked. Joyce initially feels an instant aversion to her and for a moment loses her good spirits because of her diffuse thoughts about the woman ("Joyce feels a lot of her cheer drained away," 47) and even loses her poise ("At a loss, for a moment, as to what to do or where to go next," 47). After the party, when interrogating her stepson while washing the dishes, she learns that the woman is Christie O'Dell, who is married and has just published her first short story collection. Passing a bookstore some days later, Joyce recognizes the woman's likeness on a poster and purchases her book; the saleslady informs her that the young author will give a reading in the bookstore in a few days' time. At home, reading in bed at night with her husband, the title of a short story in the book Joyce bought arouses her attention: "*Kindertotenlieder*," also the name of a song cycle by Gustav Mahler. First next to her reading husband, who regularly engages Joyce in conversations about his reading material, and later, withdrawing herself from his vicinity to the kitchen, Joyce devours the story "*Kindertotenlieder*"—and at this point, Munro's story develops a riveting intensity: Captivated as Joyce is reading Christie O'Dell's story, the reader is equally fascinated by the gradual revelation that Christie could be/is Christine, Edie's daughter, as the events Christie describes in her short story are decidedly reminiscent of a possible past reality of which only Christie could know. From the perspective of a child, Christie's story recounts the triangular relationship of a music teacher with her husband and the child's mother, who intrudes in the marriage and outrivals the music teacher. Everything that follows could have happened as told in the story "*Kindertotenlieder*": The girl is infatuated with the music teacher, who is oblivious to this fact and tries to use the girl to get information about the relationship of her ex-partner with the girl's mother, with whom the girl now lives in the music teacher's former house. Christie's short story mesmerizes Joyce. Some days later, she visits the bookstore to obtain Christie O'Dell's autograph, excited, as she apparently takes Christie's story at face value and thus construes it as being autobiographical. She brings a present for the author that is inspired by the story "*Kindertotenlieder*," chocolate tulips, wanting to find out if the author will recognize her. She does not seem to: Christie is restrained with Joyce, much as she is with the other readers

4. The Noble Genre

waiting for her to sign their book copies: "Christie O'Dell sits there and writes her name as if that is all the writing she could be responsible for in this world.... [She] has raised her eyes to greet the next person in line, and Joyce at last has the sense to move on.... Walking up Lonsdale Avenue, walking uphill, she gradually regains her composure. This might even turn into a funny story that she would tell some day. She wouldn't be surprised" (61).

"Fiction" thus ends in a self-reflexive manner. Important questions remain unanswered: Why does Joyce react so highly emotionally to the story "*Kindertotenlieder*"? At the book signing, she remarks to Christie: "'It means a great deal to me. I brought you a present'" (60). Is this merely the effect of recognition? Or does she take Christie's story at face value and is flattered and touched by the impact she had on the girl at the time, in keeping with such an autobiographic reading? Or is her love for Jon revived, the emotions and strong pains of that former phase of her life? And why does Christie O'Dell behave in such a distant manner toward Joyce? Did she recognize her? If not, then her distanced attitude toward a mere reader, from her perspective, is legitimate. But why, then, did Christie immediately leave the conversation group of the young people earlier, when Joyce joined them at the party? Was Christie overwhelmed by Joyce's sudden appearance or did she want to avoid her? If Christie does recognize Joyce, which would be more plausible, her distance toward Joyce suggests several possible explanations: The revelation of her past feelings for Joyce may be discomfiting for her in front of Joyce, if the story is autobiographically grounded. Or—bearing in mind the story's title, "Fiction"—the adult writer Christie O'Dell fictionally developed this story of one-sided infatuation between a schoolchild and her music teacher, although she based the story on the triangle constellation of lovers she experienced as a child. With her artistic story, through this narrative, Munro likely wants us to consider that despite all the autobiographic inspiration of her stories, they remain elaborate pieces of fiction and are by no means descriptions or memories of life. At the same time, "Fiction" is a literary mirror for how profoundly her own and fictional experiences intertwine in Munro's work—for without her specific life experiences, Christie O'Dell would not have written her story "*Kindertotenlieder*" the way she did.

With the unexpected ending of "Fiction" in mind, in form of a story within a story, and going back to the first part of Munro's story in search of possible indications for such a plotline related to the relationship between the music teacher Joyce and her student Christie, Edie's daughter, in Joyce's Rough River period, only very few illuminating aspects can be found, as that part is written from the focalizing perspective of Joyce. In Part I, it is mentioned that Joyce also teaches Edie's daughter and so makes a special effort for the recital, hoping Jon (with Edie) might be in the audience. The following *one* potential indication is not recognizable as such in its multiple significance upon the first reading; depending on which of the two perspectives (Joyce's or Christie's) the very same situation is observed from, this hint could consolidate the fictional "reality" in different ways: It is in fact emphasized in Part I that Joyce was extremely committed to preparing even the youngest and least gifted of the girls for the school recital: "Even with the youngest or the dullest children she taught, her tone had become caressing, full of mischievous laughter, her encouragement irresistible" (41). However, this passage is clearly placed in the context of Joyce's former partnership with Jon, so that all of Joyce's actions are aligned with Jon, even though she is ultimately self-involved. In this case, then, she is interested in a successful concert in order to impress Jon and she wants to motivate her students especially for this reason (and Part I tellingly makes no mention that Edie's daughter allegedly has the main role in the school concert—as it is later rendered in Christie's story within the story). Such a divergence of perspective by two characters with regard to the objectively same situation is—in Munro's words—an example of the aforementioned "shift of emphasis that throws the story line open to question"—the reader, who depends on the narrative filtering of the events through the characters and the focalizers, is confused which events are "true." The question remains unanswered, with a further complicating reference to yet another fictionalization at the very end of the text (namely to the story we are reading).

We should thus avoid confusing literary texts, even those apparently rooted in autobiographical events, with reality. A further example of this can be found in yet another metafictional passage of the story "Fiction" in which Munro self-deprecatingly and self-ironically refers to the lesser acceptance of the short story, long in the shadow of the novel, when she writes from Joyce's perspective about Christie O'Dell's short story collection: "*How Are We to Live* is the book's title. A collection of short stories, not a novel. This in itself is a disappointment. It seems to diminish the book's authority, making the author seem like somebody who is just hanging on to the gates of Literature, rather than safely settled inside" (49–50).

It is a further irony that with passages that enforce genre hierarchies or indeed discriminate against certain genres as in this self-ironic example from the exquisite story "Fiction," Munro herself has contributed to the fact that similar derogatory statements about the genre of the short story should now finally belong to the past: For in 2013, the highest international distinction for literature went not only to Alice Munro, and not only to Canada, but in similarly overdue fashion to not only Alice Munro's favorite literary form, the short story.

PART TWO: APPROACHES

5

"Pen Photographs"
On Short Story Poetics and the Canadian Short Story Cycle

As such classical works of world literature as Boccaccio's *Decamerone*, Chaucer's *Canterbury Tales*, Ivan Turgenev's *A Sportsman's Sketches*, Alphonse Daudet's *Lettres de mon moulin*, Joyce's *Dubliners*, and Sherwood Anderson's *Winesburg, Ohio* demonstrate, cyclical narratives are an age-old literary format. A more common text form in the twentieth century, the short story cycle has become especially prominent in North American literature. The short story cycle, which can be situated between the novel and the short story collection, has sometimes even been considered Canada's national literary genre: Canadian literary critic J. R. Struthers thus called it "almost a patented Canadian technique" (1982, 1). At the same time, James Nagel (see especially the Introduction and the Conclusion) stresses about the American brand of the genre in as late as 2001: "The short-story cycle is the most neglected and the least well understood of all the major genres in American literature" (246).[1]

This chapter engages with questions of genre theory, literary history, and literary sociology; it also casts a brief comparative glance at other national literatures and cultures relevant in this context (here the American and the British), of particular relevance for postcolonial literatures such as the Canadian. I will explore the cultural origins of this genre in Canada, reaching back to the beginnings of literature in Canada. I will also illustrate the poetological relevance of the short story cycle as it still holds today but which may also be linked back to the time of its formation in Canada. The work of Alice Munro will serve as an illuminating example for the poetological significance and potential of this genre.

Cultural and Historical Origins of the Short Story Cycle in Canada

The nineteenth century saw the fundamental beginnings of Canadian literature and Canadian short fiction in particular. A British colony until 1867, Canada gained political independence roughly a century after the United States. Pioneers originally spread across the territory to widely dispersed settlements, contributing to what Northrop Frye in the 1960s called a "garrison mentality," which had a considerable impact on Canadian myths and Canadian literature (see Frye 1976). The region was difficult to settle and remains far less inhabited than the neighboring United States; even today, Canada's population is one tenth that of the United States, although Canada's land area exceeds that of its southern neighbor. The rough terrain of the northern country, the isolated pioneers, their relative scarcity, as well as the profoundly colonial practice in regard to copyright issues (which gave preference to reprints of British and American works; see Parker 2005, 148–49) made it very difficult for a book market to develop in Canada. These circumstances contrasted with those of the mother country Britain, where up to the end of the nineteenth century the book trade was more developed than the literary magazines, thus favoring longer narratives. In the United States, bootlegged copies of British novels sold rapidly prior to the country's acceptance of international copyright conventions in 1891. Nevertheless, James Fenimore Cooper became a nationally and internationally bestselling author in 1821. Unlike in Canada, the U.S. book trade had thus developed well by the end of the nineteenth century. The significance of such aspects of, and discrepancies in, literary sociology has remained palpable in Canada: Canadian authors have only been considered truly successful when they have been published in New York and/or London, with at least some of their works translated into other European languages. This underscores not only the country's colonial past, but also the fact that the relatively limited size of the potential national readership puts a strain on domestic book production, which continues to rely on government subsidies.[2]

Especially in the nineteenth century, Canadian authors thus had to rely on other publication media. After the first printing machine had been brought from Boston to Halifax in 1751, the newspaper was flourishing in the Atlantic provinces around the turn of the century. For the most part, the regional newspaper became the main forum of cultural exchange in colonial Canada. Numerous newspapers reserved their front pages for literary texts—short texts or serial publications were therefore in great demand. Literary magazines, which started to develop in Canada by the end of the eighteenth century, are not of immediate concern in the present context: titles such as *The*

New Brunswick Religious and Literary Repository (1829–32) indicate that these magazines were mainly published by clergy, who attempted to import culture to Canada through reprints of British and American literature instead of supporting domestic literature. Necessarily, the best early works of Canadian literature were first published in newspapers.

In this context, a specifically Canadian precursor of the short story and the short story cycle developed: the "letter to the editor." Such "letters" addressed to the editor of a newspaper would frequently be expanded to a series of letters by the same author and often included fictional sequences of narrative. An early example of this specifically Canadian literary form is Thomas McCulloch's *Stepsure Letters*, serially published in 1821–1822. As the name suggests, Stepsure is a virtuous Canadian who reports of himself and his fellows in a Canadian small town in a satiric, didactic, and moralizing manner. (McCulloch was a clergyman who had immigrated from Scotland.) The *Stepsure Letters* were eventually collected as a book in 1862, 40 years after their original publication in a newspaper.

A highlight of this narrative form is the letter series published by Canadian-born Thomas Chandler Haliburton under the name Sam Slick in the magazine *The Nova Scotian* between 1835 and 1836. The texts were published several years afterwards as a book entitled *The Clockmaker; or, The Sayings and Doings of Samuel Slick of Slickville* (1836). Sam Slick is an American clockmaker and traveler who relates his picaresque experiences in the Atlantic provinces of Canada, satirically contrasting American business rationale with Canadian provincial naivety and lethargy. The series of stories or anecdotes was extraordinarily successful in Canada (in translation also in France and Germany) as well as in Britain and the United States, where bootlegged copies had appeared shortly after the original publication. With these texts, Haliburton became the first successful Canadian writer, influencing the likes of Stephen Leacock in Canada and Mark Twain in the United States, and can be seen as the forefather of the Canadian short story cycle.

The Strickland Sisters, who had emigrated from England in 1832, published autobiographical and didactic pioneer literature in Canada under their married names, Catharine Parr Traill and Susanna Moodie. Mostly prose sketches published in serial letter form, the most important collections of Traill and Moodie appeared in 1836 and 1852 with the significant titles *The Backwoods of Canada* and *Roughing It in the Bush*, respectively. Following further waves of immigration, new literary magazines were established in the mid-nineteenth century, gradually replacing newspapers as the principal venue for publication of home-grown literature. Moodie and Traill mainly wrote for *The Literary Garland*, Canada's first literary magazine to remunerate published contributions. Especially when issued in serial form, short texts could be financially rewarding. *The Literary Garland* was thus an attractive platform for the best Canadian writers and also gained international recognition. Edgar Allan Poe, for instance, published some of his short stories in this Canadian literary magazine.

In sum, precursors of the short story and of the short story cycle had flourished in Canada around the middle of the nineteenth century, followed by short story cycles in the modern sense in the postcolonial period, notably Duncan Campbell Scott's *In the Village of Viger* (1896) and Stephen Leacock's *Sunshine Sketches of a Little Town* (1912) (see also the introduction).

Characteristics of the (Canadian) Short Story Cycle

The outlined conditions and history of short fiction and, in particular, sequences of short fiction in early Canadian literature go hand in hand with practically all the aspects relevant for the short story cycle's further development up to the present day, which I will outline in five points.

First, the individual narratives of short story cycles are complete, self-contained texts. Sequencing stories into ensembles can exploit the possibilities of long prose forms, such as the detailed depiction of one, several, or even of many individualized figures, or the presentation of a local or regional background. A short story cycle can thus be conceived of as a chain of short stories that accommodates varying degrees of autonomy of the individual short stories on the one hand and the integration of these stories into a larger totality on the other. Examples of elements connecting the individual stories are the ongoing presence of the same protagonist or narrator, a constant setting, recurring motifs, or a particular ideological orientation throughout the cycle. Generically, short story cycles are thus situated between the largely disconnected collection of short stories and the novel. Their trademark characteristic, as Forrest Ingram stresses, is "the dynamic pattern of recurrent development" (1971, 200).

Secondly, short story cycles allow for multiple publications—frequently with repeated remuneration. The first publication of individual stories in newspapers or magazines often precedes the later cyclical compilation in books, which usually still sell better than short story collections, on account of the greater cohesion of the former. Such financial considerations must be taken into account, especially with vulnerable book markets such as the Canadian one.

Thirdly, the detachment from Britain in literature, a process that in Canada extended well into the twentieth century, could best be executed in Britain's least prominent genre, short prose or the short story. The major success of Haliburton's sketches and anecdotes in Britain supports this observation. A specifically Canadian voice was in a better position to mature in short prose and the short story, rather than in the genre of the novel, where it would have to compete with existing British masterpieces.

The proximity of Canada's southern neighbor, where the short story had attained international literary renown since the middle of the nineteenth century, may also have played a role in the Canadian development of the short prose form, as is exemplified in Poe's aforementioned contributions to Canada's *Literary Garland*. Canadian writers were familiar with Poe's short stories and his short story theories around the mid-nineteenth century. Forerunners and early examples of the short story *cycle* developed in the United States in the nineteenth century as well—see, for instance, Washington Irving's *The Sketch Book of Geoffrey Crayon, Gent.* (1819–1820), Sarah Josepha Hale's *Sketches of American Character* (1829), and Herman Melville's *The Piazza Tales* (1856). But it was Sherwood Anderson, the author of the classic and early paradigmatic American example of the short story cycle, *Winesburg, Ohio* (1919), who stressed about his own work: "I have even sometimes thought that the novel does not fit an American writer, that it is a form which had been brought in. What is wanted is a new looseness; and in *Winesburg* I have made my own form" (Anderson 1969, 289; on Anderson see also Chapter 2). This also underscores the generic similarities in the processes of literary detachment of both Canada and the United States from their former mother country.

Fourthly, whereas in the United States the short story evolved out of sketches, anecdotes, folk tales, romantic stories, allegories, and essayistic exempla, the predominant literary precursor of the short story and the short story cycle in Canada was the prose sketch, usually taking the form of a series of sketches. The descriptive and indeed documentary quality of these early text formats, which characterizes the Canadian short story cycle to this day, dates back to the conditions at the formation of these narrative and generic conventions. As indicated, the early cyclical forms developed in Canada in pioneer times. Literature was mostly written by immigrants, who mainly addressed British and American readerships, due in part to financial considerations. The fascination and challenges offered daily by the *terra incognita* flowed into literature in a factual, documentary manner, occasionally to such an extent that the factual outweighed the fictional, as is the case in the series of sketches by Moodie and especially Traill. Distinctive local color, the depiction of perceptible regional features of the landscape, characters, and language all became integral components of Canadian short story cycles. After Confederation in 1867 and the concomitant rising sense of nationhood, and fostered by its impressive size and the plurality of regions, the young nation's idiosyncrasies were reflected more strongly at home, but also in addressing a foreign readership. After Haliburton's *Clockmaker* had put Nova Scotia on the literary map (1836), D. C. Scott's *In the Village of Viger* (1896) conveyed the local color of idyllic rural Quebec. Stephen Leacock's 1912 *Sunshine Sketches*, commissioned by the *Montreal Star*, depicted small-town life near Kingston, Ontario. More recently, Alice Munro's representation of provincial Ontario was apparently so authentic in *Lives of Girls and Women* (1971) that the locals of Munro's hometown were said to have complained about the book for quite some time. Set some 5,000 kilometers west of Ontario, Jack Hodgins's *Spit Delaney's Island* (1976) and *The Barclay Family Theatre* (1981) capture the scenery and characteristics of Vancouver Island in Western Canada (despite its somewhat misleading subtitle, "*Selected Stories*," *Spit Delaney's Island* is a short story cycle).

These texts offer snapshots of certain regions and their inhabitants in rounded-off episodes that merge to form a larger picture. Their cyclical structure allows for the presentation of a multitude of situations, characters, and character types, without having to connect individual episodes through techniques of integration such as transition or condensation, or the alignment of situations and characters along a teleological plot line, all characteristics of at least the traditional novel. The cyclical form thus supports an external plurality that is—unlike in the novel—essentially an aspect of the text's structure rather than of its scope. The designations "pen photographs" or "mental photographs," used in *Stewart's Quarterly*, a Canadian magazine from the 1860s, to characterize the sketch, may also conveniently describe the individual parts of the Canadian short story cycle, a kind of "pen photo album," which descriptively captures regions and characters, with their respective life circumstances and problems.

Finally, there is a fifth aspect of short story cycles that harkens back to the conditions at the formation of this genre in Canada. The approximation of short story sequences to the form of the novel through the reinforcement of connecting elements stems from the long-held preference for novels over short stories by publishers and sometimes also by the writers themselves. A main reason for this tendency is the purported increase in book sales of adaptations of short stories to cycles or to novels. Canadian writer Margaret Laurence, for instance, was asked by her American publisher to rework her story collection *A Bird in the House* into a novel. The product was eventually a short story cycle (1970), one of the best-known in Canadian literature.

Alice Munro's Short Story Cycles and the Genre's Poetological Significance

Even more striking is the example of Alice Munro, that Nobel-winning "master of the contemporary short story" (from the citation of the prize-awarding Nobel committee) who has claimed to be unable to pen a novel.[3]

In her early creative period, at the beginning of the 1970s, Munro lamented the low prestige short stories had when compared to novels.[4] Thus, even after she had received the galley proofs of her works *Lives of Girls and Women* (1971) and *Who Do You Think You Are?* (1978), Munro still struggled to attain a greater unity in both collections by means of agonizing revisions, retrospectively labeling her endeavors "the most confused revision in history" (in Struthers 1983, 29). Yet after laborious re-structuring, additions, name changes, and rewriting, *Who Do You Think You Are?* was finished, the short story cycle that led to Munro's breakthrough in the United States and in Britain under the title *The Beggar Maid*. As for the earlier *Lives*, many critics have considered it to be the best Canadian *novel*. However, this terminological discord, if not confusion, suggests that Munro produced a short-long prose genre hybrid that in fact evades conventional terminological categories. Munro herself called *Lives* a "novel" in the book's preface and elsewhere, as well as a "discontinuous narrative," only later speaking of "a collection of self-contained stories." Critics have variably spoken of a "novel," "para-novel," "episodic novel," "open-form novel," "story-novel," "story-cycle," "collection of short stories," "story-sequence," or even a "sequence-of-stories-as-novel." This calls to mind William H. New's general observation: "Whatever the virtues of any system of classification, those people who write good stories repeatedly write their way out of genre, into a text—out of a system, into territory that the next critic will attempt to codify through a new set of combinations" (1987, 8).

Munro contributed considerably to the rehabilitation of the short story on the Canadian market in the 1980s (see Nischik 1987), after the short story's emancipation from the novel in the United States in the late 1970s and 1980s.[5] With critics, reviewers, prize committees, and the general readership alike, Munro's short story collections have been highly successful in Canada, Britain, and the United States (on her reception in Germany, see Chapter 4). Ever since she received the Nobel Prize in 2013, sales of Munro's works have skyrocketed internationally. Yet already for *The Moons of Jupiter* in 1982, Penguin had paid the highest price ever for the paperback publication rights of a Canadian narrative, including novels. Financially, short story collections were thus on a par with novels in Canada even then.

The suggestion that the heyday of Canadian short story cycles may be a thing of the past in light of the changed infrastructural, medial, and financial conditions nowadays would neglect the genre's poetological potential. Its functionality can be illustrated by taking as an example Alice Munro's short story cycles. Despite her declared attempts at composing a novel, Munro has consistently stuck to the structural framework of the short story, which reveals essential differences in approach, perception, and structure with regard to short and long narrative forms (see Munro in an interview with John Metcalf of 1972: "I'll always have to work within a shortened, a tighter form than the traditional novel.... I am essentially a short story writer.... I think it is something about the way that things appear to you," 61). This leads to the important consideration of how the short form can structurally and substantially affect the long form and the overall statement. At the core of the following, then, are the poetological preconditions and possibilities of the short story cycle, which will be assessed with regard to *Lives of Girls and Women*,[6] the work of Munro's that most closely resembles a novel without, however, departing from the short story format.

Lives works within the traditions of the coming of age novel and of the artist novel. Against the geographical and social backdrop of rural Ontario, the narrative renders Del Jordan's development from childhood to adolescence and ultimately to a respected author. The book consists of eight independent stories, mostly ordered chronologically, which highlight crucial moments in Del's life, such as the experience of diverging gender role expectations and attributions, which Del has difficulty adjusting to, the crisis-like confrontation with religion and faith, and the disillusioning initiation into sexuality and romantic relationships. The depiction of such experiences of initiation and self-discovery occurs in separate stories that are not bridged by connecting links, which formally underscores the impression given by the content: namely that Del's maturation to adulthood and to the status of a writer is full of fractures rather than being characterized by a linear, easily traceable development, such as the novel form tends to suggest, especially in coming of age novels and the bildungsroman. In a similar context, Nadine Gordimer once stated:

> Each of us has a thousand lives and a novel gives a character only one. *For the sake of the form.* The novelist may juggle about with chronology and throw narrative overboard; all the time his characters have the reader by the hand, there is a consistency of relationship throughout the experience that cannot and does not convey the quality of human life, where contact is more like a flash of fireflies, in and out, now here, now there, in darkness. Short-story writers see by the light of the flash [1976, 179; emphasis original].[7]

Short story writers, Gordimer thus proposes, see by the light of the flash. To keep with the metaphor, they create "pen photographs," written records of the moment that discursively leave out the connections of development beyond the recorded instant. As Gordimer continues: "Theirs is the art of the only thing one can be sure of—the present moment.... A discrete moment of truth is aimed at" (1976, 179). The plurality of people and situations, of impressions and experiences that overwhelm the sensitive and empathetic Del and that seem disconnected, indeed contradictory, are best encapsulated in a discontinuous, cyclical format.

The cyclical structure further enhances the focus on pivotal moments and crises in Del's life. The emphasis lies on the significance of the single episode, not its impact on Del's overall development. This is related to the distrust prevalent in the twentieth century in the possibility of representing consistent entities, which can, after all, hardly be detected in reality: this is one way of accounting for the remarkable number of short story cycles in the twentieth century. Critically (and metafictionally) assessing her own autobiographically colored debut novel, Del notes in "Epilogue: The Photographer" at the end of *Lives* that many inconsistencies and explanatory gaps remain in her narrative, and that even facts that appear to be simple remain untold or offer multiple interpretive possibilities, developing their own dynamics, and resisting compression into orderly plot sequences ("Treachery is the other side of dailiness," to quote from *Who/Beggar*, 19). The young author Del has to accept that her attempts at conclusively capturing reality through her literary endeavors are bound to fail: "And what happened, I asked myself, to Marion? ... *What happened to Marion?* What happened to Bobby Sherriff when he had to stop baking cakes and go back to the asylum? Such questions persist, in spite of novels. It is a shock, when you have dealt so cunningly, powerfully, with reality, to come back and find it still there.... The hope of accuracy we bring to such tasks is crazy, heartbreaking" (247, 249). As Munro highlights time and again in her fiction, works of art are not in a position to adequately convey life's complexity and intensity, nor can they do away with the impenetrability and incompleteness of everyday experience. Munro's preference for the short story and the cyclical structure of narratives can thus be taken as an implicit comment on the relation between reality and literature as well as on the estetics of the novel and the short story.

Furthermore, the fragmentary short form more adeptly conveys the intensity of perception and inner experience than the more comprehensive long form. Synchronic concentration replaces diachronic development. Figuratively speaking, the short story cycle is a series of close-ups. Such a form is particularly suitable for the narrative of a protagonist distinguished by profound sophistication and intensity in perception, experience, and intellect. As Del writes in "Epilogue": "And no list could hold what I wanted, for what I wanted was every last thing, every layer of speech and thought, stroke of light on bark or walls, every smell, pothole, pain, crack, delusion, held still and held together—radiant, everlasting" (*Lives*, 249).

In a 1981 interview, Munro characterizes her writing as "the perfect literary equivalent to a documentary movie," which again reveals her to be a part of a long Canadian literary tradition. However, the comparison to photography seems to me more appropriate than that to film.[8] *Lives* and its form of conception can also be seen as an attempt to write against the transience and fluctuation of life: the cycle's episodes appear as textual snapshots in a fractured, constantly changing development that must be recorded to be graspable and presentable, yet that is doomed to remain a series of incomplete half-truths. The short story cycle thus appears to be an attempt to come to terms with the dialectic of movement and standstill, synchrony and diachrony (T. S. Eliot's "still point of the turning world").[9]

The cyclical composition, the snapshot-like depictions of Del's experiences, the lack of direct connections between the discrete parts, the temporal gaps—all of these factors reinforce a salient function of the narrative transmission: Del's experiences are told in retrospect, as pictures in her memory; indeed, one usually recalls through associative pictures rather than in causal, linear plot lines. An orientation toward a goal is not noticeable in either the individual stories nor in the cycle as a whole; a sense of an ending, so typical of novels, does not emerge. On the contrary, through temporal interlacing, a clash of disparate interpretations, as well as a foregrounding of explanatory gaps, Munro repeatedly highlights the momentariness, incompleteness, changeability, and ultimately the unfathomable depth of human experience. As Georg Lukács pithily put it: "The soul is designed with greater breadth and depth than the fortunes life has to offer it."[10]

In this chapter I have analyzed significant factors of Canadian literary history and literary sociology that may explain the outstanding position of short story cycles in Canadian literature. The example of Alice Munro's contributions to that Canadian genre tradition has further made apparent the poetological demands and possibilities of this genre hybrid, which will keep this text format flourishing regardless of questions of literary sociology. For Alice Munro, the form proves to be an ideal expression of her artistic endeavors. Much as she writes at the end of *Who Do You Think You Are?/The Beggar Maid*, for her, the cyclical composition represents "those shifts of emphasis that throw the story line open to question, the disarrangements which demand new judgments and solutions, and throw the windows open on … unforgettable scenery" (177).[11]

6

Multiple Challenges
The Canadian Artist Story and Gender

A subgenre of the short story that is particularly prominent in Canada is the artist story, and in the following I will deal with it using a gender-based approach. In addition to embedding the Canadian artist story generically and historically as well as defining and further categorizing it, the chapter then differentiates between three categories of artist stories and illustrates the significance of gender at work in three exquisite examples of this subgenre.

When looking into short stories about artists, to begin with, a look across the Atlantic at German literature is beneficial. German literary scholarship differentiates between the related terms "Bildungsroman," "Entwicklungsroman," and "Künstlerroman." It is symptomatic of this generic tradition's importance in German literature that the German term "Bildungsroman" has been imported untranslated into the English language, whereas the other two generic concepts have been translated as "developmental novel" and "artist novel." While the term "Bildungsroman" is closely linked to weighty novels of German Classicism and Romanticism with their esthetics of the genius (for instance, Johann Wolfgang von Goethe's *Wilhelm Meisters Lehrjahre*, 1795–1796; *Wilhelm Meisters Wanderjahre*, 1829; Gottfried Keller's *Der grüne Heinrich*, 1854–1855), the term "artist novel," although it may overlap with "Bildungsroman" (see *Der grüne Heinrich*), is relatively unrestricted with respect to literary period. The artist novel in general deals with the development and preoccupations of an artist—be it a painter, musician, writer, etc.— and often shows the artist as an outsider trying to reconcile the demands of their artistic vocation with the social context and the sheer demands and necessities of life. As the German Romanticist Ludwig Tieck put it: "He who succumbs to art has to give up what he is or could be as a human being."[1]

A generic offshoot of the artist novel is the artist novella, a shorter piece of fiction that concentrates on a significant episode (or a few episodes) in the life of an artist rather than rendering the whole panorama of their development or life. The artist novella, too, has a time-honored tradition in German literature, with canonical texts such as E. T. A. Hoffmann's *Das Fräulein von Scuderi* (1819), Eduard Mörike's *Mozart auf der Reise nach Prag* (1855), or Thomas Mann's *Tonio Kröger* (1903).

Since the end of the nineteenth century, finally, the artist short story developed—more indigenous to North American literature (for example, "The Real Thing," 1892, by Henry James)—in which compression replaces extension and brevity usually correlates with an increase in semantic density as well as stylistic and structural sophistication. The artist short story does not have a generic tradition in Germany—significant contributions belong to the second half of the twentieth century, since the short story as a literary genre came into its own in Germany only after the end of World War II due to the increased reception of American literature in Germany at the time.

Against the backdrop of the history of world literature, the Canadian artist *novel* (see Margaret Laurence, *The Diviners*, 1974; Margaret Atwood, *Lady Oracle*, 1976; Atwood, *Cat's Eye*, 1988; and many others) could be called an imported genre. The artist *story* is a relatively recent but important literary format of Canadian literature (especially from the 1960s onward), which is significant—also on an international scale—for its remarkable quantity in Canada, for its overall quality, and, last but not least, for the varied treatment of gender, particularly by female authors.

That art and the artist in society should have become such important themes in Canadian short fiction from the 1960s onward is not surprising in view of the precariousness of the state of literature and the artist-audience-relationship in an emergent literary market at the time (see Chapter 3). A clear example is the work of John Metcalf, literary and cultural critic, anthologizer and editor, and himself a writer of short fiction. His preoccupation with the state and quality of Canadian literature since the 1970s resulted not only in many, partly polemical, essays, but also in the fact that more than one third of his approximately 50 pieces of short fiction are explicit examples of artist stories, with many more being indirectly related to art or the artist (on Metcalf's impact on Canadian short fiction in general and his artist stories in particular, see Chapter 12). Although there are excellent examples of artist stories written by male Canadian writers,[2] it is artist stories written by female Canadian writers that are particularly intriguing. This is due to the fact that leading authors like Margaret Atwood, Alice Munro, Carol Shields and, to a lesser extent, Mavis Gallant clearly see a double challenge for their fictional female artists: the challenge for the artist in general is enhanced by that of the female gender in particular, thus combining in a "double eccentricity." The result is a wide array of artist stories by these and other writers (such as Margaret Laurence, Audrey Thomas, Jane Urquhart, Jane Rule, and Dionne Brand), whose foregrounding of gender may partly explain the success of these writers also, for instance, in Germany and in German translation. Luise von Flotow and Brita Oeding thus report in their survey of German translations of Canadian fiction in the 1980s and 1990s:

> During the 1980s, a total of thirty-eight books of adult fiction by Canadian authors were translated and published in German, and in the 1990s the overall figures rose further still, bringing seventy-seven books of adult Canadian fiction onto the German-language market. The number of women writers in each decade easily outmatched the number of male writers with twenty-six books by women and twelve by men in the 1980s and fifty-one books by women versus twenty-six by men in the 1990s [2007, 82].

The explanation the authors give for this 2:1 ratio in favor of women writers is based on Even-Zohar's polysystem theory (1990, 1997), which argues that literatures work as necessarily constrained systems: "just like biotopes they might lack necessary elements at certain times. This lack is often filled by translations" (von Flotow and Oeding 2007, 83). Von Flotow and Oeding argue that German-language "feminist writing" at the time (see Elfriede Jelinek, Verena Stefan, Karin Struck, etc.) "tended to be aggressively provocative and to demand 'women's liberation' rather than produce a good story line, use interesting narrative techniques, focus on writing style and quality, let alone employ humour" (ibid.). In contrast, Canadian fiction by female writers tended to meet all these challenges and at the same time provided "surprising new inspirations for contemporary women's lives" (ibid., 91), not least for German readers. This holds equally true for the rather demanding subgenre of the artist story, which usually displays self-reflexive, metapoetical characteristics and which can often also be discussed in the context of auto/biography, as the following text analyses will show.

In my treatment of three exemplary artist stories that ingeniously link problems of the artist with those of gender, I distinguish between artist stories that predominantly feature (a) gender-affliction, (b) gender-consciousness, and (c) gender-affirmation.

Canadian artist stories with female protagonists that may be regarded as gender-afflicted saw a vogue in the 1970s and 1980s, the period of feminism's so-called Second Wave. In these stories, the female characters feel severely hampered by their social status as *female* writers, that is, by the social influences surrounding them and/or by their internalization of strict gender roles.

A complex case in point is Alice Munro's story "Dulse" (1978; collected in *The Moons of Jupiter*, 1982). The protagonist Lydia works as an editor for a publisher in Toronto and also calls herself a poet, though always in a reserved manner: "She was also a poet, but she did not refer to that unless it was something people knew already" ("Dulse," 36). From the beginning, her self-conception as a poet is rather shaky, lacking in determination: "She did not think of making a living writing poetry ... because she thought, as she had thought innumerable times in her life, that probably she would not write any more poems" (37). As an alternative for writing poetry, she even considers the most menial, and often women-dominated, jobs for earning money: "She was thinking that she could not cook well enough to do it for pay but she could clean ... how much an hour did cleaning pay?" (37). The writing motif in this story is strengthened by the fact that Lydia considers her ex-lover Duncan, with whom she has just broken up, a "writer. He writes historical books" (43). What is more significant in this context is the story's allusion to the biographical fact that American writer Willa Cather repeatedly spent some time with her female lover on the island off the southern coast of New Brunswick (Grand Manan Island) where Lydia goes on a short trip and where the story "Dulse" is set. Cather serves as a foil to the fictional Lydia, in that Cather is presented as a self-determined, resolute woman living according to her own wishes and preferences and, even back at the beginning of the twentieth century, not paying too much heed to prescriptive gender conventions which restrict the lives of women in particular. Toward the end of the story, the two different types of writers are contrasted in Lydia's conversation with Mr. Stanley, an ardent admirer of Willa Cather. He relates that Cather once gave a female resident of the area helpful advice concerning her marital problems, thus conveying the impression that Cather could handle not only art but also life successfully. The highly self-doubting Lydia, however, tries to challenge this positive view of the all-capable artist by telling Mr. Stanley that Cather never lived with a man, and thus allegedly could not have been informed in matters of marriage. Stanley, not knowing that Lydia is a writer herself, retorts: "'She knew things as an artist knows them. Not necessarily by experience'" (57), thereby invoking the superior—that is, perceptive, imaginative, creative, intelligent—knowledge of the writer as "seer." Yet Lydia, with her negative conception of herself both as a person/woman and as a writer, cannot subscribe to Mr. Stanley's very positive view of the writer: "'But what if they don't know them [i.e., "things"]?' Lydia persisted. 'What if they don't?'" (57).

Lydia indeed fails to come to terms both with her writing and with her life, particularly her love life, due to her complete lack of self-confidence and self-determination. Having always chosen the wrong partners, to whom she feels fatally attracted because they cooperate in, and thereby perpetuate, her dismal self-image, by the time she makes the trip to the island she is in a full-fledged crisis. She is pursued by memories of her recent separation from Duncan, the writer of history books, who ensured his own dominance in their relationship by constantly putting Lydia down:

6. Multiple Challenges 99

> At least he indicated that he could love her, that they could be happy, if she could honor his privacy, make no demands upon him, and try to alter those things about her person and behavior which he did not like. He listed these things precisely. Some were very intimate in nature and she howled with shame and covered her ears and begged him to take them back or to say no more.... She thought she saw a quiver of satisfaction, a deep thrill of relief, that ran through him when she finally broke under the weight of his calm and detailed objections [53].

Rather than loving Lydia and accepting her as she is, Duncan wants to force upon her his idea of a perfect female partner. Instead of believing in herself and warding off his attempts at colonizing her ("She could not make the connection between herself and things outside herself," 41), Lydia resorts to the unfortunate method of "pleasing," as she strains and eventually deforms herself to comply with his wishes; thereby, she even gives up her friends and former lifestyle and orbits around Duncan only. Focusing on him alone and hewing to his conceptions of her rather than becoming aware of her own wishes, she truly behaves as a member of the proverbial "second sex," derived from the norm-providing "first sex." The more she tries to please him, the unhappier she becomes, and eventually she has to consult a psychiatrist.

Although the extracts rendered from the sessions with the "doctor" (55) are enlightening—at least for the reader, if not for Lydia—it is not the psychotherapy but rather her short trip to the New Brunswick island that seems to mark a change in Lydia's stagnant life (Carscallen in 1993 aptly calls this story an "Exodus story," 205). This change is symbolically highlighted through the noun/object providing the title of this story, "Dulse." In the hotel on the island, Lydia meets several men who work for the New Brunswick telephone company: Lawrence, Eugene, and Vincent, each representing different types of men. At night, Lydia eventually imagines love affairs with each of them— finally preferring Vincent to the other men. Vincent, with a "look of secrecy and humor" (46), is not an intellectual (compare Lawrence's comment on her ex-lover: "'That's what he does, collects old stuff and writes about it? ... I guess that's interesting,'" 44), but used to be a hard-working farmer. Lydia feels as if she shared similar roots with Vincent: "He was the sort of man she had known when she was a child living on a farm not so different from his.... She knew his life. With him she could foresee doors opening, to what she knew and had forgotten; rooms and landscapes opening" (52). Lydia comes close to realizing, in a sort of epiphanic insight, that her constant opting for self-damaging methods of forming and keeping up a "love" relationship has been the hinge of her unhappiness and lack of success: "Should she have stayed in the place where love is managed for you, not gone where you have to invent it, and re-invent it, and never know if these efforts will be enough?" (52). The seaweed called dulse, which Vincent had introduced her to earlier and that he leaves behind for her as a present, may be interpreted as a secret message to her, becoming an expressive symbol at the end of the story, a subtle hint in which direction Lydia should turn: "Look how this present slyly warmed her, from a distance" (59). The seaweed is presented, or may be regarded, as moist ("oily-looking even when dry," 58), "salty" (47), healthy and nourishing ("good for you," 47), linked to nature and symbolizing a warm vitality and perhaps even an indirect ("slyly") suggestion from Vincent at a fulfilled sexuality, making her feel good "from a distance."

In Munro's story "Dulse," then, Lydia the writer is overwhelmed and severely hampered by Lydia the unhappy lover for the largest part of the story. The main reason for her lack of satisfaction and success in both regards is her glaring lack of self-assurance and self-interest, which is put in a decisively gendered context in this moving story about a middle-aged poet who "at the end of the summer" (36; the story's first words) may well be about to enter a new, more self-determined, and rewarding phase of life—which might also have a reviving effect on her work and self-conception as a writer.

Although Munro's earlier story "The Office" (collected in *Dance of the Happy Shades*, 1968) also shares characteristics that may be classified under gender-affliction, it is rather the protagonist's pronounced awareness of gender differences and challenges that informs this text.[3] Significantly, this story begins where "Dulse" ends, here with an *explicit* realization by the female writer and first-person narrator that she must change something in her life: "The solution to my life occurred to me one evening while I was ironing a shirt. It was simple but audacious. I went into the living room where my husband was watching television and I said, 'I think I ought to have an office'" ("Office," 59).

This opening passage already indicates the female writer's predicament: While at home, traditionally a female sphere, she is also a housewife ironing her husband's shirt while he relaxes watching television. The female protagonist is quite aware of the gender differences also with regard to her profession of writing, and so she explains to her husband quite lucidly:

> A house is all right for a man to work in. He brings his work into the house, a place is cleared for it; the house rearranges itself as best it can around him. Everybody recognizes that his work *exists*. He is not expected to answer the telephone, to find things that are lost, to see why children are crying, or feed the cat. He can shut his door. Imagine (I said) a mother shutting her door, and the children knowing she is behind it; why, the very thought of it is outrageous to them.... So a house is not the same for a woman.... She *is* the house; there is no separation possible [60; original emphasis].

Such interrelations between space, independence, writing, and gender were first raised in 1929 by Virginia Woolf in *A Room of One's Own*, where she stated: "A woman must have money and a room of her own if she is to write fiction" (Woolf 2001, 6). In the Munro story, the noun "room" is substituted by "office," thereby lending the desired space of one's own more dignity, and stressing that writing is a profession that needs focused attention and seriousness of purpose—both are hard for a female writer to set aside in a domestic sphere in which the role definitions of wife and mother may easily overwhelm that of the writer. Ironically, the first-person narrator is unlucky enough to rent an office whose peace is constantly invaded by the landlord Mr. Malley. He considers her writing a mere hobby and presumes the protagonist to be in need of a muse: a male muse, namely himself. Even the "official space" of an office does not rule out deep-seated prejudices against women and, even more so, against a female writer. For a while, the first-person narrator politely complies with Mr. Malley's wishes to talk to her, criticizing herself for her inconsequential behavior at the same time and feeling ill at ease. The situation escalates when the landlord, realizing that he cannot control this woman the way he would like to, paints over her bathroom with obscene signs, insinuating it was the narrator or her friends rather than himself. With this outrageous act the landlord eventually develops into "a madman in the bathroom," his self-complacence severely threatened by a woman who is relatively independent from any male influences on her actions. She leaves this "office" for good after his glaring act of aggression, but is shown to be the eventual winner of this battle for influence and self-determination; as she reflects in hindsight: "I have not yet found another office. I think that I will try again some day, but not yet. I have to wait at least until that picture fades that I see so clearly in my mind.... Mr. Malley with his rags and brushes and a pail of soapy water, scrubbing in his clumsy way ... at the toilet walls.... While I arrange words, and think it is my right to be rid of him" (73–74). At the end of the story, then, the received gender attributions have been turned on their head, at least in the protagonist's imagination: While she thinks of Mr. Malley cleaning the bathroom in his house, she herself sits at her home desk writing, "arranging words," apparently having settled in her symbolic writing space irrespective of an office of her own for the moment. By writing about her painful past experience with the landlord, she gets "rid of him" on a symbolic level—she has defended and occupied her space in spite of Mr. Malley's constant attempts to sabotage her wish to write.

Whereas in these two Munro stories the female writer has to fend for herself through conflicts with male antagonists and times of inner crisis, Margaret Atwood's story "Significant Moments in the Life of My Mother," which opens her collection *Bluebeard's Egg* (1983), takes a decisive step toward an awareness of the female tradition in writing and thereby toward an affirmative view of female gender. Margaret Atwood herself, when asked whether her muse was male or female, once answered: "Oh, she's a woman" (in Sullivan 1998, 37). The many personal cues invite Atwood connoisseurs to read this story through an auto/biographical lens as well.

"Significant Moments in the Life of My Mother" is rendered as a retrospective account by a nameless female first-person narrator, who focuses mainly on the representation of her (nameless) mother. The mother's stories and remarks transmitted to her children are either vividly rendered in direct speech and embedded with comments by the narrator, or are summarized by the narrator. In either case, the narrator enters into a sort of indirect retrospective dialogue with her mother, whose apparently cheerful mentality colors the writing. By telling stories to her children and to others, the mother is rendered as a highly communicative and expressive character, observant, mentally alert, caring, not taking herself too seriously, and with a pronounced sense of humor.

The doubly narrated episodes, which are added to each other apparently at random, at first seem to belie the "significant moments" in the life of the mother, as indicated in the title. The stories mainly belong to the narrator's family and the traditionally female-dominated domestic sphere, such as the story about a cat "wet[ting] itself copiously" (19) on the mother's lap. Nevertheless, these domestic events are obviously worth a story, and on different levels of reception: because of the manner in which the narrator's mother retells the episodes, and how their telling characterizes her; because of her daughter's interpretation of the stories, attaching further significance to them; and because of the influence and effects this particular mother must have had on her narrator-daughter, who is a budding writer, as the story as a whole and particularly its ending suggest.

The narrator's mother seems to be a born storyteller in several respects. She obviously loves telling stories, she is entertaining and witty, and she is very clearly aware of and attentive to her listeners. She tells certain stories only to a female audience, as the narrator stresses. The mother relates events she finds noteworthy, but largely refrains from commenting upon them. Whether or not she pursues effects beyond informative, expressive, or entertaining ones remains open. From the perspective of the daughter/narrator, at any rate, who "analys[e]s" (26) and evaluates these stories in retrospect and draws her own conclusions, the mother seems to have been not only an active oral storyteller, but at the same time an educator as well (and the mother's profession in the story is indeed school-teaching).

The narrator's mother also exerts an influence on her daughter in the art of storytelling. That domestic storytelling in this text is related to artistic storytelling, to writing, if *ex negativo*, becomes clear in reflective passages such as the following: "There is, however, a difference between symbolism and anecdote. Listening to my mother, I sometimes remember this" ("Significant Moments," 27). By offering a meaningful characterization as she contextualizes her mother's stories, the daughter-narrator attaches a weightier cognitive significance to her mother's storytelling and, in the writing process, transfers an esthetic value to the stories, thereby indeed transforming the anecdotes and episodes into "significant moments." In this step from oral to written storytelling, from the mother as domestic storyteller to the daughter as conscious narrator and writer, lies the metafictional gist of "Significant Moments" and its Chinese-box-like set-up. Whereas the mother's narrations stick factually to "real events," the narrator makes use of her imaginative ("… which I pictured as…" 17), analytical, and esthetic capacities to make sense of these events not only as a daughter but also as a writer. By writing a short story about her mother's stories—and hereby I also enter an auto/biographical reading of the text—she "translates the world into words."[4]

This transformative power of art is suggested by a mise-en-abymic rendering of a mundane object turned into something marvelously extraordinary: "It was in this house that I first saw a stalk of oats in a vase, each oat wrapped in the precious silver paper which had been carefully saved from a chocolate box. I thought it was the most wonderful thing I had ever seen, and began saving silver paper myself" (14). This fascinating image of the metamorphosing capacity of art links the first part of my analysis of Atwood's story—its involvement with storytelling, its metafictional impact—with the second part—its auto/biographical aspects and the female line of influences sketched in this story. For the wonderful image of the wrapped stalk of oats—which results in the first-person narrator's beginning to save silver paper, too (in order to be able to effect such metamorphosis herself)—is, significantly, situated in her *mother's* family house, where "its secret life … was female" (13). In connection with her mother's oral storytelling, we can see the coordinates of a female line of tradition. It is the female connection that influences the daughter most in the story. The world in which the girl grows up is a gendered world, in her own as well as her parents' perception, with the female sphere appearing more exciting to her, definitely inspiring her to a greater extent, for while "the structure of the house was hierarchical, with my grandfather at the top … its secret life … was female" (13), or "'Your father was upset about it,' says my mother [about hair-cutting], with an air of collusion. She doesn't say this when my father is present. We smile, over the odd reactions of men to hair" (15). Such gender differences and allegiances are reported by the narrator in retrospect in a friendly tongue-in-cheek manner, brimming with mild irony in both gender directions ("Not everyone shares this belief about men; nevertheless, it has its uses," 22).

It is toward the end of the text that the mother's stories start to focus on her daughter. The text thus symbolically passes from the life and times of the mother on to the daughter, and her relationship to her mother (for instance: "'You always kept yourself busy.… You always had something cooking. Some project or other,'" 28), but only relatively briefly so. The more the daughter develops into an intellectual ("I read modern poetry and histories of Nazi atrocities, and took to drinking coffee," 28), the more a gap of silence seems to develop between mother and daughter: "My mother has few stories to tell about these times. What I remember from them is the odd look I would sometimes catch in her eyes. It struck me, for the first time in my life, that my mother might be afraid of me...: at any time I might open my mouth and out would come a language she had never heard before. I had become a visitant from outer space, a time-traveller come back from the future, bearing news of a great disaster" (29).

Thus the story ends. It may be considered ironic (or even somewhat tragic) that the mother's legacy to her daughter, the joy in and disposition toward storytelling, eventually seems to estrange mother and daughter from each other, as if they originated not from the same family but from different worlds (another example: "Off in the distance, my mother vacuumed around my feet while I sat in chairs, studying," 28–29). But I would argue that, ultimately, the story is not to be understood entirely in the light of this final turn toward mutual estrangement. Rather, what makes up the most substantial part of this text and what lingers is the loveable mother and her engaged and vivid storytelling to her daughter, through which she plays a decisive role in the daughter's development. What the daughter could (and, in a possible autobiographical reading of the story did) learn from her mother is, among other things, that the art of storytelling partly consists of the right selection and arrangement of material and includes the art of omission ("I realized that she never put in the long stretches of uneventful time that must have made up much of her life: the stories were just the punctuation," 16); that a good storyteller is a good listener and perceptive observer ("In gatherings of unknown people, she merely listens intently, her head tilted a little.... The secret is to wait and see what she will say afterwards," 17); that storytelling may (or perhaps should) be connected with fun and delight ("my mother's eyes shine with delight while she tells this story," 21; "Having fun has always been high on my mother's agenda," 18); and that being a good performer is conducive to effective storytelling ("When she tells them [the stories], my mother's face turns to rubber. She takes all the parts, adds the sound effects, waves her hands around in the air. Her eyes gleam," 17). The narrator's mother provides the model for her daughter's muse in that she supplies the first female voice.

"Significant Moments in the Life of My Mother" is a clever (meta)fictional treatment by a female writer of the "translation of the world into words." It is a celebration of the art of storytelling, demonstrating Atwood's anti-Romantic, rather pragmatic view of artistic creativity (see also her *Negotiating with the Dead: A Writer on Writing*, 2002). At the same time, it is a wonderful, moving homage of a daughter to her mother, of an intellectual writer to a domestic oral storyteller, and, I daresay, of Margaret Atwood to her mother.

The story demonstrates—with the author and narrator apparently also having a lot of fun along the way—how high-quality literature may spring from the traditionally female sphere of the domestic (successful fellow-writers like Alice Munro or Carol Shields stress a similar point) and how well aware Atwood has been of the long-neglected female influences in life and art,[5] of the female tradition of storytelling and writing in which she firmly places herself with this story, "saving silver paper [her]self" (14).

With this text we have come full circle in my treatment of artist stories, which can only begin to suggest the wide range of contemporary Canadian artist stories written by female writers. Even if we consider stories by the same writer—Atwood is a prominent case in point: compare her "Significant Moments" with her artist stories "Loulou" (*Bluebeard's Egg*) and "Lives of the Poets" (*Dancing Girls*)—we see their impressive variability in thematic orientation and technique. With the innovative and liberating view of female gender in "Significant Moments," it is no coincidence that this story is the most recent (published in the 1980s) of those discussed here. At the same time, championing the female tradition in "Significant Moments," Atwood in a gendered context of writing toward the end of the twentieth century shares a conviction that Johann Wolfgang von Goethe (in *Wilhelm Meisters Lehrjahre*) had formulated two centuries earlier in view of the artist in general, who at the time was presupposed to be a male artist: "Man's greatest achievement is when he determines circumstances as much as possible, and is determined by them as little as possible."[6] Comparing Munro's "Dulse" and "The Office" and Atwood's "Significant Moments in the Life of My Mother"—which range from gender-affliction and women's complicity in their own oppression, via gender-awareness and women's attempt to alter their received fate, toward gender-affirmation and women's positive view of their gender—we are told the story of female artists increasingly meeting the multiple challenge of taking their lives and their artistry confidently into their own hands.

7

Gender and Genre
Margaret Atwood's Short Stories and Short Fictions

Although her novels are more widely read, Margaret Atwood belongs to the rare breed of writers who have excelled in practically all literary genres. My 2009 book *Engendering Genre: The Works of Margaret Atwood* thus features comprehensive chapters on her poetry, her short fictions and prose poems, her short stories, her novels, her involvement with film, her works of literary and cultural criticism, and her comics. Focusing on the question of how Atwood has developed these genres to be gender-sensitive in content and form,[1] I show that genre and gender intertwine in Atwood's oeuvre in an interplay of complicity and critique. In focusing on gender issues, Atwood often ends up revising the traditional design and demarcation lines of (sub)genres with respect to both content/theme and form. Highlighting this process—which I call "engendering genre"—I illuminate not only the role gender may play in constituting genre and, conversely, the role genre may play in constituting gender in Atwood's works, but also her self-conscious play with intersections of gender and genre (see Nischik 2009). In a more approachable manner, "engendering genre" in Atwood's works also refers to the foregrounding of gender in specific textual formats, which will be the main focus of this chapter, as I discuss the complexities of gender and genre in representative short stories and short fictions by Atwood.

The very versatility and variability of genre that characterizes Atwood's oeuvre as a whole is best seen when focusing on her short prose. Indeed, Atwood is arguably at her most experimental in her short prose. In order to come to grips with the variability of these texts, one may roughly categorize her short fiction into, first of all, short stories proper and, secondly, so-called short fictions, prose poems, and "fictional essays" or "essay-fictions" (see also Chapter 14). The second category, in particular, encompasses such a variety of different subgenres and formats of fictional short prose not easily classifiable that scholars and critics have resorted to a considerable number of different terms and generic labels—some of them rather original but not particularly useful, such as "short shorts" or "gems." Especially noteworthy for their formal and stylistic variability are Atwood's "short fictions"—the collective term most frequently used for these varied literary texts that are shorter and altogether less "narrative" in orientation than short stories proper. In bending, twisting, crossing, and transcending genre boundaries, Atwood's works are in line with what postmodern esthetics and genre theory have diagnosed as "the arbitrariness and undecidability of generic boundaries" (Delville 1997, 57). As Atwood's short fictions combine genre and gender issues, they are in line with, for instance, Judith Butler's research on the social constructedness of gender and the relativity if not arbitrariness of gender boundaries. As I will demonstrate in my chronologically structured assessment of Atwood's short fiction oeuvre, Atwood's works emphasize that genre and gender should not be taken for granted but are subject to change, responsive as they are to social, ideological, and cultural developments (see also Chapter 11).

Not surprisingly, Atwood started out in this genre with the production of short stories proper, and she has remained faithful to this kind of short prose with the publication of a short short collection in every decade since. Five of her to date eight collections of short prose belong to this first category: *Dancing Girls* (1977), *Bluebeard's Egg* (1983), *Wilderness Tips* (1991), *Moral Disorder* (2006), and *Stone Mattress* (2014, though this last collection lies outside this book's time range). The 15 years' gap between her acclaimed third short story collection, *Wilderness Tips*, and her short story collection *Moral Disorder* may also be explained by her exploration of new generic territories during this period with her collections of short fictions as well as prose poems and fictional essays in *Murder in the Dark* (1983), *Good Bones* (1992), and *The Tent* (2006). Even as Atwood returns to the short story in *Moral Disorder* (and the later *Stone Mattress*[2]), this collection also marks another generic debut in her oeuvre, since *Moral Disorder* is her first short story cycle.

The 14 short stories of her first collection *Dancing Girls* had first been published separately between 1964 and 1977, thus demarking the early phase of Atwood's writing. When considering the character constellations and the themes of these stories, Atwood's words in a poem of the same period come to mind: "This is not a debate / but a duet / with two deaf singers" ("Two-Headed Poems," 227). For these early short stories portray characters in unfitting, unfulfilling, or disintegrating relationships. A lack of self-confidence, the feeling of being trapped inside the wrong body—such feelings of inadequacy lead many characters in *Dancing Girls* into dysfunctional relationships that confirm their negative self-perception, whether through their partners' open lack of interest, their attitude of dominance, or their sexual betrayal.

The stories demonstrate how the characters' failure to come to terms with themselves results in their inability to form meaningful relationships: the protagonists are, ultimately, defeated by themselves, not by their partners.

A case in point is the opening story of the collection, "The Man from Mars," which was first published in 1977, two years after the end of the Vietnam War. This is a typical Atwood story in that it combines intellectually challenging writing with high readability and many humorous twists, despite the seriousness of the topic and of the events rendered. The story's title, "The Man from Mars," suggests the perceived alien status of a male Vietnamese student, who is staying in Canada pretending to study. The appearance and, especially, the behavior of the nameless Asian man are so utterly different from what the female protagonist Christine has experienced in her shielded middle-class life that he appears to be the "Other" in this story. In Christine's family, in which the multicultural aspects of Canadian society are kept at bay, foreigners and, one gathers, non-white Canadians are referred to as "person[s] from another culture" (10). The seedy young man from Vietnam, after Christine's initially kind behavior toward him, starts to follow her around, persistently, mysteriously, obsessively: "She was aware of the ridiculous spectacle they must make, galloping across campus, something out of a cartoon short, a lumbering elephant stampeded by a smiling, emaciated mouse, both of them locked in the classic pattern of comic pursuit and flight" (22). Since Christine is quite an unattractive young woman, the stranger's motives remain utterly opaque. But due to his unswerving persistence, his obsessive tracking of Christine on the university campus eventually "render[s] her equally mysterious" (23). Although he is even less attractive than Christine, the Vietnamese immigrant temporarily reinstates overweight, plain Christine as feminine in the eyes of the Canadian men around her. In the end, the story takes an ironic twist as it is Christine—for once having been at the center of a man's attention—who finally ponders on the deported Asian's motives and worries about him as she obsessively searches for news on his homeland in reports on the Vietnam War. Blending questions of gender and ethnicity, "The Man from Mars" challenges conventional cultural constructions of both. By presenting the story from Christine's perspective and rendering the strange young man through her eyes, Atwood enables the reader to participate in the construction and deconstruction of prejudice and misconception. The story clearly demonstrates how fragile, painful, and sometimes irresolvable the relationships between the sexes may be, even more so when coupled with the attempt at transcultural understanding. "The Man from Mars," the Asian stranger, remains a rather enigmatic figure until the end, not only for Christine but also for the reader.

The 12 stories included in Atwood's second short story collection, *Bluebeard's Egg*, were written in the 1970s and early 1980s. This collection no longer focuses on individual psychological problems as the stories in her first collection did, but instead places emphasis on socio-psychological themes. Individuals are increasingly seen as a part of their social surroundings and as members of specific groups. Whereas in the first collection, the characters are often presented in what for them would be exceptional surroundings and exceptional circumstances—indeed, they can be viewed as Atwood's early "tourist characters"—in *Bluebeard's Egg* the characters are usually shown at home or within their family circles. The volume, which Atwood dedicated to her parents, contains several "family stories"—such as "Significant Moments in the Life of My Mother," "Unearthing Suite," and "Loulou; or, The Domestic Life of Language"—which are marked by a warmth quite unlike the dark mood surrounding the alienated, desperate characters of Atwood's first short story collection. The family unit, of course, is usually the location of people's earliest significant experiences with gender and gender relations. An especially compelling family story (which is at the same time, though less obviously, also an artist story) is the opening story, "Significant Moments in the Life of My Mother," which was first published in *Bluebeard's Egg* (for an analysis of this story see Chapter 6).

Published in 1991, *Wilderness Tips*, Atwood's third collection of short stories, features 10 texts written in the 1980s. These stories, thematically moving away from the family-orientated previous collection, tend to present characters in their work context. "Hairball" and "Uncles," for instance, focus on talented female characters who have succeeded professionally even in the face of resentment and nasty envy among their male colleagues. The story "Death by Landscape," following in the footsteps of "Significant Moments," features an additional thematic, gender-related aspect within Atwood's short prose. As she does in her novel *Cat's Eye*, published three years previously, in 1988, in "Death by Landscape" Atwood places gender problems in a same-sex context that goes beyond the mother-daughter and father-son relationships that she had explored earlier. In this story, the tentative friendship that for several years links the Canadian schoolgirl Lois with the American girl Lucy in retrospect turns out to carry more emotional power than any of Lois's subsequent relationships, including that with her husband Rob. The lasting bond between the girls is strengthened by Lucy's mysterious, unsolved disappearance into the Canadian wilderness during a summer camp excursion. After her husband's death, the adult Lois reviews her life up to that point, recognizing that it has taken two paths: an "official" life that Lois has lived physically, and an "unofficial" inner life of the mind—a typical dichotomy with Atwood's characters. In this story, the "untold story" develops into the conscious, dominant path: "She can hardly remember getting married, or what Rob looked like. Even at the time she never felt she was paying full attention. She was tired a lot, as if she was living not one life but two: her own, and another, shadowy life that hovered around her and would not let itself be realized—the life of what would have happened if Lucy had not stepped sideways, and disappeared from time" (127–28). Here, as in the story "Weight" in the same collection, the male-female relationships and conflicts in many early stories are reduced in importance, because for the female protagonists their emotional and (in "Weight") intellectual friendships with other women turn out to be the deepest, most personal, and most formative relationships in their lives. Relationships between men and women, on the other hand, are marked too strongly by conventional gender patterns (not to say rituals) of behavior, and seem rather to get in the way of the female characters' individual development in this collection (cf. also Chapter 11).

Since the 1980s, Atwood, as mentioned above, has employed new textual formats for her challenging rewritings and explorations, short texts that are altogether hard to classify and have few genuine forerunners in Canadian literature. Although the texts collected in *Murder in the Dark*, *Good Bones*, and *The Tent* do include pieces that operate within the generic parameters of the short story, it would be inaccurate to describe them simply as short short story collections or prose poetry collections. Short dialogues, dramatic monologues, and "essay-fictions" are among the text formats featured in these collections.

Representative of Atwood's contribution to the postmodern development of generic hybridization and intensified intertextuality is also her involvement with the prose poem, especially in *Murder in the Dark: Short Fictions and Prose Poems* and in *Good Bones*. The prose poem had mainly evolved through the works of French author Charles Baudelaire, also known for his misogyny and his reification of women in his writing. In several of the pieces in *Good Bones* and *Murder in the Dark*, Atwood gets in an intertextual, revisionist dialogue with Baudelaire, for instance in her prose poems "Worship" and "Iconography" in *Murder in the Dark*. These texts can be read as critical cross-referencing of Baudelaire's prose poems "Un hémisphère dans une chevelure" and "Un cheval de race" from *Le spleen de Paris* and of his poems "Le serpent qui danse" and "Le chat" from *Les fleurs du mal*. Atwood's "A Beggar" in *Murder in the Dark* refers back to Baudelaire's "Assomons les pauvres" from *Le spleen de Paris*; her text "The Bad News," the opening work of *Good Bones*, recalls Baudelaire's "Au lecteur" from *Les fleurs du mal*; Atwood's "Let Us Now Praise Stupid Women" in *Good Bones* includes a direct reference to the latter well-known text by Baudelaire; and her prose poem "Men at Sea" from *Good Bones* is an inversive writing back to Baudelaire's poem "L'homme et la mer" from *Les fleurs du mal*.[3] In such texts, Atwood responds to Baudelaire in various ways: most fundamentally, in her elaboration of the hybrid genre of the prose poem, which did not really have a generic tradition in Canada when Atwood adapted the form in *Murder*; secondly, by way of specific intertextual references to Baudelaire's poems and prose poetry in her prose poems; and thirdly and most importantly, in her revisionist handling of themes Baudelaire had dealt with, most notably in Atwood's very different treatment of gender. In fact, it is Baudelaire's self-serving and self-enhancing reified and sexualized portrayals of women that most spurs on Atwood's revisionist rewriting of this canonical French writer, by first cleverly subverting Baudelaire's themes and evaluations and eventually employing full-fledged inversion techniques.[4] As Atwood progresses from *Murder in the Dark* to *Good Bones*, she uses increasingly bold and drastic counter-representations hinging on gender, which are stirred and at the same time tempered by her injections of playful and comic elements.

The development in Atwood's technique of gender representation from, largely, subversion to inversion may be seen, for instance, by a comparison of "Liking Men" (from *Murder*) with "Making a Man" (from *Good Bones*). These two texts also demonstrate that Atwood is by no means only—or even mainly—concerned with the representation of female characters. In "Liking Men," there is a facetious undercurrent of irony right from the beginning— "It's time to like men again. Where shall we begin?" (53)—as Atwood subverts the traditional Baudelairean approach in which the male author's portrayals of women self-servingly reify them, that is, make them into depersonalized objects. In Atwood's text, an unusual reversal of roles takes place, with the female author portrayed as reifying men. With Baudelairean symmetry, "Liking Men" is split into two halves by the triggering phrase "You don't want to go on but you can't stop yourself" (53). After various parts of the male body have been rejected as too problematic for liking, the speaker ironically singles out the seemingly harmless and utilitarian feet as *pars pro toto* objects for "liking men." But, alas, even in this context of male feet, a positive approach— "You think of kissing those feet ... you like to give pleasure" (53)—may hardly be kept up in the speaker's train of thought as she then remarks on less likable or even obnoxious styles of behavior connected with men: the associations evoked by footwear, though benign at first, inexorably lead, from "dance shoes," "riding boots," "cowboy boots," and "jackboots," to scenes of war and rape in which man is the aggressor. Improving upon Baudelaire, who resorts to stereotypical representations of women, the first-person narrator in "Liking Men" attempts to differentiate between man as a category (which includes rapists and war mongers) and men as individuals: "Just because all rapists are men it doesn't follow that all men are rapists ... you try desperately to retain the image of the man you love and also like" (54). This attempt at a circumspect, non-stereotypical view of men takes the first-person narrator back to the man's birth and his socialization, that is, to the social context and conditions that have influenced his life story. Despite the ironic undercurrents of "Liking Men," Atwood in this piece, quite in contrast to Baudelaire's very partial view of gender, thus aims at a balanced, non-stereotypical acknowledgment of the individuality of men while remaining aware of the social and socio-psychological conditions that breed misogynistic behavior. Nevertheless, "Liking Men," with an unflattering and unimpressed view of men, subverts the Baudelairean intertexts with their heroization of man and reduction of woman (cf. also Baudelaire's poem "L'homme et la mer" from *Les fleurs du mal* with Atwood's subversive treatment of the text in her prose poem "Men at Sea" from *Good Bones*; see note 3). "Liking Men," then, points both intra- and intertextually to the constructedness and thereby mutability of gender roles and gender images. Atwood's unconventional, subversive portrayal of men, women, and gender relations has a fundamentally didactic as well as political intention, as can be seen even more clearly in her later collection *Good Bones*.

"Making a Man" from *Good Bones* is a humorous attack on, and inversion of, women as commodities of popular culture. While Atwood in her intertextual method in these collections frequently gets into a dialogue with authors from world literature, as is the case with Baudelaire, or also Shakespeare (see Atwood's take on *Hamlet* in "Gertrude Talks Back"; see note 3), "Making a Man" turns to intertexts of popular journalism and mocks its commodification of women. Mimicking the style of women's magazines in giving readers tips on how to "make a man," the text takes the form of a recipe that presents various creative methods for baking, sewing, or even—ironically suggestive—inflating figures of men, thereby smugly parodying the stylistic conventions of cookbooks and other how-to books. The first, the "Traditional Method" of "making a man," irreverently parodies the biblical creation myth. The third, the "Clothes Method," is laced with word play and a critique of traditional gender roles: "Clothes make the man! How often have you heard it said! Well, we couldn't agree more! However, clothes may make the man, but women—by and large—make the clothes, so it follows that the responsibility for the finished model lies with the home seamstress" (55). The fifth and last method, "The Folk Art Method," in its imagery stresses the reductive reification of man in this text, though nicely packaged in a rather cute style: "You've seen these cuties in other folks' front yards, with little windmills attached to their heads. They hammer with their little hammers, saw with their little saws, or just whirl their arms around a lot when there's a stiff breeze" (57). Such stylized representations of men take the anti-essentialist constructedness of gender images at face value and demonstrate Atwood's playful intertextual poetics of inversion at work in the smallest of places.

"The Little Red Hen Tells All," similar to "Gertrude Talks Back," also from *Good Bones*, is an illuminative example of Atwood's gender revisionism concerning the representation of women. Again, as in "Death by Landscape," Atwood juxtaposes an "official," conventional story with an "unofficial" version.

In this case, however, the differences between the two versions are directly explored and, so to speak, made public. The parable-like tale of the hen telling "all" is also an example of Atwood's repeatedly revising received stories from popular culture, such as fairy tales and myths, with an eye to the gender models or stereotypes perpetuated by such influential tales. "The Little Red Hen Tells All" is based on a children's tale widely known in the English-speaking world. Atwood reproduces the basic structures of this fable but adds imaginative amplifications and ambivalent word-play—for example, "A grain of wheat saved is a grain of wheat earned" (12)—as well as precisely integrated comments on the plot, which, with apparent casualness, expose the popular tale's intellectual implications, by commenting, for instance, on the capitalist ideology supporting production and maximization of profits: "Sobriety and elbow-grease. Do it yourself. Then invest your capital. Then collect" (11). Atwood's most important reinterpretation in this story, however, concerns gender difference. By highlighting the gender of the female "narrator-hen," Atwood brings to light the ideological impact of the tale, both in its original and its new version.

For gender roles in the original folk tale (which is, ironically, often passed on orally from mothers to their children) are, on closer inspection, rather strangely conceived. The egocentric, hoarding, greedy behavior of the female "narrator," the hen—"*I'll eat it myself, so kiss off*," says the hen (13)—does not comply with the typical female behavioral patterns of nourishment and generosity; it rather resembles the typical behavior of a "rooster." Atwood further parodies the original story by eventually supplanting this selfish demeanor with traditionally associated "feminine" qualities, such as freely putting oneself in second position and thinking of others first. The conflict is thus transferred from the external to the internal: because of her gender-specific socialization, the hard-working hen acts contrary to her own (economical) interests and needs in a way that is much in favor of the common good, but verges on her own self-denial. The capitalist ideology of the folk tale is thus modified in Atwood's retelling through a foregrounding of gender difference. In her adaptation to a gender-conscious era, Atwood makes clear the pitfalls of gender differentiation, to which "hens"/women fall victim far more often than do "roosters"/men. Her story also makes clear that women's self-effacing behavior grows out of gender-specific socialization and is responsive to social context.

Atwood's most recent book of "short fictions," *The Tent* (2006), again includes a variety of textual formats: there are two works one can rightly call poems, mainly because they are printed with indentations, two short dialogues, verging on mini dramas, three fables, several episodic rewritings of previous literature and of mythology, as well as a hybrid textual format we may call "essay-fictions." The latter format tends to color this collection, with the predominant impression of the volume being a reflective rather than a narrative one. Gender is not particularly foregrounded in this later collection (for a more detailed, genre-oriented discussion of this collection, including an analysis of several of its texts, see Chapter 14).

That gender is not particularly foregrounded applies also, to some extent, to *Moral Disorder*, which was published in the same year as *The Tent*. With this short story collection—the individual stories of which were first published between 1996 and 2006—Atwood formally returns to the short story proper, linking the individual stories thematically in such an integrative way that we may speak of this work as Atwood's first short story cycle. *Moral Disorder* is clearly also her most "autobiographical" book, with Atwood the writer and family person in her mid-sixties taking stock and looking back. The individual stories step by step sketch the development of the protagonist Nell from childhood to adulthood and older age within her family context—two of the 11 stories deal with Nell's childhood, one with her youth, eight mainly with an adult Nell, who is present in all stories. The structure of the book is predominantly chronological, within a largely retrospective framework and a sometimes montage-like alternation between narrative past and narrative present, a technique used in "The Headless Horseman," "The Labrador Fiasco," and "The Boys at the Lab." Yet the introductory story, "The Bad News"—told in the present tense—shows an aging Nell with her long-time husband Tig, thus opening the book with the latest chronological story, to signal an essential aspect and tone of the collection as a whole: "The Bad News" exudes a sense of loss—loss of reckless optimism, of vitality—and a sense of fear and anxiety. In a way closing the circle with Atwood's first short story collection *Dancing Girls*, danger seems to lurk everywhere, and in this later collection danger also exists on a larger, political scale. Afraid of old age, illness, and a potential loss of mental capacity, Nell is in a tense, often anxious mental state, with gender in this later life period apparently no longer a pressing issue for her (for a more detailed reading of "The Bad News" see Chapter 8).

It is significant that the two stories in which gender does figure prominently are part of the first third of the book, which mainly deals with a young/er Nell in her childhood and youth. These periods, of course, are crucial for gender socialization, especially given the stories' setting in the 1950s and 1960s, when gender was a particularly defining and restrictive issue for women especially. "The Art of Cooking and Serving" and "My Last Duchess" in *Moral Disorder* thus belong to the relatively few stories in Atwood's short story oeuvre—similar to "Betty" in *Dancing Girls*, "Hurricane Hazel" in *Bluebird's Egg*, "Uncles" and "Death by Landscape" in *Wilderness Tips*—that show gender at work in the crucial younger, formative stages of life and that emphasize that gender is not in-born but is transmitted, constructed, and performed.

The story with the telling title "The Art of Cooking and Serving," the second story in *Moral Disorder*, is an initiation story telling of the daughter Nell's initiation into domestic life and mothering, and of her eventual distancing from her family as she comes to reject her mother's influence. The story shows how conventional gender expectations and restrictions are part of Nell's upbringing, for instance by the fact that knitting is one of Nell's prime pastimes, not least because her mother is expecting a "late" child. Lillie is an unplanned baby and turns out to be "one of *those*" (22), as the doctor puts it, a nervous and nerve-racking child who hardly ever sleeps and who exhausts her family, especially her mother. Before the baby's sex is known, Nell reflects on the gendered color system for babies, blue for boys and pink for girls (11–12). She is praised by others for knitting diligently for the baby and is called "a good little worker" (20), which reinforces gendered socialization patterns that train little girls in the direction of motherhood. Whereas Nell, "with single-minded concentration" (14), is fully integrated into the family preparations for the birth of the third child, Nell's brother is hardly mentioned and his task under the new circumstances is not exactly taxing: "We would all have to pitch in, said my father, and do extra tasks. It would be my brother's job to mow the lawn, from now until June" (13).

When Nell is not knitting the layette for the baby or cleaning the house, another pastime of hers is to read a cookbook published in 1929–30, 10 years before Nell was born (just like Atwood herself). Sarah Field Splint's (real) how-to manual *The Art of Cooking and Serving* sets Nell's thoughts into motion: "Did I want to transform, or to be transformed? Was I to be the kind homemaker, or the ... untidy maid? I hardly knew" (19). In her insecure, transgressive, liminal state of development (on liminality and the short story see chapters 8 and 9), she is, on the one hand, thankful for guidance from role models, but, on the other hand, cannot decide on one or the other—probably because both of them are heavily engendered and she is looking for other options. Yet when Nell openly rebels against her mother and the nurturing role her mother is steering her toward in a gender-essentialist manner, she is punished. To act against ingrained gender roles in an open manner may entail pain, in more than one sense: "My mother stood up and whirled around, all in one movement, and slapped me hard across the face" (23). Nevertheless, the end of the story sees young Nell drifting away from the domestic, nurturing role supposedly cut out for her, mentally turning toward a new kind of outside world of peer groups, "to all sorts of ... seductive and tawdry and frightening pleasures I could not yet begin to imagine" (23).

Whereas this distancing between mother and daughter in puberty is a common developmental step, the mother's pregnancy is rendered in rather unusual, problematic terms in this story, thereby also working against any kind of euphemistic motherhood myth. For one thing, as mentioned before, Lillie is a late, unplanned baby. Due to the advanced age of Nell's mother, her pregnancy is viewed with trepidation. Second, the newborn baby totally disarranges the family with her constant wailing. Third, Nell's mother becomes exhausted physically and mentally after giving birth to Lillie. Perhaps no wonder, then, that Nell eventually opts against this kind of female familial restriction by explicitly rejecting responsibility for her younger sister. Again, the men in the family seem to have little to do with the baby; they are not shown to support the mother in her caring for the child and do not seem to particularly care. "The Art of Cooking and Serving" thus renders traditional gender roles in problematic terms, showing these roles to work against women's independence and freedom of choice. Giving birth to a child and nurturing it are shown to be the concerns of women—who must either accept the prescribed role and live with the consequences or, painfully, opt out of it, as does Nell at the end of the story, leaving her overtaxed mother in the lurch.

As Atwood deals with the girlhood and youth of the protagonist Nell in her largely chronological short story cycle *Moral Disorder*, she emphasizes the social constructedness of gender and the performance status of femininities and masculinities in Nell's troubled coming of age (cf. also Chapter 11). And she also, in this work, moves to other concerns as Nell comes to realize the reality of her aging: "These are the tenses that define us now: past tense, *back then*; future tense, *not yet*. We live in the small window between them" (4). Interestingly, over the course of some four decades Atwood's treatment of gender issues in her short stories and short fictions has developed largely according to the various stages of "victim positions" she differentiated early on in her 1972 work *Survival*: *"Position One: To deny the fact that you are a victim"*; *"Position Two: To acknowledge the fact that you are a victim, but to explain this as an act of Fate ... the dictates of Biology (in the case of women, for instance)"*; *"Position Three: To acknowledge the fact that you are a victim but to refuse to accept the assumption that the role is inevitable"*; and finally *"Position Four: To be a creative non-victim"* (36–38). Especially in *Murder in the Dark* and in *Good Bones*, Atwood's subversive and inverse views on gender conceptions become even more incisive and outspoken, though not without a light-hearted, humorous treatment of a complex issue.

Atwood's way of dealing with gender relations in her short stories and short fictions may be read as "Instructions for the Third Eye," to take up the title of the resonant rounding-off text in *Murder in the Dark*. Atwood admonishes us, female and male readers alike, to transcend the dualistic thought pattern of either/or, which chains us to fixed identity positions and gender roles, and to be open to liberating, non-essentialist views of gender relations. In her more recent short story cycle *Moral Disorder*—although its protagonist in her younger years repeatedly feels subjected to gender clichés—eventually an altogether non-essentialist view of gender relations seems achieved, so much so that over larger parts of this collection gender is seldom foregrounded. As Nell reflects close to the end of "The Entities" in *Moral Disorder:* "All that anxiety and anger, those dubious good intentions, those tangled lives, that blood. I can tell about it or I can bury it. In the end, we'll all become stories" (188).

8

Multiple Liminality
Aging in the Canadian Short Story

As the chapter title suggest, the aims of this chapter are multiple. Uniting various aspects of Literature and Culture Studies, the chapter investigates the concept of liminality in Canadian short fiction specifically within the framework of age studies, pivoting on the life period of old age. Further concerns of this chapter are the cross-connections between the concept of liminality and the short story as well as the contention that the short story is a "liminal" genre. I also consider the extent to which old age can be seen as a liminal period. Last but not least, I show liminality at work in selected contemporary Canadian short stories that deal with aging, and classify these stories into four categories: Aging as a Journey, Liminal States of Consciousness and Old/er Age, Liminal Locations of Aging, as well as Old/er Age and Death as Liminal Periods. My text selection is culled from a text corpus of some 40 short stories in total that deal with aging, by canonical writers of the Canadian short story such as Margaret Atwood, Mavis Gallant, Thomas King, Alice Munro, Jane Rule, Carol Shields, and Audrey Thomas.

On Liminality

The term "liminality" is derived from the Latin *limen*, meaning "threshold." The concept was originally introduced to cultural anthropology by ethnographer Arnold van Gennep in 1909 in his book *Les rites de passage*. He defined *rites de passage* as "rites which accompany every change of place, state, social position and age" (van Gennep in Turner 1969, 94). Victor Turner would later use the notion of "state" to encompass all of these latter categories, "state" referring to "any type of stable or recurrent condition that is culturally recognized" (Turner 1969, 94). Van Gennep detected a universal pattern in the social rituals or ceremonies that mark an individual's or a social group's passing from one state to another. He identified three general stages of this process, the middle of which he called the "liminal phase."[1] In this phase, which occurs in all ritual passages that societies use to demarcate transitions from one state to another, the individual (whom Turner calls the "passenger") is "in-between," no longer part of the previous state and not yet part of the next one. In such periods, the passenger "passes through a cultural realm that has few or none of the attributes of the previous or coming state" (Turner 1969, 94). The passenger's self-conception and behavior are modified, their sense of identity dissolves and changes to some extent. As a result, such transitional periods tend to be characterized by disorientation, indeterminacy, ambiguity, intensity, and the openness for change.

Van Gennep's concept of liminality became more widespread when his book was translated into English as *The Rites of Passage* in 1960. After British anthropologist Victor Turner had taken up the term and elaborated it in the 1960s and 1970s, it became popularized in the 1980s and 1990s (Thomassen 2015, 47). Turner freed the term from its original, more narrowly anthropological application to small-scale tribal societies and identified parallels with modern, (post)industrial ones. He thus widened the use and applicability of the term so that it has now permeated the social sciences and the humanities to such an extent that social scientist Bjørn Thomassen, for instance, recently went so far as to call liminality "a master concept in the wider political and social sciences" (2015, 39).[2]

Victor Turner later differentiated between the terms "liminal" and "liminoid" (see Turner 1982, esp. 53–55). Liminal periods (or events or experiences), according to Turner, are a part of a social ritual and are identity-related: they are transitional periods with strong transformative potential. When the ritual subject moves past such a period, a meaningful change has taken place. "Liminoid" experiences share certain characteristics with liminal experiences, yet they are "optional and do not involve resolution of a personal crisis or change of status" and thus lack the element of transition constitutive of liminal experiences (Thomassen 2015, 47). The terms as I will use them in the following can be illustrated with an example: Going to a rock concert may be a liminoid experience for a concert-goer as it is something quite out of the ordinary, a setting in which social rules and propriety are relaxed or even ignored, where the concert-goer may feel immersed in an intense and special communal situation, temporarily removed from the normal course of her life; but when she comes home again, her status and sense of self usually remain unchanged. Only when, for instance, the concert inspires in her a deep love for rock music and she resolves to become a rock musician herself, does the concert-going experience become liminal: it would thus have been identity-related and would have changed the person's state—life would not be the same for her anymore. Turner argued that in our Western consumerist societies, truly liminal rites of passage have become scarce and are often displaced by liminoid experiences (thus marriage has often been replaced by "living together"). In accordance with scholarly practice today, I will use a more wide-ranging concept of liminality than van Gennep's, and in part also Turner's, while remaining mindful of the term's socio-anthropological dimension. In line with Bjørn Thomassen in a different context, I will thus also ask: "What happens in liminal situations that unfold outside the spatial and temporal boundaries of expert-led ritual passages?" (2015, 41).

Liminality may generally refer to time and to space, marking areas of transition between two individual "states" in a temporal and/or a spatial sense. Examples of liminal periods are traveling, falling in love, getting engaged, and taking final exams. Airports, hotels, hospitals, caring homes, and border regions are liminal locations or liminal zones. A liminal experience is thus not always ritualistic and externally induced, as in the case of a wedding ceremony and celebration. A liminal experience may simply come about, such as when falling in love or becoming or being old. Formulations such as "being 'stuck in liminality'" (Thomassen 2015, 54) point to the relevance of in-between situations as such, but equally to the significance of people's reactions to liminal experiences. Liminality is thus also about how we deal with essential processes of change (ibid., 40). Finally, one may distinguish between the subject, space, time, and scale of liminality, the latter referring to the level or intensity of the liminal experience.

Liminality and the Short Story

In the sparse research on liminality in connection with the short story (the main publication in the area being Achilles and Bergmann 2015; see also Chapter 9 of this volume on border stories), it has been argued that the short story is a liminal literary genre, or even "the liminal genre *par excellence*" (ibid., 4). I cannot support Achilles and Bergmann's argumentation that the short story is a liminal genre because of its alleged hybrid status between essay and sketch, poem and novel, and elitist and popular culture (ibid.). Similar arguments could apply to other or even to all literary genres, and such a broad, all-encompassing view of liminality would deprive the short story of its indisputably independent standing as a major literary genre. Not merely a transitional genre that points toward other genres, the short story is clearly a genre in its own right.

It is, however, a genre with strong affinities to liminality, with respect to both its themes and structures. Katherine Orr (2015), too, acknowledges liminality's essential role for the short story: "At the core of the short story lies flux: a quality as important to the form and the subjects explored by its writers. In contrast to the larger landscapes of the novel, the short story situates both characters and readers on the brink, foregrounding the ... intensity of threshold experience" (251). The short story generally makes up in structure, theme, and intensity what it lacks in length in comparison to the novel. Short stories thus often spotlight pivotal situations, "slices of life" charged with significance, which in themselves point beyond the narrated events. These are transitional episodes such as in initiation stories, which suggestively condense the past, present, and future, situations of crisis and of turning points, indeed, thresholds in the characters' lives. Narrative techniques of transition such as episodic and epiphanic structures, flashbacks, or transitional settings technically support and enhance the liminality of the themes the genre favors. The short story is thus strongly informed by a poetics of liminality and can be characterized as "a forum for certain crisis and potential change, a privileged terrain for scenarios of reorientation" (Achilles 2015, 41).

Age Studies, Aging, Old/er Age

One such "scenario of reorientation" is the period and experience of growing old. We begin to age the day we are born. Aging is thus a life-long process that eventually leads to old age (if one does not die prematurely) and then, inevitably, terminates with the ultimate threshold, death—in this sense, "we are *all* terminal cases" (Rooke 1992, 249). The aging process is often divided into developmental phases: infancy, childhood, adolescence, adulthood, middle/"best" age, and old age. For the later and for the last life periods, I myself use the term "old/er age"[3]—with a slash after "old" to combine two terms, "older" and "old," into one, as particularly the latter term, "old," is a classification that is fuzzy and subjective, as well as still rather negatively connoted. "*The magic age of 65*" (Erber 2013, 11), formerly the statutory age of retirement in many Western societies, was long regarded as the beginning of disengagement, but the retirement age has been in a state of flux (see also Kunow 2012). Old/er age for me encompasses roughly the years after 70 and until death. There are various alternative circumscriptions for this chronologically late/r period of life, such as "third age" or "fourth age" (Woodward 2012, 2), or, a term I also find appropriate, "older adulthood" (e.g., Aiken 2001, 4). While old/er people have been addressed in texts since antiquity (such as in Plato's *Republic*, Seneca's *Epistulae morales* [letter 26], or Cicero's *On Old Age* [orig. *Cato Maior de Senecute*]), the period of old/er age was not theoretically considered on a larger scale until relatively recently: in earlier centuries, people died on average at a much younger age and the demographic proportion of "old/er" people was so trifling (less than 2 percent) that they were considered negligible (see Achenbaum 2005, 24). A considerable rise in average life expectancy and the population aging that goes hand in hand with it, have only been a fact in Western societies from the twentieth century onward, due to healthier nutrition, better hygiene and sanitation, advanced medical treatment, and a higher general standard of living. The increase in life expectancy in Western societies throughout the twentieth century—"the great watershed in the history of ageing" (ibid., 25)—and into the twenty-first century has been so remarkable that it has been dubbed a "demographic revolution" (e.g., Jahnson 2004, 1). For instance, on the African continent in 2010, only 3 percent of the population was older than 65, whereas on the North American continent, it was already 13 percent in the same year; Europe had the highest proportion of people above 65 in 2010, namely 16 percent (Population Reference Bureau; see Erber 2013, 14). There are numerous projections as to how dramatically this number will rise in Western societies within the next few decades, owing to the combined effect of diminishing birth rates and increasing life expectancy. Whereas Western societies' higher life expectancy can be regarded as a "societal achievement" (Jahnson 2004, 1) and is, or should be, a source of joy (at least if one ages in good health and with economic welfare), there has been a predominantly negative public discourse about potential side-effects of becoming older: an increase in diseases, particularly mental diseases such as Alzheimer's and other forms of dementia, accompanied by increasing health costs ("greying means paying"; Kunow 2012, 64), as well as shortages of, and costs for, caring homes and caregivers. As Gerald F. Manning put it some 25 years ago: "A series of fearful 'Ds' may seem to accompany the coming of age: diminishment, decline, disengagement ... demise" (1993, 470).

Yet aging and old/er age are not only—and not even predominantly—an indelible chronological and biological fact, resulting in what Margaret Gullette in 1997 critically called a "decline narrative," but rather a cultural construct that is subject to socio-cultural change. Rüdiger Kunow accordingly calls aging and old/er age "relational phenomena," which structure interpersonal relationships in a culturally specific way (2012, 56). In a process of social standardization, one is also *made* increasingly older in the course of one's life—individuals thereby being pressed into cultural aging and perhaps even into an identity crisis because of a resulting self-image that is often split between a personal "not-old" Self and a public "old" Self (ibid., 57). Many scholars argue that the "problems of old age" will not be resolved if the public discourse does not change its predominantly negative conception of "old age," a stance that Robert Butler in 1975 called "ageism," "a process of collective stereotyping which emphasizes the negative features of ageing" (Featherstone and Hepworth 2005, 357). Scholars nowadays also differentiate between "ageism" and a more subtle form, "new ageism" (the latter "is evident in *compassionate stereotypes*, which foster a view of older adults as helpless and in need of advocacy") and warn: "Unlike racism and sexism ... all of us could become targets of ageism if we live long enough" (Erber 2013, 13).

Though the scientific study of old/er age can be traced back to the nineteenth century (see Erber 2013, 3), it took until the 1970s and 1980s for the topic to reach the humanities, when a "literary gerontology" started to develop. At that time, Kathleen Woodward still bemoaned that the variable of age had been ignored in literary criticism and postulated that it needed to be added to the prominent analytical variables of race, class, and gender (see Wyatt-Brown, 1992, 331–32). Since the end of World War II, and in a literary context since the 1970s, age studies have indeed been on the rise. In a recent book review published in *The New York Times* of Michael Kinsley's *Old Age: A Beginner's Guide*, Phillip Lopate (2016) states: "Longevity breeds literature"—which implies that writers also tend to live longer nowadays and are thus more concerned with the late/r life period, as are their readers. In other words, old/er age has been culturally upgraded, or, as Mary Sohngen already put it back in 1977, "old age is in" (70).

In age studies and also in literary gerontology since the 1980s, there has been a reorientation away from the predominantly negative views of old age—which, for instance, Simone de Beauvoir still maintained in her book *La Vieillesse* in 1970 (Engl. *Old Age* [1972]; 20 years later, Rooke in 1992 calls the book "dated ... resoundingly," 244). Age studies nowadays allow for a more balanced and constructive, also positive approach to aging: "Nowadays, old people ... do not define their age in terms of how many years they have lived, but in terms of what they can still do. They become more participative and active and see their age more like a second adulthood rather than a second childhood" (Jahnson 2004, 1).[4] Indeed, gerontologists today consider various other kinds of age that need not go hand in hand with chronological age. In fact, "chronological age by itself is ... rarely an accurate indicator of a person's biological, psychological ... social [and functional] age" (Aiken 2001, 4).[5] Whereas the earliest scientific perspective on aging may be called "*normative*" (it focused on "behavioral functioning" that was "considered normal, or average"), nowadays scholars also consider "*successful aging*" ("a distinction can be made between an average outcome and an ideal outcome") and, "the newest perspective, '*positive aging*,'" which refers to the obvious fact that "a person can experience happiness and well-being even in the face of objective adversity" (Erber 2013, 27). There are earlier differentiations based exclusively on chronological age, such as between "young-old (ages 65–74), old-old (ages 75–84), and oldest old (ages 85+)" (ibid., 12), with the fastest growing group in Western societies nowadays being the oldest age group. All this underscores that old/er age is becoming the second-longest life period after adulthood (if one differentiates between these two periods, see above). Owing to its "elastic boundaries," it has repeatedly been claimed to be "the most heterogeneous" period of life: "Today's generation of elders varies enormously in physical, mental, psychological, and social capabilities" (Achenbaum 2005, 25).

In recent decades, the subject of aging has featured in an increasing number of literary texts, and old/er characters have been assigned major roles in them (see already Rooke 1992). Literary texts on aging usually work against ageism, still in contrast to much of the public discourse. As Anne W. Wyatt-Brown summarizes in her survey "Literary Gerontology Comes of Age" in 1992, "fiction provides a fairly balanced view of old age" (333). Fictional texts narrate stories about aging individuals and thus individualize facts, problems, as well as opportunities that arise with growing old/er. Literary texts exemplify how individual old/er characters deal with aging and how they are treated in their social context. Literary texts may thus raise the readers' awareness of the life period of old/er age and may make them more empathetic toward old/er people: "The understanding we gain through literature can actually change the emotional climate of old age" (Rooke 1992, 244), while also fulfilling one of literature's main functions, that of contributing to collective memory, specifically of how we deal with old/er age.

To what extent can this late stage of life be considered a liminal period? One of its specificities, in comparison with the other life stages, is that the duration of life left for the individual tends to be shorter than the one that already lies behind. The longer this period of typically unpredictable duration lasts, the more one can speak, with Victor Turner (1969) in a different context, of a seeming "permanentization" of liminality. The older one gets, the more aware one becomes of the inexorable finiteness of life. This increasing "proximity to darkness" lends "a special intensity" (Rooke 1992, 248) to the late phase of life. Its transitional state is accounted for by the fact that, on the one hand, one no longer counts as middle-aged but as an old/er adult—although one may functionally, socially, psychologically, and even biologically still rather belong to the previous age group. On the other hand, at the very end of this life period, when, significantly, "passing" (i.e., dying), one has reached the end of individual existence or, if one believes in "life after death," a totally new, metaphysical state.

In scholarly treatment of literature and aging, the genre of the short story, in spite of its having embraced the topic of old/er age particularly in recent decades, has received little attention[6]—although, as I will demonstrate in what follows, there are many expressive and excellent short stories that address this topic, and although the short story lends itself particularly well to a rendering of liminal states and liminal spaces.

Textual Analyses

"In Transit": Aging as a Journey

Several stories in my text corpus symbolically align the process of aging with the metaphor of life as a journey; and indeed, traveling is an often mentioned form of liminality. The traveler is "in transit," in-between with regard to both space and time, changing places while aware that the journey will come to an end eventually. Mavis Gallant's programmatically entitled story "In Transit" (1965) is an excellent example of age-related liminality in the short story. In very short narrative space (1,650 words), the story skillfully shows how aging is a life-long process. It is set in a place that is the epitome of transit, namely the waiting room of an airport, here in Helsinki. With respect to narrated time, too, the story on the present time level encompasses only a few moments, rendering a fleeting encounter between two married couples, a young French and an old American one, the only four people left in the waiting room after a group of Japanese tourists has departed for Oslo. The story's central motif of being in transit is stressed in a number of ways. For instance, the old American man, seemingly disoriented, reads out to his old wife the different destination signs to European cities he sees: "'Oslo.' 'Amsterdam.' 'Copenhagen' … I don't see 'Stockholm'" (310). Eventually, they are said to be "going through the Amsterdam door, whatever their tickets said" (311). The freshly married young French couple, too, experience several noteworthy moments on their honeymoon. Thus the beautiful young French wife ("She had been told she looked like Catherine Deneuve," 313), while walking with her husband along the Helsinki harbor the previous day, is mistaken by a group of tourists for the French actress Catherine Deneuve. Many of the tourists ask for her autograph, which is for her a fleeting source of happiness: "Everything flew and shrieked around them—the seagulls, the wind, the strangers calling in an unknown language something she took to mean 'Your name, your name!'" (ibid.). The state and experience of liminality could hardly be expressed in more concise and diverse a manner: The young French wife was married just a few days previously—weddings of course being ritualized liminal events—and travels with her husband in a foreign country, Finland. A tourist herself, she is surrounded at the harbor, another liminal space, by many other tourists who speak a foreign language she does not understand. And her identity is mistaken, so for a few moments she may feel as if she were a famous film star. The fact that this harbor scene is described retrospectively as a memory adds a further liminoid layer, and the scene also shows how liminal experiences are often identity-related and may be suffused with ambiguity. For the young French wife does not actually feel happy. On the contrary, she is seen to be highly insecure and doubtful, if not even unhappy, during their wedding trip to Helsinki; she is jealous about any contact her husband had or has with other women, afraid that she may one day lose him: "'How do I know you won't leave me?'" (313).

The unfavorable prospects for their just-begun shared life-journey—in parallel, Finland is only the first part of their wedding trip—are underscored by the way the old American couple is rendered through the young Frenchman's perception in the airport waiting room. He may pick up only a few fleeting sentences the American couple exchanges, but these suffice to reveal their marital strains toward the end of their joint life. The American couple thus mirrors the problems already noticeable at the early stage of the young French couple's marriage. Stressing the enhanced experiential intensity liminal situations and places (such as traveling and airports) tend to foster, the old American couple there and then dramatically draws the sum of their long married life together. Thus the old woman abruptly replies to her husband, when he is reading out the destination signs to her: "'What I wonder is what I have been to you all these years.' She had removed her glasses and was wiping her eyes. How did she arrive at that question here, in the Helsinki airport, and how can he answer? 'In the next world we will choose differently,' the man said. 'At least I know you will'" (310). This brief yet momentous exchange is perceived by the young Frenchman on his wedding trip, after all, and, while he cautiously ruminates on the first symptoms of his own recent marriage already being *en route* to a similar development, he becomes acutely aware of the fundamental meaning of marriage, as mirrored by the old couple: "They are chained for the rest of this life. Too old to change? Only a brute would leave her now?" (310). As the other three characters in this short story, the young Frenchman is in a multiple liminal state and becomes intensely aware of the transitoriness of love, marriage, and (life) journeys. The discourse that pinpoints his liminal feelings employs a simile referring to yet another liminal state, namely that of dreaming: "…as if love and travel were opposed to living, were a dream" (313). The atmosphere of being in transit, being in-between, which this story exudes, is also captured by the old American man trying to console his wife by drawing her attention to a restaurant in the airport, while their plane tickets are inspected: "'It is part outside and part inside, see? It is inside *and* outside'" (311). The old American couple, too, is inside and outside: inside and outside their marriage, looking back on a frustrating relationship in this life and contemplating what might come after life, "in the next world" (319), inside and outside their apparently joyless lives, in which they do not seem to care anymore where they are headed, as is symbolically rendered by the seeming arbitrariness of their choice of a flight gate, in transit to another world.

"What Is Remembered"[7]: Liminal States of Consciousness and Aging

Gallant's story "In Transit" demonstrates that one of the relativizing, non-quantifying circumscriptions of old/er age is that with it comes a more intense involvement with the past rather than with what still lies ahead. Memory is thus an important aspect of aging, even more so, and cruelly, when memory fails, for instance with afflictions like Alzheimer's disease and other forms of dementia.[8] Memory, as other states of consciousness such as fantasy and dreaming, creates liminoid or, as the case may be, liminal spaces and states, for they punctuate the flow of life by creating transient internal worlds, alongside the factual world of "real life" (Gallant, "In Transit," 313). The heightened intensity that is emblematic of such states of consciousness becomes evident in our emotional responses to remembering the death of loved ones (such as shedding tears), or in the frightening occurrences typical of nightmares. A contemporary author who masterfully renders such states of consciousness in the short story, also in connection with aging, is Alice Munro. Since it can be said that her stories follow, if very broadly, the trajectory of her own life, it is unsurprising that aging would figure prominently in several stories of the (in August 2016) 85-year-old writer, who retired from writing at 82 in 2013, mere months before being awarded the Nobel Prize in Literature, as it happened.

For the purpose of a closer textual analysis, I chose "In Sight of the Lake," from Munro's final collection, *Dear Life* (2012). Compared to many other Munro stories, this text has a relatively simple structure. Yet its surprise ending, only a few lines long, shows that the entire previous narration represented a dream by an old female resident of a caring home, who had fallen asleep before the caretakers come to her at the end of the story to prepare her for the night, thereby awakening her from what had developed into a nightmare. The difficult questions about this largely chronologically narrated story refer to the personal significance of the numerous elements of the old woman's dream. The reader of this story is thus invited to engage in literary dream analysis. Next to many other references of significance for the dreamer and her (former) life, her dream incorporates two main concerns: first, the old woman's forgetfulness and sense of feeling lost; second, the panic she has of being confined in a caring home for good.

The narrated dream ("narrated by an extradiegetic narrator but clearly focalized through the woman," Simal 2014, 71) visualizes the old woman traveling on her own to a small town some 20 miles away from her hometown. Her aim is to consult a doctor specialized in, as it is put, "elderly patients who are off their nut" (218). She repeatedly insists, however, that it is not her mind but "just memory" (ibid.) that has been letting her down. The transmitted dream in a way confirms both aspects. For one, the dreamer keeps forgetting the doctor's name on her trip, having taken a wrong note instead of the one with the doctor's name and address with her. She feels rather lost in the small town until she is sent to the town's caring home by a kind man, because the sought-for doctor might work for this institution, called "Lakeview Rest Home." Both the euphemism involved in the designation "rest home" and the at first sight serene lake symbolism used for the institution's name prove apt for this story, for "apart from evoking appeasing images of serene old age, lakes have traditionally conjured up ominous threats of drowning and dissolution" (Simal 2014, 77). When the woman arrives at the caring home, its architecture is at first described in positive, even inviting terms ("a bright dome that has a look of welcome, of cheerful excess," 229). But her dream soon develops into a nightmare when the dreamer finds the reception hall deserted, lacking light switches despite the progressing evening, and finally, making her panic, with a front door (which had opened automatically as she was coming in) not budging when she wants to get out again, so that she feels trapped inside the institution.

The product is a Chinese-box-like internal structure, or a *mise-en-abyme*: the old woman's existentially challenging situation at the end of her life in a caring home is mirrored and dramatized by her dream, which visualizes her situation in a short story, that is, her "narrated" dream. Her multiple liminal situation—living in a caring home at her old age—is thus further enhanced in the liminal form of a dream that turns into a claustrophobic nightmare pinpointing her anxiety about her situation. The idea of death being close at hand at this late stage of life (see the repeated references to a funeral home and to death) as well as the fact that the dreamer's mind seems indeed still largely intact, are revealed in the subsequent passage, when the dreamer's nightmare ends in a remarkable attempt at dealing constructively with her situation:

> She opens her mouth to yell but it seems no yell is forthcoming. She is shaking all over and no matter how she tries she cannot get her breath down into her lungs. It is as if she has a blotter in her throat. Suffocation. She knows that she has to behave differently, and more than that, she has to believe differently. Calm. Calm. Breathe. Breathe. (232)

The following final two lines of this passage render the liminal situation when the dreamer is awakening, in-between dream and reality: "She doesn't know if the panic has taken a long time or a short time. Her heart is pounding but she is nearly safe" (ibid.).[9]

The ending of the story, briefly and factually suggesting that the story up to this point was the dream of an old woman living in a caring home, provides a suitable link to my third subcategory of stories of aging.

"Salon des Refusés": Liminal Locations of Aging

Caring homes, psychiatric wards, and to some extent also hospitals are typical liminal locations of aging. Such institutions belong to spaces that Michel Foucault calls heterotopias (Foucault 1984), which can be regarded as "spatialized forms of liminality" (Achilles 2015, 36). Caring homes are often dreaded locations for old people where they go or are put in the last stages of their lives, institutions that are a part of the social support system yet are nevertheless pushed to the margin of, and largely neglected by, the work-hard, play-hard society. This is the final stage on the life journey for those who cannot help themselves anymore and who cannot be helped by relatives or caregivers at home. In literature, the caring home is frequently rendered as the "antechamber to the grave" (Rooke 1992, 255),[10] as relay stations where individuals in the terminal period of their lives are put, with the borderlines to psychiatric wards or hospitals sometimes becoming fuzzy.

A case in point is the aptly titled story "Salon des Refusés" (1967), French for "exhibition of rejects." The term originally referred to an exhibition of paintings that were officially rejected by the jury of the famous Paris Salon, that of 1863 being the most well-known. Audrey Thomas's ironic use of the term as the title of her short story comes from a wider use of the term to pertain to works rejected at competitive art exhibitions. While the original Parisian Salon des Refusés significantly also included paintings that are considered masterpieces today (such as Édouard Manet's painting *Le Déjeuner sur l'herbe*), in Thomas's story we are shown a depressing cabinet of curiosities of 32 elderly women, the residents of a special ward on the third floor of a caring home or a psychiatric clinic. The story structurally mirrors an exhibition of paintings by sequencing, in montage-like fashion, fleeting "pictures" of individual patients who all seem demented, alternated with episodes that feature the conversations, perceptions, and fantasies of the mostly female caregivers. The often shocking sketches of the residents' deficient states of mind and miserable living situation in the ward crassly demonstrate how in the final period of their lives these old women are indeed caught between life and death. Vegetating in another world, both physically and mentally, they are cut off from normal life—sedated with medicine several times a day and seeming to no longer recognize even their relatives or other visitors, who are only permitted to see them on special visitors' days. Some of the residents act aggressively toward the very caregivers they depend on for their sheer physical survival, and one resident persistently refuses to eat by pressing her mouth shut, so that she is physically forced to open it, in her aggression almost biting off one of the nurse's fingers.

This story, too, is characterized by multiple liminality—with regard to the location, a caring home or psychiatric ward, to the women's final phase of life, to their peculiar memories and fantasies, and also to the frustrated caregivers' daydreaming of escaping from their burdensome job. This internal liminal structure of the story comes to the fore once more in its episodic, matter-of-fact ending. While the night nurse dozed, herself in-between wakeful and sleeping states, Eleanor La Douce, one of the old residents, "climbed on top of the washbasin and quickly and efficiently hanged herself from the steel light fixture. Swaying gracefully, as though to an old and lovely melody, Eleanor waltzed slowly toward the waiting arms of General La Douce" (173), her deceased husband. While the old woman has thus transitioned from life to death through her quickly executed suicide, in the process of dying envisioning the reunion with her late husband, the last short paragraph of the story abruptly switches to one of the caregivers, who, off duty at night, lies in her bed at home, asleep. She is dreaming blissfully of oranges, a symbol of warm and sunny Florida, to which she also hopes to escape in her frequent daydreams while carrying out her burdensome work in the caring home.

The suicide at the end of Thomas's gloomy text points toward the fourth group of stories of aging, those that focus on the late/r life period and death as liminal periods.

"The Bad News": Old/er Age and Death as Liminal Periods

Whereas the first text group I dealt with uses the travel metaphor to signify the course of life, in the final story to be discussed, belonging to my last story group, the late/r life period and death are correlated with history. Margaret Atwood's story "The Bad News" opens her short story cycle *Moral Disorder* (2006), arguably her most autobiographically tinged book. The story is structured into two plot strands. We first get a view of the long-term partnership between an aging couple, which is then followed by images of the narrator imagining herself[11] and her male partner back to the times of the Romans in southern France, particularly in Glanum, a historical site the couple had visited on "a vacation of sorts" some years earlier ("when?," 6). The first plot strand, in the narrative present, centers around "bad news," at first sight in connection with the ubiquitous bad news in newspapers, but on a personal level in connection with fear and images of old age and dying. Fearing not only physical decline ("Everything takes longer than it did back then," 2), but also possible dementia, the narrator states in memorable terms: "This has become my picture of my future self: wandering the house in the darkness, in my white nightdress, howling for what I can't quite remember I've lost. It's unbearable. I wake up in the night and reach out to make sure Tig [her partner] is still there, still breathing. So far, so good" (8). Also by repeatedly using terms of transition such as "still" and "not yet," the narrator shows herself as very much aware that she is living in a transitional phase of her life, limited, of necessity, by death:

> Communication hasn't failed us, not yet.... It's the silent *not yet*. We don't say it out loud.
> These are the tenses that define us now: past tense, *back then;* future tense, *not yet*. We live in the small window between them, the space we've only recently come to think of as *still*, and really it's no smaller than anyone else's window. (4)

This last phrase, alluding to the inevitable human fate of growing old (unless one dies young), leads the narrator to a constructive *carpe diem* awareness. Without deflecting transience, this relatively positive turn toward the couple's later life period is also stressed when the narrator imagines both of them back to the Roman town of Glanum in today's Saint-Rémy-de-Provence in southern France. The narrator's *joie de vivre*, accompanied by her fear of illnesses and gradual decay, are paralleled by her fantasies about the historical area and time of Glanum and the fear of invasion by "the barbarians":

> It's such a beautiful day. The air smells of thyme, the fruit trees are in flower. But this means nothing to the barbarians; in fact, they prefer to invade on beautiful days.... Still, they're very far away ... they won't get here for a long time. Not in our lifetime, perhaps. Glanum is in no danger, not yet. (9)

These final words of the story, "not yet," again stress its central concept of liminality, linking the present and the future ("Everything is interim," 3). The ending stresses the narrator's attempt at also seeing the positive aspects of the later life period ("It's such a beautiful day," "in no danger," etc.). By constructing a parallel between the life course of individuals, here of the aging couple, as well as the fate of historical tribes and the course of history, Atwood's story stresses the inevitable transience of individual life periods and of lives just as of historical periods. The aging narrator's silent prayer to her slightly ailing partner, "Oh, make things stay the way they are" (8), is bound to remain fruitless: The story's final sentence ("Glanum is in no danger, not yet"), although soothingly putting it *ex negativo*, points toward the inexorable eventual decay of life, just as historical Glanum was eventually destroyed by the fatal Germanic invasions.

Conclusion

In the course of related research of mine on the concept of liminality in North American literature (see Chapter 9), I focus specifically on North American short stories that feature crossings of the international border between Canada and the United States. In this at first sight clearly spatial context, I nevertheless differentiate between the physical border crossing as such and the characters' mental border crossing that on a more abstract level accompanies their physical border crossing. In the present context of stories of aging, liminal spaces are also of relevance both in a concrete spatial understanding and in an abstract mental one. As for the physical relevance of space, I dealt with liminal locations of aging such as the caring home. In addition, the conceptualization of aging as physical movement through space (and time) was demonstrated with stories that correlate aging with traveling. In stories of aging, mental liminal states are especially prominent and significant. As shown, these texts frequently feature memories, or the deficiency of memory, as well as other liminoid or liminal states of consciousness, such as dreams and fantasies, as decisive expressions of aging and old/er age.

Let me conclude with an evaluative look at old/er age. The stories I discussed here, which were first published between 1965 and 2012, as well as my analysis of them, mostly focus on the negative aspects potentially pertaining to old age: the physical and mental instability, if not frailty or incapacity, often accompanying old age; old people's marginal position in society and their dependency on the help of caregiving (though not necessarily caring) strangers, who are (poorly) paid to do so; the inescapable fact that in old/er age the passed/past time of people's lives is much longer than the uncertain amount of time they still have to live; the physical and mental proximity of death, which even seems more desirable than the conditions of life at an old age for those that contemplate suicide or euthanasia.[12]

Yet the stories in my text corpus also feature positive aspects of aging: If healthy, elderly people after retirement may attain a degree of freedom and flexibility hardly possible during their working years (e.g., Audrey Thomas, "Miss Foote," in *Path of Totality*). Old/er age also makes possible a long partnership, a familiar, supportive feeling of togetherness and bonding in a fulfilling love relationship (e.g., Margaret Atwood, "The Bad News"). Especially in a long-lasting partnership, the old/er partners may become particularly attentive to and appreciative of the emotional and also practical value of such a partnership (e.g., Alice Munro, "The Bear Came Over the Mountain," in *Hateship*). There are also several artist stories in my text corpus: Aging artists may look back on a long career of creativity and the success, renown, and admiration that may bring with it (e.g., Jane Rule, "Puzzle," in *Inland Passage*). Even if there is restriction in physical mobility, as with the residents of caring homes, their minds, if intact, may still travel and have the time for it, in positive fantasies and nourishing memories (e.g., Alice Munro, "What Is Remembered," in *Hateship*). Although other stories are more positive, even in the most somber story I have dealt with, Audrey Thomas's "Salon des Refusés," there are a few positive signs within the depressing context. One such instance occurs at the beginning of the story, involving a resident repeatedly referred to as "Toot-toot," as this onomatopoeia is apparently all she ended up being

8. Multiple Liminality 133

able to say. When Toot-toot wakes up in the morning, she immediately reacts to "the pale sunlight of a winter dawn, cold as a false smile, sidl[ing] through the [window] bars and deposit[ing] small parcels of light on the floor" (159). Dearly wanting to touch the squares of light on the floor and wanting to take them into her bed to play with them, the old woman reaches out too far and falls off the bed. But no matter: "Toot-toot ... lay happily [on the floor], fondling the light, a royal child playing with building blocks of gold" (ibid.). However, this fleeting moment of happiness ends with Toot-toot crying quietly (160), because her equally demented roommate Eleanor La Douce pounces on her verbally and, shrieking maniacally, scolds her as a whore.

Another example of the merging of negative and positive images and, literally, of light in the dark appears toward the end of Audrey Thomas's story. The recreation room is described from the perspective of one of the caregivers, significantly called Mother Brown, who also considers the supposed reason why this room is never used for its purpose in this ward: "Recreation room—but why should we be concerned with recreation in the case of thirty-two old ladies? They would neither understand nor appreciate. Better left in their beds, where they can bloom like hothouse flowers in their fantasies of past and future" (171). In atmospheric accordance with this cynical, inadequate, and here also egotistical view of old women, "the walls [of the recreation room] are the colour of milky tea and porridge ... cheap and serviceable, the colour of No-Hope and muddy rivers" (171). Against this dreary background, there is the nurse's brief mention of an art object she passes over quickly, without any further comments: "On one wall of the room is a reproduction of Van Gogh's *Starry Night*" (ibid.). One can imagine how this colorful painting of the Dutch post-impressionist painter would stick out particularly in the bleakness of that so-called recreation room. It may be argued that *The Starry Night* (1889) encapsulates not only van Gogh's involvement with nature, but also his view of life and death. Toward the end of his life, he evidently reflected a great deal on distant stars (see Winkler 1992, 258). In a reconciling view of death and eternity, the emphasized, overwhelming night sky in this painting almost displaces the man-made village with the relatively small abodes of the mortal human life. Around the time van Gogh painted *The Starry Night* during his stay in Saint-Rémy-de-Provence roughly a year before his death, he wrote a telling letter to his brother Theo, which provides a visual and memorably positive perspective on the late/r life period as well as dying. As the Canadian writers whose stories I discussed in this chapter, van Gogh in his letter stresses the liminal conditions of aging and dying with an unusual take on the travel metaphor:

> I know nothing whatever about it [dying], but looking at the stars always makes me dream, as simply as I dream over the black dots representing towns and villages on a

> map. Why, I ask myself, shouldn't the shining dots of the sky be as accessible as the black dots on the map…?
>
> Just as we take the train to get to…. Rouen, we take death to reach a star…. Tuberculosis and cancer are the celestial means of locomotion, just as … buses and railways are terrestrial means. To die quietly of old age would be to go on foot [qtd. in Winkler 1992, 258].

"Walking to the Stars" (ibid.) or—to quote the title of Mavis Gallant's story—"In Transit" as metaphorical circumscriptions of the processes of living, aging, and dying: perhaps we need artists to reconcile ourselves with the fact that, in whatever period of our lives we may be, we are all subject to transience—to the liminality that comes with aging, until one day "we take death to reach a star."

9

Liminal Spaces, Liminal States

Crossing the Canada–U.S. Border in Canadian Border Stories

In this chapter, I investigate how the Canada–U.S. border has been tackled in Canadian border stories. I draw on the results of my recent larger comparative investigation of Canadian *and* American border narratives in contextualizing the present, more selective analysis (see Nischik 2016, Chapter 3; for a short survey of border studies and crucial studies on the Canada–U.S. border see 61–65 in that chapter). While a few articles on some novels (such as Thomas King's *Truth and Bright Water*, 1999) address the northern North American border, the short story has (again) been neglected in this context, apart from a few articles about individual stories, especially Thomas King's "Borders" (which is one reason why I will not deal with this story in detail here; see in particular Gruber 2008). Yet the short story format seems particularly suited to border narratives, especially when it comes to stories dealing with the crossing of the border as such. For the short story, much more so than the novel, is the genre of the poetics of the significant moment, of initiation, transition, being on the threshold, liminality, indeed of crossing the border between two "states" (here applicable in more than one sense of this word; on liminality and the short story see at greater length Chapter 8).

Nevertheless, I found it somewhat surprising that, at least considering the utter ideological significance the Canada–U.S. border has for what scholars such as Gibbins and New have even called "borderlands Canada," as well as considering the political significance the northern border has gained for the post-9/11 United States, there do not seem to be many (Canadian or American) stories (quite in contrast to stories of aging, see Chapter 8) that passed my thematic and qualitative filter: the border crossing as such has to be a theme in the stories, if only, as in the one case of Alice Munro's "Miles City, Montana," *ex negativo* (see below). After all, Canada and the United States not only share the world's longest border, but also enjoy the world's largest bi-lateral trade agreement (in terms of amount of trade). The Canada–U.S. border stretches for 8,891 kilometers across land and water and comprises 119 official border crossing points. In 2010, 140,728 cars and other vehicles crossed the border daily, and roughly 300,000 people altogether per day. There were 39,254,000 trips by Canadians to the United States in 2009 (which means, statistically speaking, that, with some 33 million people living in Canada, on average every Canadian crossed that border at least once a year), and, a much smaller amount, 20,213,500 trips by Americans to Canada in 2010, as well as over 15,700,000 people who flew on scheduled flights between Canada and the United States in 2010. There were as many as 21,277,000 same-day return trips by Canadians to the United States in 2009, whereas "only" 8,858,000 same-day trips by Americans to Canada in 2009 (*CBC News* 2011). Crossing the Canada–U.S. border, in spite of increased border hassles after 9/11, seems, at least statistically speaking, a matter of course for many North Americans, especially for Canadians–which may in fact be the reason why this border crossing, according to my research, has not figured prominently in the North American short story. However, there are quite a number of relevant and highly significant stories. I researched about the same number of Canadian and American stories dealing with this border crossing. As to the direction of mobility, the stories of my text corpus are rather balanced, too: roughly as many stories deal with crossing the border from Canada to the United States as the other way round (5 vs. 6 in my text corpus).

I will classify my text corpus—which in this chapter, as mentioned before, is a small selection of Canadian stories only—into several thematic subcategories while stressing here that the analytic "borderlines" differentiating these text types are not distinct but relative; it is the predominantly important thematic aspect that results in the classification of each story into one category rather than another. The guiding questions of my analysis will be: What is the image of Canada and the United States evoked in these stories? Why do their characters want to cross the border? Why is the crossing of international borders, or, rather, of this particular border, rendered as such an intense, if not often existential, experience? What do these stories tell us about the continuing relevance of nation-states, or, rather, of these two nation-states, in the late twentieth and early twenty-first centuries? And is there such a collective entity as "North America" in sight in these stories at all?

The Personal Is Political: Crossing the Border for Political Reasons

The first type of stories represents a paradigmatic case of border narratives: if a border is an official demarcation line between two states or countries and thus, first and foremost, a political entity, crossing the border, in this context leaving one country for the other, may be politically motivated. (This political motivation becomes clear in several American stories that are set against the historical background of the U.S. involvement in the Vietnam War.) It is somewhat ironic that the only Canadian story in my text corpus belonging to this first thematic subcategory—perhaps because hardly any Canadians leave Canada for the United States for political reasons—was written by an author who, although both of Native *and* white origins, regards himself as a Native (and a Canadian) writer.[1] The Indigenous population of North America by and large negates the importance of the border between the United States and Canada, regarding it as a political construct illegitimately imposed on them by the European "invaders" (as Thomas King's story "Borders," in *One Good Story*, ingeniously demonstrates in narrative terms). But the text example I chose for this first subgroup, Thomas King's story "The Closer You Get to Canada, the More Things Will Eat Your Horses" (1989, in *Short History*), significantly belongs to his (relatively few) stories about whites (see Nischik 2012, 37), and is thus not—at least not directly—concerned with particularly Indigenous issues. Rather, the story paints a dystopian, partly satirical view of a United States that is $\Delta 118$, as a part of its suggested culture of violence, by a seniors law. This law puts people older than 55 years into "Senior Game Preserve[s]" (94), which one has to enter through turnstiles, and for six weeks of each spring's "hunting season" (99) forces them to function as "game" in a hunting "game" that allows younger men behind hunting blinds to kill the seniors while they have to cross a meadow trying to reach the cover of the woods, just as animals do. This annual ritual is formally and systematically regulated and organized, precisely because it is part of a law in the dystopian United States sketched in the story. As 72-year-old Mason explains to his granddaughter during one of her visits (with reference to an existential Indigenous issue in the Native subtext running through the story):

> "It has to do with nature. You see, a long time ago, there were a great many animals.... People used to hunt these animals for food, but, after a while, they just hunted them for sport.
> Well, the animals began dying off. There were many reasons. Pollutants killed quite a few. Diseases killed some, too. But most of the animals were hunted until there just weren't any more.
> Human beings are natural hunters, you see" [96].

In the gloomy scenario rendered in this story, with all the animals extinct, it thus became the elderly who had to step in as hunting objects, as "game" for the younger. As Joe, a fellow senior, says to Mason, "'Mason, we're killers. Man's a killer. How do you think we got ourselves into this crazy mess in the first place'" (102).

This dystopian story based on legalized ageism and a heartlessness and brutality presented as inherent to man—or at least to the (U.S.) society represented here—is given another twist, as all seniors living in the Fernhill[2] Senior Game Preserve who are mentioned in the story have family names that are identical with, or very similar to, the brand names of guns: Mason Walthers, Henry Culler, Joe Beretta, Mrs. Winchester, Myrtle Smith and Liz Wesson, Howard Luger, Wilma Remington, Benny Ruger, Ben Ingersoll, Freddy Sharp, Amy Browning, and George Savage.[3] This parabolic twist stresses that violence, or the agents and means of violence, may backfire on the perpetrators. It also stresses that man-made technology may turn back on its creators, and that the species that killed off all the animals for the sheer joy of killing thereby endangered its own species (an ecological conviction engrained in Indigenous culture). In other words, and as a sideways critique of the lack of gun-control laws in the United States, human beings are eventually killed with their own weapons.[4] The text indeed ends with a potential victim turning aggressor: Mason manages to overwhelm one of the young hunters and with the hunter's gun—in a way following Joe's macabre "teaching" earlier in the text[5]—Mason cold-bloodedly kills off many of his friends and fellow seniors, "until all the shells were gone, and the meadow ran with colour, as though the Ruby Hearts had come early" (106).

This ending with the provocatively implied comparison of human blood and a midsummer flower[6] that has "come early" on the meadow—flowers in spring being a sign of a new cycle in nature, which conforms to the logic of the seniors law policies on which the plot is based—picks up an isotope of (past) idyll which runs through the story. This idea of pastoralism, of a better past with unspoiled nature with which people lived in harmony, is clearly connected to Canada on several levels of the story. For one thing, Mason's granddaughter Sarah yearningly looks at picture books with (by then extinct) horses ("'The horse book is my favourite book,'" 96), which Mason associates with the neighboring country Canada: "'You think they still have a few horses in Canada, Joe?'" (102). Although Mason probably poses this question with a rhetorical, implicitly negating purpose, Canada's formerly claimed "belatedness" in comparison with the United States nevertheless clearly shines in positive terms in the dystopian context of the story.

Furthermore, Canada does not have a seniors law as the United States does in this story. King thus puts his text into the historical tradition of Americans trying to escape across the border to Canada for sociopolitical reasons, such as the Underground Railroad (see Tyrer 2009) in connection with slavery (from the late eighteenth century until 1865), the Loyalists during and after the American Revolution, and the draft dodgers during the Vietnam War: "Joe always had grand ideas of escaping and heading for Canada. Canada didn't have a seniors law. There had always been rumours of some families smuggling their parents and grandparents across the line" (98). Repeatedly in this story of oppression Canada thus shines as the safe haven for U.S. seniors tortured and endangered by their own government and fellow citizens. Even shortly before Mason kills off his pal Joe, too, the latter, still dreaming his Canadian Dream, shouts to Mason utterly amazed: "'Canada, Mason, Canada! What the hell are you doing?'" (106). Crossing the border to Canada thus remains just a dream of liberation, a dream never reached by any of the seniors in the story due to Mason's killer instinct. Bound to die himself soon anyway, due to arthritis slowing him down in the annual "hunting" event, his mind has been so corrupted by the violence that surrounds him in his country (see also his defense of the seniors law) that he, at the first opportunity, turns into a serial killer himself—note also the similarity of his name with the name of the notorious American serial killer Charles Manson.

Interestingly enough, the area where the "Fernhill Senior Game Preserve"[7] is situated is the border region between the United States and Canada. The border to Canada, a physically noticeable border in this dystopian story, whose crossing would bring freedom for the American seniors, is quite close but guarded: "'Maybe we could cut through the wire.... Maybe there's a way to get over the fence'" (102). Yet, in accordance with the at first sight cryptic title of the story, the nearer the seniors get to the border, the more dangerous their situation becomes on the U.S. side as their fellow American coldbloodedly massacres his often physically handicapped, defenseless fellow seniors shortly before they can reach the life-saving northern border.[8]

It is noteworthy that the movement in the stories that deal with border crossings in the first, "political" subgroup of stories is uni-directional: the characters go (or hope to go) to Canada in order to flee from a United States that, due to its war politics and inhuman social policies, is life-threatening for them—no matter whether these stories are written by Canadian or American writers. In line with the tradition of black spirituals created in the context of slavery, in which Canada was surreptitiously encoded as "heaven" (see Gruber 2014, 66), Canada in these border narratives is indeed envisioned as a safe haven for Americans who are threatened legally and endangered physically by their own government and fellow citizens for the morally wrong reasons.

The Border as a Liminal Space and Threshold

Crossing a national border means crossing from one "state" into another and this crossing the border of political states is often paralleled with metaphysical, metaphorical, or mental states. To put it in spatial terms, the material, "objective" form of space, here the border and the two countries at stake (what Edward W. Soja calls "Firstspace" or "perceived space") is coupled with or paralleled by a mental space, a subjective thinking about space, for the border-crossing character (what Soja calls "Secondspace" or "conceived space"). Again and again, these border narratives speak of "different worlds" at stake when they refer to the crossing of the border between Canada and the United States. To reach this new world may be desired, may be opted for out of sheer existential necessity, or may be seen in its significance only in hindsight, as the story representing the second subgroup will make clear. The border itself, along with the border region, is the bridge between these two states or worlds and it thus not only has a demarcating function, but also a linking function. To enter into a border region consciously means entering a liminal space and, often in these stories, a liminal state of mind, which is characterized by ambiguity, indeterminacy, and comingling, versus the demarcation, separation, and exclusion traditionally associated with the notion of borders.[9] Particularly if the crossing of the border is indeed seen by the characters as an important, if not momentous, change in their lives, we may speak of a threshold situation[10]: crossing the border opens, or would open, a new life, for better or for worse, for them.

Such a threshold situation, which the retrospective first-person narrator still feels the consequences of years later, is rendered in Miriam Waddington's short short story "I'm Lonesome for Harrisburg" (1982, in *Summer*). Like Waddington herself, who studied social work in Toronto and Philadelphia, Pennsylvania, the narrator goes from Toronto to Philadelphia by train and shows a pronounced sensitivity toward social conditions.[11] Assuming that the story is an autobiographically inspired text, we can date the narrator's train journey to the 1940s, with the first era of industrialism over, the memory of the depression years still fresh, and the U.S. involvement in World War II imminent or already ongoing.

Focalization is bound to the first-person narrator throughout the text, and, for the most part, focalization takes place vividly on the level of the experiencing I. On the level of the narrating I—and the fact that the experiencing and the narrating I's assessment of what happened in Harrisburg do not differ fundamentally shows what a lasting effect this episode has had on her life—the narrator explains at the beginning that the very significant meaning Harrisburg, Pennsylvania, has for her is the result of a 20-minute stay in Harrisburg Station when she was changing trains on her journey from

Toronto to Philadelphia at the time. The setting of the train as a moving location in itself symbolizes change, and the fact that the route via Harrisburg actually means an unusual detour (see the conductors' repeated comments on this) signals the exceptional character of the coming change for the Canadian narrator. The central place of action, Harrisburg Station, a railway station where travelers change trains, again has a symbolic meaning in her life, here as a threshold with a "before," "now," and "after." In this liminal situation at the American train station, in which she becomes intensely aware of all the details of the dreariness of this place, the narrator loses her childhood naivety: "The minute we pulled into Harrisburg I knew that Toronto was gone.... To me it was like waking up in a new world.... And it was here that pain and evil, no longer a legend of childhood, became tangible and entered me" (85, 86). The shabby and dreary sight of the train station in the old, run-down industrial town of Harrisburg opened her eyes to the dark side of life and made her lose her naive childhood feeling of safety in a benevolent world. Poverty, ugliness, sadness, and tragedy (see her being reminded of an illustrated story about a mine accident in her school reader) suddenly become part of the "emotional map" (86) of her life, and her childhood trust in a solely benevolent world is disillusioned. She never leaves the station building and actually does not really see much of Harrisburg, but the shabby indoor scenery and the few glimpses of the dreary world outside the station suffice to bring about her change of perception. In short, the 20 minutes it takes to change trains at Harrisburg Station mean so much to the narrator because in the United States, during her first trip to a "foreign country" (85), her naive, idealistic childhood perception of the world turns into the disillusioned, realistic perspective of a grown-up.

The story also demonstrates that border crossing narratives, by definition, usually deal with, more or less, *both* countries involved and often lend themselves to an imagological approach to literature. (On imagology, the study of images and, particularly, the stereotyping, of foreign countries as rendered in literary texts, see Chapter 4 in Nischik 2016.) For this story, as the previously discussed story by King, sets off the United States against Canada and does so in an evaluative manner, presenting a certain image of one's own and the other country. In "I'm Lonesome for Harrisburg" by far most of the information given is about the narrator's perception of (a part of) the United States. Canada, in contrast, here Toronto and Ontario, features only briefly in the story. Yet the narrator stresses the positive and long-lasting influence Toronto had on her perception of the world, again in the symbolic terms of the train journey: "All night long Toronto's warm, benign presence had dominated, at first Buffalo, then the towns of upstate New York, and had even succeeded in blotting out the dawn that was just rising over the Pennsylvania hills outside of Harrisburg" (85). The two adjectives "warm" and "benign" suffice to express the all-encompassing feeling of security the narrator attributed to Toronto and Canada, the place of her childhood, a feeling of security and trust in the world that is lost after becoming aware of the dreary reality of Harrisburg/the United States. At the end of the story, in a second direct reference to Canada, the narrator sketches her country not only as an urbanized one (see Toronto) but also in its rural aspects: "All that happened to me in Harrisburg. It was nothing and it was everything. It was the place where Toronto changed into Philadelphia and where I forsook the soft black fields of Ontario forevermore. It was, as I now know, my debut into darkness, and I am lonesome, as everyone always is, for that moment when change began" (86).

The narrator's perception of the United States is not straightforwardly a negative one, as formulations like "debut into darkness" might suggest, but rather an ambivalent one, as is often the case in Canadian-American relations. The narrator is attracted to the bustle of Harrisburg Station, but, at the same time, she sees that this is no vital liveliness: everything is old or old-fashioned in style or material ("old-fashioned nickel plated coffee urn," "cobbled" streets), exhaustion prevails (the waitress is tired, the hobo is asleep), and the appearance of the whole scene seems to be coated, blurred—the red color of the wall is covered with soot and the sky is only visible through the dim frosted glass roof covering the station. When arriving in Harrisburg, the narrator feels the "wakeful and struggling spirit" (85) of the U.S. heartland of heavy industry, but, at the same time, she recognizes for the first time in her life the seamy side of industrialism with its poverty and decay. The United States appears as a country that has achieved a lot but has also lost its innocence. In contrast, in the narrator's memory, Canada—the place of the narrator's childhood—appears youthful, not yet burdened with the problems of "adult" life. Waddington's contrastive symbolic representation of the two neighboring countries is sensitive—she does not build up a rivalry nor does she express feelings of inferiority, contempt, or hate concerning either side. The relationship between Canada and the United States is rendered in this story as similar to the relationship between children and adults, with the Canadian narrator's train travel and epiphany at Harrisburg Station paralleling this development and marking the threshold between sheltered innocence and a more powerful, though disillusioned, sense of reality. This story, first published in 1982, with its treatment of an existentially disillusioning threshold experience located in the United States, may also, of course, be a Canadian writer's literary response to one of the worst nuclear crises in history, when in March 1979 the nuclear power plant on Three Mile Island, 10 miles from Harrisburg, became a gruesome disaster to be surpassed later only by Chernobyl and Fukushima.

The retrospective setup of the Waddington story, which represents the second subgroup, points to how borders may also become memory spaces, especially when linked to threshold experiences. The memory of significant border experiences creates spaces attributed to the past (note that such a space has title prominence in the story), with the physical borderline becoming fluent, which may result in a mental overlapping of past and present: the past invades the present, the present is built on, or infiltrated by, the past. The utter significance of the threshold experience of the border crossing, or the possible failure of the border crossing, remains and makes a memory space of the border.

(National) Dreams and Nightmares: The Border Before and After 9/11

A question guiding this section is whether the border crossing as such is handled differently in stories before and after 9/11. Also, the stories in this third group focus, more or less explicitly, on the American Dream, on individual dreams in connection with it or the border crossing, and on nightmares that may be the flip side of dreams.

Alice Munro's story "Miles City, Montana" (in *Progress*), first published in 1985 and with its main strand of action set in 1961, features the journey of a Canadian family from Vancouver, BC, to Sarnia, Ontario, on the south shore of Lake Huron. It is noteworthy that the first-person female narrator and her family (husband and two daughters) decide to travel on the American side of the border, dipping down south in the United States as far as Bozeman, Montana, and eventually, they hope, Milwaukee, Wisconsin, in a long car trip for which they sensibly estimate five days of driving one way. This route through the United States is much more direct, faster, and cheaper on gas than driving around the Great Lakes on the northern, Canadian side. Nevertheless, for the narrator other reasons are involved in this choice of route: "We were driving east across the United States, taking the most northerly route, and would cross into Canada again at Sarnia, Ontario. I don't know if we chose this route because the Trans-Canada Highway was not completely finished at the time or if we just wanted the feeling of driving through a foreign, a very slightly foreign, country—that extra bit of interest and adventure" (88).

The border crossing as such from Canada to the United States seems so uneventful, a mere matter of course, that it is not even mentioned in the story. In fact, the narrator—like Alice Munro herself, who admits to having been mainly influenced by writers from the American South[12]—views the United States in largely positive terms and, in a reference to Jackie Kennedy as a fashion model, lumps both North American countries together as "this continent" (87). The narrator very positively reacts to the vistas she sees along the way and, when they drive through the "grainland and grassland" (92) of Douglas County in the state of Washington, she wonders why she loves it so much. Referring to Ontario—the couple's home province where they both grew up—her husband ventures as a response: "'It reminds you of home'" (92). Similarly, about some of the cities in Montana they drive through the narrator states: "These busy, prosaic cities reminded me of similar places in Ontario" (96). It is thus indeed the "very slight" foreignness of the United States for the Canadian narrator that nevertheless adds an extra bit of attraction and adventure for her. The young family, ironically, gets their share of "adventure" when their three-and-a-half-year-old daughter Meg almost drowns in a swimming pool in Miles City, Montana, also due to the negligence of the American lifeguard who is kissing her boyfriend during her lunch hour rather than paying attention to the two Canadian girls whom she has kindly allowed in the pool outside of the pool's opening hours. It is only through "some kind of extra sense that mothers have" (105) and the father's courageous rescue that their little daughter is saved.

The couple's view of the United States does not seem to alter due to this life-threatening experience there—the story ends with them continuing on their planned route through the United States, and they are also planning to later drive back to Vancouver via the United States ("We missed seeing Kalispell and Havre. And Wolf Point, I like the name," 104). Yet there is an essential ambivalence in the story nevertheless: although the U.S. lifeguard was kind enough to let the family in so that the two children could cool down briefly during the guard's lunch-break, the guard is negligent enough not to pay particular attention to the two small girls splashing in the pool (and her boyfriend's "smiling" at the narrator after the girl is saved by her father is judged by the narrator to be "unfeeling"; see also: "I noticed that he had not turned the radio off, just down," 101). The story also presents an interesting inversion compared to the default view that Canadians often regard the United States as utterly different, whereas Americans, if they are aware of Canada at all, regard Canada as some sort of natural extension of the United States. As the narrator negotiates with the lifeguard about whether she might briefly let her two daughters into the pool, Americans' proverbial ignorance of things Canadian is pinpointed: "I was going to say that we were driving from British Columbia to Ontario, but I remembered that Canadian place names usually meant nothing to Americans. 'We're driving right across the country,' I said" (98). This story of the 1980s gives the overall impression that Canadians may blend into the United States because it is only "very slightly" foreign, that crossing the North American border is physically and mentally no problem, but that the positive attraction of an allegedly more interesting and adventurous United States may turn out to be a dangerously ambivalent affair from a Canadian perspective. As the narrator muses at one point after the pool incident, "if only we hadn't taken this route" (103).

In contrast to the protagonists of the Munro story, the female first-person narrator of travel writer Laurie Gough's[13] "The Border Crossing" (first published in 2002) expects and does encounter trouble at the border, when she travels from her hometown of Guelph, Ontario, to California, her dream state, where she wants to stay for the summer or, perhaps, eventually even for good. The reason she expects trouble crossing the border is not on account of her innocent self but because of the appearance of her travel companion Debbie, a 28-year-old graduate student at the University of Guelph who responded to her posting on the university ride board for a co-ride, and sharing of costs, on this long car trip. When the narrator collects Debbie on the day of the trip, she is struck by her morbid looks (long black polyester dress, army boots, and loads of black make-up), which she finds totally inappropriate, also because it is one of the hottest days of the year: "Decked out in this sort of Goth get-up ... especially when we're about to cross the border from Canada into the US, and I can't imagine the American border patrols will take kindly to her freakish attire" (15). Then too, Debbie has a whip in her leather case for when she wants to visit her "boyfriend" in St. Louis, whom she only knows from the Internet and has never met in person. (As Debbie says to the narrator later at the border: "'But they don't trust the internet. Don't tell them I met Alex on the internet,'" 21.) In connection with Debbie dressing "as a witch" (19), "as if she's on her way to a satanic cult meeting" (23), and the whip, the narrator presumes that Debbie is part of the sado-masochism scene—in any case, at first glance, not a very trustworthy-looking person with her gothic attire.

Yet when they cross the bridge at Sarnia, Ontario, "over the St. Clair River where it flows out of Lake Huron," and at the end of the bridge arrive at the immigration booth "without having to wait in a line" (20), it is the narrator, a white woman in her early thirties, who is first questioned and eventually bullied and ridiculed by the first of two, both white-haired, border patrols. The guard at the booth gets suspicious, or pretends to get suspicious, apparently not because of Debbie's appearance (whom he hardly seems to notice on the passenger seat), but because the narrator truthfully names two different destinations for the two travelers: California and St. Louis, Missouri. At the inspection station, where the first border guard authoritatively sends them ("'Pull your vehicle over there and step inside the main building,'" 21), the second border guard (see this foreshadowing characterization: "this one's hair shoots up in mean military spikes," 21) seems to have malicious fun in questioning, ridiculing, and trying to intimidate the narrator. For instance, we read that "He turns around to the people behind him at the computer screens and shouts, 'She is trying to tell me she's a teacher!' ... 'So if you're a teacher you're really smart. You should know all the capital cities'" (22). The narrator of Gough's story, however, does not let herself be intimidated; apparently calm, she sensibly responds to the continuing provocations of the second guard, although the reader is informed that she begins to feel her "pumping heart" as the two travelers are sent to the inspection station (21). It is only when the narrator cleverly plays the trump card of her dual citizenship—she was born in Madison, Wisconsin, so she also holds American citizenship and can prove this by producing her birth certificate—that the bullying second border guard, whom she comes to think of as "an American Border Bastard" (23) or "Mr. Border Bastard" (23–26), very reluctantly (24) lets her off the hook—not without immediately pouncing on her travel companion Debbie after already having questioned the narrator for 45 minutes.

The two eventually have to go back to Canada across the bridge and "all over the city of Sarnia" (25) to buy a return ticket from St. Louis back to Guelph for Debbie as well as to a branch of her bank to obtain an updated statement of her bank account (which luckily shows $15,000 and so indicates that she comes from a well-off family) to present at the border. When they arrive back at the border trying to enter the United States a second time, now with much more trepidation than the first time, they are lucky enough to run into a friendly, younger, "more relaxed" (26) U.S. border guard ("he doesn't have a military haircut"), who very soon wishes them "a good one." The narrator's response to his easygoing behavior is utter surprise and a great feeling of liberation: "I squeal the brakes, not actually meaning to, but it feels right for the occasion. We're free" (27).

This story first published one year after 9/11 might suggest that the potential of being hassled at the border, particularly on the American side, may have increased since 9/11—here, it is two white women in the same car who are both treated with rude suspicion by two U.S. border guards. By means of the surprise ending, in which the third, lenient, friendly border guard waves them through, the story also stresses that, even after 9/11,[14] it is simply a matter of luck which kind of border guard one happens to run into ("Mr. Border Bastard must be the keeper of some rare wickedness stored in a bitter heart," 25). And, finally, this story suggests that (at least for the narrator) the American Dream, the time-honored myth of an exciting, fulfilling, better life in the United States, is still alive even after 9/11 (including the implied border hassles that have to be expected). The narrator's first feelings on the American side of the border clearly point in this direction: "An incredible lightness takes over my body and everything around us—the highway and the sudden and numerous interstate signs, the duty free store, the green grass on the boulevards, the ATM machines, the convenience stores, the blinding sun setting low on the horizon—feels like the hatching of a strange and marvelous dream. I'm allowed to be here. I'm American" (27).

As the narrator, who holds both Canadian and U.S. citizenship, announced at the beginning of the story: "I just left my life behind and am heading to the other side of it. The other side of it is called California, the land of iced organic defatted decaf soy mochas at every small town street corner, T-shirts any day of the year, taco stands in the desert, orange trees on front lawns and avocado trees in the back; the land of redwoods and palms and palm readings down the road, mountains almost everywhere and a twelve hundred mile view of the sea" (15). At the start of her trip, her American (Californian) Dream of abundance, everyday sunshine, freedom, high living standards, natural beauty, and the feeling that everything is possible is painted in very positive terms. After her annoying border experience, at the end of the story, the dream seems to have shifted more to a materialistic view (the stores, the ATM machines)—having had to overcome an obstacle at the border at the end of the story makes her sense of relief and joy upon entering the United States even more palpable. But the American Dream is still very much alive for the narrator. Myths die hard and are larger than petty, bullying border guards—or reality, this story seems to suggest.

Conclusion

We see that border narratives figure as either "travel literature" or feature migration, in the context of an (intended) emigration from one to the other North American country. Only one third of the Canadian and American stories I have examined here and in my comparative study of North American border narratives (Nischik 2016, Chapter 3) deal with (a planned) emigration. The large majority of the stories thus belongs to "travel literature," where the motivation for the border crossing is either pleasure or a professional reason. The fact that the travelers and the migrants chose the other country as the destination for their pleasure trip or as their anticipated new home largely explains why the overwhelming majority of the stories see the other North American country in positive terms, no matter what the direction of mobility is and irrespective of whether the writer is Canadian or American (or holds dual citizenship). The only two stories with a pronounced critical view of the other country (the United States in this case) in my text corpus are Thomas King's "The Closer You Get to Canada…" and Miriam Waddington's "I'm Lonesome for Harrisburg"; the latter text, as shown above and as the very title of the story suggests, refrains from crude stereotyping but presents a fair view of both countries in the context, as, in its satirical and thus more pointed way, does the former story.

The notable exception is the altogether negative depiction of American border guards, irrespective of being described by Canadian or American writers. One may argue that a country with such—rightly or wrongly—positive self-conceptions (and with such a national trauma as 9/11 behind it) is particularly careful whom they let into "my country," as a border guard in Gough's story patriotically (or, in the context, also somewhat provocatively) formulates it (23; see also note 14). The stories that feature border guards almost always render American guards, as perhaps the more memorable, what with their guns and their authoritative, if not intimidating or even rude behavior, at least in these stories. Only Thomas King's story "Borders" (see for this Gruber 2008) features both American and Canadian border guards—and characterizes them contrastively according to national stereotypes: the female Canadian border patrol is much nicer, more polite, and more communicative with the traveling Natives[15] than the American border guards, who, with their weapons, their swagger, and their eventually rather rough treatment of the Natives remind the youthful narrator of American cowboys.

A few other stereotypical depictions of both countries are suggested in the stories of my corpus. In the case of the United States, it is noteworthy that these depictions are altogether relativized in the very same story or at least when one surveys these stories as a whole: the United States is rendered as a violence-prone country, yet also as a country of extraordinary civil community service and civil spirit; a country where everything seems bigger, more advanced, and more exciting, yet, at the same time, with a polarization between the rich and the poor; a country with the most positive national myths, where nevertheless danger, harassment, and poverty may lurk; a country with strong patriotic views, which are simultaneously shown to be a burden for some of the American travelers. Somewhat similarly, Canada is rendered as a northern country which may nevertheless be as hot as to temperature as the United States and to enter it one has to go *south* at some places (this refers to U.S. writer Joyce Carol Oates's story "Crossing the Border," which repeatedly stresses the geographical fact that at the Ambassador Bridge linking Detroit with Windsor one actually has to go *south* to enter Canada; for a reading of this Oates story, see Nischik 2016, Chapter 3); a country that does not collectively imagine a "Canadian Dream," but nevertheless may make something like such a dream come true; a country associated with "innocent" benevolence, which, however, has to face up to a disillusioning reality (related to the United States in the Waddington story). Nevertheless, it is striking that altogether, throughout a large majority of stories, Canada is seen in an unreservedly more positive light. In six stories of my Canadian and American text corpus, Canada is represented as the better, more desirable alternative to the United States (again, no matter whether the writer is Canadian or American). In these stories Canada is presented as a peaceful, more innocent, less politically burdened, and economically well off direct alternative to the

9. Liminal Spaces, Liminal States 149

United States, a safe haven for Americans who have to fear legal impositions from their own government for morally suspect reasons.

Apart from these comparative imagological aspects inherent to the motif of border crossing, the intensity of the border crossing experience as such, the liminal space and state that are created when one crosses from one country to the other, are at the center of almost all these stories. With the exception of Munro's "Miles City, Montana," all of these stories render the other North American country as a different world, thereby somewhat negating the quote from the Munro story that refers to the United States as a "foreign, a very slightly foreign, country." The other-world view is caused in the stories either by the different politics and social policies of the two neighboring countries, by their different stages of industrial development, or by their different national mythologies, which are all shown in their considerable impact on individual lives. In addition to these general differences suggested between the United States and Canada, practically all stories set up a parallel of "border crossing" on personal, mental, and developmental levels so that the crossing of the international border doubly appears as marking a momentous change in the lives of the characters. This parallelism suggests that the problems involved in crossing the border that separates nations and cultures correlate with the difficulties involved in crossing other kinds of borderlines. We can say with Herb Wyile, commenting on Thomas King's "Borders," that these border narratives are a "literalization of liminality" (1999, 120), thus literalizing Victor Turner's concept of liminality as a transitional space or phase that exists at the intersection between, but at the same time outside of, two cultures or stages.[16] As the stories variously demonstrate, in this liminal (border) space, established paradigms are relativized for the characters or even seem to become meaningless.[17] In this intensified liminal state—see, for instance, the catalyzing behavior of the often identity-challenging "border guards"—being in-between two countries/states, inside and outside the border/s, the characters are made intensely aware of the demarcating and separating, yet, at the same time, also bridging and enabling function of borders. In this manner, these contemporary border narratives and narratives of nation, which are a far cry from suggesting a collective space called North America, may be seen as representative of what Laura Moss in a different context has called an updated "transnational-nationalism" (2006, 22): For these border narratives display an awareness of the very different (material and mental) spaces that the Canada–U.S. border delineates, yet, at the same time they transcend that border through the very act of a desired, and often also fear-inducing, border crossing on a North American continent marked by intense travel and trade—both material and immaterial in kind.[18]

10

Cultural Locations of Ethnicity

Vancouver Short Fiction by First Nations and Chinese Canadian Writers

This chapter foregrounds the multicultural diversity of Canadian short fiction and analyzes a crucial thematic aspect linked to ethnic identity in short fictional prose of two prominent ethnic groups in Canada, the Indigenous and the Chinese Canadian population. It does so by focusing on fictional texts dealing with Canada's westernmost metropolis, Vancouver, thereby in general also stressing the relevance of the city in Canadian short fiction as of modernist times (see also Chapter 1).

Introduction

Vancouver, one of the most beautiful cities in the world and a favorite destination for immigrants, has known the presence of First Nations and many other ethnic groups, especially the Chinese, as a significant part of its population from the beginning of the (non–Native) settlement in the 1860s.[1] As early as in the 1880s, Chinese immigration to the area was so considerable that a Head Tax, a financial restriction on Chinese immigration, was introduced in 1885, making the Chinese the only ethnic group ever to pay a tax to enter Canada. The Head Tax escalated from $50 to $500, to be followed by the Exclusion Act, banning Chinese immigration, in 1923 (repealed in 1947).[2] The Chinese had thus become the only people Canada ever excluded explicitly on the basis of race (see *CBC News* 2004). On the other hand, the establishment of Vancouver's Chinatown (today the largest in the country) as early as 1885 and the heavy immigration of often wealthy Hong Kong

10. Cultural Locations of Ethnicity 151

Chinese in the 1990s—before Britain handed Hong Kong back to China in 1997 and after new Canadian immigration laws in 1978 and 1985 had attracted Hong Kong Chinese—are further markers of the complex history of the Chinese presence in Vancouver. Indeed, Vancouver is the only Canadian city in which the Chinese population forms by far the largest ethnic minority—so that Vancouver is sometimes even called "Hongcouver" (see Lu 2000, 20). Today, four in five immigrants to the city come from Asia, and the various ethnic groups have tended to cluster in the city. As a result, Vancouver has been called a "city of neighbourhoods"—with Chinatown in East Vancouver and in Richmond, "Little India" as a five-block section of Main Street around 49th Ave., "Japantown" ("Little Tokyo" or "Little Yokohama") north of Chinatown, "New Japantown" ("Little Ginza") on Alberni Street (between the West End and the Financial District in Downtown), "Koreatown" (in the West End, Robson Street, and Cardero Street), "Little Italy" (Commercial Drive, Burnaby-Heights, Hastings Street), "Greektown" (1945–1980s, in the Kitsilano area), the German population in South Vancouver, and the Iranian community on the North Shore. However, the high number of people with Chinese descent in Vancouver, especially due to the large immigration wave from Hong Kong around July 1, 1997, brought the Chinese to almost every Vancouver neighborhood, thereby desegregating the city (on the development of Vancouver's "hybrid urbanism," which also colors the city's architecture, see Lu 2000).

Quite in contrast, the Indigenous population in Vancouver is relatively small, making up only some 2.2 percent of the population,[3] yet with writers like Pauline Johnson, Lee Maracle, and Eden Robinson they have found prominent Vancouverite literary voices. Most of Vancouver's Aboriginal population, some 5,000 people, live in Downtown Eastside, the center of this neighborhood (one of the poorest in Canada) being the intersection of Main Street and Hastings Street. The majority of the inhabitants "are people too poor to live anywhere else in Canada's highest rent city" (Culhane 2003, 596).[4]

What consequences does this ethnic and cultural makeup have for (short) fiction set in Vancouver? I would first like to demonstrate to what extent Vancouver fiction is indeed also fiction by and about ethnic minorities (here focusing on First Nations and Chinese Canadian texts). I will also show how Vancouver (short) fiction has incorporated specific ethnically defined spaces and boundaries, but also border crossings and dissolutions into its representations of the city. Ethnic demarcations and the attempt at transcultural dissolution of ethnic boundaries in attitudes, actions, and social set-ups are often also externalized into what may be ambivalently called "cultural locations of ethnicity." "Location" thus refers to specific places, such as community centers, connected with certain ethnic groups, but also, in a figurative sense, to the cultural space allocated to specific ethnic groups in the city context. This chapter, though it harks back to the origins of Vancouver fiction, focuses on twentieth and twenty-first century Vancouver short fiction as well as on specific spaces, borderlines, border transgressions, and border dissolutions ethnic groups have brought forth and that thus engendered the multicultural/transcultural phenomenon of Vancouver and Vancouver short fiction. Attention will also be paid to the question of how these cultural locations of ethnicity coincide with Canada's official policy concerning a peaceful cohabitation of various ethnic groups in a multicultural mosaic. Are locations such as Chinatown or specific "ethnic" meeting places seen as equal parts of a larger mosaic in these texts? Or are they rather pejoratively characterized as "urban reserve[s]" and "colour bar[s]," "accommodat[ing] sentinels—not people, but sentinels, alone on a bridge, guarding nothing," as First Nations writer Lee Maracle put it,[5] thereby challenging Canada's official self-conceptions? And what kinds of developments can be detected in this context by comparing earlier with recent First Nations and Chinese Canadian Vancouver stories?

The literature analyzed in this chapter is drawn from the two anthologies of Vancouver short fiction available, Carole Gerson's *Vancouver Short Stories* (1985) and *The Vancouver Stories*, edited by Derek Fairbridge and with an introduction by Douglas Coupland (2005). Both anthologies were put together by white editors; the earlier anthology's proportion of stories by ethnic minority writers is one fourth, the later anthology's proportion has increased to more than one third. In both books writing by and/or about ethnic minorities in Vancouver mainly comprises stories by Indigenous and Asian Canadian writers.[6]

First Nations Short Fiction About Vancouver

When it comes to First Nations short fiction about Vancouver, the earliest writer is Pauline Johnson (1861–1913; daughter of a Mohawk father and an English mother). Born and raised on the Six Nations Reserve in Brantford, Ontario, Johnson moved away only at the age of 22, after her father's death. She eventually settled in Vancouver in 1909, where she became friends with the Squamish Chief Joe Capilano, whose narration of stories inspired her to put these Native myths to paper. The resulting short prose texts were first printed in 1910 as a series in the Vancouver Saturday *Province Magazine* and then collected as *Legends of Vancouver* in book form in 1911. Pauline Johnson became so closely connected to the place that when she died in Vancouver at the height of her fame, thousands attended her funeral procession. Her ashes were buried in Stanley Park, and she remains the only person ever buried there—a very special case of cultural location of ethnicity, which honored her as the first (semi-)Indigenous female writer of fiction and poetry writing in English about Indigenous issues.

Pauline Johnson's short prose text "The Two Sisters," first published in 1910, shows her celebration of the topography of this beautiful area, the generally close intertwining of the natural setting/the land and First Nations' myths, and a positive conception and truly outstanding location of Native ethnicity. In a way that is not unusual for Vancouver fiction as a whole, which often oscillates between urban and pastoral iconography,[7] in this early text it is rather the natural context of what later became the city of Vancouver that provides the setting. The focus is on the striking twin mountain peaks overlooking Vancouver as part of the North Shore Mountain range, which also lent their (Western) name, "The Lions," to the Lions Gate Bridge. In the story, Pauline Johnson gives the reason why these peaks are called the "Lions" in Western discourse: "[they] recalled the Landseer Lions in [London's] Trafalgar Square" (10).[8] In a gesture of postcolonial mentality, a British monumental artefact is thereby blended with a Canadian natural site. The Native legend that Johnson renarrates in her text explains why in Native mythology and discourse these twin peaks are called "The Two Sisters": "Many thousands of years ago," when "Indian Law ruled the land ... Indian customs prevailed. Indian beliefs were regarded" (11), the Segalie Tyee (high-ranking chief) decided to immortalize the Chief's two daughters by forming them into mountain peaks, since on their day of honor, entering womanhood, the special wish they wanted their father to fulfill was for him to invite the tribe he was at war with to their festivities. With this generous deed, the two sisters brought "Peace and Brotherhood"[9] (15) to the region: "And on the mountain crest the chief's daughters can be seen wrapped in the suns, the snows, the stars of all seasons, for they have stood in this high place for thousands of years, and will stand for thousands of years to come, guarding the peace of the Pacific Coast and the quiet of the Capilano Canyon" (15). Native ethnicity here symbolically melts with the land, becoming a permanent fixture of the natural setting. The Native legend sets an entirely different imaginative world and view of history in place of white historiography, and it makes quite clear why the First Nations insist on calling themselves that way. As often, allegiances show in naming practices: Whereas the whites' naming of these prominent mountain peaks is part of Canada's colonial history, the First Nations' version points back to an autonomous time before European contact and features the Indigenous population as being a part of nature.

Though not of Native descent herself, Emily Carr's (1871–1945) writing and paintings (of Indian artefacts and the British Columbian coastal rain forest) display much sympathy and identification with the local First Nations culture and people. Born and raised in Victoria, British Columbia, Carr lived in Vancouver for several years (between 1906 and 1913) before returning to

Victoria. Her story "Sophie" (from the Governor General's Award-winning collection *Klee Wyck*, 1941) is largely (auto-)biographical, since the Native Sophie Frank, a basket-seller, was in reality one of Carr's best friends (cf. "we began a long, long friendship—forty years," 48). In this text of intercultural female friendship, the white and Native worlds do overlap (much more than in the previously discussed story), yet with clearly different cultural locations assigned to each of them. Whereas the first-person narrator lives in what she calls "my Vancouver studio" (48), Sophie stays in the "North Vancouver Mission" (48), an Indian Reserve on the North Shore in North Vancouver, close to Burrard Inlet. When the narrator visits Sophie, the difference between the two cultures is rendered also in spatial terms: "Across the water we could see the city. The Indian Reserve was a different world—no hurry, no business" (50). The seeming inevitability of the situation of the Natives in this story, their cultural dislocation within Vancouver society, yet also the different points of view, are shown in connection with the hospital having a separate "little Indian ward" (53) of four beds. Sophie, when sick in the ward, does not at all appreciate the mattress of her bed there ("'Bad bed.... Move, move, all time shake. 'Spose me move, bed move too,'" 54), and yearns for the kitchen floor she is used to sleeping on ("'Me like kitchen floor fo' sick,'" 54). That the story is written from a white perspective[10] also shows in its use of designation: "Behind the village [that is, the reserve] stood mountains topped by the grand old 'Lions,' twin peaks, very white and blue" (49). Moreover, the difference between white and Indigenous cultures in this text is exemplified by envisioning the futures awaiting the respective communities: Whereas the white mothers may proudly look at their "thriving white babies," the Indigenous women, due to their extremely high child mortality rate, are described as "the mothers of all those little cemetery mounds" (54). Thus Sophie, having given birth to as many as 20 babies, had to see them all die young—the Natives' future, the story seems to suggest in an emulation of the "Vanishing Indian" myth, is sadly doomed ("Every year Sophie had a new baby. Almost every year she buried one.... By the time she was in her early fifties every child was dead," 49). Finally, the separateness of both worlds is stressed at the very end of the story when Sophie, though very much longing to do so after her constant child losses, does not dare to touch the "thriving white babies," "resolutely" (54) having reconciled herself to the seemingly unbridgeable gaps between the white and the Natives' cultural positionality in Vancouver.

The more recent story "Polka Partners, Uptown Indians and White Folks" (1999) by Lee Maracle is based even more on a semantics of space that culturally locates the Indigenous population in the city. Lee Maracle, who spent part of her life in Vancouver, is the daughter of a Salish father and a Métis mother, and a member of the Stoh:lo Nation. The strict separation and

10. Cultural Locations of Ethnicity 155

compartmentalization between white and First Nations city life is suggested in spatial terms from the beginning of this story:

> When I was a petulant youth, it never ceased to amaze me how we [First Nations people] could turn the largest cities into small towns. Wherever we went we seemed to take the country with us. Downtown—the skids for white folks—was for us just another village, not really part of Vancouver. We never saw the myriads of Saturday shoppers battling for bargains, and the traffic went by largely unnoticed except that we had to watch out not to get hit when crossing against the light. Drunk or sober, we amble along the three square blocks that make up the area as though it were a village stuck in the middle of nowhere [179].

A first opposition set up at the beginning here is between "large city"/ "downtown"/"Vancouver" on the one hand—connected to Western (materialistic) culture—and "small town"/"the country"/"village" on the other—the community-centered First Nations' reconception of the same area, the Downtown Eastside (see the reference to Pigeon Park [182], located at the corner of Carrall and Hastings Street). Through this reconception, the Natives partly import a tribal mode of living, mentally and by way of behavior, into the metropolis, thereby reclaiming the land the way it was before the city of Vancouver engulfed it.[11] This opposition of large city vs. village is connected to further dichotomies established at the beginning of the story, the ones between "buildings"/"downtown" vs. "earth"/"nature," as well as between non-home and "home":

> It was fall. Ol' Mose had that wistful look on his face—he was thinking about home, missing it. The colour of earth death, the scent of harvest amidst the riot of fire colours, like a glorious party just before it's all over—earth's last supper is hard to deal with in the middle of the tired old grey buildings of the downtown periphery. I can see the mountains of my home through the cracks between the buildings that aren't butted one up against the other. It seems a little hokey to take a bus across the bridge and haul ass through nature's bounty, so I don't do it any more [179–80].

What is probably referred to as "home" here, along similar lines as in the story by Emily Carr, is the Indian Reserve in North Vancouver.[12] This location, situated close to the water of Burrard Inlet and not far from the North Shore coastal mountains ("the mountains of my home"), can be seen by the narrator "through the cracks between the buildings" (180)—the city partly displaces and screens off "nature's bounty" and "my home," but the emotional perceptions of the Indian Reserve, of "home" persist ("wistful," "hokey"): "Time crawled by all winter. I spent most of it staring at my mountains just across the water ... and wishing I was lost there" (184).

Indigenous life in Vancouver at the beginning of the story is presented as being rooted in cultural enclaves. The meeting point of the First Nations characters is a café, the "4-Star"[13]: "Every urban reserve has its café.... We talk, laugh and behave like we were visiting our neighbours rather than dining out" (180–81). A disturbance in this domestic routine is initiated by a (better-situated) "uptown Native" (181),[14] whom the female narrator fondly comes to call "Polka Boy" and whose crossing over into their downtown area is referred to by the narrator as "slumming" (181). In a broader context she comments on the importance of regional origin: "Vancouver had become a collector of Natives from all over. Where you were from determined how we treated you in some way I couldn't explain.... His mouth formed a perfect smile, white teeth even and well cared for. He is beginning to look like a polka partner from the other side of the tracks that form my colour bar" (182–83). The uptown Native's project to establish an "office"/"community centre" for the downtown First Nations people in their area is an attempt at cultural upgrading and at integrating Native life more into the urban context. The narrator is skeptical from the outset, and, as further developments sadly demonstrate, her wavering and pessimism are justified:

> Why the hell did anyone want a centre, an office? We had the café. It was a hangout for those of us not quite cognizant of the largesse of the city, but aware we were not truly alone. Bridge Indians. Not village, not urban. An office is urban. Somehow Jimmy the waiter, the cranky manager and their café kept us just a little village. It was a place where we could locate our own in any city. Like an urban trail to the local downtown village. This guy [the uptown Native] wanted to sever the trail [185].

> No one would allow the total transformation of this end of town into a real community. Its attraction, its magic, lay in remaining a peripheral half-village that could accommodate sentinels—not people, but sentinels, alone on a bridge, guarding nothing [187].

However, whereas some of the Indigenous characters, like Tony and Frankie ("He had never left our reserve," 187) "didn't buy the dream" (187) and refrain from participating in this center project, the narrator, as most others, is eventually drawn in and supports it ("soon I was in the centre of it, as though it had been my idea all along. It was a star-quality performance for an Indian who would never see Hollywood," 187). She plucks up the courage and gains a more positive outlook on life at the center, "without me thinking about the beauty of the colours of impending earth death or yearning for my mountains" (193). She thus speaks of "the joy of our work" (194) and does not yearn for "home" any more, although the former unity of the Native group is thereby temporarily split up ("Tony and Frankie's faces haunted me. It occurred to me that they had been sitting at the back of the café alone for the first time," 187). After the "community centre's" first successes and support from local politicians, the project, about to be enlarged into a special clinic for First Nations people, is to be shifted uptown: "The clinic didn't get its funding and we are moving uptown.... The city said they could not justify funding a racially segregated clinic" (194). The Native activists' attempt to prolong a segregational attitude into institutions is abortive (or, one could also argue, the attempt at affirmative service/action for those who are not eligible for "universal health care" comes to nothing).

The narrator's ambivalence in this transformational context also becomes clear in her stance on "Polka Boy": She feels attracted to him and does recognize him as a harbinger of change, potentially for the better, eventually following him in his Native center project downtown. She puts him off, however, after the failure of the project and seems to aim at a conscious reversal to her former style of living at the end of the story, to the surprise of the uptown Native: "Everything after that is mechanical and unmemorable. I pay the hydro bill, experience rudeness from some prissy white girl and tell her that I understand. She works in an office. She looks as confused as Polka Boy when I leave" (201).[15]

The First Nations stories (written by or, in any case, about Indigenous people) collected in the two anthologies of Vancouver fiction thus show a significant development. The literary representation of Indigenous life in these stories starts with a retrograde turn to the pre-contact past of Indigenous people's history (when they lived by themselves—though not peacefully—in the area, in close contact with nature). It proceeds to a presentation from a white point of view which, though sympathetic to Native life, emphasizes its poverty, tragic hopelessness, and clash with a white style of living. And it culminates in a strongly segregated view of white and Native city life in Lee Maracle's 1999 story. In all three anthologized stories, place is an important signifier for Indigenous people's cultural location: from the melding with nature in "The Two Sisters" by Pauline Johnson, to an oppositional, though linked set-up of spaces in Emily Carr's "Sophie," to, finally, an enclave-like, segregational set-up of Native locations in Lee Maracle's more recent story "Polka Partners, Uptown Indians and White Folks." The deficiency of cultural integration is especially striking in the latter, most recent story, since cultural and class demarcation lines run right through an ethnic group, not just between Natives and whites: in this case uptown (more integrated) and downtown (more segregated) Indigenous city dwellers. The narrator of this story ultimately regards the uptown Native as an "apple" (red on the outside, white on the inside) and eventually distances herself from him as well as his attempt to transcend internal and external ethnic borderlines.

Chinese Canadian Short Stories About Vancouver

Whereas the view of the chances for integration of First Nations people into Vancouver's multicultural society in these selected stories is a largely pessimistic, if not hopeless one, the two stories by Chinese Canadian writers to be discussed in the following are involved with the diaspora situation, the tensions between present vs. past and between various generations, and the more or less successful integration of first- and second-generation Chinese into Canadian society.

Sky Lee, born in Port Alberni in 1952, lived in Vancouver for a while around 1967, before settling on Salt Spring Island, British Columbia. Her story "Broken Teeth" (1981) is a family story of three generations, focusing on mother-daughter and father-daughter relationships. Whereas the first-person narrator was born in Vancouver, her mother had immigrated from Hong Kong. The relationship between mother and daughter is strained. The daughter visits her mother's house merely out of a sense of duty: "I mean my mother's house on east first avenue, just off the freeway. Actually I don't live there. I don't feel part of it anymore…. I [have] other memories" (144). The daughter associates her mother's house in Vancouver with feelings of guilt, reproaches, and intimidation, which keep making her feel ill at ease there: "I always marched up those shaky pink backstairs too quickly, with the secret hope that maybe my mother would not be home. Thus, my token home visit would be duly recorded and in turn, reported to her. But by then, I would be sure to be gone" (144). The daughter has largely severed the emotional bonds to her mother and also to her family history originating in Hong Kong. In fact, her mother does everything to turn her daughter away, although she intends just the opposite. By constantly reproaching her daughter with a lack of interest and involvement in her life, the mother initiates the principle of self-fulfilling prophecy: The daughter distances herself from her mother, her family, and her Chinese cultural heritage and stresses that she is a local ("I didn't know because I was local born," 145). Nevertheless, she does feel responsible for taking care of her mother (see her cutting her mother's hair).

Within this framing narrative, an embedded story partly explains the mother's expecting positive, caring emotions from her daughter. After a passage of dysfunctional dialogue between mother and daughter that again shows how much they are at cross purposes, the mother narrates her traumatic experiences when she was an eight-year-old child back in Hong Kong, which clearly demonstrate the gender bias toward males in traditional Chinese culture: Rushing toward her parents who are waiting for her, the narrator's mother as a child falls down a staircase and onto her little brother playing at the bottom of the staircase. Instead of sympathizing with her, severely hurt as she is, her father beats her up because she fell upon her brother, who seems to be the only important child for the father ("'Damned bitch! Knock over my son, willya. I'll show you,'" 147). The daughter's plight, which is much stronger than the son's, is disregarded: She is bleeding heavily, has broken all her front teeth, and is in severe pain. Yet her mother, too (the narrator's grandmother, that is), hardly sympathizes with her daughter ("She was shrieking all over the county. 'We're done for. She's killed my son,'" 147), once again exemplifying the small value attributed to women/girls in traditional Chinese culture.[16]

It is only when the narrator's mother emigrates to Canada that her teeth are fixed and that her physical pain stops. Yet because of the lingering traumatic experience of gendered devaluation and humiliation, she constantly expects signs of love or at least affirmation from her own daughter—who tragically reacts by being just the opposite, namely aloof, toward her mother. The more the narrator's mother wants family commitment from her daughter, the more the daughter withholds it. This is also demonstrated by the ending of the story, which shows the mother admonishing her daughter and talking about the grandfather's funeral. While the daughter, feeling Canadian, is silent about the death of a family member from China she has never met, the mother is still linked to Chinese traditions (see her shopping in Chinatown; her keeping faith with her dead father, honoring him in his death, irrespective of his having mistreated her as a child; her blaming her mother, rather than her father, for the brutal injustice done to her when she was a child): "'And I'll have to go shopping down in Chinatown. How about Sunday then. A big dinner on Sunday. Mind you—you remember to come back on Sunday to eat and pay your respects then'" (148).

The most recent and last story under consideration here is Madeleine Thien's "A Map of the City" (from *Simple Recipes*, 2001). This story significantly gives the "mapping" of the city title-prominence.[17] The fates of two generations of a family with a Chinese-Indonesian background are sketched and set off against each other. The narrator Miriam's parents had emigrated to Vancouver from Indonesia, their only child Miriam was born in Vancouver. As in Sky Lee's story "Broken Teeth," the degree of integration into Canadian society differs between first- and second-generation immigrants. Miriam's father—to whom, as a child, she has a close relationship that grows more problematic in her adult years—cannot quite adapt to the new surroundings. As an owner of a restaurant and later of a second-hand furniture store on Hastings Street, his business ventures eventually fail. A substantial part of the story is situated in the father's furniture store, referred to as "a neighbourhood furniture store" (312), geared to local customers on Hastings Street, where Chinatown and the poorest quarter of Vancouver, the Downtown Eastside, are located (yet also more mainstream neighborhoods, since this street leads to Simon Fraser University in Burnaby, an eastern suburb of Vancouver). Miriam's father tries his very best to make his small business a success—accumulating knowledge on Western public life and politics from the newspaper and trying hard to be communicative with his customers, though apparently in a forceful, awkward, and later "despair[ing]" (328) manner: "'Trudeau,' he said to one customer, then shrugged his shoulders, or 'Bill Bennett,' or 'Thatcherism,' the word hanging disturbingly in the air" (315). He not only tolerates his daughter's scribbling on the furniture, but in other ways, too, his attitude and actions contribute to his lack of success. The store, and his increasingly desperate clinging to it (eventually against his wife's pragmatic advice), become a symbol for his attempt to make it in the country of immigration. When the store proves to be a failure, also because he could offer his customers only rather run-down furniture, he knows that "this was the last business he would ever own" (329)—his Canadian Dream, if it ever existed, has not come true. Miriam's mother, in contrast, adapts better to the new surroundings, is promoted in her job, and seeks out the advantages of living in Canada compared to her former homeland, which she, after all, wanted to leave ("I was miserable there," 326):

> Despite the violence and the political tension, my parents missed Indonesia. It came out in small ways, their English interrupted by a word of Chinese, a word of Indonesian.... But those were the only Indonesian words I learned. At home, they spoke Indonesian and Chinese only to each other, never to me. My mother would stand on the porch watching kids race their bikes up and down the back lane, and say, out of the blue, "But isn't it so much cleaner here?" [322].

The father's attachment to his former homeland is shown by means of a covering-up *pars pro toto*-statement in a scene in his store when he, tellingly,

> reached into his desk and pulled out a handful of photographs. I had seen them before, Indonesian plantations spread out under wide skies. He tapped his index finger down, pointing out the house where my parents lived before coming to Vancouver.... My father ran his hands over the trees in the backdrop, told me about the fruit, strange and exotic things, rambutan and durians.... "Do you miss it?" I asked him.
> "What's to miss?" he said, smiling gently.
> I didn't know.
> "I only miss the fruit," he said, putting the photos away. "The country, I've almost forgotten" [315].[18]

As in the stories by Pauline Johnson and Lee Maracle, the dichotomy between the former (rural) home and the new metropolitan life is also rendered by contrasting natural with urban iconography, the latter being predominant. There are several scenes when the characters drive through the city, either in the parents' Buick or on Will's, Miriam's later husband's, motorcycle. Significantly, during these drives, the mother is called "the navigator," with "a map of the city unfurled on her lap" (324), which suggests that she has a clearer purpose in her country of immigration than the father. She wants to "read," to understand the city, to find her way through it, whereas the father seems more like a drifter, who often, symbolically, looks backwards into the rear-view mirror (323–24). The different degrees of adaptation of father and mother to the new country eventually contribute to the parents' separation and their ending up on their own in Vancouver.

10. Cultural Locations of Ethnicity

It is the daughter, born in Vancouver, who makes the city her own and feels at home there: "I was the only one of us born in Canada, and so I prided myself on knowing Vancouver better than my parents did—the streets, Rupert, Renfrew, Nanaimo, Victoria. Ticking them off as we passed each set of lights" (321). While she remains aware of her familial and cultural background (see especially the framing beginning and ending of the story, as well as Will's statement: "'It's plain. You miss them [your parents] all the time,'" 308), it is her attachment to Vancouver that is rendered intensely, "physically," even sensuously, with recourse to urban as well as natural iconography:

> I have lived in Vancouver all my life.... When I was twenty-one, the familiarity of this city comforted me. I was waitressing then, working odd jobs. Every night my girlfriends and I stayed late at the bar, lighting cigarettes, throwing shots of vodka straight back. Men came and went; it was nothing. Some nights, we dropped our clothes on the sand and swam in the ocean.... Other times, I drove along the coast, the sky blacked out. I'd park and watch the big green trees rolling back and forth in the wind and the sight would make me fleetingly happy. Legs stretched out, I would lie back onto the roof of my car and listen to the sound of my clothes flapping [317].

Another instance where Miriam seems an integrated part of the city—mapping it in various directions, responding to the city visually and emotionally, as if in a trance—is the important first outing with Will. They have a memorable ride on Will's motorcycle through and beyond the scenic city, symbolizing freedom and Miriam's distancing herself from her parents: "On the way back to the city, the moon was low and full, a bright orange round above the skyline. The mountains bloomed against sky, one after the other like an abundance of shadows. I remember watching one silent tanker floating on the water. We sped over the Lions Gate Bridge, a chain of lights. I grasped his chest, kept my eyes wide open and thought, *Things should always come this easy*" (319). We do not even get to know which ethnic group Will, Miriam's husband, belongs to. In this generation and in this city, this does not seem to be so essential any longer.

Whereas the second-generation immigrant Miriam found her happiness in her city of birth, Vancouver, she continues to be aware that this was not equally the case for her immigrant-parents, especially her father—yet even he seems to have eventually reconciled himself with his life. The story thus ends on a realistic note, acknowledging the heights and the depths of the immigrant experience, but also the fact of having "arrived." The imagery used to situate these different experiences is again mainly spatial (as well as temporal), as if Miriam was indeed mapping out the city and her family's potential and real locations in it:

> When I hang up the phone, I feel a surge of hope, of fierce protectiveness over him [Miriam's father]. Perhaps, knowing everything that has brought us here, I would

redraw this map, make the distance from A to B a straight line. I would bypass those difficult years and bring my father up to this moment, healthy, unharmed.

But to do so would remove all we glimpsed in passing, heights and depths I never guessed at. That straight line would erase our efforts, the necessary ones as well as the misguided ones, that finally allowed us to arrive here [329–30].

Conclusion

Having surveyed stories about ethnic minorities in the two existing anthologies of Vancouver short fiction, both compiled by white editors and published in 1985 and in 2005 by two Vancouver publishing houses, I want to emphasize five results of my analysis. First of all, there is an increase of stories about ethnic minorities in the more recent book (from one fourth in the earlier to more than one third in the later anthology), mirroring the changes in canon formation in recent years, supported by official government policies.[19] Second, these Vancouver stories about ethnic minorities are predominantly about First Nations and Chinese Canadian characters. Third, by far most of the stories analyzed here—namely Pauline Johnson's "The Two Sisters," Emily Carr's "Sophie," Lee Maracle's "Polka Partners, Uptown Indians and White Folks," and Sky Lee's "Broken Teeth"—especially those focusing on First Nations characters, display a strict separation of (cultural) locations and spheres for whites and non-whites.

Fourth, the only story of the anthology selection where ethnic borderlines are dissolved (by the second-generation immigrant daughter) is the most recent story of 2001, by Madeleine Thien. Her protagonist Miriam roams freely around Vancouver, without any apparent external or internalized ethnic demarcation lines (as, by contrast, in the story originally published two years earlier by Indigenous writer Lee Maracle). As has been observed above, it is not even mentioned which ethnic group Miriam's husband Will belongs to. One could argue that the second-generation immigrant Miriam is a fictional representative of Canada's official multiculturalism policy: She acknowledges her family history and cultural roots, but regards Vancouver and Canada as her own city and country and realistically acknowledges all the "heights and depths ... that finally allowed us to arrive here" (330).

Finally, one could go one step further and argue that Miriam represents a new, future-oriented integrationist model following upon the earlier "Anglo-conformity" and "melting-pot" models and the more recent "multiculturalism" model.[20] For Vancouverite Miriam, in contrast to her immigrant parents, ethnic affiliation does not seem to be the primary basis for identity formation any more. In Miriam's flexible construction of her individual identity in the urban context, irrespective of collective identity categories such as ethnicity, she transcends difference and becomes a representative of a "rooted cosmopolitanism" (on this concept see Appiah 2005, Chapter 6). Miriam conceives her identity largely irrespectively of the ethnically defined one of especially her father, whom she keeps remembering in his restrictive furniture store on Hastings Street. For Miriam, pluri-ethnic Vancouver becomes a place for disentangling herself from collective identities. She makes the whole city her own, maps out the city for herself, thereby overcoming her father's restrictive and culturally nostalgic, or rather melancholic, way of life, and putting a dynamic, flexible way of constructing an urban identity, based on individual experience, in its place. Quite in contrast to the kind of identity formation displayed in Lee Maracle's story, in the story by Madeleine Thien, where one comes from no longer determines who one is. Just as Miriam unconventionally chooses Will (see 317–19) rather than behaving according to custom by letting him choose her, she transcends traditional affiliations in a city that for her apparently becomes a post-ethnic one: traditional, ethnically ascribed affiliations are displaced by chosen, experiential ones.

In this new context of a "rooted cosmopolitanism," Miriam's flexible, individualistic approach to identity construction comes closest to the ideals addressed in the September 2005 Installation Speech of Canada's then-Governor General Michaëlle Jean (an immigrant from Haiti): "Our country is vast and it is blessed with a wealth of colours and the varied music of its tongues and accents.... Every one of us rekindles in his [or her] own way the sense of belonging to this space that we all share, a space that contains the world."

Part Three: Analyses

11

(Un-)Doing Gender
Alice Munro, "Boys and Girls"

This chapter is linked to Chapter 7 in the Approaches section in that it zooms in on the pronounced gender awareness displayed in Alice Munro's short stories, by analyzing one of her early stories in this regard. Before this close textual analysis, the chapter contextualizes its gender focus by addressing further essential characteristics of Munro's short story oeuvre (for this, see in greater detail also chapters 4 and 5).

On Alice Munro and Her Works

Coral Ann Howells (1998) opens her book on Munro's oeuvre with the question "Is it true that in order to appreciate Alice Munro's stories we need to begin by looking at a map of Canada?" A map of Canada is certainly not necessary to appreciate Munro's fictional worlds, but she indeed prefers to "map" a certain Canadian region in her writing: southwestern Ontario (sometimes abbreviated as "Sowesto"), more specifically the area around London, Ontario, close to Lake Huron. Munro's longtime preoccupation with that particular region and her interest in local history and topography in her writing are linked to her own life. She was born on July 10, 1931, on a farm in the outskirts of the small town of Wingham, Ontario (some 30 kilometers from London in Huron County), the eldest of three children of a former school teacher and a fox farmer with a family history going back to Scottish pioneers (see Chapter 4 for a concise biography of Munro). At the end of the 1960s, after the publication of 17 stories of hers in Canadian magazines, Munro had her literary breakthrough with her first story collection *Dance of the Happy Shades* (1968), which won Canada's most prestigious literary prize, the Governor General's Award for Fiction. In 1971, *Lives of Girls and Women* was published, a book of linked stories which brought Munro international recognition.

Since then, all of her short story collections have been national and international bestsellers: *Something I've Been Meaning to Tell You* (1974), *Who Do You Think You Are?* (1978; published under the title *The Beggar Maid: Stories of Flo and Rose* in England and the United States[1]; it won Munro another Governor General's Award), *The Progress of Love* (1986; winning a third Governor General's Award), *The Moons of Jupiter* (1982), *Friend of My Youth* (1990; Ontario Trillium Book Award, Commonwealth Writers' Prize), *Open Secrets* (1994; W. H. Smith Award in England), *The Love of a Good Woman* (1998; National Book Critics Circle Award from the United States), *Hateship, Friendship, Courtship, Loveship, Marriage* (2001), *Runaway* (2004; Giller Prize and Commonwealth Writers' Prize), *The View from Castle Rock* (2006), *Too Much Happiness* (2009), and *Dear Life* (2012), plus seven volumes of selected stories: *Selected Stories* (1996), *No Love Lost* (2003), *Vintage Munro* (2004), *Carried Away* (2006), *New Selected Stories* (2011), *Lying Under the Apple Tree* (2014), and *Family Furnishings: Selected Stories, 1995–2014* (2014). In 1977 began Munro's longtime affiliation with *The New Yorker*, where many of her stories were first published, thus popularizing her writing among American readers in particular.

Both nationally and internationally, Munro's tremendous success as a short story writer has done much to enhance the profile of the Canadian short story. She is Canada's leading short fiction writer, unrivaled in that genre in Canada, with the possible exception of Margaret Atwood, and she has, over some six decades, established an impressive oeuvre. By far the most frequently anthologized writer of Canadian short fiction, many critics argue that Munro is the best living short story writer. The many literary prizes she has received (see also the PEN Malamud Award for Excellence in Short Fiction and the Canadian Authors Association's Jubilee Award for Short Stories in 1997), even the highest of them all, the Nobel Prize in Literature in 2013 (see Chapter 4), attest to her extraordinary success as a writer of short fiction with both critics and academics as well as the general reading public.

Munro is exceptional also in that she has published only short fiction (apart from several essays, mostly on aspects of writing, and some interviews). The closest she has come to the genre of the novel are her two short story cycles *Lives of Girls and Women* and *Who Do You Think You Are?* Both have a quaint publication history as they are the two instances in which Munro, at the insistence of her publisher for her to write a novel—mainly for financial reasons, after the big success of her prize-winning first short story collection—tried very hard to forge her episodic technique and individual story units into the form of a novel (see Munro's amusing recollections in the interview with Struthers 1983, 29 *passim*). During these painful processes of revision, Munro became aware that it was short stories she wanted to write more than anything else (see Munro in Hancock 1987, 190) and that it was this genre that best suited her talent and writing habits—considering her laborious revising technique and her intense preoccupation with style as well as her view of the world as consisting of discontinuous chunks rather than a consecutive storyline (see Chapter 5). And although the stories in her more recent story collections (as of *Friend of My Youth*, 1990) have become generally longer, Munro kept faith with her preferred literary format until she retired from writing in 2013 (as it happened, shortly before receiving the Nobel Prize).

The appeal of the short story format to Munro is directly linked to her particular writing esthetics: explanatory gaps, supplementarity (Howells 1998, 10-11), the construction of "worlds alongside,"[2] the contrasting of disparate interpretations, multiple views on a given event (by the same or by various characters), juxtaposition of the past and present, and the deferral of fixed meaning—all stress the fluidity, incompleteness, variability, and the ultimate inexplicability of human experience. The short story as a format that privileges slice-of-life representations, episodic and condensed time structures, suggestive, deliberately fragmentary representations, and open endings is thus the perfect literary form to transport Munro's "snapshot"[3] views of her fictional world (see also Chapter 5).

Next to the generic choice and the esthetics connected with it, the multifaceted Munrovian fictional world has been marked by three main characteristics: her regional attachments, her preference for female protagonists and her privileging of a female perspective and corresponding themes, as well as the autobiographical or, as she prefers to call it, the "personal" (Munro in Struthers 1983, 17) dimension of her work.

Munro understandably shrinks away from her frequent classification as a "regional writer": "I use the region where I grew up a lot. But I don't have any idea of writing to show the kind of things that happen in a certain place. These things happen and the place is part of it. But in a way, it's incidental" (Munro in Hancock 1987, 200). Although several of her stories have a varied, even international setting and although her living for a long time on the Canadian west coast (see biographical sketch in Chapter 4) resulted in several stories with a western Canadian setting, it is her rural home region and the small-town life of southwestern Ontario that have most frequently formed the backdrop to her writing.[4] Her frank, detailed, unsparing depiction of this region and its inhabitants, her way of looking beyond appearances, and her unflattering revelation of backward mentalities and crankiness of character have led some inhabitants of Wingham to reject her writing.[5] Howells however rightly points out about Munro's favorite setting that "what she emphasises is not its familiarity but its strangeness" (1998, 13). Munro's gender awareness and her focus on the female perspective have made her a favorite author with astute (female) readers and critics alike. As early as in 1972, Munro stated that she was generally sympathetic to the Women's Liberation movement. Both her preferred geographic settings and her gender awareness combine in the often personal sources of her writing (on the strong autobiographical dimension in Munro's works see Thacker 2005). One important thematic strand is the significance of family relationships, especially of mother-daughter relationships, which in Munro's writing—somewhat in contrast to Atwood's (see Chapter 6)—are usually highly problematic and psychological "works-in-progress." Munro's mother's early death from Parkinson's disease when Munro was only 28 years old has been reworked in early (e.g., "The Peace of Utrecht," in *Dance*), middle-period (e.g., "Friend of My Youth," in *Friend*), and late/r stories of Munro's career, even in the final story of her final collection, *Dear Life* (2012). Among other gendered and partly autobiographical themes in Munro's stories are the restrictive socialization patterns, especially of girls in rural or small-town settings. Yet Munro is also a "writer's writer," who, making use of postmodern techniques, integrates poetological problems into her fiction, experiments with the short story form in her non-linear, digressive, sometimes montage-like narrative style, re-works Joycean multiperspective and epiphanic techniques, and blends the quotidian with the extraordinary.

Commenting on developments in Munro's writing over several decades, Howells rightly states that "her topics have not changed but her narrative methods have" (1998, 68). It is striking that in more recent collections, beginning with *Love*, the protagonists tend to be older, having grown older with Munro herself (see also Thacker 1988, 154). The crucial thematic aspect is still, however, the challenge of controlling one's own life in negotiation with inhibiting restrictions, such as social norms, vicissitudes and conventions, or old/er age. The technical turning point in Munro's writing career may be identified as the collection *The Moons of Jupiter* (1982). Although Munro has always adhered to indeterminacy in her stories, it is in this collection that this principle is amplified, structuring not only her verbal discourse but also her narrative method: "multiple and often contradictory meanings have room to circulate in structures of narrative indeterminacy ... unsettling the story at every stage of its telling, as she allows more and more possible meanings to circulate in every story while refusing definite interpretations or plot resolutions" (Howells 1998, 11, 10).

Analysis of Munro's Story "Boys and Girls"

I want to turn now to one of Munro's excellent early stories for analysis, in order to demonstrate that many of the characteristic aspects of Munro's writing have been present from her early works on. Also, the story selected for closer analysis here was written at the time of the beginning of the Second

Wave of the women's movement, when questions of gender identity and gender roles were generally more virulent than they seem to be nowadays, not least thanks to the achievements of the women's movement.

"Boys and Girls" was first published in 1964 and then included in Munro's first story collection *Dance of the Happy Shades* (1968). The first paragraph of the story immediately maps out the Munrovian fictional territory, with several general features of her writing addressed above noticeable right from the beginning:

> My father was a fox farmer. That is, he raised silver foxes, in pens; and in the fall and early winter ... he killed them and skinned them and sold their pelts to the Hudson's Bay Company or the Montreal Fur Traders. These companies supplied us with heroic calendars to hang, one on each side of the kitchen door. Against a background of cold blue sky and black pine forests and treacherous northern rivers, plumed adventurers planted the flags of England or of France; magnificent savages bent their backs to the portage [111].

Apart from the clearly Canadian setting with a postcolonial historical background, we notice the autobiographical dimension to this first-person narrative told by an 11-year-old girl growing up on a fox farm near Jubilee—if a strong personal orientation is assumed, with Munro born in 1931, the story would be set at the beginning of the 1940s, when Munro's father was indeed still a fox farmer in Wingham.[6] The rural setting of the farm surrounded by fields is only scantily sketched: "This was the time of year when snowdrifts curled around our house like sleeping whales and the wind harassed us all night, coming up from the buried fields, the frozen swamps" (112). Relevant as such information concerning place and time may seem, it is rather the highly traditional gender mentality of the unnamed girl's parents and of other characters, like the hired man or the salesman (that is, representing inner family as well as external social attitudes and prejudices), that stresses the story's setting with respect to time and place (Carrington speaks of a "closed rural society" [1989, 15]).

A further autobiographical aspect of the story is the girl's habit of creating stories that imaginatively mirror her own state of development, at the same time revealing a budding writer (though this potential further development is, characteristically, left open in the story): One could even argue that the child's fantasies are the prototypes of Munro's "linked stories":

> Laird [the narrator's brother] went straight from singing to sleep.... Now for the time that remained to me, the most perfectly private and perhaps the best time of the whole day, I arranged myself tightly under the covers and went on with one of the stories I was telling myself from night to night. These stories were about myself, when I had grown a little older; they took place in a world that was recognizably mine, yet one that presented opportunities for courage, boldness and self-sacrifice, as mine never did [113].

This is an apt example of the potential compensatory function of literature in general and in particular of the narrator's imaginative ability (which sets her apart from the rest of her totally unimaginative family, who are stuck in conventional thought patterns), as well as of Munro's supplementary narrative constructions, her "worlds alongside."

The narrator's later reference to her story compositions shows the effect of her ongoing socialization into received gender patterns and thereby points to the central theme of this story, the constructivist aspect of gender identity—how male and female children are socialized according to different role patterns, forming them into two different genders, "boys and girls":

> In these stories something different was happening, mysterious alterations took place. A story might start off in the old way, with a spectacular danger, a fire or wild animals, and for a while I might rescue people; then things would change around, and instead, somebody would be rescuing me. It might be.... Mr. Campbell, our teacher, who tickled girls under the arms. And at this point the story concerned itself at great length with what I looked like—how long my hair was, and what kind of dress I had on; by the time I had these details worked out the real excitement of the story was lost [126].

In a mise-en-abymic structure (a writer telling about a budding writer telling autobiographically based stories), we see the results of initiation into the female gender role as conceived at the time.[7] While the narrator is still very young, she is allowed to do as she pleases, and she much prefers her father's (money-earning) outdoor activities to her mother's domestic sphere and chores: "My father was tirelessly inventive and his favourite book in the world was Robinson Crusoe" (114).[8] Indeed, the whole story hinges on an inside/outside-dichotomy linked to gendered spaces. The young daughter identifies with the male world and feels at ease with it. She even considers herself more appropriate for it than her younger brother Laird, whom she regards as a sissy for a large part of the story: "Laird came too, with his little cream and green gardening can, filled too full and knocking against his legs and slopping water on his canvas shoes. I had the real watering can, my father's, though I could only carry it three-quarters full" (114).

In contrast, the girl decisively turns against the maternal domestic sphere: "It seemed to me that work in the house was endless, dreary and peculiarly depressing; work done out of doors, and in my father's service, was ritualistically important" (117). The daughter enters into a domestic tug-of-war with her mother, even calling her an "enemy" (117), because she feels that "she was plotting now to get me to stay in the house more, although she knew I hated it (*because* she knew I hated it) and keep me from working for my father" (118). That the mother might be in need of some help and allegiance, too, is a thought that never crosses the girl's mind ("It did not occur to me that she could be lonely, or jealous," 118).[9] In turning against her mother and against her domestic confinement she symbolically rejects the traditional female gender role cut out for her as a girl. The story demonstrates how in her adolescence the girl is pushed by manifold social pressures into a role she would never have chosen herself: "One time a feed salesman came down into the pens ... and my father said, 'Like to have you meet my new hired man.' I turned away and raked furiously, red in the face with pleasure. 'Could of fooled me,' said the salesman, 'I thought it was only a girl'" (116). This gender contrast implies, of course, an upgrading of "male" and a downgrading of "female"—an evaluation that the girl, "red in the face with pleasure," internalizes when her father masculinizes her because she is doing a good job for him. Being compared to a male worker is flattering in her mind because she does not yet realize the implications this has for her own gender. Professional work outside the house is considered a male domain in this story. Through his above-quoted statement, the father unwittingly robs his daughter of her sexual identity, whereas the salesman quite unashamedly brings her down to earth by reducing her to her biological sex with derogatory gendered implications—"only a girl." Statements by her visiting grandmother rub in the fact that the female gender role is an utterly restrictive one at the time in which the story is set: "'Girls don't slam doors like that.' 'Girls keep their knees together when they sit down.' And worse still, when I asked some questions, 'That's none of girls' business'" (119).

For a while, the girl manages to resist such strict gender norms: "I continued to slam the doors and sit as awkwardly as possible, thinking that by such measures I kept myself free" (119). Her most spectacular opposition works on a more pronounced symbolic level of action. She purposefully keeps the gate open for the female horse Flora,[10] thus enabling the mare to postpone her fate of being slaughtered by the narrator's father for fox food. The girl intuitively identifies with the female horse because she, too, wants to escape a certain death—not in the literal sense of the word but in the transferred sense of the end of her free-ranging activities and options when she is pressed into a fixed female role pattern. The symbolic act of letting Flora run wild also constitutes the protagonist's first rebellion against her father, who adheres to an authoritative and conventional gender patterning. Mainly, however, the narrator's deed is a silent outcry against her own domestication. In this opposition, the girl is similar to the mare Flora, which is clearly contrasted with the stallion Mack in that she, too, refuses to be fenced in: "Mack was an old black workhorse, sooty and indifferent. Flora was a sorrel mare, a driver.... Mack was slow and easy to handle. Flora was given to fits of violent alarm.... Flora threw up her head, rolled her eyes, whinnied despairingly.... It was not safe to go into her stall; she would kick" (119).

The climax occurs at the end of the story when the family is gathered at the dinner table, symptomatically in a scene that is an epitome of ordered (or, depending on one's perspective, regulated and individually restricting) family life. Here, the gender pendulum fully swings back: Laird, in a classical act of "male bonding," tells on his older sister by disclosing that she let Flora escape on purpose. For the first time in the story, he sides with his father against her. The father, having overcome his immediate consternation about his daughter's apparently ill-advised act, reacts in a manner that is even more threatening to his daughter than either fury or reproach would be: "'Never mind,' my father said. He spoke with resignation, even good humour, the words which absolved and dismissed me for good. 'She's only a girl,' he said" (127).[11]

This reaction represents her initiation into a female gender role, with the word "girl" becoming what Jacques Derrida calls a "conflictual site" (qtd. in Heble 1994, 38). The implications are disastrous for the narrator: Girls, in the received, stereotypical gender assumptions of the time, behave irrationally and—like the mentally handicapped—cannot be held responsible for their actions; in any case, in the domestic sphere cut out for them, it will not matter much *what* they do because power is not on their side. The girl's reactions to such implications (making up the ending of the story) are even graver because they suggest the impact of socialization on the forming of mentalities: "I didn't protest that, even in my heart. Maybe it was true" (127). The girl has learned her gendered place in the social hierarchy the hard way: Humiliated by her younger brother's self-seeking act of betrayal and now domineering attitude, she has internalized not only to behave, but also to feel and think as a girl and thus to consider herself, as the ending suggests, rather insignificant. Adopting her father's belittling view of her and her letting Flora run, she betrays her own desire to rid herself of the restrictive role patterns forced upon her by the dominant gender system.

Nevertheless, even on the level of narrated time there is some hope presented at the end of the story by way of the modal adverb "maybe" ("Maybe it was true")—the girl may eventually manage to distance herself from prescribed gender roles (see also the narrator's critical reflections on the past events). These conventional gender roles, as this story illustrates, work against the interests of women by drastically reducing their options for leading a suitable and fulfilling life according to their individual—and not predominantly categorical, gender-type—characteristics and desires. Adrienne Rich has suggested that especially for women, re-visioning and then revising traditional gender roles is not only part of cultural and personal history but a step toward self-acceptance and, finally, an act of survival. "Until we can understand the assumptions in which we are drenched we cannot know ourselves," Rich states (1979, 35). As often with Munro, in this retrospectively recounted story by a narrating "I" that has a higher level of awareness than the narrator/protagonist as a young girl, questions of gender identity and an autobiographical impulse combine. Robert Thacker claims that "Munro's stories share the definition of the self—the primary urge in autobiography—as their central aim.... In fact, autobiography lies at the very core of Munro's celebrated ability to offer stories of such precision, such haunting beauty, and finally, such verisimilitude" (1988, 155). However, that Munro at once also deals with general role models and goes far beyond a potential autobiographical background of shedding internalized social patterns through the liberating experience of writing is suggested from the outset by the story's generic title in the plural form, "Boys and Girls," which points to the social significance of the individual experience rendered. The socialization forces with regard to both boys and girls are also evoked by the fact that the narrator's brother is named and thereby individualized, significantly through a speaking name that suggests his empowered gender role ("laird" is the Scottish word for "landowner"[12]). The female narrator, in contrast, remains nameless, which supports generalizing her socialization experience, while at the same time keeping her character more open to an autobiographical reading of the story, as Munro herself has suggested in various interviews concerning this and other stories.

"Boys and Girls," written at the beginning of the Second Wave of feminist involvement with literature in North America, renders gender relations in a rather programmatic manner[13]: the almost stereotypical characterization of the father and the mother; the systematic, highly symbolic opposition between interior/female and outer/male space; the divergent character of the male and the female horses; the clear-cut socializing influences imposed on the girl both by family members and by the closed rural society; and the seemingly logical mirroring of the girl's ongoing socialization process in her different nightly phantasies, that is, her imagining and telling stories to herself in bed. This early story does not feature Munro's later postmodernist technique of circulating indeterminacy but rather "the capsule summary conclusions—the 'false unity'—found so often in *Dance of the Happy Shades*" (Thacker 1988, 157). The short story demonstrates the restrictive, de-individualizing forces of an essentialist gender concept during the adolescent phase of development. At the same time, it also points out positively valued, liberating opportunities for women to rebel against dominant male codes of behavior. The girl thus feels the first estrangement from her father when she surreptitiously watches him kill a horse, apparently without any emotions on his part: "Yet I felt a little ashamed, and there was a new wariness, a sense of holding-off, in my attitude to my father and his work" (124), an attitude that later climaxes in her spontaneous rebellion against her father when she helps Flora escape. It is part of the female role that the narrator abhors the routine killing of animals, although an economic necessity on the fox farm. Her brother Laird, in contrast, is ritualistically initiated into the male role by being allowed to join his father in the hunt to capture Flora and also through having her blood on his body. He seems to be proud of symbolically having arrived at male adulthood: "Laird lifted his arm to show off a streak of blood. 'We shot old Flora,' he said, 'and cut her up in fifty pieces.' 'Well I don't want to hear about it,' my mother said" (126–27).[14]

Nevertheless, from the vantage point of the experiencing "I," the clear difference between the girl's and the boy's initiation into their respective gender roles seems to be to the girl's disadvantage: "Far from being a heroic aggrandizement, her initiation, by contrast to her brother's, is an ironic deflation of her status, which helps her understand that for a girl to grow up is to come down" (Ventura 1992, 80). The family scene at the dinner table is supposed to be a lesson for life, making the adolescent girl aware that, just as the foxes on the farm are raised in fenced pens, so the gender role she is supposed to identify with is a social "production,"[15] a construct: "A girl was not, as I had supposed, simply what I was; it was what I had to become. It was a definition, always touched with emphasis, with reproach and disappointment" (119). With even her younger brother and former pal eventually joining the restricting forces socializing and suppressing her, every character and almost every act or speech rendered in the text functions as a socializing agent or agency, pushing her in a certain direction of behavior and stressing a highly differential view of the sexes and their strictly separate spheres of action and development in this story. Even the two types of calendars mentioned in the text bluntly differentiate between men and women on a symbolic level of meaning. The historical calendar on the kitchen door showing scenes from nature and of Canada's colonial past (thus representing domestication on a national level) parallels the mother's personal domestication, with the kitchen being the epitome of a domestic existence. Henry Bailey's (the hired man's) calendars, in contrast, are stashed away in the male sphere of the barn—most likely pornographic pin-up calendars which "embody" another, more drastic and reifying form of domestication of the female, that is, through the representation of her naked body as an object for the male voyeuristic gaze and desire.

The painful, conflicting feelings that the gender instruction by the male family members at the dinner table must instill in the girl silence her for the moment, yet make her body speak: as her brother points out "matter-of-factly, 'she's crying'" (127). On the one hand, the experiencing "I" is given a ready-made explanation for her behavior with Flora that she did not understand at the time of her spontaneous decision. On the other hand, she seems to have lost the gender battle for the more attractive and dominant position in the family, being reduced to the description of "girl," a term that is twice used dismissively in the story. The conflicting feelings that such fixing, derogatory attributions must provoke under the circumstances are captured in the first-person narrator's contradictory, oxymoronic formulations, a hallmark of Munro's earlier writing in particular (see Hoy 1980), for instance: "He spoke with resignation, even good humour, the words which absolved and dismissed me for good" (127).

Conclusion

Correlating with the conflictual ending of the story, "Boys and Girls" shows competing gender concepts at work, thereby calling into question a strictly essentializing view of gender hierarchies. Already in this early story, Munro has shifted the emphasis to "throw the story line open to question" and thereby to "demand new judgements and solutions" (*Who*, 177), because the binary oppositions between male and female that constitute a thread through the story are constantly undercut (for instance, by the father calling his competent daughter a "hired man" and by the daughter feeling ill at ease with the stereotypical gender role distribution). What the girl yearns for is not an "either/or" but, in an early postmodernist stance and a plea for multiplicity, an "and" (see Ventura 1992, 84). As Dell, the female protagonist of Munro's second book following upon *Dance of the Happy Shades* was to formulate in another context and in more pronounced metafictional terms: "And no list could hold what I wanted, for what I wanted was every last thing, every layer of speech and thought, stroke of light on bark or walls, every smell, pothole, pain, crack, delusion, held still and held together—radiant, everlasting" (*Lives*, 249).

Several decades after Alice Munro published her early stories in the 1960s, featuring an astute and heightened awareness of what in 1990 came to be called "gender trouble" (J. Butler), American philosopher and literary theorist Judith Butler theoretically developed the view of gendered behavior as a learned pattern subject to the workings of the social environment (see J. Butler 1990 and 2004; from the latter, in which she elaborated gender performativity, the main title of this chapter was adapted). Munro's take on the matter, as relayed through her story "Boys and Girls," is similar, but the individualized psychological concerns of her story and her tangible sympathy with the victims of gender roles complement Butler's abstract arguments and bring home more vividly the emotional implications of socially instilled gender identities.

12

Canadian Artist Stories
John Metcalf, "The Strange Aberration of Mr. Ken Smythe"

Picking up Chapter 6, which introduces the subgenre of the Canadian artist story in the context of a gender-based approach, this chapter focuses on a single writer, John Metcalf, and his artist stories, in particular one of his many artist stories that suggests Metcalf's involvement with the state of the arts and the status of the artist in contemporary (Canadian) culture as well as with the relationship of the artist with their audience or readers.

On John Metcalf and His Works

In an interview with Geoff Hancock in 1981, John Metcalf stated:

> We now have *sophisticated* writers who make considerable demands on readers.
> Compare this with what we had before. When I arrived in Canada in 1962, the Canadian story was more tale or yarn.... Heavy on plot and light on brains, style, and elegance.... Callaghan may have *known* Hemingway but I can't see any evidence that he learned from him.[1] It was Hugh Hood with *Flying a Red Kite* who signalled that we were joining the rest of the 20th century [Metcalf 1982a, 13].

Asked by Hancock whether anything had changed concerning the short story in Canada in the previous decade, that is, in the 1970s, Metcalf replied: "It's changed out of recognition" (Metcalf 1982a, 12).

This brief extract from an interview may serve to indicate, if indirectly, that John Metcalf, at the crucial time of the development of the Canadian short story in the last third of the twentieth century, was one of the most important supporters and mentors of short fiction in Canada (perhaps surpassing even Robert Weaver from CBC Radio in this respect; see Chapter 3). For some five decades now, Metcalf has worked devotedly for this purpose, with

12. Canadian Artist Stories

unflinching determination and in several ways: as cultural critic, literary critic, anthologizer, editor of short fiction, and also as a short fiction writer himself.

As suggested in the quotation above, Metcalf immigrated to Canada in 1962. He was born in Carlisle, England, in 1938, to a schoolteacher and a Methodist minister (for biographical information, see Rollins 1985). A voracious reader at school and university, Metcalf received a BA in 1960 and a Certificate in Education in 1961. After several teaching posts in England, he went to Canada in 1962 and taught English and Canadian history at a high school in Montreal. He soon became aware of the relative dearth of Canadian literature and Canadian literary studies at the time and, after settling in Canada in 1966 for good (and becoming a Canadian citizen in 1970), he developed into one of the most outspoken and severe critics of Canadian culture, cultural policy, and of Canadian literature, with a special dedication to Canadian short fiction (see Nischik 1987).

Metcalf's main goal at the time was to make Canadians conscious of and interested in their own literature, that is, to make Canadians *read* Canadian literature (he claimed in 1986 that "one out of every five Canadians is functionally illiterate," see Metcalf 1986, 4). This strong focus on the author/work-reader relationship was complemented by his endeavors to support particular writers (and praise very few critics) and harshly criticize others in order to steer the emergent Canadian literature away from a parochial interest in the (preferably "Canadian") themes of writing (see his critical stance toward the "thematic criticism" that ruled "CanLitCrit" in the 1960s and 1970s; cf. Rosenthal 2008, esp. 291–301) and rather toward an emphasis on style and the technique of writing (see statements such as "I regard writing not as investigation of character but as an exercise in the use of language," Metcalf 1982a, 6; in the same interview he also uses the expression "CanLitCrit," 8). His intense preoccupation with the craft rather than the themes of fiction contributed its share in bringing Canadian literature up to international literary standards. In his many essays, books of cultural and literary criticism, and in his interviews, Metcalf formulated his views drastically, clearly taking sides and not shrinking from exaggeration or even harsh personal attacks on writers, critics, or journalists (see, for instance, Metcalf 1982a; 1986; 1994). He thus developed into a controversial figure, an *enfant terrible* of Canadian literary and cultural criticism. Particularly in retrospect, however, it is obvious that although the tone of his criticism often seemed inappropriately offensive, Metcalf's self-proclaimed "missionary" attempts (Metcalf 1982a, 10) contributed to the "Canadian Renaissance" in the 1960s (see Chapter 3) and especially to the rapid increase in the quality of Canadian short fiction as well as, arguably (and to a lesser extent), short fiction criticism.

The central tenet of Metcalf's cultural and literary criticism is that the quality of writing should be the only criterion for judging a work of literature—not its themes, motifs, or settings, nor whether the writing appeals to the masses ("You cannot write well for the mass because the mass can't read," Metcalf 1982a, 1). His is clearly and unashamedly an elitist, demanding view of literature: "I want to write elitist art. It's the austere that appeals to me more than anything else in art" (qtd. in Cameron 1975, 411). Metcalf thus firmly argued against the cultural policy of the Canada Council at the time, which supported Canadian literature simply because it was Canadian and preferred Canadian themes and settings. Metcalf, with his international outlook, countered: "The pervasive identification of art with nationalism is one of our central problems. It stands in the way of artistic maturity" (Metcalf 1986, 4).

A high school English teacher, Metcalf soon turned to anthologizing Canadian short fiction for teaching purposes and thereby developed into the most active and influential supporter, "popularizer," and talent scout of Canadian short fiction (see his involvement in practically all the series of Canadian short fiction over the decades, such as—partly under another name—*Best Canadian Stories*, 1971–1982, or *New Canadian Stories*, 1972–1976; see Nischik 1987). One of his earliest short fiction anthologies, *Sixteen by Twelve* (1970), was the first anthology of Canadian texts for teaching purposes in Canada; his later anthology *Making It New: Contemporary Canadian Stories* (1982b) was one of the first Canadian short story anthologies to explicitly address an international market. To date, Metcalf has some 40 short fiction anthologies to his credit (edited either for a general readership or for schools and universities), all of which have contributed to forging a Canadian short fiction canon.

In 1970 Metcalf, then still living in Montreal (he later moved to Ottawa), initiated the Montreal Story Teller Fiction Performance Group, together with Hugh Hood, Clark Blaise, Ray Smith, and Raymond Fraser. All group members apart from Fraser were or developed into important short fiction writers. The intention of this group, which officially disbanded in 1976, was again "missionary": if poetry could be read "live" to audiences, so could short fiction. The group mainly toured the Montreal area, reading out their short stories to audiences at schools, universities, community colleges, and bookshops, educating in particular young people about literature, especially the short story (see Struthers 1985).

The Montreal Story Tellers bonded over their same reader-oriented outlook, but they were not a homogeneous group of writers, with Ray Smith and Ray Fraser in particular belonging to the "postmoderns," against whose writing style Metcalf repeatedly argued. This in itself shows that Metcalf has not been as partial a critic as he may sometimes seem at first sight, owing to his often drastic outspokenness. His literary activities and his own writing style, however, clearly underline his preference for the modernist-realist tradition of writing over the antimimetic, postmodernist style (which, as he repeatedly argued, sometimes conceals bad writing). In his critical articles and especially his anthologies he has thus particularly (but not exclusively) supported those writers who conform to this tradition—writers such as Clark Blaise, Hugh Hood, Alice Munro, and Mavis Gallant.

Not the least of Metcalf's diverse achievements concerning the Canadian short story is that he is an excellent writer of short fiction himself. Although both his anthologies and his books of nonfiction outnumber his fiction volumes, he has nevertheless created a noteworthy fictional oeuvre over the years: three novels between 1972 and 1988, and altogether seven collections of short fiction (short stories and novellas) between 1970 and 2004. Even though the three volumes *Selected Stories* (1982c), *Shooting the Stars* (1993), and *Standing Stones: The Best Stories of John Metcalf* (2004) reprint stories of his from his earlier collections or anthologies, Metcalf must be regarded as a fairly productive short fiction writer, who has contributed not only several novellas[2]—a rather neglected genre in Canada—but also critically well-received short stories such as "The Teeth of My Father," "Gentle as Flowers Make the Stones," "The Years in Exile," "Keys and Watercress," and "The Strange Aberration of Mr. Ken Smythe" (all in the New Canadian Library edition of his *Selected Stories*). Metcalf's first story, "Early Morning Rabbits" (collected in *The Lady Who Sold Furniture*, 1970), won him the first prize in a CBC short story competition in 1963 and reinforced his decision to become a writer.

Although Metcalf once stated that he does not regard himself as a traditional writer,[3] he writes in the modernist-realist tradition (a pronounced example of a modernist writing style is his frequently anthologized artist story "Gentle as Flowers Make the Stones"[4]). Metcalf explains that he likes writing "factually," carefully focusing on the object, the particular as such, irrespective of its potential symbolic values (compare American writer William Carlos Williams's modernist-imagist credo "No idea but in things"); yet resonating symbolic significance can be attributed to many an object in his stories (for instance, the keys in his artist story "Keys and Watercress"). Metcalf has stated repeatedly that he is a slow writer whose first responsibility—as with many writers of short fiction—is to style, not theme, that is, to the discourse level. He arduously revises his writing ("I write each page 20 times over," Metcalf 1982a, 22) to meet his own critical standards, as postulated again and again in connection with other writers. Because of his often self-reflexive, "elitist" themes (about one third of his collected short fiction are explicitly about artists, with many others related to questions of art or writing), unusual set-ups, and demanding writing style, he has remained largely a "writer's writer," unknown to a wider audience. Thus, the American magazine *Harper's Bazaar* once referred to John Metcalf as "one of Canada's best-kept literary secrets."[5] Metcalf's concern with art, the artist, and the craft of writing in his fiction is not surprising in view of his intensive and long-term efforts to raise the standard of Canadian writing. Although he has also dealt with such topics in his satirical novels (*General Ludd*, 1980; *Going Down Slow*, 1972), Metcalf has claimed that his particular style of writing (a focus on episodes and objects, on suggestive rather than explicatory writing, with intensive dedication to structure and to verbal style) is more suited to the genre of the short story than to the novel (which he admits to having tried his hand at mainly, as with Alice Munro, because his publisher wanted him to, that is, for financial reasons). His short fiction—comprising more than 50 published pieces altogether, several of them novellas—can be classified into three groups according to the status of the protagonist: first, initiation stories, featuring boys or adolescents maturing in awareness and experience; second, stories with protagonists who have reached a certain educational and professional status, such as students or teachers; third, stories whose protagonists are actively involved with art (see Nischik 1988, 164).

Analysis of Metcalf's Story "The Strange Aberration of Mr. Ken Smythe"

The story selected for interpretation here belongs to the third category of his artist stories differentiated above. "The Strange Aberration of Mr. Ken Smythe," the opening story of Metcalf's second short story collection *The Teeth of My Father* (1975), was first published in *73: New Canadian Stories* (ed. David Helwig and Joan Harcourt). The story is situated in the Pleasure Gardens of Edinburgh and deals with a performance of popular culture in front of an international, entertainment-seeking, audience—it is thus a somewhat unusual Canadian artist story (especially for the 1970s), displaced in location and motif because it is not at all concerned with Canadian "highbrow art" or writing at first sight. Nevertheless, this story ingeniously reflects Metcalf's preoccupation with the Canadian artist and the artist-audience-relationship. The story's didactic potential is also manifested at several removes, since this easily accessible, engaging text on art in the context of entertainment may be read as a weighty allegory about the status of the artist in society and what "true" art is all about. To make his critical implications more palatable to a Canadian readership, perhaps, Metcalf chooses a decisively international setting: the third-person narrator, a traveler to Edinburgh, Scotland, visits one of the city's most frequented tourist spots, the Pleasure Gardens, to see the evening show of a local vaudeville group and the performance of a German brass band.

The third-person narrator is introduced at the very beginning of the story: "The traveller strolled up the incline of the station approach."[6] He remains unnamed and hardly characterized, apart from the fact that he is only traveling through Edinburgh and has decided to spend the time waiting for his connection train to London at the Pleasure Gardens. The manner in which the narrator—or, rather, focalizer—is introduced, proves important for the reader's overall reception of the text. We are aware of a focalizer only during the first one and a half pages of the story, where his approaching and then entering the Pleasure Gardens are reported in a simple, matter-of-fact style: "He glanced at his watch and then strolled around the curve of the paling fence to the entrance. He paid his one shilling and sixpence and sat in the corner of an empty row. He finished the ice-cream. Rolling and unrolling the blue ticket, he stared down into the cave of the bandshell. The shouting startled him" (162). The last sentence is the only overt comment about the focalizer throughout the whole story. After that, the focalizer functions purely as an unintrusive, seemingly neutral "camera-eye," through which the events unfold as if speaking for themselves; the readers are left to form their own opinions and conclusions about them.

The way space is handled in the exposition subtly hints at what is in store. Establishing a contrast between "up" and "down," the exposition also partly suggests a decline in action, behavior, character, and values. In the very first paragraph of the story, the traveler "strolled *up* the incline of the station approach" and sees "*high above* the city, Edinburgh Castle ... just beginning to lose detail in the evening light.... He stopped to look at a statue of Robert Burns" (161; italics added). In view of what is to follow, one can also see a symbolic meaning in these references. The monuments, which belong to an elevated level of culture and are probably perceived by an educated character (see his looking at the statue of one of Scotland's best-known writers, "poet of brotherhood and the common man," Rollins 1985, 185), indeed "lose detail" to black-and-white contrasts in an increasingly gloomy atmosphere after sunset, when the expected entertainment begins. After this reference to the statue of Robert Burns, the story's movement turns in a downward direction, both spatially and culturally. The traveler gazes "*down* in the Pleasure Gardens," comes, during his strolling through the city, to "a flight of steps leading *down* into the Gardens" (161), and stares "*down* into the cave of the bandshell"; "leaves drifted *down*" (162; italics added). This spatial descent is paralleled by a cultural descent: having viewed Edinburgh Castle "*high above* the city" (161; italics added), approaching the Pleasure Gardens he sees "tourists mill[ing] along the gravel paths between the fragrant rosebeds photograph[ing] each other" (161), "family groups of Americans" (161) in "plastic mac[s]" (162), "a mob of soldiers ... running across the lawn booting a football in long passes, with the boys chasing after yelling" (162). The focalizer also perceives the potentially destructive force of such mass activities: "One of the soldiers turned and punted the ball black into the sky. It *crashed* through the branches of the oak tree...; leaves drifted *down*" (162; italics added).[7]

In the short overture to the events proper, we can thus trace a subtly transmitted outlining of a factual and symbolic descent from "high" to "low" or from highbrow to lowbrow. Just as spatial and cultural descents coincide, the earlier reference to the reaction of the focalizer ("the shouting startled him," 162), too, is a foreshadowing of how he is bound to react to the subsequent gruesome events. In this brief exposition we see Metcalf's modernist craft at work, for although he seems to merely report factually, focusing strictly on objects, human figures, and visual matters, the exposition, when read in the context of the story as a whole, is a densely structured, subtly symbolic foreshadowing of events in concrete and increasingly drastic terms.

While the exposition introduces us to the make-up of the show's audience, it also, quite factually again, announces the performers in printed capital letters on "the large notice-board": "MUNICIPAL ENTERTAINMENTS ... THE GLASGOW VARIETY SHOW AND THE ESSEN INTERNATIONAL AMITY BOYS BRASS BAND" (162). The reader awaits a vaudeville show by a Scottish group followed by a German youth brass band performing German folk songs, a veritable popular culture event designed to give pleasure (as the venue's name suggests) to a varied audience, but also to raise intercultural understanding and friendship ("International Amity") through the exchange of popular national art forms.

The Glasgow Variety Show Company starts off the evening with typical vaudeville acts: "Vladimir produced playing cards, ping-pong balls, handkerchiefs, flags, rabbits, and doves from tubes, hats, pockets, and his nose. He ended by sawing Wanda in half" (164). The matter-of-fact-style of reporting on supposedly surreal vaudeville tricks of the trade exposes the banality, if not the ridiculousness of the show. Also performing are "two great stars.... Scotland's pride" (164) of the Scottish National Opera Company, who sing songs from various popular musicals, such as *Oklahoma* and *The Sound of Music*. Though the crowd is later said to become "restive" about "lengthy selections" (164) from these musicals, thus indicating their short attention span, the first part of the evening is all in all a success with the audience: "The entire company bowed; the audience broke into unrestrained applause ... the light inside the bandshell died. Whistling and stomping continued for some time in the darkness" (164).

The Scottish actors and singers, singing songs in English and performing in their home country, serve not only to "warm up" the audience for the subsequent performance of the German boy band, but the very positive reception of the Scottish performers also indicates that the disastrous way in which the performance by the German musicians develops is due to a large extent to intercultural ignorance, intolerance, prejudice, and, finally, downright nationalistic hostility.

Ironically, the German band is visiting Scotland for just the opposite reason, namely to foster international exchange and understanding. As their Scottish compere, the Mr. Ken Smythe of the story's title, explains to the audience, "these young German lads are the guests of Rotary International" (165), the "fellowship of business, professional, and community leaders ... [who] provide service to others, promote integrity, and advance world understanding, goodwill, and peace."[8] Their exchange with "a Temperance Band from Leicester ... touring Germany" indeed intends to "foster international goodwill" (165). That these enlightened words are spoken by Ken Smythe, of all people, proves a stark irony in light of the subsequent events, for it is the Scottish compere, a Second World War veteran with an RAF (Royal Air Force) badge pinned to his blazer, who will incite the audience first to restlessness, then to a slanted reception, and eventually to downright hostility toward the German band. It is through his interference that the "amity" event will eventually result in sexist and nationalistic obscenity, aggression, and chaos.

Smythe at first appears to give off a sophisticated impression, with his "sleek hair gleam[ing] in the lights" (165) and suave language marked by a strained politeness—the very spelling of his surname ("Smythe" rather than "Smith") looks pretentious. Yet right from the beginning, his cultured middle-class mannerisms strike a false note, as his first utterance on stage, which he thinks is not overheard, betrays his lower-class origin: "'What, mate?' boomed over the sound system" (165). As the events unfold, Smythe's true colors increasingly shine through. Although in his announcements he repeatedly tries to pass himself off as putting a lot of idealistic effort into youth work, it soon becomes obvious—actions speaking louder than words—that he is a most unsuitable model for young people or anyone interested in respectful personal and intercultural relationships. For one thing, he is revealed to be a drinker, covertly drinking alcohol even during the performance ("As the section sat and the trombones dipped to rest position, Ken Smythe's tilted face was revealed for a second, a square bottle at his lips," 167). Throughout the concert, Smythe gets increasingly inebriated and soon becomes a nuisance and eventually a disaster for the music performance (barging into Herr Kunst, the conductor; losing his balance, "falling sideways into the trumpet section, knocking over two music stands," 169).

Smythe's actions and speeches become increasingly unrestrained and vulgar. This is first noticeable in his behavior toward "Fräulein Hohenstaufen," his German female co-host, dressed in a clichéd (Bavarian) "native costume" ("Plump and pretty in yoke blouse and dirndl skirt, rosy cheeks and hair in coiled braids, Fräulein Hohenstaufen blushed and curtsied to the cheers and piercing whistles," 166). Smythe's increasingly sexist advances toward her on stage climax when his assault turns into nationalistic antagonism: "He put his arm around her shoulders again and pulled her close ... 'Like dumplings,' he said, looking down" (170). The fact that he chooses a Bavarian culinary specialty ("dumpling") to refer to the woman's breasts, and publically so, is indicative of his combined sexist and racist mind-set.

These developments are carefully foreshadowed earlier in the story. If one sequences the titles of the German folk songs as Ken Smythe announces them, they unmask the chauvinistic behavior of the Scottish compere in leading the masses toward first sexist and eventually nationalistic aggression: *"Auf, auf zum fröhlichen Jagen.... Happy Hunting Song"* (167). To the translation of *"Das Wandern ist des Müller's Lust," "The Millers Like to Wander,"* he adds a lewd translation of his own, which plays on the ambivalent meaning of "Lust" in German: *"The Millers' Lust." "Ein Jäger aus Kurpfalz,"* for which the translation on his card correctly reads *"A Palatinate Hunter,"* is first falsely rendered by him as *"A Passionate Hunter,"* again with sexual innuendo. Further German songs like *"Ich hab' mein Herz in Heidelberg verloren"* ("I Lost My Heart in Heidelberg") or *"Auf der Lüneburger Heide"* ("On the Lüneburg Heath," all 167) lead to the titles *"Wenn alle Brünnlein fliessen"* (168, "When All the Fountains Flow") and *"Ein Vogel wollte Hochzeit machen"* (*"A Bird's Wedding,"* 168), which are clearly given a sexual interpretation by Mr. Smythe. During the performance of *"Wenn alle Brünnlein fliessen,"* Fräulein Hohenstaufen, apparently being sexually molested by Smythe, "rose from behind the trombone section with a sudden screech"; and to his announcement of *"A Bird's Wedding,"* he insinuatingly adds: "And with a bird like our Miss Hohenstaufen here we shouldn't have long to wait, should we?'" (168).

The turning point in the story occurs when the drunken host falls into the trumpet section, finally making a fully-fledged slapstick performance out of an earnest "amity" event:

> Herr Kunst [the band's conductor] extricated him [Smythe]. Hawling him to his feet, gripping him by the upper arm, Herr Kunst guided him to the farther side of the microphone. Above the stamping and applause of the crowd, any exchange of words was inaudible...
> Ken Smythe shook himself free and stood glaring at Herr Kunst's back as the boys in the trumpet section righted the stands and finished sorting the sheet music [169].

Characteristic of Metcalf's art of omission, the reader does not get to know what exactly the conductor has said to Mr. Smythe; a highly disciplined character, Herr Kunst has probably simply tried to bring Smythe to his senses and to moderate his inappropriate behavior. However, Smythe's behavior ("glaring" at Herr Kunst) only changes from sexist to nationalistic, with his primary target now no longer Fräulein Hohenstaufen but Herr Kunst. After his—unwittingly self-revealing—announcement of the song *"Trink, trink, Brüderlein trink.... Drink, my Brothers, Drink"* (170), he uses the first opportunity to twist the mood toward nationalistic hostility, by indirectly referring to the Germans' role in the Second World War:

> "...a most typical German song named *Warum ist es am Rhein so schön.*"
> "And we all know what's typically German, don't we?" said Ken Smythe, jerking his thumb backwards at Herr Kunst.... "It wasn't so beautiful the last time *I* was there, Herr Kunst or no Herr Kunst.... Last time *I* saw the Rhine—last time I saw *Essen* ... it was through my bomb-sights.... RAF, mates" [170].

The inebriated Scottish compere and Second World War veteran, parodying Herr Kunst's highly controlled, even stiff conducting motions, eventually drifts into a military posturing ("Ken Smythe lurched out to the edge of the stage and, pulling himself erect, saluted," 172). He now quite purposefully directs the audience to turn against the German brass band. The innocent performance of a German youth band metamorphoses horribly into modern-day warfare on the battlefield of "popular culture" (see the foreboding juxtaposition of the Pleasure Gardens with the War Memorial at the beginning of the story, 161):

> Ken Smythe launched the crowd into yet another chorus.
> HITLER HAD ONLY GOT ONE BALL
> GOERING TWO BUT VERY SMALL
> HIMMLER WAS VERY SIMLAR
> BUT POOR OLD GOBALLS HAD NO BALLS AT ALL.... BOLLOCKS! roared the crowd THEY MAKE A TASTY STEW! BOLLOCKS! [173].

With Smythe's primitive sexual and nationalistic leanings fully unleashed, his revolting song reduces the most abhorred Germans in history (Hitler, Goering, Himmler, Goebbels)[9] to their sexual organs in a barbarian, cannibalistic context (see "they make a tasty stew").

Smythe is thus depicted as an extremely unlikeable character: lower-class, ignorant, sexist, vulgar, and racist. The story also illustrates that this behavior is not really (in ironic negation of the understated title) a "strange aberration" at all, but an authentic expression of his character and mind-set. Smythe's influence on the ignorant and gullible masses, which under his direction eventually turn against the German brass band, delivers a gloomy message: "Smythe emerges as a kind of everyman who is both a member of and a voice for the mob" (Rollins 1985, 186).

The reader's sympathy in this story lies with the members of the German music band, who become innocent and rather arbitrary victims of nationalistic aggression. Against this background of popular culture turning into vulgarity and obscenity, the Germans are marked positively from the outset by their names: "Heine" recalls one of the most important German writers,[10] while Fräulein Hohenstaufen's name is reminiscent of German aristocracy and tradition.[11] The most obvious reference to the allegorical meaning of this artist story is the name of the disciplined director and conductor, Herr Kunst ("Mr. Art"). Indeed, his band, though performing in a context of mass entertainment, is dedicated to its art rather than its audience, displaying the utmost discipline of appearance and behavior:

> A tall blond boy [Heine] came out and gave a stiff bow; he cradled a trumpet in his arms. The other boys, black-suited, filed onto the stage and to their section places.... Suddenly onto the stage strode a man in a black suit, halted, faced the silent band. The arm of Herr Kunst rose; the arm of Herr Kunst descended.
>
> The burst of sound was crisp and perfect, the sections rising and sitting as one man, the soloists flawless. Herr Kunst stood rigid except for the metronome pump of his elbows.
>
> During the applause ... Herr Kunst remained motionless facing the band who were turning over the sheet music on their stands [166].

To further stress the value of their performance, the instruments of the band members are described using bright and precious colors. The cymbals are said to be "glittering"; "light shone in the trombone bells, glanced off the slides" (167); and blond Heine's trumpet is twice referred to as "golden": "Light flashed golden on his trumpet" (172).

The spatial contrast introduced in the exposition of the story runs throughout the text. Of Heine's performance we read: "Heine's golden trumpet tones *soared* round and sweet *above* them" (167, italics added); at the end of the story, we read in horrible contrast how "Heine suddenly staggered, *dropping* his trumpet and half-*falling* against the boy next to him. His hands covered his face. Herr Kunst was at his side in two strides. A stone, a bottle, something thrown from the darkness. Blood was shining, trickling *down* the backs of his hands" (173, italics added).[12]

The earlier up-and-down movements of the conductor's arm and the band's exact response to it strikingly show the concentration and precision of their performance (though in the rigor of their appearance and movements, that is, their traditionally stereotypical, by now outdated Germanness, the band members are also satirized to some extent). Herr Kunst's conducting initially even seems capable of imposing some order on the increasingly noisy audience: "The arm of Herr Kunst remained raised until the noise had stopped and then descended" (167). At the end of the story, by contrast, the movements of the conductor's arms are no longer mentioned. Although the band, despite an increasingly disorderly and eventually hostile audience, keeps an admirable discipline, Herr Kunst is as powerless in controlling the hostile masses as the rest of the band: "The louder the stamping, the louder played the band" (172) changes into: "The roaring voices and the pounding feet had drowned the band although the boys still played" (173). The masses seem to prevail over the elitist artist.

It is in the ending that the allegorical meaning of this artist story becomes particularly clear, as the absolute dedication of the artists to their art clashes with an audience that is not, to put it mildly, interested in a "serious" musical performance. This is also stressed in interspersed episodes showing the reactions of an American family to the evening show. Shooting several rolls of film, peeling oranges, and eating potato chips, the Americans, like the rest of the audience, disrespect the performance of the brass band, which is obviously the result of considerable talent and intensive practice. When the trumpet player Heine is physically assaulted by someone from the audience, the Americans are only interested in getting a good picture of the blood running down the boy's face: "'The color!' screamed the mother, tugging at the edge of the father's plastic mac. 'Use the color film!'" (173). This heartless and sensationalist outburst, enhancing the shock of the violent ending, horrible enough in itself, closes out the story.

Conclusion

"The Strange Aberration of Mr. Ken Smythe" is the most dismal of Metcalf's artist stories, which are generally concerned with the precarious state of the artist in a social context that does not particularly value art or artists. The development of the action on stage and the reactions of the audience may thus be understood as an allegory illuminating this strained relationship between the artist and society, if pushed to extremes here (see also Metcalf's treatment of national clichés: Germany is associated with "highbrow" culture—Heine, Herr Kunst—yet also with the Second World War and the Nazi regime; the Scots, through Mr. Smythe, are associated with drinking, and the Americans with superficiality and a sensationalist tourist stance). The social context, the audience, appears as a backdrop against which art goes on in spite of the antagonism presented between the artist and society. The artists must carry on no matter what the hindrances, and according to their own demanding standards, not catering to an uneducated mass audience. Although in constant friction with their surroundings, Metcalf's artists never give up but keep striving to give the best they can. The story also demonstrates that Metcalf, no matter how involved with the craft of writing, does not take a purely estheticist stance, but regards himself as a political writer in the final analysis ("all writing is political, all great writing subversive," Metcalf 1972a, 154). It is important to keep in mind that this story was first published at the beginning of the 1970s, the period that has been called the "Canadian Renaissance," when Canadian culture was in a crucial formative stage (cf. Chapter 3).

Clearly, the story makes a highly negative statement about the relationship between artist and audience. Yet it also insists on high, if not elitist, standards of art, irrespective of what an uneducated audience finds palatable. One would hope that Metcalf, having clamored for a suitable reception of Canadian literature by an educated audience for decades, would not see quite such a necessity for writing such a story nowadays. In any event, "The Strange Aberration of Mr. Ken Smythe" demonstrates that John Metcalf, apart from having been an important and dedicated mentor of Canadian short fiction, is also an excellent writer himself, for whom the craft of writing short fiction is definitely not a "strange aberration," but another important means to the end of fostering nothing short of excellence in Canadian short fiction.

13

Blending Indigenous and Western Traditions of Storytelling
Thomas King's Short Fiction

The large variety of different ethnic voices contributes considerably to the wealth of contemporary short fiction writing in Canada. Picking up the multicultural threads laid out in the historical survey Chapter 3 and, in greater detail and focus, in Chapter 10 (which analyzes short fiction writing on the city by First Nations and Chinese Canadian writers), the present chapter deals with the short story oeuvre of Canada's internationally best-known writer with an Indigenous background, Thomas King.

King published his first short story in 1987. To date, two short story collections with altogether 30 of his stories have appeared, *One Good Story, That One* (1993) and *A Short History of Indians in Canada* (2005), and there are also a few uncollected stories.[1] Thomas King is mainly regarded as a novelist and as a short story writer. Although scholars have mostly dealt with his novels, it could be—and has been—argued (for instance by Gibert 2001, 75–76) that King's literary writing is most successful in the short story format, or, to put it differently, that essential aspects of his writing style are more conducive to short fiction than to longer prose. The oral tradition of Indigenous storytelling, which King adeptly integrates into his texts, is particularly prominent among these aspects, as is the author's leaning toward parabolic and satirical styles of narration. On the other hand, these aspects also inform King's novels, which tend to be written in episodic structures, too. In fact, his first published long fiction text, *Medicine River* (1989), though usually classified as a novel, has also been considered a short story cycle, even by King himself (see Lynch 2007; Rooke 1990, 3).

Under these circumstances, and considering King's status as the leading

Indigenous fiction writer in Canada, the relative sparseness of research into King's short stories comes as a surprise.[2] This chapter, then, sets out to provide a wide-angle analytical assessment of King's short stories.

Thomas King's Short Fiction Oeuvre

In surveying King's short story oeuvre, I will first point out several general traits before classifying his 30 collected stories into different groups and subsequently analyzing selected examples from each group.

First of all, Thomas King inscribes himself into the North American (originally white) written short story tradition by writing short stories proper, clearly a Western genre format. In doing so, he refrains, for instance, from postmodern experimental short fiction formats or various other experimental forms of short prose. His short stories indeed tell "stories," which are partly indebted to the realist narrative tradition. All the same, they clearly show themselves to be indebted to postmodernist techniques—King started to publish short fiction in the late 1980s, after all. Most of his stories contain a mixture of realist as well as "surreal" (supernatural, fantastic, mysterious, or mythical) elements, so that his narrative style could generally be characterized as a specific kind of (that is, Native) magic realism.

Most of King's short stories are informed by elements from Indigenous cultures and traditions.[3] One essential element is the oral tradition, often combined with Indigenous narrators. Many of his stories are seemingly "orally" *told* (despite their written format), with many characteristics of oral speech reproduced in writing. This integration of aspects of the Indigenous oral tradition into his short stories and novels—Teresa Gibert speaks of King's "written orality" (2006)—has major consequences for King's technique and style. Gibert, reverting to Walter J. Ong's fundamental study *Orality and Literacy* (1982), has stressed that "orally based thought and expression are additive rather than subordinative; aggregative rather than analytic; redundant ... close to the human lifeworld ... participatory rather than objectively distanced ... and situational rather than abstract" (Gibert 2006, 97). In his well-known article "Godzilla vs. Post-Colonial" (1990), King speaks of "interfusional literature" in referring to narratives that are written in English—and thus accessible to a wider readership—but which at the same time retain the typical voice of Indigenous storytellers and "oral discursive devices" (Gibert 2006, 4). Even in those of King's stories that do not have a foregrounded (mostly Indigenous) narrator, the narrative mode of direct speech features prominently through a high proportion of (free) direct discourse. The Indigenous "participatory" tradition of oral storytelling also explains the polyphony of voices in King's stories, which leads Gibert to call his stories "voice pieces ...

13. Blending Indigenous and Western Traditions 191

hybrid texts which have undergone the process of transforming oral/aural speech into the visual figuration that readers see when they look at a printed page" (2006, 6).

Another Indigenous aspect of King's stories, connected to but slightly different from the first one, is the foregrounding of storytelling practices within the texts themselves. Indigenous narrators who tell their stories to addressees present in the story prove highly relevant for the texts' production of meaning. The same can be said about the metanarrative elements, which draw the reader's attention to an (Indigenous) narrator telling a story, as well as about the stories' "rambling," circular characteristics. As Paula Gunn Allen has pointed out, "traditional tribal narratives possess a circular structure, incorporating event within event, piling meaning upon meaning, until the accretion results in a story" (1986, 79). An aspect that also falls into the realm of storytelling, but combines elements of both white and Indigenous cultures and storytelling traditions, is King's use of intertextuality. Repeatedly, key Western texts (like the Bible) or myths (like the creation of the world or the settling of the West) are retold from an Indigenous perspective, thereby significantly redirecting and drastically changing their received cultural significance. King's short stories, by implementing a largely Indigenous point of view, amply demonstrate to what extent content is dependent on narrative perspective.

In such juxtapositions—and sometimes confrontations—of white and Indigenous characters and cultures, stereotyping, in both directions, plays an important role. In several cases, King draws his readers' attention to stereotypes by turning clichéd characterizations of both ethnic groups on their heads, his preferred narrative techniques for this purpose being humor and irony, parody and caricature, satire, and, sometimes, slapstick elements. Margaret Atwood, in her early comments on two of King's short stories, aptly summarizes the effect of all these techniques: "They [these stories] ambush the reader. They get the knife in, not by whacking you over the head with their own moral righteousness, but by being funny. Humour can be aggressive and oppressive.... But it can also be a subversive weapon" (1990, 244).

By far most of King's short stories deal with both Indigenous and white characters at the same time. Only a few stories deal with subjects and characters not noticeably Indigenous (none in the earlier collection, six of 20 in the later collection), and almost none deal with clearly Indigenous characters only (one in the earlier, none in the later collection). King's main themes are the displacement of Indigenous people and Indigenous culture in white mainstream culture, Indigenous people's and whites' attitudes toward each other, the negative stereotyping of Indigenous people by whites (and the other way round), Indigenous reevaluation of Western history, myths, and beliefs, and, last but not least, family themes. The stories are set in present times and thus counteract the traditional white preoccupation with "Indians" and their battles and displacement in the nineteenth century. Dealing with both everyday and fantastic or mythical affairs from a predominantly Indigenous perspective, they pinpoint white prejudices and the neglect of Indigenous people in contemporary North American society and culture. Although King tells stories about individual Indigenous and white characters, these stories nevertheless have a parabolic tendency toward more encompassing statements about being Indigenous in present-day North America (this would classify King's stories as "associational" literature in the terminology he established in "Godzilla vs. Post-Colonial" [1990], in that they focus on the group rather than the individual). King's roots in both white and Indigenous cultures afford him the opportunity of a larger perspective. As he himself put it in an interview with Margaret Atwood, setting off his own work from that of fellow Indigenous writer Tomson Highway: "Mine was more of a wide-angle shot. From above and out of range, as it were. And ... Tomson was, you know, up close and personal" (in Atwood 2005, 11). Thomas King thus tells new and illuminating stories about the situation of Indigenous people in present-day North America, and does so in an engaging, speech-orientated, often humorous, and frequently magic-realist manner, mixing comic and tragic elements as well as realist and surrealist or fantastic aspects of narrative to punching effects.

Against the backdrop of these general traits, King's short stories may be roughly subdivided into four major groups, with individual stories sometimes straddling more than one group; classification then depends on which aspects seem predominant concerning an individual story:

1. Creation Stories/(Bible) Parodies
2. Trickster Stories/(Re-)Creating History
3. Fantastic Stories/Parables
4. Family Stories

This is meant as an heuristic classification that points to some of King's main thematic interests and narrative methods, and that manages to account for the majority of his stories (to capture *all* of them, one would have to add a fifth, "residual" or "various" group).

Creation Stories/(Bible) Parodies

An essential "received" narrative of all cultures is the story about how the world and (wo)mankind came into being, a *grand récit* if ever there was one. In the Judeo-Christian tradition of Western culture this refers to the biblical narratives of God's creation of the world in six days (Genesis 1), of

13. Blending Indigenous and Western Traditions   193

the Garden of Eden and Adam and Eve (Genesis 2), and of original sin and the fall from grace (Genesis 3). In Indigenous North American cultures and their oral traditions, creation stories figure even more prominently, with various stories about how the world (or North America, called "Turtle Island" by most Indigenous peoples) came into existence. Creation stories in general can be said to incorporate basic beliefs of their respective cultures, and the Judeo-Christian vs. the Indigenous North American ones could not be more different in this regard.[4] Usually those beliefs go unchallenged by the respective communities due to their profoundly identificatory, foundational, and mythical power. When seen through the eyes of members of a vastly different culture, however, essential aspects of these creation myths may not only stand out more clearly, but may also be relativized or even distorted, debunked, and ridiculed.

While a concern with creation narratives is characteristic of large parts of King's oeuvre, four of his published short stories explicitly belong to this important group: two from *One Good Story, That One* (1993)—"One Good Story, That One" and "The One About Coyote Going West"; and two from *A Short History of Indians in Canada* (2005)—"Bad Men Who Love Jesus" and "The Garden Court Motor Motel." The last story may be regarded as a contemporary update and parody of the Indigenous "Woman Who Fell from the Sky" creation myth, whereas "Bad Men Who Love Jesus" is a parodic pastiche of various biblical stories. In the first two stories, in contrast, King takes devastating shots at the biblical Judeo-Christian creation myth. "One Good Story, That One" (1988) is the most resonant story of this group, and it encompasses many of the thematic and narrative characteristics typical of King's stories.[5] For one, it is told in a clearly oral set-up. In a frame narrative that serves as a bracket around an embedded story, three young white anthropologists, driven by their scholarly interest in the exotic Other and armed with camera and tape recorder, ask an Indigenous elder to tell one of his or her[6] stories for them to record. While the storyteller—who is also the story's first-person narrator—twice starts to tell them contemporary stories of "Indians" (as King refers to Natives in his fictional writing), all the white anthropologists want is "old" Indian stories: "Those ones like old stories ... maybe how the world was put together. Good Indian story like that.... Maybe not too long" (5, 4). Accordingly, the longest part of the text is the embedded story, an allegedly Indigenous creation myth that the Indigenous elder supposedly "passes on" to the three young anthropologists. The cheerful old storyteller is a trickster, however (see below). It is no coincidence that the frame narrative concludes with the sentence: "I clean up all the coyote tracks on the floor" (10), which is not directly or realistically motivated by the events on this particular story level, but rather in the inserted story.[7] The idea of the archetypal Indigenous trickster ("Coyote come by maybe four, maybe eight times. Gets dressed up, fool around," 8) thus invades—and blurs the boundaries between—two different narrative levels of this seemingly simple, yet tricky narrative.

Instead of giving the whites an authentic traditional Indigenous story of "how the world was put together" (5), the Indigenous narrator mischievously dishes out a mock creation story to them, which is actually derived from Genesis, yet reconceptualizes this story from an irreverent Indigenous perspective. The authority of the biblical creation account is challenged right from the beginning by the Indigenous storyteller, who introduces the embedded story with the conventional fairy tale opening formula "Once upon a time" (5). Then, too, the Garden of Eden mutates into the garden of "Evening," the Indigenous female version of the biblical Eve (8). Evening, in contrast to the original biblical story, is the more active, self-assured, "generous," helpful, "smart" one in comparison to her "whiteman" (7, 8) partner, who—described as rather boring and simple-minded—is sarcastically called "Ah-damn" instead of Adam. Ah-damn on the one hand stands for white rationalization, appropriation, and colonization, as he meticulously writes down, catalogs, and "transcribes" the names of all the newly created animals, which, significantly, they themselves tell him, in their Indigenous language.[8] God also uses Indigenous names for his creations before the English translations are given (for instance, "Me-a-loo, call her deer," 6).[9] The idea or figure of God (significantly spelled in lower case in the story, "that fellow, god, whiteman," 9), sacrosanct in Christian thought, is treated with particular irreverence in this story, for instance: "Pretty soon that one, god, come by. He is pretty mad. You ate my mee-so [apple], he says. Don't be upset, says Evening, that one, first woman. Many more mee-so back there. Calm down, watch some television, she says" (9). All the revered tenets of the biblical creation account are called into question or turned on their heads: Ah-damn is "not so smart" (8) as tricky coyote (who repeatedly fools him) or Evening, and is found out by god to be a liar (9). God is shown as selfish, loud-voiced, bad-tempered, angry, and authoritarian. As a side-swipe at white colonization of the Indigenous people, the narrator equates god's "throw[ing] out" (9) of Evening and Ah-damn from Evening's garden—because god does not want to share the apples with them—with the situation of contemporary Indigenous people: "Just like Indian today" (9). God thus becomes the appropriator. Nevertheless, Evening and Ah-damn go on to live somewhere else happily enough and "have a bunch of kids" (10). Last but not least, the Indigenous storyteller "forgot" (9) the crucial issue of original sin and, trivializing, twists the biblical episode of the snake tempting Eve into a funny, sexualized attempt at an explanation of why snakes hiss.

The three white anthropologists react indeterminately to this disrespectful debunking of the Bible and their own cultural creation myth. Possibly they sense the Indigenous narrator's guile and lack of respect because they "leave pretty quick," nevertheless politely smiling, shaking hands, and making "happy noises" (10). But they may also just be too stupid (thus Truchan-Tataryn and Gingell 2006, 13) or too carried away by "Indianthusiasm" (Lutz 2002, 13) to recognize the told story as the parody and criticism of the Judeo-Christian creation myth that it is. With the Indigenous storyteller in any case getting the better of the white scholars in such a drastic way, one sees the legitimacy of Margaret Atwood's question to King: "How outrageous are you willing to be? Do you ever get attacked for going too far ... by making white people too stupid to live?" (Atwood 2005, 5).

One may presume that King gets away with his desecrating though revealing shots at foundational texts of white/Western culture not least because of the sheer fun and humor of his stories. The Indigenous storyteller speaks in a simple, truncated, seemingly child-like English.[10] The imaginative wordplay (Ah-damn, Evening, etc.) and the other outrageous deviations from the "sacrosanct" original story distance the characters and the plot elements from the biblical pre-text in such a funny way that King manages to keep these stories out of "up close and personal" (King in Atwood 2005, 11) dismay, while nevertheless teaching his white readers (if not the anthropologists in the story) a lesson about the hierarchical, highly gender-coded, and authoritarian set-up of the biblical origin myth (on the latter, see also Walton 1996).

Trickster Stories/(Re-)Creating History

The inevitable relativity of my proposed categorization of King's short stories may be highlighted by pointing out that the cunning, clever narrator of "One Good Story, That One" may also be called a trickster, a crucial agent in the Native North American storytelling tradition.[11] One may differentiate between "classical" tricksters from Indigenous mythology and human characters derived from the classical trickster figure, who perform similar (narrative) functions, the Indigenous narrator in "One Good Story, That One" belonging to the latter category. In King's stories, the classical trickster figure is always Coyote, a "choice [that] may well be explained by Coyote's position as the closest thing there is to a pan-tribal trickster in First Nations mythologies; also, Coyote is the trickster non–Native readers would most likely be familiar with" (Korkka 2002, 147). While the trickster figure in Native discourse defies being pinned down academically in a definitive way, it is safe to say that it is "a brilliant tribal figure of imagination that has found a new world in written languages" (Vizenor 1993, 68). The classical Indigenous trickster may be both a culture hero and an antihero, often trying to "fix the world"—which may turn out to have both beneficial and chaotic or disastrous effects. Tricksters are shape-shifters and seem to exist outside any norms and rules. Anything seems possible with them, and they thus open up liberating, liminal spaces of imagination, which invite readers, too, to transgress borderlines and reevaluate received cultural tenets (see Gruber 2008, 96). However, the tricks tricksters play—in contrast to those of the trickster narrator in "One Good Story, That One"—may also fail dismally and backfire on them or on the culture they represent. As King himself points out, though: "Whatever the damage, contemporary characters, like their traditional trickster relations, rise from their own wreckage to begin again" (King 1987, 8), thus representing typical agents in the cyclical form of Indigenous storytelling.

King's classical coyote tricksters appear in "The One About Coyote Going West" and "A Coyote Columbus Story" (both in *One Good Story, That One*, 1993) and in an "updated" Coyote story in *A Short History of Indians in Canada* (2005), "Coyote and the Enemy Aliens." King's human trickster figures are diverse, with the Blackfoot female protagonist in King's most frequently anthologized story "Borders" (in *One Good Story, That One*) being a good example of a conscious trickster (see Gruber 2007) and Joe, the protagonist of "Joe the Painter and the Deer Island Massacre" (in *One Good Story, That One*), exemplifying a probably unconscious and in any case white trickster character.[12] All these trickster stories are involved with the rewriting/reconstruction of official "white" history from an Indigenous (or, in the case of "Joe the Painter," an unconventional white) perspective. The tricksters and the trickster discourse in these stories lure us into reconsidering the white man's heroic metanarratives, not coincidentally also called master narratives, and to see them from a new perspective.

A trickster story with a clearly historical context and reference is "A Coyote Columbus Story" (1992). The story, again, consists of a frame narrative and an embedded story and is also told by an Indigenous first-person narrator. In contrast to "One Good Story, That One," this narrator mostly speaks standard English, with some exceptions such as "Yes, I says" (121).[13] The story opens with a matter-of-course mixing of contemporary reality and time-honored myth, as is typical in King's narratologically hybrid stories: "You know, Coyote came by my place the other day. She was going to a party. She had her party hat and she had her party whistle and she had her party rattle. I'm going to a party, she says. Yes, I says, I can see that" (ibid.). This contemporary Coyote is clearly a female character, then, who soon tells the narrator that the party is in celebration of Christopher Columbus: "That is the one who found America. That is the one who found Indians" (ibid.). Confronted with the question whether the American continent was "discovered" (the white view) or "invaded" (the Indigenous view) by Europeans, the seemingly naïve Coyote is confused about which stance to take, not least because she read a (white-authored) history book that apparently does not tell the whole story. The Indigenous narrator thus tells her an inserted story about Old

13. Blending Indigenous and Western Traditions   197

Coyote (also female) and Christopher Columbus, interspersed with fragments of the biblical creation story, thus mixing two entirely different historical time periods and genres. The embedded story, told by the Indigenous storyteller, supplants the white view of history with a Native perspective: "But what happened to the Indians? There was nothing in that red history book about Christopher Columbus and the Indians.... If Christopher Columbus didn't find America and he didn't find Indians, who found these things? Those things were never lost, I says. Those things were always here. Those things are still here today" (126–27).

The story that the Indigenous narrator tells Coyote to make her take a more "politically correct" view of Native-white history and relations contrasts a playful and friendly yet rather reckless, foolish, and naïve Old Coyote with an interest-oriented, teleologically-minded Christopher Columbus, who sets foot on the American continent looking for China. Columbus's main motivation for his travels is an economic, exploitative one: "We got to find China. We got to find things we can sell.... Where is the gold?" (123). But since the Europeans do not find anything worth the trip, only "a monkey ... a parrot ... a fish ... a coconut" (124), they eventually decide to take all the Indigenous people with them and sell them in Europe. The noble European founding myth of America is deconstructed by rendering Columbus's arrival on the American continent as the threshold to when the dismal colonization of North America's Indigenous peoples by the Europeans started.[14] The story has a trickster-like twist to it (as also indicated toward its ending: "This world has enough problems already without a bunch of Coyote thoughts with tails," 127)—which reveals that it was Old Coyote who thought up Columbus in the first place, for the simple reason that she had no one else to play ball with her:

> Wait a minute, says old Coyote. What happened to my friends? Where are my Indians? You got to bring them back. Who's going to play ball with me?
> But Christopher Columbus didn't bring the Indians back and Old Coyote was real sorry she thought him up. She tried to take him back. But, you know, once you think things like that, you can't take them back. So you have to be careful what you think [126].[15]

Is this twist in the Coyote tale/tail a hint by the author that the Natives may be considered partly responsible for their fate? That they did not have a powerful agenda for their continent? That they were too friendly and naïve toward the invading Europeans at the outset? That they have internalized, as a result, a colonial mentality and cannot get rid of it, although they had the original advantage of being there first and having more knowledge of the continent? Or is this rather a swipe at individuals who are selfish and greedy, as tricksters tend to be, and who are not at all concerned with communal issues? It is with relativizing twists like these that King's hybrid cultural roots may be said to shine through occasionally—"wide-angle shots" (see above) indeed.

Fantastic Stories/Parables

Although King has also published stories written in a realist narrative style (see below), he has come to be associated mainly with the magic realist style most of his stories adhere to. As he told Constance Rooke: "I really love magic" (Rooke 1990, 69). The fantastic elements run the gamut from surrealist to supernatural to grotesque or even to slapstick style in his short fiction. As Eva Gruber comments, the "use of the grotesque produces texts that inherently defy the validity of conventional logic and accustomed frames of reference. The notion of the grotesque is based on surprise and incompatibility, that is, on the linking of elements from different areas and the sudden departure from reality to reveal a surreal, illogical, and unpredictable world" (2008, 107). The "logical" and deeper connection and meaning of such at first sight incompatible story elements have to be sought and decoded by the reader, who discovers that such unheard-of stories boil down to attractively narrated and poignantly resonant, meaningful parables of Indigenous life in North America. Consider three stories from *One Good Story, That One* (1993). In "How Corporal Colin Sterling Saved Blossom, Alberta, and Most of the Rest of the World as Well," suddenly and mysteriously stiff Indigenous characters are abducted—that is, saved from white treatment—by blue, silent, alien coyotes in space ships (see Davidson, Walton, and Andrews 2003, 18–26). In "Totem," totem poles, making all sorts of noises, keep popping up out of the blue into the silence of a museum. And in "A Seat in the Garden," an Indigenous man constantly haunts a garden, yet remains a spectral, untouchable figure.[16] In a pair of stories in *A Short History of Indians in Canada* (2005), animals all of a sudden massively invade the city, only to vanish totally ("Rendezvous"), or "little bombs" are used to configure human relationships ("Little Bombs").

Of this rich group of stories, I have selected "A Short History of Indians in Canada" (2005) for closer analysis. The title of this short short story is both apt and ironic. It is obviously a *short* history, because it is a very short story (encompassing only 617 words). It is a *short history*, because it is made short shrift of, from a white, reductive perspective. And it is a short *history*, as it may indeed be seen as a parable that reductively and sarcastically condenses Native history in Canada onto a few pages. The story is set in Toronto, most of it on Bay Street, in the city's financial district, at nighttime. Bob Haynie, a businessman, is a first-time visitor to Toronto and is "looking for some excitement" at night ("Short History," 1). The doorman of his hotel sends him to Bay Street, without further explanation, where the businessman is in for quite a surprise. It is "raining" Indians, so to speak. They are flying in flocks through the air and, simultaneously allured and blinded by the lights, into the sides of the highrises, dropping down—dazed, injured, or even dead—onto the pavement. The ornithological comparison of Natives with birds in the story is obvious ("flock of Indians," "fly"). Two municipal workers, Bill and Rudy, soon arrive to take care of the "falling Indians," so that "by the time the commuters show up, you'll never even know the Indians were here" (4). At nighttime, then, the Natives from various tribes, injuring or even killing themselves, are regarded as quite an attraction for whites ("A family from Alberta came through last week and didn't even see an Ojibway," 4), but in the morning, once traffic and white business life start again, they become a nuisance: "The dead ones we bag, says Rudy. The live ones we tag, says Bill. Take them to the shelter. Nurse them back to health. Release them to the wild" (3). Indigenous people, the story slyly suggests, are out of place in the city. Lured by the glittering wealth of the metropolis, they cannot thrive or even survive there because they seem to be uncivilized creatures of "the wild." They are regarded as "nomadic ... and migratory" (3) by the whites, as not belonging to the civilized city. They are the exotic Other, judged as one judges birds, "by the feathers," as is explained in guide books ("We got a book," 2).

At the end of the story, when the businessman out for some nocturnal fun returns to his hotel, thanking the doorman for his "spectacular" tip, King adds another sarcastic twist in that the white doorman calls upon "the cliché of the Vanishing Indian as an endangered species" (Gruber 2008, 108): "Not like the old days. The doorman sighs and looks up into the night. In the old days, when they came through, they would black out the entire sky" (4). This condescending remark reveals the story's scathing sarcasm, especially as it comes from a white Canadian and thereby from a member of the group that— in contrast to official ideology—has contributed to the decimation of the Native population, only to sentimentally and hypocritically bemoan it afterwards (see Gruber 2008, 108).

This short piece of comical tragedy exemplifies King's treatment of the situation of Indigenous people without the use of an Indigenous narrator (the story is written from a white perspective, and is nevertheless indirectly scathingly critical of it), without the use of Native mythology, and—all dialogues being by whites only—without any interference into the English language by Native language structures and vocabulary. Nevertheless, the story is one of the best examples of King's "voice pieces." There are no quotation marks for the large proportion of direct speech and dialogue in this text, which keeps the narrative mode of report to a minimum, is free from authorial comments, and uses hardly any description. Moreover, the writing frequently works with onomatopoeic words such as "Smack!" and "Whup!" to mimic the sound of the Natives crashing into the buildings and then down onto the sidewalks, so that one may extend Gibert's expression of "voice pieces" and speak of "sound pieces." The story is a good example to show that many of King's stories should be read out loud to experience the full effects of their oral/aural style. As Gibert proposes: "In this story, as in many others contained in the same volume, oral features function as narrative techniques that have been chosen by the author in order to deliberately promote more active, cooperative, or communal ways of reading/listening" (2006, 7).

Family Stories

The only group of stories that by and large does not explicitly concern itself with specifically Native themes is the group of family stories. This is also the text group in which King mostly adheres to the realist tradition of storytelling, without any admixture of surreal elements (which in his other groups of stories are usually connected to Indigenous people or Indigenous mythology). Since most of these family stories are not particularly striking or unusual as to their themes, motifs, and narrative styles, it is perhaps no wonder that they comprise a lesser-known part of King's short fiction oeuvre. Nevertheless, three stories of this group ("Trap Lines" and "Magpies" in *One Good*, "The Dog I Wish I Had, I Would Call It Helen" in *Short History*) have been anthologized. Not coincidentally, two of these reprinted stories do center on Indigenous families, with "Magpies" and "Trap Lines" also integrating some Native folklore concerning burial and hunting rites.

Almost one third of King's stories, that is, eight of the 30 stories in his two short story collections, belong to the group of family stories and, although less known, most of them are among his best, including "Magpies," about how to bury the grandmother properly—according to Native or Christian burial rites—and "Trap Lines," an elaborately constructed and moving father-son story, both from *One Good Story, That One* (1993). Whereas all 10 stories in this earlier collection are concerned with themes of Native life, the second collection, *A Short History of Indians in Canada* (2005), also features several stories that hardly, if at all, focus on Indigenous issues. This also shows in the five family stories from the later collection, none of which are predominantly concerned with Indigenous characters. In fact, the moving family stories "The Dog I Wish I Had, I Would Call It Helen," "States to Avoid," and "Domestic Furies" seem to feature only white protagonists, with only Faye, a one-night stand for the deserted husband in "States to Avoid," being the (Indigenous) exception. And although the mother-daughter story "Not

Counting the Indian, There Were Six" (in *Short History*) gives an Indigenous character title prominence, the family at the center of the story is white. The eponymous "Indian" is only an off-stage presence, as one of in fact seven husbands whom daughter Beth had been married to before she drowned while scuba-diving. Most of King's family stories revolve around the separation of couples and, sometimes, the effects of these separations not only on the partners themselves, but also on the children.[17]

A representative story of this group is "Domestic Furies" (2005). The three protagonists—mother, father, and son—are apparently white. The story is rendered in the first-person by an almost 11-year-old narrator whose focus alternates between his mother and his father, just as he himself alternates spending time with each of them. Reminiscent of Raymond Carver's minimalist narrative style, the story effectively omits and simultaneously evokes the very issues the reader would be most interested in: Why did the father leave the mother? Why are they separated although they are obviously still preoccupied with, if not haunted by, each other? Why do they not talk directly with each other but communicate mainly via the child? What effects does this state of affairs have on their child? What did the parents say to each other when they briefly met after the theater performance? What is the outcome and consequence of this conversation? What about the irritatingly open ending? The story very adeptly manages to render the speechlessness between two former partners who obviously cannot live with nor without each other. Their son helplessly tries to mediate between them, but again and again clashes with the walls of silence and ambivalence that the parents have erected around themselves, as illustrated by the following "conversation" between mother and son: "My mother ... told me about how life was always full of surprises, that some of them were good and some of them were bad. 'Does that mean Dad is coming home?' 'What did I just say?'" ("Domestic Furies," 189). With stories such as these, King proves that the quality and attraction of his short stories are by no means only to be associated with his clever and humorous handling of Indigenous themes from a predominantly Indigenous perspective, but that he also succeeds in the (originally white) short fiction tradition of (psychological) realism.

Conclusion

In his short fiction, across the board, Thomas King's tragicomic stories about the pitfalls of being Indigenous in a white-dominated North American context have enriched the tradition of Native North American writing just as much as they have Canadian literature in general. The thematic and technical range of his short fiction is considerable. King's stories demonstrate his sheer inventiveness, playfulness, unpredictability, knowledge of Indigenous and white mythology, history, and literature, his commitment to the Indigenous cause, and last but not least his *joie de narration*. King—who says that in his Indigenous material he writes for rather than on behalf of the Indigenous community (Gibert 2001, 69; see also Rooke 1990, 72–73)—proves himself as an engaged storyteller, with, in the final analysis, a political agenda. His storytelling also proves his fellow Indigenous writer Gerald Vizenor right when he claims that "writers in general are tricksters in the broadest sense of disruption…. I don't think it's worth the energy unless the formulas can be broken down, unless the expectations of the readers are disrupted" (qtd. in Bruchac 1987, 294). With his "wide-angle shots" at white complacency and hypocrisy toward Indigenous people, Thomas King tells stories that may wound, but, not least due to their overriding humorous impact, do not antagonize white readers. On the contrary, his stories may contribute to greater understanding and tolerance between very different cultures sharing the same continent.

14

Crossing Generic Borders
Margaret Atwood's Short Prose Collection The Tent

Versatile writer Margaret Atwood is a generic wizard (as I elaborated in *Engendering Genre: The Works of Margaret Atwood*, 2009). A highly successful writer of novels, short stories, short fictions, and one short story cycle, poetry and prose poetry, literary and cultural criticism, children's fiction, and even comic strips, a few screenplays, libretti, a stage drama, and a graphic novel (see Nischik 2009, 1–3), Atwood seems to be out to constantly reinvent herself and her literary art. A case in point are her works of fictional short prose, which one may divide into, first, short stories proper and, second, so-called "short fictions," prose poems, and fictional essays. The latter category in particular—which includes the three collections *Murder in the Dark*, *Good Bones*, and *The Tent*—exemplifies such a variety of different subgenres and not neatly classifiable formats of fictional short prose that scholars and critics have resorted to a considerable number of different terms and generic labels (such as "short shorts" or "flash fiction," see S. Wilson 2003, 20–22; Nischik 2009, 50) to get a generic grasp of these texts. In fact, if one wanted to present an audience, a readership, or a class with the formal variability of short fiction by way of referring to the works of a single writer, there would probably be no more suitable example than Atwood, especially concerning her three collections of "short fictions," the collective term most frequently used for these varied texts, which are shorter than short stories (for a treatment of Atwood's short prose oeuvre especially from a gender perspective, see Chapter 7).

Also and especially in her short fiction, then, Atwood has produced "boundary works"[1] of large interest for anyone involved with questions of genre and with short fiction. Her genre-bending works are in line with what postmodern esthetics and genre theory have diagnosed as "the arbitrariness and undecidability of generic boundaries" (Delville 1997, 57). Atwood herself, when asked about genre affiliation concerning one of her short texts ("Happy Endings" from *Murder in the Dark*), answered in a reserved manner, calling these kinds of works "permutational fiction," "mutations," and "aberrations," and stressing that she did not know "what sort of creature" a certain of her pieces was. She also indirectly referred to the fact that her handling of genre is connected to her frequent undermining of conventions and of the reader's expectations:

> This is the way such a mutant literary form unsettles us. We know what is expected, in a given arrangement of words; we know what is supposed to come next. And then it doesn't.
>
> It was a little disappointing to learn that other people had a name for such aberrations, and had already made up rules [Atwood 1988 and 1989; qtd. in S. Wilson 2003, 22].

At the risk of disappointing the author further (but certainly not with the intention of making up rules), I will look at Atwood's more recent collection of fictional short prose, *The Tent*. It appeared in the same year as her first short story cycle, *Moral Disorder* (2006), thereby stressing the range of her short fiction production as well as her productivity in this genre. *The Tent* is made up of three sections and comprises 35 pieces. In fact, the back cover describes the book as containing "fictional pieces," and I would agree that this is a fittingly inclusive term in the context—for these texts are "fictional" (referring to their general category of expression) and they are small fragments ("pieces," referring to their form). As to the panorama of various text formats represented in *The Tent*, there are two short pure dialogues, which verge on drama (even leaving out any narrative inquit forms: "Bottle"; "Take Charge"); two poems ("The Animals Reject Their Names and Things Return to Their Origins"; "Bring Back Mom: An Invocation"); three fables ("Our Cat Enters Heaven"; "Chicken Little Goes Too Far"; "King Log in Exile"); as well as several episodic rewritings of previous literature ("Horatio's Version," concerning *Hamlet*) and of mythology ("It's Not Easy Being Half-Divine"; "Salome Was a Dancer"; "Resources of the Ikarians"; "Nightingale"). Although several of these texts have a pronounced narrative impulse (especially the fables and the adaptations of myths), indeed do tell imaginary, very short stories, the predominant impression the volume conveys is at least as much a reflective as a narrative one. This is also due to the fact that the majority of the texts (those not mentioned by title so far) belongs to a text format that is hard to classify since it derives from what Linda Hutcheon, in a different context, has called "interzones" (Hutcheon 1992, 12): These particular texts are not quite short short stories, not quite parables, not quite essays. I suggest the term "essay-fictions"[2] for this majority of hybrid texts in *The Tent* and would like to focus on these particular texts in what follows.

14. Crossing Generic Borders

The hybrid term "essay-fiction" tries to capture the fact that many of these texts are written in the reflective "I" (or even "you") form and show us a mind at work pondering some problem or state of affairs rather than narrating a sequence of events. Yet these "musings" or "mini-musings"[3] are not passed off as coming straightforwardly from the author's pondering mind, as in a traditional essay. Instead, they are clothed in fictional, literary frameworks—such as the frame of a "narrated" event, as in "Winter's Tales," or a quasi-poetical use of language, as in "No More Photos"—which also in fact brings some of these texts close to, or even makes them indistinguishable from, prose poetry. Atwood thus bridges the difference between what H. G. Widdowson in another context has described as "static focusing, which seeks significance in the representation of a certain state of being" and "narrative projection, which seeks significance in dynamic relationship between events" (qtd. in Stanzel 1990, 27). The narrative impulse in these texts is toned down in favor of metaphorical, symbolic, parabolic meaning rather than referential meaning (cf. Stanzel 1990, 23), extending the range of significance toward the abstract, toward generalization, and sometimes even toward the archetypal. It is striking that these essay-fictions in *The Tent* are often concerned with an aging writer persona and with aspects of the writer's craft and profession, thus giving these texts an autobiographical as well as metapoetical twist, while at the same time working against this by the fictional/narrative elements used.

A good example is "Encouraging the Young" (17–19). The text begins straightforwardly, like an essay, about an older writer's stance toward the ambitious young (writers): "I have decided to encourage the young. Once I wouldn't have done this, but now I have nothing to lose. The young are not my rivals" (17). But even in the first paragraph, the *poet* shines through by adding in metaphorical style: "Fish are not the rivals of stones" (17). The rather factual first paragraph is followed by a second paragraph that starts to twist the writer's self-expression in an odd, unreal direction by doing away with a reasonable, proportionate distribution of praise: "I will encourage them en masse. I'll fling encouragement over them like rice at a wedding. They are *the young*, a collective noun.... I'll encourage them indiscriminately, whether they deserve it or not. Anyway, I can't tell them apart" (17). This rather factual statement is immediately followed by a poetical version: "So I will stand cheering generally, like a blind person at a football game: noise is what is required, waves of it, invigorating yelps to inspire them to greater efforts" (17). The older writer's persona writes from an apparently superior, cynical stance: "There you are, young! What is a big, stupid, clumsy mess like the one you just made—let me rephrase that—what is an understandable human error, but a learning experience? Try again! Follow your dream!" (18). The "I's" (ironically) self-congratulatory attitude—"What a fine and shining person I am ... now I'm generosity itself. Affably I smile and dole" (18)—is at the end of the text openly called into question by the writer herself: "My motives are less pure than they appear. They are murkier. They are lurkier ... and I see that I am dubious" (19). The writer persona then indirectly compares herself to an old, fairy-tale witch who beckons with an "increasingly knobbly forefinger," as she lures the ambitious young to "*a lavish gingerbread house, decorated with your name in lights*" (19; original emphasis). In other words, "Encouraging the Young" develops into a literary Hansel and Gretel story, in the writer's mind, with the writer as an ensnaring witch who knows that the ambitious young can hardly resist the glaring temptations of fame: "*Wouldn't you like to walk into it* [the lavish gingerbread house] ... *stuff your face on sugary fame? Of course you would!*" (19; original emphasis).

Is "Encouraging the Young" Atwood's partly factual, partly fictional response to hoards of younger writers clamoring for her attention and support? Is cynicism an understandable reaction under the circumstances? Or is this text a warped reflection of envy on the aged writer's part toward "the young," who have everything still ahead of them? Is this text purely fictional or does it rather show us Atwood's/a writer's mind at work, analyzing her own attitudes and motives, as in an essay, but with fictional padding and twists? Significantly, the last sentence of the text is resoundingly ambivalent, casting, at second glance, also a new, positive light on the text as a whole: "I won't fatten them in cages, though.... I won't drain out their life's blood. They can do all those things for themselves" (19). Even though it is put in negative terms, this concluding sentence may suggest that the younger writers are not dependent on the older one, after all, but can strike out on their own. The narrator's superior, if not seemingly arrogant stance toward the young is thus relativized at the end of the text and further complicates its meaning. The "actions" told by the narrator are self-reflective, showing us a writer's ponderings, rather than telling a story.

The essay-fiction "Voice" also oscillates between the essayistic rendering of apparent "facts" on the one hand and the clothing of these "facts" in clearly fictional terms on the other hand. The piece may be regarded as a kind of fictional, autobiographical mini-essay concerning the writer's career, focusing on the most important asset for her profession, her "voice," that is, her writing talent and expressive prowess. The text starts out straightforwardly, as if it was part of a writer's autobiography: "I was given a voice. That's what people said about me. I cultivated my voice, because it would be a shame to waste such a gift" (21). But then, as in the text just discussed, the writing soon turns poetical ("I pictured this voice as a hothouse plant, something luxuriant, with glossy foliage and the word *tuberous* in the name, and a musky scent at night," 21). To render the exceptionality of this writer's talent, the text thus resorts to imaginative, metaphorical rather than referential or reportorial techniques as we would expect in a traditional autobiographical text. The essay-fiction develops an extended metaphor about the writer in attentive, even loving communication with her "voice," which is discursively rendered as a separate entity of the writer, similar to a life-long companion, with the voice being partly personified: "We went everywhere together.... We sit in this hotel room, my voice and I ... I've given it all my love, but it's only a voice, it can never love me in return" (21, 22, 23).

Mainly through personification, animalization, and animation of the writer's "voice"—which one would usually regard as something abstract, that is, as the writer's talent—the text has an alienating effect on the reader, just as the writer seems to have an ambivalent, alienated stance toward her talent. The alienating effect particularly derives from those passages where the writer's "voice" is compared to a plant (vine), animal (frog), or dangerous creature (vampire), which hampers, constricts, and threatens the writer, and in the final image of the text even endangers her life:

> I nurtured it, I trained it, I watched it climb up inside my neck like a vine [21].
>
> What people saw was me, what I saw was my voice, ballooning out in front of me like the translucent greenish membrane of a frog in full trill [21–22].
>
> Soon it will be time for us to go out. We'll attend a luminous occasion, the two of us, chained together as always.... Then we'll descend to the foyer, glittering like ice, my voice attached like an invisible vampire to my throat [23].

In a highly condensed manner, the text thus presents a writer's career by focusing, synecdochically, on the writer's relation to her "voice." This almost exclusive focus on and nurturing of her writing capabilities proves professionally highly successful,[4] yet it is at the same time constricting and even life-threatening. The text also addresses the writer's fear of her being completely dependent on her "voice," in other words, that her personal fate is linked to her writing output. The aging writer, who presents herself as heartless (completely dominated by her "voice"; cf. also "glittering like ice," 23), is nevertheless painfully aware that in due course decay—of her writerly capabilities, to which she seems to reduce her person—is inevitable: "It's begun to happen, the shrivelling. Only I have noticed it so far. There's the barest pucker in my voice, the barest wrinkle. Fear has entered me, a needleful of ether, constricting what in someone else would be my heart" (22).

To briefly undergird the thin generic borderlines in this short prose collection, I would argue that the strong title piece "The Tent," for instance, is a prose poem rather than an example of essay-fiction, the main reason being that this text does not even try to give the impression that the writer straightforwardly and "truthfully" addresses a reader and tells her or him about the writer's stance on a certain topic. Right from the beginning, "The Tent" proceeds on a metaphorical, parabolic level and also clearly foregrounds language, as a poem or indeed prose poem does: "You're in a tent. It's vast and cold outside, very vast, very cold. It's a howling wilderness.... Many things are howling out there, in the howling wilderness" (143). "The Tent" is a highly condensed rendering of the writer's position in the world as Atwood envisions it. The presentation of this view in an imaginative, metaphorically distanced rather than "factual" manner is signaled from the very first word on: "You." Thus, the reflecting writer does not use the essayistic first-person form here (as in the previously discussed texts), but distances her rendering even further by using the "conative" (Jakobson 1964, 355) form of address "you." Matt Del-Conte has shown how second-person narration is defined along the axis of narratee and by a frequent coincidence of narratee and speaker-protagonist.[5] The second-person point of view as used in Atwood's collection *The Tent*[6] indeed largely does *not* invite the reader to imagine her- or himself in the narrator's place, as is often the case with you-narration (cf. Bruce Morrissette qtd. in DelConte 2003, 208). Rather, Atwood's "you" is a personalized, yet distanced and self-reflective "you," stressing the self-referential impression given by this collection as a whole: that of an intellectual, authorial mind in conversation with itself.

With this self-reflective kind of you-form of address[7] we come full circle, because many of the essay-fictions in *The Tent*, too, show us a writerly mind trying to come to terms with challenging issues, such as aging or the tortuous creative process (cf. Rao 2009, who stresses the motifs of the forest and, particularly, the maze in *The Tent*). Atwood does this in a self-referential, meditative, only partly "fictional" manner, most often using the first-person form. As these are essay-fictions and not straightforward essays, this "I" is still a persona and should not, of course, be fully equated with Atwood, the writer—clearly, one should give imaginative and fictional strategies their due. Yet the writer's persona in *The Tent*'s essay-fictions seems so quintessentially Atwoodian, with recognizable "facets of self and self-image" (Washington 2006), that several reviewers have compared this collection to literary notebooks, sketch books, or scrapbooks.[8] Indeed, some of these pieces are so condensed and quizzical that Atwood sometimes seems to speak more to herself than to her readers. She playfully experiments with form and with how to merge significant bits of reality with a fictional vision and presentation.[9] In doing so, that is, in blending elements of the essay with that of (short) fiction, Atwood probes the borderlines between factual and fictional narration, which Jean-Marie Schaeffer has differentiated as follows: "Factual narrative *is* referential whereas fictional narrative has no reference (at least not in 'our' world) ... factual narrative advances *claims* of referential truthfulness whereas fictional narrative advances no such claims.... In factual narrative author and narrator are the same person whereas in fictional narrative the narrator (who is part of the fictional world) differs from the author (who is part of the world we are living in)" (Schaeffer 2009, 98; original emphasis).[10] Atwood's hybrid writing style in *The Tent* may be visualized with one of her drawings, seven of which are included in that volume. The one that accompanies her essay-fiction "Voice," for instance, pinpoints the condensed mixture of factual and fictional presentation that I have discussed: A female figure climbs up a staircase, to some extent realistically enough, but then perhaps also symbolically advancing to the sky—representing success, fame, and happiness, but also death—with her surrealistically visualized, revered, and extraordinary "voice" leading the way.

I have indicated above how Atwood further inscribes her writing into the history of short prose with her collection *The Tent*. Here, too, she proves most experimental in the short prose format. Whereas her earlier collection *Murder in the Dark* (1983) contains predominantly prose poems, her more recent collection *The Tent* often features essay-fictions, in which the narrative impulse is reduced in favor of a reflective one. In an indirect, "fictionalized" manner, these texts show us "a writer's mind working to understand itself" (Morano 2003, 37–38) and trying to come to terms with problematic issues by using self-referential, meditative methods. Atwood's essay-fictions distinguish themselves from the simple essay form by the pronounced fictional admixtures that designate these texts as a hybrid subgenre of short prose. In her bending, twisting, crossing, and transcending of genre boundaries, Atwood proves to be an experimental if not avant-garde practitioner of a genre that already Brander Matthews, one of the earliest American theorists of the short story, had hyperbolically characterized as having "limitless possibilities."[11]

Chapter Notes

Introduction

1. "Writers in French Canada (Quebec as well as French-speaking parts of Ontario, Manitoba, and New Brunswick) were producing short pieces as early as the 1830s, although recognizable short fiction really began with the Abbé Henri-Raymond Casgrain in the 1860s" (Gadpaille 2001, 2899). See also Eibl 2008a.

2. See, for instance, Gadpaille 1988 on Crawford's story "Extradited": "in spite of a ragged narrative and Crawford's infelicitous way with words," 11–12; or Dean 2000, xiv: "Parker's habit of inventing locales, 'Indian' legends and 'Indian tribes,' is stunningly racist as well as frighteningly inaccurate.... The traces of racist and masculinist ideologies are clearly identifiable in Roberts' representation of animals, and in Thomson's French Canadians."

Chapter 2

1. For a general comparative evaluation of modernism in the United States and Canada see Nischik 2016, 27–36.

2. Scofield 2006, 107. This rise in significance not only refers to the commercial magazines but also to the little magazines. Cf. also Willa Cather's statement: "Writing ought either to be the manufacture of stories for which there is a market demand—a business as safe and commendable as making soap or breakfast foods—or it should be an art, which is always a search for something for which there is no market demand, something new and untried, where the values are intrinsic and have nothing to do with standardized values" (1992 [1920], 939–40).

3. In fact, numerous short prose narratives were written and published in Canada already around the middle of the nineteenth century, though they have been largely ignored by processes of canon formation and had less of an influence on the development of the short story genre in Canada. These earlier narratives include sketches of pioneer life by authors such as Susanna Moodie and Catharine Parr Traill, popular sentimental fiction by May Agnes Fleming, and pieces of social critique by Harriet Vaughn Cheney, and others. For a collection of women's short fiction of the early to mid-nineteenth century, see McMullen and Campbell 1993. For a brief survey of the short story in Canada before modernism see the introduction.

4. See, for instance: "Most of his novels are now seldom read. Even during his lifetime, it seems to have been understood that whatever enduring name Anderson would have would depend on his short fiction" (Small 1994, xi).

5. See Turgenev's book of related sketches *Annals of a Sportsman*, an Anderson favorite; see Small 1994, 8–9.

6. On literary relations between Stein and Anderson see Wagner 1980.

7. For a long list of U.S. writers apparently influenced by Anderson, see Papinchak 1992, ix. Cf. also Raymond Carver's statement: "The short story writer's task is to invest the glimpse with all that is in his power" (1986, 27).

8. Qtd. in Curry 1975, 85. *The Writer's Book* was left uncompleted at the time of Anderson's sudden death in 1941, but one of the most important aspects of this text is the insight it provides concerning Anderson's esthetics of the short story; see ibid., lii–lxv.

9. "The Rabbit-pen" (which remained uncollected) was Anderson's first short story to be published and the only one to appear in the respected commercial magazine *Harper's*, in 1914. It was written to prove that he was able to publish successful commercial stories. This story was a kind of antithesis to the modernist short story he then set out to create.

10. Knister was appointed Canadian correspondent for this magazine and became associate editor of *The Midland*. He was also the first Canadian writer to publish in *This Quarter*, alongside such writers as Ernest Hemingway, James Joyce, and Ezra Pound.

11. So far, three collections of Knister's stories are available; see Knister 1972, 1975c, 1976a. Knister's collected poetry also appeared posthumously: *Collected Poems of Raymond Knister*, ed. Dorothy Livesay (Toronto: Ryerson, 1949). Knister wrote most of his poetry in the 1910s. In the 1920s he concentrated on fiction and nonfictional prose.

12. See also: "My poems and stories were so Canadian and came so directly from the soil that Canadian editors would have nothing to do with them" (Knister 1975a, 162).

13. See a contemporary review: "Mr. Knister has performed adequately a heavy task and a real service. He has brought together in one volume seventeen of the best Canadian stories, including old favorites which everybody knows, but including also to our great debt some treasures which would be lost to practically all of us if they had not been rescued from the files of periodicals" (J. D. Robins 1928 qtd. in Burke 1979–80, 54).

Knister dedicated the book to Duncan Campbell Scott, whom he thought the best writer of short stories Canada had had up to this point (see Scott's *In the Village of Viger*, 1896). Knister's anthology includes stories by Morley Callaghan, Merrill Denison, Norman Duncan, Stephen Leacock, Thomas Murtha, Gilbert Parker, Margery L. C. Pickthall, Charles G. D. Roberts, Mazo de la Roche, Duncan Campbell Scott, and Edward William Thomson, as well as lesser-known writers.

14. Knister was born and raised on his parents' farm in southwestern Ontario. He also worked on this farm for several years (1920–1923), which were indeed the years in which he became a short story writer; see his so-called "farm stories."

15. Knister, like Anderson, spent a few months at college—in his case Victoria College at the University of Toronto—but then left college and retreated to the parental farm owing to an influenza epidemic at the time, never to go back to college.

16. In 1924 Knister completed a list of his readings of world literature since he was 14, and he claimed that he had read about one hundred books a year; see Knister 1975a, 161; Trehearne 1989, 65–66.

17. "The best of the American short-story writers, among whom may be mentioned ... Sherwood Anderson" (Knister 1975b, 148).

18. See the parallels between "I Want to Know Why" and a statement on horses in Anderson's *Memoirs*: "Tears came into my eyes and a lump into my throat. It was my first love. Oh the beautiful, the courageous and aristocratic creatures. I grew sick with envy of the drivers" (qtd. in Small 1994, 209).

19. Knister's "The First Day of Spring" does not count among his most radically modernist stories, yet it is one of his best. "Elaine" (1925), for instance (his fifth story), overuses ambiguity, allusion, ellipsis, and the portrayal of consciousness to the point of obscurity, as does "The Loading" (1924). Stylistic inconsistencies, such as unclear pronoun referents, clumsy sentence rhythms, and awkward expressions occasionally disturb the quality of Knister's innovative stories.

20. An even earlier publication was "A Divine Gesture" in *The Double Dealer* (May 1922), yet this story is not generally listed in the Hemingway bibliographies and did not make it into his short story collections.

21. The original *in our time* published in Paris in 1924 consisted of 18 short vignettes. Two pieces, "A Very Short Story" and "The Revolutionist," were expanded into longer stories while the remaining 16 vignettes became the interchapters between stories in the later *In Our Time*, published in New York in 1925.

22. Hemingway's short story oeuvre: *Three Stories & Ten Poems* (Paris: Contact, 1923); *in our time* (Paris: Three Mountains Press, 1924); *In Our Time* (New York: Boni and Liveright, 1925); *Men without Women* (New York: Scribner, 1927); *Winners Take Nothing* (New York: Scribner, 1933); *The Fifth Column and the First Forty-nine Stories* (New York: Scribner, 1938); *The Nick Adams Stories* (New York: Scribner, 1972); *The Complete Short Stories of Ernest Hemingway* (New York: Scribner, 1987). All of these collections contain original material, although sometimes partly also reprints from earlier publications; other collections not mentioned here contain only reprints.

23. Morley Callaghan's short story collections: *A Native Argosy* (New York: Scribner, 1929); *Now That April's Here and Other Stories* (New York: Random House, 1936); *Morley Callaghan's Stories* (Toronto: Macmillan, 1959); *The Lost and Found Stories of Morley Callaghan* (Toronto: Exile, 1985). Further later collections (*The Morley Callaghan Reader*, 1997; *The New Yorker Stories*, 2001; *The Complete Stories*, vols. 1–4, 2003) encompass only reprints from his earlier collections.

24. See Callaghan's report of these events in Callaghan 1979 [1963], 241–55. Callaghan still wrote in 1981 about this boxing fight and its aftermath, including the many different reports of the fight Hemingway had supposedly given over the years (Callaghan 2008b [1981], 357). On biographical issues concerning Callaghan see Boire 1994.

25. Hemingway 1932, 183; see also Hart 1957.

26. The only exception was Raymond Knister, whom Callaghan regarded as a kindred spirit (and vice versa); see the critical brief note in Callaghan 1979, 56–57; and, more positively, Callaghan 2003a [1964]; Weaver 1958, 6–8; on Knister's view of Callaghan see Knister 1975a, 165–66.

27. In the *Paris Review* interview, Hemingway mentions James Joyce and Ezra Pound along with Stein as writers he "respects" (see Hemingway 1958, 71); he does not mention Callaghan in the interview (nor does he do so in his memoirs of the Paris years, *A Moveable Feast*, 1964).

28. Translation of "'Ha perduto qualque cosa, Signora?'" in the story (324).

29. See in the story: "As though making the first move in a game, Joe leaned forward suddenly, and the boy, lowering his head, shuffled a few feet away" (155).

30. Cf. Sherwood Anderson's example of an apple in his description of his writing credo above, or Callaghan's own use of an apple in his own such description: "Strip the language and make the style, the method ... all the one thing.... Cézanne's apples. The appleness of apples. Yet just apples" (Callaghan 1979 [1963], 148).

31. On these narratological questions see, for instance, Cohn 1983, Chapter 2; Nischik 1991, Chapter 5.1 and 5.2, esp. p. 148.

32. Similarly, see Morley 1978: "Contrary to Fraser Sutherland's thesis in *The Style of Innocence*, I would argue that the link [between Hemingway and Callaghan] was never stylistic. Certainly the young Callaghan admired Hemingway's prose. The real link, however, was a psychological one" (9).

33. On Anderson's early influence on Callaghan see Callaghan himself: "Sherwood Anderson published some of his stories in *The Smart Set*.... So I had this well of literature, of contemporary American literature, laid at my feet when I was nineteen (Callaghan in 1962, qtd. in Woodcock 1993, 14); see also Callaghan's essay "Saroyan and Anderson" in Callaghan 2008a, 311–14, for instance: "Anderson had meant so much to me when I was twenty. He gave me a whole world" (311). Callaghan indeed called Anderson, not Hemingway, his literary "father" (see Callaghan 1979 [1963], 49); see also Weaver 1958, 14–15; and Goetsch 2007, 96, 101–3.

34. See also G. Carr 1987, 187, 151–54. For a general comparative assessment of modernism in Canada and the United States see Nischik 2016, 27–36.

35. Cf. Norris 1984, 1: "Modernism is a development that came comparatively late to Canadian poetry and became the dominant mode in the 1940s, although there had been moderate intimations of it since 1914. By the time Modernism had fully established itself in this country, literature in most European countries and even in the United States had begun its 'Post-Modernist' period."

36. Irvine 2005, 1. Female Canadian modernists dealt with in Irvine 2005 are Louise Morey Bowman, Katherine Hale (see Campbell 2005), Anne Marriott, Elizabeth Smart, and Cecil Buller, indeed names (with the exception of Smart) largely unknown

even to many Canadianists. See also Irvine 2008; Brandt and Godard 2009.

37. Only in the twentieth century did realism decisively enter the Canadian short story, with Sara Jeannette Duncan and Frederick Philip Grove (cf., however, D. C. Scott's *In the Village of Viger*).

Chapter 3

1. She retired from writing in 2013, a few months before she was awarded the Nobel Prize; see Chapter 4.

2. Jean Barman, *The West Beyond the West: A History of British Columbia*. Third ed. Toronto: University of Toronto Press, 2007, 534; Carolyn Heiman, "Checkout Time for Crystal Court: Condo Tower Proposed for Site of Affordable Downtown Motel." *Times Colonist* [Victoria, British Columbia] 20 Nov. 2007: A3.

Chapter 4

1. Alice Munro in an interview; source could not be reconstructed.

2. See Resnick 2012, 122: "A writer's writer ... is a writer that other writers read, and admire, and study, and try to learn from. And sometimes fall a little bit in love with."

3. In Germany, for instance, *Too Much Happiness* was number 29 in the hardcover list on October 2, 2010, but after winning the Nobel Prize, it made it to number one on the paperback list on October 28, 2013. In a review of *The Beggar Maid* on December 4, 1981, in the German weekly newspaper *Die Zeit*, Munro was called a "still unknown Canadian author here" (my translation), although this could only refer to the German general readership at the time, since in German academic circles she was already well known; in a review from December 2, 2000, in the *Frankfurter Allgemeine Zeitung* of *The Love of a Good Woman*, however, Munro is called a "renowned author" (my translation) in Germany.

4. It is, perhaps, significant that Munro has received genre-related prizes to a lesser extent (yet there are also fewer of them), such as the PEN Malamud Award for Excellence in Short Fiction or the Canadian Authors Association's Jubilee Award for Short Stories (in 1997).

5. On *The New Yorker*'s potential influence on Munro's work, see Beran 1999. See also Munro's "Author's Note" prefacing *The Love of a Good Woman*: "Stories in this collection that were previously published in *The New Yorker* appeared there in very different form."

6. As Howells concurs: "with an accompanying sense of individual lives scrolling out over many decades" (Howells 2003, 54).

7. The quote is from Eliot's poem "Burnt Norton," in *Collected Poems 1909–1963*. London: Faber and Faber, 1963, 191.

8. "So lying alongside our world was Uncle Benny's world like a troubling distorted reflection, the same but never at all the same" (Munro, "The Flats Road," in *Lives*, 26).

9. See Munro's answer to an interviewer's question regarding the revision of *Who*: "Oh, it's the most confused revision in history" (Struthers 1983, 29 *passim*).

10. Considering that Munro had a say, of course, in the choice of stories for her *Selected Stories*, Howells comments: "Only *Lives of Girls and Women* was ever published as a 'novel' and its omission from her *Selected Stories* would indicate that she wishes it to be considered as a novel" (Howells 1998, 157, n.35).

Chapter 5

1. Theoretical and text-analytic considerations of the short story cycle in general have been undertaken, for instance, by Ingram 1971; Mann 1989; Dunn and Morris 1995. On the American short story cycle see Kennedy 1995. On the short story cycle specifically in Canada see Godard 1989 and Lynch 2001. Kuttainen 2010 deals with the Canadian, Australian, and American "Short Story Composite."

2. On the history and the problems of printing and the spread of literature in Canada see MacLaren and Potvin 1989, especially the contributions by Frank Davey, "Writers and Publishing in English-Canada," 13–25, and by George L. Parker, "Publishing in Nineteenth-Century Canada: Copyright and the Market for Books," 57–66; the Canadian subvention practice is illuminated in Ray Ellenwood, "Government Funding: The

Effect on Writers, Translators and their Associations," 77–84. See also Lamonde, Fleming, and Black 2005.

3. See Munro's statement in a 1982 interview with Geoff Hancock: "I will probably, from now on, just go on writing books of short stories which are not connected as long as my publisher will consent to publish them. Of course, you know you are not very popular with a publisher if you do this. For years and years I would convince myself that I really had a novel there and I would take these ideas I had and bloat them up and I would start writing them and they would go all—they would just fall. It was just a total waste of time. And I'd become very depressed. So it took me a long time to reconcile myself to being a short-story writer" (Hancock 1987, 190).

4. "I feel very confused about the whole short story thing because … it wins one so little respect.… I now hesitate to put all that effort into something that is going to be regarded as fragmentary … and also from a practical viewpoint books of short stories are just not going to go anywhere in the bookstores. I know this" (Munro in Metcalf 1972b, 61).

5. In 1978, a short story collection (by John Cheever) made it to the bestseller lists; in 1984, the front page of *The New York Times Book Review* pronounced the definitive emancipation of the short story from the novel.

6. For an analysis of the integrative structural elements in *Lives*, see Garson 1994.

7. See also Munro in an interview: "This is why I'm not drawn to writing novels. Because I don't see that people develop and arrive somewhere. I just see people living in flashes. From time to time.… None of these stories will seem to connect. There are all these realities.… There are just flashes of things we know and find out. I don't see life very much in terms of progress" (in Hancock 1982, 88, 101).

8. On photography in general in Munro's work, see York 1988, 21–50. On the relation of literature and photography, see Rabb 1995; Bryant 1996; Breitbach 2012.

9. The quote is from Eliot's poem "Burnt Norton," in *Collected Poems 1909–1963*. London: Faber and Faber, 1963, 191. See also William Faulkner's remarks on the act of writing: "You catch this fluidity which is human life … and you stop it long enough for people to be able to see it" (in Gwynn and Blotner 1959, 239).

10. My translation from Lukács, *Die Theorie des Romans: Ein geschichtsphilosophischer Versuch über die Formen der großen Epik*. Darmstadt: Luchterhand, 1977, 98.

11. The proximity of Munro's narrative style (especially in her later works) to postmodernism is evident; on this, with reference to her short story collection published in 1986, *The Progress of Love*, see Howells 1990; for an extensive analysis of Munro's oeuvre following a post-structuralist approach, see Blodgett 1988.

Chapter 6

1. This is my translation of the original quote, which is taken from Ludwig Tieck, *Franz Sternbalds Wanderungen* (1798): "Wer sich der Kunst ergiebt … muß das, was er als Mensch ist und seyn könnte, aufopfern" (329).

2. Of the many by Metcalf, for instance, I will only mention "Keys and Watercress," "Gentle as Flowers Make the Stones," and "The Strange Aberration of Mr. Ken Smythe" (all in *Selected Stories;* see Nischik 1988 and, for the analysis of the latter artist story, Chapter 12); or see Rohinton Mistry's "Swimming Lessons" (*Tales from Firozsha Baag*) about the cultural shifts in the immigrant experience of a writer, Guy Vanderhaeghe's "Things As They Are?" (*Things As They Are?*) about a writer whose dream and ideal is a flawless Chekhov story, or Hugh Hood's "Where the Myth Touches Us" (*Flying a Red Kite*) about competition in writing and the father-son relationship.

3. Munro herself stated in 1978: "'The Office' is the most straightforward autobiographical story I have ever written" (Munro 1993, 192).

4. This quote is taken from Atwood's story "Unearthing Suite" (*Bluebeard's Egg*): "Perhaps it was then that I began the translation of the world into words. It was something you could do without moving" (275).

5. See also, for instance, Atwood's stories "Death by Landscape" and "Weight" in *Wilderness Tips* (1991) and "My Last Duchess" in *Moral Disorder* (2006).

6. My translation into English from Johann Wolfgang von Goethe's *Wilhelm Meisters Lehrjahre* (1795–1796), 433; German

original: "Des Menschen größtes Verdienst bleibt wohl, wenn er die Umstände soviel als möglich bestimmt und sich sowenig als möglich von ihnen bestimmen läßt."

Chapter 7

1. See my "Introduction" to *Engendering Genre* (2009), 1–15.
2. Atwood herself in the "Acknowledgments" in the book calls these texts "tales" (271).
3. For further details see Chapter 2 on Atwood's short fictions and prose poems in my book *Engendering Genre* (2009).
4. I earlier called this technique Atwood's "inverse poetics of intertextual minuteness" in my book *Engendering Genre* (2009, see Chapter 2 in that book).

Chapter 8

1. In addition to the stage of transition, the other two stages in ritual passages are "separation" (from the previous state) and "incorporation" (into the next state); see van Gennep 1977, e.g., 166. See also: "Van Gennep also noted that rites of separation, transition, and incorporation are not equally important or elaborated in specific rituals, and that the tripartite structure is sometimes reduplicated in the transitional period itself: in liminality proper, the sequence of separation, transition, and incorporation is often present" (Thomassen 2015, 43).
2. To give another example: Arpad Szakolczai states that liminality "is not only important for anthropologists but should be a key term of social thought and philosophy" (in Horvath, Thomassen, and Wydra 2015a, 33). See also: "Today the concept of liminality is used in such diverse fields as conflict studies, international relations, literature, business studies, consultancy, psychiatry, education, theater, leisure, arts, and popular culture" (Horvath, Thomassen, and Wydra 2015b, 7).
3. In line with German scholar Silvia Bovenschen, one may add here: "This is familiar: an older woman is younger than an old woman. How great must be the fear of old age that it even violates grammar" (Bovenschen 2015, 145; my translation into English).

4. See also: "A constructive attitude towards aging is that one recognizes advantages as well as disadvantages in growing old. Among the advantages, or at least the possibilities, of older adulthood are decreased responsibilities, increased discretionary time and income, an opportunity to attend less to trivial matters and focus more on things of greater importance, less susceptibility to the anxieties, vanities, and social pressures of youth and middle age, an increased acceptance of life and death, and less preoccupation with what other people think" (Aiken 2001, 4).
5. See also: "From a strictly medical viewpoint, age is assessed in terms of *functional capacity*—the ability to engage in purposeful activity ... a person can be old at either 40 or 80 years of age, depending on his or her overall health, attitude, and other circumstances" (Aiken 2001, 4). See also Erber 2013, 8–10.
6. See, for instance, in a preface to a book on aging in literature: "Literature, like other art forms, has given us a portrayal of aging throughout history. In poetry, drama, novels ... one can find conceptual attitudes toward aging" (Prisca von Dorotka Bagnell in Bagnell and Soper 1989, xxiii).
7. This is the title of a story dealing with memory in Alice Munro's collection *Hateship, Friendship, Courtship, Loveship, Marriage* (2001).
8. Alice Munro's "The Bear Came Over the Mountain" (1999, in *Hateship*) is a moving story about an aging female Alzheimer's patient and the drastic repercussions this disease, whose onset is usually in old/er age, has for her identity as well as her marriage and her husband. The story has also been successfully adapted to a film by Canadian director Sarah Polley under the title *Away from Her* (2006), starring Julie Christie and Gordon Pinsent.
9. For an interesting reading of this story from a slightly different perspective see Simal 2014, 71–75. The article traces how the narrated events, rendered from the patient's perspective, depict her developing Alzheimer's symptoms and "what it must feel like to be partially aware of the crumbling of memory ... of the gradual closedown of her brain ... that slow dimming of the mind's 'lights,' as she is unable to utter a word, 'to yell' for help" (74, 73).
10. See, for instance, Munro's stories

"The Peace of Utrecht" (*Dance*) and "Spelling" (*Who*).

11. Although the narrator's sex is not explicitly mentioned in this story, given the autobiographical bent of the short story cycle that it opens, we can presume that it is female.

12. See psychiatrist George Vaillant's statement: "Suicide ... reflects a fear of living, not of dying" (qtd. in Wyatt-Brown 1993, 8).

Chapter 9

1. Thomas King thus explains: "I am not originally from Canada, and the Cherokee certainly aren't a Canadian tribe. Now that becomes a problem only if you recognize the particular political line which runs between Canada and the U.S., and if you agree with the assumptions that that line makes. I think of myself as a Native writer and a Canadian writer. I doubt if I could call myself a Canadian Native writer, just because I'm not from one of the tribes up here" (King in Lutz 1991, 107).

2. The name "Fernhill," ironically, has idyllic connotations—it sounds like a soft, nice, comforting place to be. "Fern Hill" is also the title of a poem by Dylan Thomas which features a farm of that name and—again ironically in the context of the King story—deals with growing up.

3. Compare: "Carl Walther GmbH," "Culler Firearms, Inc.," "Fabbrica d'Armi Pietro Beretta," "Winchester Repeating Arms Company," "Smith & Wesson," the "Luger," a famous pistol produced by "Deutsche Waffen- und Munitionsfabriken," "Remington Arms Company, Inc.," "Sturm, Ruger & Company, Inc.," "Ingersoll Life-Line Company," "Sharps Rifle Manufacturing Company," "Browning Arms Company," and "Savage Arms."

4. One could perhaps also argue that due to the seniors' names being identical with brand names of guns, them being subjected to the life-threatening circumstances sketched in the story may be a kind of punishment for the amount of violence they brought into the world through their involvement in gun manufacturing. This interpretation would also provide a more special meaning to Joe's statement, "How do you think we got ourselves into this crazy mess in the first place" (102). I favor a more general interpretation that reads the seniors, too, as representative of a violence-prone U.S. American society. This also fits with such general statements as Joe's that "Man's a killer" (102).

5. See Mason, who earlier defends the seniors law system and at the end of the story radically becomes one of its prime agents: "'Joe, even if you did get to Canada, it wouldn't change a thing. People die. It's a natural process. What does it matter if you get run down by a drunk driver or shot by someone having a good time? At least here you're part of a delicate balance that keeps human beings from blowing themselves up'" (98).

6. Compare earlier in the text: "Mason especially liked the Ruby Hearts, a tiny, bright-red perennial that appeared suddenly in splashes and pools in the tall grass" (101).

7. "Preserve," rather than "Reserve," is another satirical allusion by King reminding us of historical parallels to the hoarding together of Natives in "Reserves"/"Reservations" in Canada/the United States, as is the undertone of how white society altogether does not value and care for the elderly as opposed to Native respect of elders.

8. The somewhat strange title of the story is actually a quotation from the Western film *The Missouri Breaks* of 1976, starring Jack Nicholson and Marlon Brando (United Artists Corporation, dir. Arthur Penn). The film, mainly set in Montana, features a deadly conflict between the rustler Logan and his gang and Braxton, a horse-breeder. At one point, Logan's gang crosses the Missouri River and the border to Canada to steal the horses of the Mounties ("supposed to be the best police in the world"), while the Mounties are distracted by a church service. On their way to Canada, the gang has to overcome several natural obstacles: the difficult crossing of the Missouri River, the mountains ("I wonder why they had to put Canada way the hell up here?"), and, not least, their fear of wild animals such as bears ("The closer you get towards Canada, the more things eat your horses"). Eventually, the Mounties on U.S. territory take all their stolen horses back from the rustlers, nonviolently, whereas Logan brutally kills Clayton and Braxton, Logan eventually being the lone survivor. The many parallels of the story by Thomas King to the filmic intertext *The Missouri River* are striking.

9. Liminality involves two discrete spaces (and/or phases), linked by a "limen" (Latin for "threshold," see also following note). In its positioning "in between," liminality lies between binaries (similar to Soja's "Thirdspace") and is characterized by indeterminacy, openness, "not any more here," and "not yet there," a space and phase where familiar conventions and norms are relativized or even seem to become invisible. The term "liminal" goes back to the second phase, the "liminal phase," in Arnold van Gennep's *Rites de passage* (1909; Engl. 1960), who defined these as "rites which accompany every change of place, state, social position and age" (qtd. in Turner 1969, 94)—border crossings thus may also be regarded as linked to *rites de passage* (on liminality see in greater detail Chapter 8). The concept of liminality is related to, but not the same as, Mary Louise Pratt's concept of the "contact zone," which refers to "social spaces where cultures meet, clash, and grapple with each other, often in contexts of highly asymmetrical relations of power, such as colonialism, slavery, or their aftermaths" (Pratt 1991, 34).

10. We may say, with Walter Benjamin, that the concept of "border" stresses the absolute, demarcation, separation, and exclusion, whereas the concept of "threshold" (Latin *limen,* see previous footnote on "liminality") stresses ambiguity and de-limitation; see Nischik and Rosenthal 2002. On the other hand, both borderlines/borders/border regions as well as thresholds may be seen as areas of transition between two "states" in the sense that through the act of crossing the border, the border becomes a threshold. I use the word "threshold" here mainly to refer to essential if not momentous changes, which, as the stories of this group also demonstrate, tend to be fully realized for their life-changing importance retrospectively.

11. Given these biographical resemblances between author and narrator, it is safe to assume that the text is at least autobiographically tinged, if not altogether autobiographical. I will therefore refer to the narrator as "she," although the text itself does not provide any direct information about the narrator's sex (except through her propensity for crying and her pronounced empathy, which are typically attributed to women).

12. On the American influence on Munro's work see Thacker 1994. Autobiographical references in the story indicate that the narrator is probably a writer (see p. 88), and the near drowning of the family's youngest daughter accords with Alice Munro's own experience with her two daughters as described in her daughter Sheila Munro's (auto-)biographical book *Lives of Mothers and Daughters: Growing Up with Alice Munro* (Toronto: McClelland and Stewart, 2001).

13. Born in the United States, but raised and now living in Canada, with dual citizenship.

14. It should be added here that this story of a travel writer was first published in 2002, but that the text in one of the two available published versions starts with a sub-headline printed in bold, "June 20, 1998," thus suggesting that the trip rendered in the narrative actually took place before 9/11. One may nevertheless ask in this case why the story of a travel writer who, according to this version of the story, writes about a trip of hers back in 1998 is published four years after that trip, that is, soon after 9/11. Does the author want to suggest by the addition of the travel date at the beginning of one of the two versions that the kind of random harassment and display of power has happened all the time in Canada–U.S. border crossings, particularly in cars?

15. The rendering of the Canadian female border patrol in King's story "Borders" suggests Canada's supposedly more liberal and tolerant attitude toward its Indigenous population; see, however, Gruber 2014.

16. This sentence on Victor Turner's concept is a slight adaptation of Gruber 2008, 359.

17. Similarly, see Wesley in connection with travel narratives: "Unconnected to formerly secure location, the traveller is rendered marginal ... but this forced detachment can also transform character in 'those who surrender themselves to the condition of motion' to produce an alternative to the static social self that is left behind" (1994, 178).

18. In the final analysis, these border narratives support what geoscientist Heather Nicol stated in the context of the post 9/11 politics of "risk society" and her explanation of the "continuing lack of transnational development among North American states," in contrast to Europe: that the "Good Old-Fashioned Nation States of North America" are not so old-fashioned, after all, because

"risk societies" (should) insist on keeping up and guarding their national borders (2006, 65).

Chapter 10

1. The first European settlement—by Irish, British, Scottish, and Welsh settlers—was probably established in 1862, from which Vancouver quickly developed from 1863 onward. Sources disagree on the exact dates. See also: "As early as 1891 the census of Canada documented more than 42 countries of origin among the 14,000 people living in the young city. Orientals even outnumbered Whites from continental Europe: 840 to 560" (Lu 2000, 23).

2. After Canada had signed the United Nations Declaration of Human Rights after the Second World War, the Chinese Exclusion Act contravened to this charter and was consequently repealed.

3. Indigenous peoples are not officially considered a visible minority group by Statistics Canada.

4. This is also the area where most of the at least 69 missing (and probably often murdered) women of Vancouver come from. See the arrest of Robert William Pickton, a pig farmer from suburban Port Coquitlam, in 2002, who was eventually found guilty of six of the murder charges in 2007 and was sentenced to jail for 25 years. See also Culhane 2003, 598.

5. In her story "Polka Partners, Uptown Indians and White Folks" (1999) (see Fairbridge 2005, 180, 183, 187).

6. Other stories about ethnic minorities in Vancouver in these two anthologies—by Shani Mootoo, Gabriel Szohner, Joy Kogawa, and Kevin Roberts—deal with East Indian, German, Japanese, and Australian characters. On a pluralistic approach to majority and minority writing in Canada see Padolsky 1997, for instance: "Canadians, regardless of origin, share the common characteristic of ethnicity, but differ in whether the ethnicity is of majority or minority status in Canadian society.... A pluralistic approach to majority and minority writing in Canada thus offers a much needed and highly promising perspective on Canadian literature. It brings majority ethnicity into focus and minority writing into an equitable, common framework" (26, 38).

7. See Gelfant 1995 concerning Ethel Wilson's fiction; on Wilson, see Chapter 1.

8. The four British bronze Landseer Lions at the base of Nelson's column in Trafalgar Square in London (unveiled in 1867) are called after Sir Edwin Henry Landseer (1802–1873), their creator. On the relevance of naming in a Canadian context see Kroetsch 1989.

9. Gender in this story, which is based on old legend, is handled highly traditionally, with an essentialized, mainly biological view of women.

10. See: "The room [the Indian ward at the hospital] was bright. It seemed to me that the four brown faces on the four white pillows should be happier and far more comfortable here than lying on mattresses on the hard floors in the village, with all the family muddle going on about them" (53). "I have asked her why she did this or that thing—Indian ways that I did not understand" (49).

11. The Squamish traditional territory "includes some of the present day cities of Vancouver, Burnaby and New Westminster, all of the cities of North Vancouver and West Vancouver.... In many instances, a location has particular meaning to our people because of the existence of oral traditions that served to explain that place in the Squamish universe and in our relationship to the land. In addition, the land bears witness to the settlements, resource sites, and spiritual and ritual places of our ancestors, including villages, hunting camps, cedar bark gathering areas ... and cemeteries" (Squamish Nation).

12. Lee Maracle herself grew up in a poor neighborhood in North Vancouver, yet off the Indian Reserve. See her statements in her autobiographical *Bobbi Lee: Indian Rebel* (1990): "Most of the people we knew lived on the Indian Reserve. The people outside the Reserve in our neighbourhood were mainly squatters, living on houseboats or shacks on the mud flats.... Another family lived between our house and the Reserve" (26).

13. This name is probably an ironic reference to the white practice of classifying restaurants and hotels with a certain number of stars to indicate their quality. See also the Indigenous characters' behavior discouraging whites to come to this café: "One lone old white man sits in front of him eat-

ing his soup. Jimmy doesn't bother looking at him at all. 'Nobody I know,' and I laugh at the remark he always whispered to me whenever a white man entered" (201).

14. See the comments on "uptown" Natives in some other context: "Everyone there had been uptown, dressed in the Sunday best of white folks.... They pinched out their words, pronouncing every single letter" (184).

15. On Maracle's representation of First Nations characters in this story, cf. Salman Rushdie's defense of Hanif Kureishi, who had been criticized by the Asian community for his *My Beautiful Launderette* and for the reason that it might provide for white racist propaganda: "The reason for my defence is that there is nothing in it that is imaginately false, and because it seems to me that the real gift that we can offer our communities is not the creation of a set of stereotyped positive images to counteract the stereotyped negative ones, but simply the gift of treating black and Asian characters in a way that white writers seem very rarely able to do, that is to say as fully realized human beings, as complex creatures, good, bad, bad, good. To do anything less is to be kept captive by the racist prejudices of the majority" (qtd. in Rutherford 1992, vii).

16. On this see Margery Wolf 1985: "In traditional [Chinese] society, even illiterate farmers knew about the Three Obediences by which women were to be governed: as an unmarried girl a woman must obey her father and her brothers; as a married woman she must obey her husband; and as a widow she must obey her adult sons. During the three stages of a woman's life defined by male ideology, she was the property of different groups of men who were responsible for her care but who could, as with any property, dispose of her as they saw fit" (2).

17. The text included in the anthology of Vancouver fiction is a shortened version of the original publication. My analysis is thus based on this shortened anthologized version.

18. See also his singing along to the John Denver song "Take Me Home, Country Roads" (313). See also Christine Lorre's convincing characterization of the father's stance toward his home country as melancholy, the mother's stance as mourning: "she misses things Indonesian, but over time she builds her life anew in Canada" (2002, 95).

19. See Padolsky 1997: "If the Canadian government's policy of multiculturalism and the Quebec government's policies towards 'communautés culturelles' have not solved all the problems of Canadian ethnic minority groups, they have nevertheless helped to foster public awareness of the increasing role of minority writers within Canadian and Quebec literatures and cultures in general. With the help of this official recognition and support, Canadian minority writing is being published at an unprecedented rate along with a growing body of accompanying scholarly materials" (24). Cf. also Kamboureli 1994.

20. See Palmer 1994, 297–98, *passim*; see also Morris 2007: "Since Confederation in 1867 three concepts of national identity have arisen in Canada.... The changing expectations towards immigrants corresponded to 'Anglo-conformity' around the turn of the century, to the Canadian 'melting pot' after World War II, and to the currently influential model of multiculturalism. The various approaches have had decisive impacts on every-day urban life and the forms of its representation in cultural products" (87–88; my translation).

Chapter 11

1. Because the publishers thought that while the provocative original title would make sense to Canadian readers, it would not appeal to an American or British audience.

2. This quote is taken from Munro's story "The Flats Road"; see Chapter 4, note 8.

3. See Munro's poetologically self-referential reference to "snapshots" in her story "The Ottawa Valley": "I didn't stop there ... because I wanted to find out more, remember more. I wanted to bring back all I could. Now I look at what I have done and it is like a series of snapshots" (*Something*, 197).

4. See Howells: "To return to that map of Canada, if we began by locating a group of small towns in southwestern Ontario (Wingham, Clinton and Goderich on Lake Huron) we would delineate Munro's geographical territory" (1998, 2).

5. Note though Munro's disclaimer on the bibliographical page of *Lives*: "This novel [*sic*] is autobiographical in form but

not in fact. My family, neighbors and friends did not serve as models.—A.M."

6. In her second book, *Lives*, the first-person narrator's father is also a fox farmer, and this book of linked stories is also set in Jubilee, a fictional homage to Wingham, as has often been argued. For a later autobiographically inspired story on the father-daughter relationship see "The Moons of Jupiter" (in *Moons*), first published in 1978, two years after Munro's father's death during heart surgery.

7. See also Goldman: "No longer the valiant hero, she becomes the victim in need of rescue" (1990, 65).

8. On the significance of Robinson Crusoe in the context see Goldman 1990, for example: "Robinson Crusoe, the economic man *par excellence*, is an apt hero for the narrator's 'tirelessly inventive' capitalistic father" (73, n.1).

9. See Hallvard Dahlie's statement on Munro's biographical mother: "Like many of the unfulfilled and despairing mothers of Munro's fiction, she expended her energies during the formative years of the three Laidlaw children in the nurturing of a family under conditions of deprivation and hardship" (Dahlie 1993, 188–89).

10. On the significance of this name for the female horse see Heliane Ventura: "The name given to the mare reinforces her female status. Flora is one of the minor Greek goddesses of agriculture. Like Demeter, she represents the bounties of nature, its seasonal fertility. Her liberation inaugurated by her passing through the opened gate can be likened to a new birth which reiterates the primordial act through which the individual takes possession of the world" (1992, 86).

11. See also the film *Boys and Girls* (1982) based on the Munro story, which was produced by the National Film Board of Canada and won an Oscar in 1984 for Best Short Film and Live Action. It is advertised on the internet as "the paramount short film on sexism."

12. See also Ventura: "Laird is a potential laird, the male heir to the family who will by-pass the law of primo-geniture to occupy the whole territory, inside and outside, in keeping with male prerogatives on the farm" (1992, 82).

13. See Munro's interesting—and also self-critical—contemporary comments on this story of 1970, for instance: "I wrote it rather too purposefully perhaps, to show something" (Munro 1993, 185).

14. See also Goldman: "As they lift him [Laird] into the truck, the little boy becomes a man: he joins the hunting party.... The mark of blood and the domination of the Other continues to function as a crucial element in the rites of manhood. The boy cements his alliance with the father on the basis of their mutual triumph over nature" (1990, 71).

15. See also Goldman: "The construction of gendered subjects constitutes a form of production. Yet unlike other systems of production, the mechanisms which assist in the creation of gendered adults remain invisible; they seem natural, and for this reason they are taken for granted" (1990, 69, 62).

Chapter 12

1. For a comparison between Morley Callaghan's and Ernest Hemingway's esthetics of the short story, see Chapter 2.

2. See "The Lady Who Sold Furniture," "Girl in Gingham," "Private Parts: A Memoir" (in *Shooting the Stars*); "Polly Ongle" and "Travelling Northward" (in *Adult Entertainment*).

3. "Most critics seem to have me pegged as a very traditional writer. I'm not sure why.... I don't follow any school or manner.... I just *discover* the right shape" (Metcalf 1982a, 22).

4. In *The Teeth of My Father* (1975) and *Selected Stories*; for an interpretation of this story and a survey of Metcalf's artist stories see Nischik 1988.

5. Printed on the back cover of Metcalf, *Shooting the Stars* (1993).

6. "The Strange Aberration of Mr. Ken Smythe," 161; the text quoted from is that of the *Selected Stories* edition (1982e).

7. This particular reading of the story corresponds with Jurij M. Lotman's conception of space in fiction as not only pertaining to topographical locales, but also to the totality of homogenous objects (phenomena, conditions, functions, figures, variables, etc.) between which there are relationships similar to those of common spatial relationships. Lotman concludes that it thus becomes possible for designations of spatial relationships to structure reality in and via

narrative. Concepts such as "high–low," "right–left," "close–distant," "open–closed" serve to establish cultural models with not just spatial content, acquiring meanings such as "good–bad," "valuable–valueless," "advantageous–disadvantageous," "recommendable–not recommendable" in fiction (Lotman 1972).

8. Quoted from the homepage of Rotary International; see www.rotary.org/myrotary/en/document/577, p. 2, last accessed February 1, 2016.

9. These names signify the inner circle of power of the Nazi regime: Adolf Hitler (1889–1945) of the National Socialist German Workers Party (NSDAP or Nazi Party) became chancellor and leader ("Führer") of Germany in 1933/1934 and started the Second World War in 1939. Hitler's racial policies culminated in the Holocaust, that is, the genocide of at least 11 million people, including more than six million Jews. Hermann Wilhelm Goering (1893–1946), one of the main leaders of Nazi Germany, was the founder of the Gestapo (the Nazi's secret state police), who helped to keep Hitler in power by brutally executing opponents. Heinrich Himmler (1900–1945) was the commander of the German Schutzstaffel (SS) and controlled the Gestapo. He was also founder and officer-in-charge of the Nazi concentration camps. Joseph Goebbels (1897–1945) was Hitler's Propaganda Minister, known for his zealous and energetic speeches, his virulent anti-Semitism, and his efficient use of the mass media.

10. Heinrich Heine (1797–1856), poet and politically active journalist and essayist, represents German (post)Romanticism. He is one of the most translated German authors.

11. The Hohenstaufen family brought forth several kings and emperors of the twelfth and thirteenth centuries, including Friedrich I, also known as "Barbarossa." The name Hohenstaufen derives from the castle Stauf near Göppingen in southwestern Germany.

12. This spatial orientation also applies to Smythe to a certain extent. His movements are, not surprisingly, mainly downward. The deterioration in his state is indicated by his *dropping* his file cards during an announcement (167); he is then seen "*falling* ... into the trumpet section" (169); later the drunk man "*sinks* from view" (171, italics added).

Chapter 13

1. For instance, "Simple Sufferings," "Prairie Time," and "Looking for Home: Chapter One." See the bibliography in Gruber 2012, here 319–20.

2. Notable exceptions are, for instance, Gibert 2001, 2006, 2009; Truchan-Tataryn and Gingell 2006; Walton 1996; Turcotte 2003; Andrews and Walton 2006; and (one of the earliest treatments of all, by a fellow writer) Atwood 1990.

3. See also King's answer to the question "What do you think you value most of your Native heritage?": "That's like asking someone what they like best about their mother when she's sitting in the same room, listening. It sustains me. I value that" (Rooke 1990, 76).

4. On Native North American creation myths, see Pijoan 2005 as well as Bastian and Mitchell 2008. On the substantial differences between the Native North American and the Judeo-Christian creation myths, see Walton 1996.

5. Accordingly, it is also the most frequently discussed of King's stories: see, for instance, Walton 1996; Davidson, Walton, and Andrews 2003, 55–61; Gruber 2008, 194–97; Gibert 2001, 71–73; Gibert 2006, 5–6; Truchan-Tataryn 2006; and Turcotte 2003, 212–17.

6. Priscilla Walton consistently uses the female pronoun for the Indigenous storyteller, though there are no indicators for either gender in the story. Rather, "this figure of the Elder, this voice of wisdom, is both male and female" according to Indigenous traditions (see Dvořák 1998 on the Indigenous narrators in King's *One Good Story, That One*, here especially 13).

7. See also Dvořák 1998, 14: "Our narrator is but passing on a tale that has been told many times before in countless places and periods.... We are faced with a strategy of embedding in which a chameleon narrator shifts from receiver to teller, or rather a Chinese box spiral in which the *I* puts on or peels off masks, changing identities, compressing periods, telescoping geographical locations as well as levels of diegesis."

8. As Priscilla Walton points out, "Ahdamn's affinity with white culture, which is written, is contrasted with Evening's affinity with Native American culture, which has

always been associated with nature" (1996, 53).

9. It is not quite clear, however, whether this is supposedly "god's" or the narrator's statement. Note also how "beaver" in a pun is equaled with the translation "Khan-yah-da" (8), close to the pronunciation of "Canada."

10. "This narrative mimicking is intended to reproduce a sense of the syntax, tone and diction that characterizes the English speech of Natives" (Gibert 2006, 5). For exactly how Native and English aspects of language interfere in the narrator's direct speech and for the oral markers of his "written" direct speech, see Gibert 2006; Truchan-Tataryn and Gingell 2006, 6; and Dvořák 1998, 13.

11. For a survey of the Native North American trickster figure and trickster discourse, see Gruber 2008, 95–103; see also Shackleton 2003; and Canton 1998, 96; on King's use of trickster characters see also Shackleton 2012.

12. On this story, see Hirsch 2004, 159–63, here especially 162–63; Atwood 1990, 244–47; and Davidson, Walton, and Andrews 2003, 130–32.

13. See Gibert 2001, 74: "The storyteller speaks fluent English while retaining the basic traditional oral narrative devices, such as word-repetitions, gaps, discontinuities, and a phatic rhetoric address."

14. Dvořák points out "a deliberate, even systematic use of anachronism that deflates the noble heroic deeds of white history books through contiguity with the modern and the trivial. How better to question the historicity of the founding myth than to … recontextualize it, and reweave the strands along with contemporary cultural references?" (1998, 15–16).

15. Note that "A Coyote Columbus Story" was first published in 1992 as a picture-book with 31 drawings to illustrate King's text. On the differences between the two versions, see Wilke 2003; see also D. Wolf 2012.

16. On this story see Gibert 2009, 256–62; Turcotte 2003, 217–21; and Davidson, Walton, and Andrews 2003, 93–94.

17. These motifs are probably in part biographically motivated (see Rooke 1990, 65). In most of these cases, children stay with their mothers in the stories, as did King himself when his father left the family. King's own son Christian, however, was raised by his father after his parents' separation (concerning King's first of two marriages).

Chapter 14

1. This term is used by Gary Saul Morson in his book *The Boundaries of Genre* (1981) (qtd. in Delville 1997, 57).

2. See, in a different context, Weber 1980, 1; thus also Michelle Gadpaille concerning six pieces in *Murder in the Dark* (Gadpaille 1988, 96). For related terms such as "fictional nonfiction," the "nonfiction short story," "creative nonfiction," and "historiografiction," see Abildskov 2003; Morano 2003; Orlovsky 2003; Tilden 2004.

3. These two terms are resorted to in the reviews of the book by Birrell 2006; Washington 2006; Zipp 2006.

4. For instance: "My voice was courted. Bouquets were thrown to it. Money was bestowed on it. Men fell on their knees before it" (22).

5. Cf. DelConte 2003, 204; see also Monika Fludernik: "If there is address, there must be an *addresser*, an *I* (implicit or explicit), and hence a narrator, and this narrator can be a mere enunciator or also a protagonist sharing the *you*'s fictional existence on the story level" (1993, 219).

6. The purest "you-texts," without using also the "I"-form, are, next to "The Tent," "Gateway" and "Winter's Tales."

7. See also Fludernik 1993, who calls second-person fiction "a story form that seems to contradict expectations of customary patterns of verisimilitude" (220), "I" being the more "natural" form in such contexts.

8. See also Morano 2003 in a different context: "Short stories that straddle the genre of the essay subvert or complicate the reality warp so that the narrative 'I' seems at times to transcend character and refer directly to the author; in so doing, these pieces help readers become aware of the writer's negotiation between personal experience and the creation of characters' lives" (45).

9. Cf. Shuli Barzilai's (2008) fascinating analysis of the piece "Thylacine Ragout"—a story largely inaccessible for readers without quite some Internet research concerning factual references. Cf. also Washington: "Some [texts] are just plain weird. It's hard

to know what to make of 'Thylacine Ragout,' for instance, the tale of cloning and eventual devouring of the never-explained thylacine" (2006).

10. Schaeffer continues: "The poststructuralist criticism of the fact/fiction dichotomy has pointed out that every (narrative) representation is a human construction.... But the fact that discourse in general, and narrative discourse in particular, are constructions does not itself disqualify ontological realism or the distinction between fact and fiction" (99). For further explanations, see Schaeffer.

11. Matthews 1994, 48; in the vein of Edgar Allan Poe, Matthews stated issues at the time that are (still) surprisingly relevant in the present context, for instance: "A Short-story deals with a single character, a single event, a single emotion, or the series of emotions called forth by a single situation.... The writer of Short-stories must be concise, and compression, a vigorous compression, is essential.... If to compression, originality, and ingenuity he add also a touch of fantasy, so much the better ... the Short-story and the Sketch ... melt and merge one into the other, and no man may mete the boundaries of each, though their extremes lie far apart ... the Short-story has limitless possibilities" (ibid., 45–48).

Works Cited

Abildskov, Marilyn. 2003. "Playing It Straight by Making It Up: Imaginative Leaps in the Personal Essay." In *The Postmodern Short Story: Forms and Issues*, ed. Farhat Iftekharrudin, Joseph Boyden, Mary Rohrberger, and Jaie Claudet, 25–34. Westport, CT: Praeger.
Achenbaum, W. Andrew. 2005. "Ageing and Changing: International Perspectives on Ageing." In *The Cambridge Handbook of Age and Ageing*, ed. Malcolm L. Johnson, 21–29. Cambridge: Cambridge University Press.
Achilles, Jochen. 2015. "Modes of Liminality in American Short Fiction: Condensations of Multiple Identities." In *Liminality and the Short Story: Boundary Crossings in American, Canadian, and British Writing*, ed. Jochen Achilles and Ina Bergmann, 35–49. New York: Routledge.
———, and Ina Bergmann, eds. 2015. *Liminality and the Short Story: Boundary Crossings in American, Canadian, and British Writing*. New York: Routledge.
Aiken, Lewis R. 2001. *Aging and Later Life: Growing Old in Modern Society*. Springfield, IL: Charles C. Thomas.
Allen, Paula Gunn. 1986. *The Sacred Hoop*. Boston: Beacon.
Anderson, Sherwood. 1919. *Winesburg, Ohio*. New York: Modern Library.
———. 1921. *The Triumph of the Egg*. New York: Huebsch.
———. 1923. *Horses and Men*. New York: Huebsch.
———. 1925. *The Modern Writer*. San Francisco: Lantern Press.
———. 1933. *Death in the Woods*. New York: Liveright.
———. 1962. "I Want to Know Why." In *Sherwood Anderson: Short Stories*, ed. Maxwell Geismar, 5–13. New York: Hill and Wang. First published 1919.
———. 1968. *A Story Teller's Story: A Critical Text*, ed. Ray Lewis White. Cleveland: Press of Case Western Reserve University. First published 1924.
———. 1969. *Sherwood Anderson's Memoirs*, ed. Paul Rosenfeld. Chapel Hill: University of North Carolina Press.
Andrews, Jennifer, and Priscilla L. Walton. 2006. "Rethinking Canadian and American Nationality: Indigeneity and the 49th Parallel in Thomas King." *American Literary History* 18: 600–17.
Appiah, Kwame Anthony. 2005. *The Ethics of Identity*. Princeton: Princeton University Press.
Arnason, David. 1983. "The Historical Development of the Canadian Short Story." *Recherches Anglaises et Américaines* 16: 159–64.
Atwood, Margaret. 1972. *Survival: A Thematic Guide to Canadian Literature*. Toronto: Anansi.
———. 1983. *Bluebeard's Egg*. Toronto: McClelland and Stewart.
———. 1983. "Significant Moments in the Life of My Mother." *Bluebeard's Egg*, 11–29. Toronto: McClelland and Stewart.
———. 1983. "Unearthing Suite." *Bluebeard's Egg*, 267–85. Toronto: McClelland and Stewart.

_____. 1984. *Murder in the Dark: Short Fictions and Prose Poems*. London: Jonathan Cape. First published 1983.
_____. 1984. "Liking Men." *Murder in the Dark: Short Fictions and Prose Poems*, 53–54. London: Jonathan Cape. First published 1983.
_____. 1984. *Dancing Girls and Other Stories*. London: Virago. First published 1977.
_____. 1984. "The Man from Mars." *Dancing Girls and Other Stories*, 9–31. London: Virago. First published 1977.
_____. 1990. "A Double-Bladed Knife: Subversive Laughter in Two Stories by Thomas King." *Canadian Literature* 124–125: 243–50.
_____. 1991. *Wilderness Tips*. Toronto: McClelland and Stewart.
_____. 1991. "Death by Landscape." *Wilderness Tips*, 107–29. Toronto: McClelland and Stewart. First published 1985.
_____. 1992. *Good Bones*. Toronto: Coach House Press.
_____. 1992. "The Little Red Hen Tells All." *Good Bones*, 11–14. Toronto: Coach House Press.
_____. 1992. "Making a Man." *Good Bones*, 53–58. Toronto: Coach House Press.
_____. 1993. "Afterword." In Margaret Laurence, *The Diviners*, 383–89. Chicago: University of Chicago Press. Afterword first published 1974.
_____. 1998. "Two-Headed Poems, xi." *Eating Fire: Selected Poetry 1965–1995*, 226–27. London: Virago.
_____. 2002. *Negotiating with the Dead: A Writer on Writing*. Cambridge: Cambridge University Press.
_____. 2005. "In Conversation with Thomas King and Margaret Atwood." In Thomas King, *A Short History of Indians in Canada*, 5–17 of "About the Book" section. Toronto: HarperCollins.
_____. 2006. *Moral Disorder*. Toronto: McClelland and Stewart.
_____. 2006. "The Art of Cooking and Serving." *Moral Disorder*, 10–23. Toronto: McClelland and Stewart.
_____. 2006. "The Bad News." *Moral Disorder*, 1–9. Toronto: McClelland and Stewart. First published 2005.
_____. 2006. "The Entities." *Moral Disorder*, 167–88. Toronto: McClelland and Stewart.
_____. 2007. *The Tent*. New York: Anchor Books. First published 2006.
_____. 2007. "Encouraging the Young." *The Tent*, 17–19. New York: Anchor Books. First published 2006.
_____. 2007. "The Tent." *The Tent*, 143–46. New York: Anchor Books. First published 2006.
_____. 2007. "Voice." *The Tent*, 21–23. New York: Anchor Books. First published 2006.
_____. 2014. *Stone Mattress*. London: Bloomsbury.
Bagnell, Prisca von Dorotka, and Patricia Spencer Soper, eds. 1989. *Perceptions of Aging in Literature: A Cross-Cultural Study*. New York: Greenwood.
Baker, Carlos. 1963. *Hemingway: The Writer as Artist*. 3rd ed. Princeton: Princeton University Press.
Barzilai, Shuli. 2008. "Unfabulating a Fable, or Two Readings of 'Thylacine Ragout.'" In *Once Upon a Time: Myth, Fairy Tales and Legends in Margaret Atwood's Writings*, ed. Sarah A. Appleton, 127–50. Newcastle upon Tayne: Cambridge Scholars Publishing.
Bastian, Dawn E., and Judy K. Mitchell. 2008. *Handbook of Native American Mythology*. New York: Oxford University Press.
Beran, Carol L. 1999. "The Luxury of Excellence: Alice Munro in the *New Yorker*." In *The Rest of the Story: Critical Essays on Alice Munro*, ed. Robert Thacker, 204–32. Toronto: ECW Press.
Berndt, Kathrin. 2010. "The Ordinary Terrors of Survival: Alice Munro and the Canadian Gothic." *Journal of the Short Story in English* 55 (special issue on "The Short Stories of Alice Munro," ed. Héliane Ventura): 19–33.
Birdsell, Sandra. 1982. *Night Travellers*. Winnipeg: Turnstone.
_____. 1984. *Ladies of the House*. Winnipeg: Turnstone.
_____. 1987. *Agassiz Stories*. Winnipeg: Turnstone.

_____. 1997. *The Two-Headed Calf.* Toronto: McClelland and Stewart.
Birrell, Heather. 2006. "Review of *The Tent.*" *Quill and Quire* (January 2006).
Bissoondath, Neil. 1985. *Digging Up the Mountains.* Toronto: Macmillan.
_____. 1990. *On the Eve of Uncertain Tomorrows.* Toronto: Lester and Orpen Dennys.
Blaise, Clark. 1974. *Tribal Justice.* Toronto: Doubleday Canada.
_____. 1984. *A North American Education.* Toronto: General Publishing. First published 1973.
_____. 1984. "A Class of New Canadians." *A North American Education*, 3–15. Toronto: General Publishing. First published 1970.
_____. 1986. *Resident Alien.* Markham, ON: Penguin.
_____. 1992. *Man and His World.* Erin, ON: Porcupine's Quill Press.
Blodgett, E. D. 1988. *Alice Munro.* Boston, MA: Twayne.
Boire, Gary. 1992. "Morley Callaghan 1903-1990." *Canadian Literature* 133: 208–9.
_____. 1994. *Morley Callaghan: Literary Anarchist.* Toronto: ECW Press.
Bonheim, Helmut. 1980-81. "Topoi of the Canadian Short Story." *Dalhousie Review* 60 (4): 659–69.
Bovenschen, Silvia. 2015. *Älter werden: Notizen.* Sixth edition. Frankfurt am Main: Fischer. First published 2006.
Bowering, George. 1974. *Flycatcher.* Ottawa: Oberon.
_____. 1982. "Sheila Watson, Trickster." In *The Mask in Place: Essays on Fiction in North America*, ed. George Bowering, 97–111. Winnipeg: Turnstone.
_____. 1983. *A Place to Die.* Ottawa: Oberon.
Brand, Dionne. 1988. *Sans Souci and Other Stories.* Stratford, ON: Williams-Wallace.
Brandt, Di, and Barbara Godard, eds. 2009. *Wider Boundaries of Daring: The Modernist Impulse in Canadian Women's Poetry.* Waterloo, ON: Wilfrid Laurier University Press.
Breitbach, Julia. 2007. "The Beginnings of Canadian Modernism: Raymond Knister, 'The First Day of Spring' (written 1924/25)." In *The Canadian Short Story: Interpretations*, ed. Reingard M. Nischik, 67–82. Rochester, NY: Camden House.
_____. 2012. *Analog Fictions for the Digital Age: Literary Realism and Photographic Discourses in Novels after 2000.* Rochester, NY: Camden House.
Bruchac, Joseph. 1987. *Survival This Way: Interviews with American Indian Poets.* Tucson: University of Arizona Press.
Bryant, Marsha, ed. 1996. *Photo-Textualities: Reading Photographs and Literature.* Newark: University of Delaware Press.
Burke, Anne. 1979-80. "Raymond Knister: An Annotated Checklist." *Essays on Canadian Writing* 16: 20–61.
Butler, Judith. 1990. *Gender Trouble: Feminism and the Subversion of Identity.* New York: Routledge.
_____. 2004. *Undoing Gender.* New York: Routledge.
Butler, Robert. 1975. *Why Survive?* New York: Harper and Row.
Callaghan, Morley. 1929. *A Native Argosy.* New York: Scribner/Toronto: Macmillan.
_____. 1936. *Now That April's Here and Other Stories.* Toronto: Macmillan.
_____. 1959. *Morley Callaghan's Stories.* Toronto: Macmillan. First published 1935.
_____. 1959. "The Shining Red Apple." *Morley Callaghan's Stories*, 154–58. Toronto: Macmillan of Canada. First published 1935.
_____. 1979. *That Summer in Paris: Memories of Tangled Friendships with Hemingway, Fitzgerald and Some Others.* Harmondsworth: Penguin. First published 1963.
_____. 1985. *The Lost and Found Stories of Morley Callaghan.* Toronto: Exile.
_____. 2003a. "Morley Callaghan on Raymond Knister." In *After Exile: A Raymond Knister Poetry Reader*, ed. Gregory Betts, 120–21. Toronto: Exile. First published 1964.
_____. 2003b. *The Complete Stories*, vol. 2. Toronto: Exile.
_____. 2008a. *A Literary Life: Reflections and Reminiscences 1928-1990.* Holstein, ON: Exile.
_____. 2008b. "Everything He Wrote Seemed Real: Hemingway." *A Literary Life: Reflections and Reminiscences 1928-1990*, 353–57. Holstein, ON: Exile. First published 1981.

———. 2008c. "In a Jugular Vein: Hemingway." *A Literary Life: Reflections and Reminiscences 1928–1990*, 23–27. Holstein, ON: Exile. First published 1964.

———. 2008d. "Introducing Ernest Hemingway." *A Literary Life: Reflections and Reminiscences 1928–1990*, 42–44. Holstein, ON: Exile. First published 1926.

Cameron, Barry. 1975. "The Practice of the Craft: A Conversation with John Metcalf." *Queen's Quarterly* 182: 402–24.

Campbell, Wanda. 2005. "Moonlight and Morning: Women's Early Contribution to Canadian Modernism." In *The Canadian Modernists Meet*, ed. Dean Irvine, 79–99. Ottawa: University of Ottawa Press.

Canton, Jeffrey. 1998. "Coyote Lives: Thomas King." In *The Power to Bend Spoons*, ed. Beverley Daurio, 90–97. Toronto: Mercury.

Carr, Emily. 1985. "Sophie." In *Vancouver Short Stories*, ed. Carole Gerson, 48–55. Vancouver: University of British Columbia Press. First published 1941.

Carr, Graham. 1987. "'All We North Americans': Literary Culture and the Continentalist Ideal, 1919–1939." *American Review of Canadian Studies* 17 (2): 145–57.

Carrington, Ildikó de Papp. 1989. *Controlling the Uncontrollable: The Fiction of Alice Munro*. De Kalb: Northern Illinois University Press.

Carscallen, James. 1993. *The Other Country: Patterns in the Writing of Alice Munro*. Toronto: ECW Press.

Carver, Raymond. 1986. "On Writing," *Fires: Essays, Poems, Stories*. London: Picador, 22–27.

Cather, Willa. 1992. "On the Art of Fiction." In *Stories, Poems, and Other Writings*, ed. Sharon O'Brien, 939–40. New York: Library of America. First published 1920.

CBC News. 2004. "Chinese Immigration." http://www.cbc.ca/news/background/china/chinese_immigration.html. Accessed May 19, 2013.

———. 2011. "The Canada–U.S. Border: By the Numbers." *CBC News Online*. December 7; www.cbc.ca/news/canada/the-canada-u-s-border-by-the-numbers-1.999207. Accessed August 8, 2013.

———. 2013. "Alice Munro Is 1st Canadian Woman to Win Nobel Literature Prize." October 10. http://www.cbc.ca/news/arts/alice-munro-is-1st-canadian-woman-to-win-nobel-literature-prize-1.1958383. Accessed August 11, 2016.

Clarke, Austin. 2003. *Choosing His Coffin: The Best Stories of Austin Clarke*. Toronto: Thomas Allen.

Cohen, Matt. 1972. *Columbus and the Fat Lady*. Toronto: Anansi.

———. 1983. *Café Le Dog*. Toronto: McClelland and Stewart.

———. 1994. *Lives of the Mind Slaves: Selected Stories*. Erin, ON: Porcupine's Quill Press.

Cohn, Dorrit. 1983. *Transparent Minds: Narrative Modes for Presenting Consciousness in Fiction*. Princeton: Princeton University Press.

Crean, Susan. 1991. "Divining Jane Rule: A Profile of her Progress." *B.C. Bookworld* 2: 11.

Culhane, Dara. 2003. "Their Spirits Live within Us: Aboriginal Women in Downtown Eastside Vancouver Emerging into Visibility." *American Indian Quarterly* 27 (3–4): 593–606.

Curry, Martha Mulroy, ed. 1975. *The "Writer's Book" by Sherwood Anderson: A Critical Edition*. Metuchen, NJ: Scarecrow Press.

———. 1976. "Anderson's Theories on Writing Fiction." In *Sherwood Anderson: Dimensions of His Literary Art: A Collection of Critical Essays*, ed. David D. Anderson, 90–109. East Lansing: Michigan State University Press.

Dahlie, Hallvard. 1993. "Alice Munro (1931–)." In *ECW's Biographical Guide to Canadian Novelists*, ed. Robert Lecker, Jack David, and Ellen Quigley, 188–91. Toronto: ECW Press.

Davey, Frank. 1976. "Impressionable Realism: The Stories of Clark Blaise." *Open Letter* 3: 65–74.

Davidson, Arnold E., Priscilla L. Walton, and Jennifer Andrews. 2003. *Border Crossings: Thomas King's Cultural Inversions*. Toronto: University of Toronto Press.

Dean, Misao. 2000. "Introduction." In *Early Canadian Short Stories: Short Stories in English before World War I: A Critical Edition*, ed. Misao Dean, xi–xvii. Ottawa: Tecumseh Press.

De Beauvoir, Simone. 1977. *Old Age*. Translated by Patrick O'Brien. Harmondsworth: Penguin. French original *La Vieillesse*, 1970.

DelConte, Matt. 2003. "Why *You* Can't Speak: Second-Person Narration, Voice, and a New Model for Understanding Narrative." *Style* 37 (2): 204-19.
Delville, Michel. 1997. "Murdering the Text: Genre and Gender Issues in Margaret Atwood's Short Short Fiction." In *The Contact and the Culmination*, ed. Marc Delrez and Bénédicte Ledent, 57-67. Liège: L3-Liège Language and Literature.
Duncan, Sara Jeannette. 1903. *The Pool in the Desert*. New York: Appleton.
Dunn, Maggie, and Ann Morris. 1995. *The Composite Novel: The Short Story Cycle in Transition*. New York: Twayne.
Dvořák, Marta. 1998. "When Coyote Meets Adam: Or Thomas King's New Space." *Journal of the Short Story in English* 30: 11-18.
Eibl, Doris. 2008a. "The French-Canadian Short Story." In *History of Literature in Canada: English-Canadian and French-Canadian*, ed. Reingard M. Nischik, 264-69. Rochester, NY: Camden House.
———. 2008b. "The French-Canadian Short Prose Narrative." In *History of Literature in Canada: English-Canadian and French-Canadian*, ed. Reingard M. Nischik, 450-55. Rochester, NY: Camden House.
Eliot, T. S. 1928. "Hamlet and His Problems." *The Sacred Wood: Essays on Poetry and Criticism*, 95-103. London: Methuen. First published 1919.
———. 2003. "Tradition and the Individual Talent." In *The Norton Anthology*, vol. D. Sixth edition, 1425-28. New York: Norton. First published 1919.
Engel, Marian. 1975. *Inside the Easter Egg*. Toronto: Anansi.
———. 1985. *The Tattooed Woman*. Markham, ON: Penguin.
———. 1985. "The Tattooed Woman." *The Tattooed Woman*, 1-9. Markham, ON: Penguin. First published 1975.
Erber, Joan T. 2013. *Aging and Older Adulthood*. Third edition. Chichester: Wiley-Blackwell. First published 1988.
Even-Zohar, Itamar. 1990. *Polysystem Studies*. Durham: Duke University Press.
———. 1997. "Factors and Dependencies in Culture: A Revised Draft for Polysystem Culture Research." *Canadian Review of Comparative Literature/Revue Canadienne de Littérature Comparée* 24 (1): 15-34.
Fairbridge, Derek, ed. 2005. *The Vancouver Stories: West Coast Fiction from Canada's Best Writers*. Vancouver: Raincoast.
Featherstone, Mike, and Mike Hepworth. 2005. "Images of Ageing: Cultural Representations of Later Life." In *The Cambridge Handbook of Age and Ageing*, ed. Malcolm L. Johnson, 354-62. Cambridge: Cambridge University Press.
Fludernik, Monika. 1993. "Second Person Fiction: Narrative *You* As Addressee and/or Protagonist." *AAA—Arbeiten aus Anglistik und Amerikanistik* 18 (2): 217-47.
Foucault, Michel. 1997. "Of Other Spaces: Utopias and Heterotopias." In *Rethinking Architecture: A Reader in Cultural Theory*, ed. Neil Leach, 330-36. New York: Routledge. First published 1984.
Frye, Northrop. 1976. "Conclusion." In *Literary History of Canada: Canadian Literature in English*, ed. Carl F. Klinck et al. Second edition, vol. III, 318-32. First published 1965.
Gadpaille, Michelle. 1988. *The Canadian Short Story*. Toronto: Oxford University Press.
———. 2001. "Canadian Short Fiction." In *Critical Survey of Short Fiction*, ed. Charles E. May and Frank N. Magill. 2nd rev. ed., vol. 7, 2898-2907. Pasadena, CA: Salem Press.
Gallant, Mavis. 1956. *The Other Paris*. Boston: Houghton Mifflin.
———. 1982. *My Heart Is Broken*. Toronto: General Publishing. First published 1964.
———. 1973. *The Pegnitz Junction*. Toronto: Macmillan of Canada.
———. 1974. *The End of the World and Other Stories*. Toronto: McClelland and Stewart.
———. 1979. *From the Fifteenth District*. Toronto: Macmillan of Canada.
———. 1981. *Home Truths: Selected Canadian Stories*. Toronto: Macmillan of Canada.
———. 1981. "Virus X." *Home Truths: Selected Canadian Stories*, 173-216. Toronto: Macmillan of Canada.
———. 1985. *Overhead in a Balloon: Stories of Paris*. Toronto: Macmillan of Canada.

———. 1997. "In Transit." *The Selected Stories of Mavis Gallant*, 310–13. London: Bloomsbury. First published 1965.
———. 2009. *The Cost of Living: Early and Uncollected Stories*. New York: New York Review Books Classic.
Garner, Hugh. 1952. *The Yellow Sweater*. London: Collins.
———. 1952. "Preface." *The Yellow Sweater*, n.p. London: Collins.
———. 1963. *Hugh Garner's Best Stories*. Toronto: Ryerson.
———. 1966. *Men and Women*. Toronto: Ryerson.
———. 1971. *Violation of the Virgins and Other Stories*. Toronto: McGraw-Hill Ryerson.
———. 1976. *The Legs of the Lame*. Ottawa: Borealis Press.
Garson, Marjorie. 1994. "Synecdoche and the Munrovian Sublime: Parts and Wholes in *Lives of Girls and Women*." *English Studies in Canada* 20 (4): 413–29.
Gelfant, Blanche. 1995. "Ethel Wilson's Absent City: A Personal View of Vancouver." *Canadian Literature* 146: 9–27.
Gerson, Carole, ed. 1985. *Vancouver Short Stories*. Vancouver: University of British Columbia Press.
Gibbins, Roger. 1989. *Canada as a Borderlands Society*. Orono, ME: Borderlands.
Gibert, Teresa. 2001. "Narrative Strategies in Thomas King's Short Stories." In *Telling Stories: Postcolonial Short Fiction in English*, ed. Jacqueline Bardolph, 67–76. Amsterdam: Rodopi.
———. 2006. "Written Orality in Thomas King's Short Fiction." *Journal of the Short Story in English* 47: 97–109.
———. 2009. "The Politics and Poetics of Thomas King's Textual Hauntings." In *Postcolonial Ghosts/Fantômes post-coloniaux*, ed. Gerry Turcotte, Mélanie Joseph-Vilain, and Judith Misrahi-Barak, 253–68. Montpellier: Presses universitaires de la Méditerranée.
Gibson, Graeme. 1973. "Alice Munro." *Eleven Canadian Novelists*, 237–64. Toronto: Anansi.
Givens, Imogen. 1979–80. "Raymond Knister—Man or Myth?" *Essays on Canadian Writing* 16: 5–19.
Godard, Barbara. 1989. "Stretching the Story: The Canadian Short Story Cycle." *Open Letter* 7 (6): 27–71.
Godfrey, Dave. 1967. *Death Goes Better with Coca-Cola*. Toronto: Anansi.
Goethe, Johann Wolfgang von. 1953. *Wilhelm Meisters Lehrjahre*. Berlin: Aufbau-Verlag. First published 1795–96.
Goetsch, Paul. 2007. "Psychological Realism, Immigration, and City Fiction: Morley Callaghan, 'Last Spring They Came Over' (1927)." In *The Canadian Short Story: Interpretations*, ed. Reingard M. Nischik, 95–103. Rochester, NY: Camden House.
Goldman, Marlene. 1990. "Penning in the Bodies: The Construction of Gendered Subjects in Alice Munro's *Boys and Girls*." *Studies in Canadian Literature* 15: 62–75.
Gordimer, Nadine. 1976. "The Flash of Fireflies." In *Short Story Theories*, ed. Charles E. May, 178–81. Athens: Ohio University Press. First published 1968.
Gough, Laurie. 2002. "The Border Crossing." *Prism International* 40 (2): 15–27.
Gregory, Horace, ed. 1972. *The Portable Sherwood Anderson*. Revised edition. New York: Viking. First published 1949.
Grove, Frederick Philip. 1971. *Tales from the Margin: The Selected Stories of Frederick Philip Grove*. Ed. and intr. Desmond Pacey. Toronto: McGraw-Hill Ryerson.
Gruber, Eva. 2007. "Nativeness as Third Space: Thomas King, 'Borders' (1991)." In *The Canadian Short Story: Interpretations*, ed. Reingard M. Nischik, 353–64. Rochester, NY: Camden House.
———. 2008. *Humor in Contemporary Native North American Literature: Reimagining Nativeness*. Rochester, NY: Camden House.
———, ed. 2012. *Thomas King: Works and Impact*. Rochester, NY: Camden House.
———. 2014. "Comparative Race Studies: Black and White in Canada and the United States." In *The Palgrave Handbook of Comparative North American Literature*, ed. Reingard M. Nischik, 65–84. New York: Palgrave Macmillan.

Gullette, Margaret. 1997. *Declining to Decline: Cultural Combat and the Politics of the Midlife*. Charlottesville: University Press of Virginia.
Gunnars, Kristjana. 1983. *The Axe's Edge*. Toronto: Press Porcepic.
_____. 1992. *The Guest House and Other Stories*. Concord, ON: Anansi.
Gwynn, Frederick L., and Joseph Blotner, eds. 1959. *Faulkner in the University: Class Conferences at the University of Mississippi 1957-1958*. Charlottesville: University Press of Virginia.
Hale, Sarah Josepha. 1829. *Sketches of American Character*. Boston: Putnam and Hunt.
Haliburton, Thomas Chandler. 1993. *The Clockmaker: The Sayings and Doings of Samuel Slick of Slickville*. Ed. Robert L. MacDougall. Repr. edition. Toronto: McClelland and Stewart. First published 1836.
Hancock, Geoff. 1979-80. "An Interview with Jack Hodgins." *Canadian Fiction Magazine* 32-33: 33-63.
_____. 1982. "An Interview with Alice Munro." *Canadian Fiction Magazine* 43: 74-114.
_____, ed. 1983. *Illusion One: Fables, Fantasies and Metafictions*. Toronto: Aya Press.
_____, ed. 1986. *Moving Off the Map: From 'Story' to 'Fiction.'* Windsor, ON: Black Moss.
_____. 1987. "Alice Munro." *Canadian Writers at Work: Interviews with Geoff Hancock*, 187-224. Toronto: Oxford University Press. First published 1982 (see above).
Hart, Robert C. 1957. "Hemingway on Writing." *College English* 18 (6): 314-20.
Heble, Ajay. 1994. *The Tumble of Reason: Alice Munro's Discourse of Absence*. Toronto: University of Toronto Press.
Hemingway, Ernest. 1923. *Three Stories and Ten Poems*. Paris: Contact.
_____. 1924. *in our time*. Paris: Three Mountains Press.
_____. 1925. *In Our Time*. New York: Boni and Liveright.
_____. 1927. *Men without Women*. New York: Scribner.
_____. 1932. *Death in the Afternoon*. London: Jonathan Cape.
_____. 1933. *Winners Take Nothing*. New York: Scribner.
_____. 1935. *Green Hills of Africa*. New York: Scribner.
_____. 1938. *The Fifth Column and the First Forty-nine Stories*. New York: Scribner.
_____. 1958. "The Art of Fiction XXI." George Plimpton interviewing Ernest Hemingway. *Paris Review* 18: 61-89.
_____. 1964. *A Moveable Feast*, ed. Mary Hemingway. New York: Scribner.
_____. 1964. "Cat in the Rain." *The Essential Hemingway*, 323-26. Harmondsworth: Penguin. First published 1925.
_____. 1972. *The Nick Adams Stories*. New York: Scribner.
_____. 1987. *The Complete Short Stories of Ernest Hemingway*. New York: Scribner.
Hirsch, Bud. 2004. "'Stay Calm, Be Brave, Wait for the Signs': Sign-Offs and Send-Ups in the Fiction of Thomas King." *Western American Literature* 39 (2): 145-75.
Hodgins, Jack. 1981. *The Barclay Family Theatre*. Toronto: Macmillan.
_____. 1992. *Spit Delaney's Island*. Toronto: McClelland and Stewart. First published 1976.
Hood, Hugh. 1962. *Flying a Red Kite*. Toronto: Ryerson.
_____. 1967. *Around the Mountain: Scenes from Montreal Life*. Toronto: Peter Martin Associates.
_____. 1971. *The Fruit Man, The Meat Man and The Manager*. Ottawa: Oberon.
_____. 1971. "Getting to Williamstown." *The Fruit Man, The Meat Man and The Manager*, 9-21. Ottawa: Oberon.
_____. 1976. *Dark Glasses*. Ottawa: Oberon.
Horvath, Agnes, Bjørn Thomassen, and Harald Wydra, eds. 2015a. *Breaking Boundaries: Varieties of Liminality*. New York: Berghahn.
_____. 2015b. "Introduction: Liminality and the Search for Boundaries." In *Breaking Boundaries: Varieties of Liminality*, ed. Agnes Horvath, Bjørn Thomassen, and Harald Wydra, 1-8. New York: Berghahn.
Hoy, Helen. 1980. "'Dull, Simple, Amazing and Unfathomable': Paradox and Double Vision in Alice Munro's Fiction." *Studies in Canadian Literature* 5: 100-15.

Howells, Coral Ann. 1990. "Alice Munro's Art of Indeterminacy: *The Progress of Love*." In *Modes of Narrative: Approaches to American, Canadian and British Fiction*, ed. Reingard M. Nischik and Barbara Korte, 141–52. Würzburg: Königshausen and Neumann.
———. 1998. *Alice Munro*. Manchester: Manchester University Press.
———. 2003. "Intimate Dislocations: Alice Munro, *Hateship, Friendship, Courtship, Loveship, Marriage*." *Contemporary Canadian Women's Fiction: Refiguring Identities*, 53–78. New York: Palgrave Macmillan.
Hutcheon, Linda. 1992. "Canada's 'Post': Sampling Today's Fiction." Foreword by Hutcheon to *Likely Stories: A Postmodern Sampler*, ed. George Bowering and Linda Hutcheon, 9–15. Toronto: Coach House Press.
Ingram, Forrest L. 1971. *Representative Short Story Cycles of the 20th Century: Studies in a Literary Genre*. The Hague: Mouton.
Irvine, Dean, ed. 2005. *The Canadian Modernists Meet*. Ottawa: University of Ottawa Press.
———. 2008. *Editing Modernity: Women and Little-Magazine Cultures in Canada, 1916–1956*. Toronto: University of Toronto Press.
Irving, Washington. 1968. *The Sketch Book of Geoffrey Crayon, Gent*. London: Dent. First published 1819–1820.
Jahnson, Christa, ed. 2004. *Old Age and Ageing in British and American Culture and Literature*. Münster: Lit Verlag.
Jakobson, Roman. 1964. "Closing Statement: Linguistics and Poetics." In *Style in Language*, ed. Thomas A. Sebeok, 350–77. 2nd edition. Cambridge: MIT Press. First published 1960.
Jean, Michaëlle. 2005. "Installation Speech—The Right Honourable Michaëlle Jean Governor General of Canada on the Occasion of Her Installation [on 27 September 2005]." http://archive.gg.ca/media/doc.asp?lang=e&DocID=4574.
Johnson, Pauline. 2005. "The Two Sisters." In *The Vancouver Stories: West Coast Fiction from Canada's Best Writers*, ed. Derek Fairbridge, 9–15. Vancouver: Raincoast. First published 1910.
Kamboureli, Smaro. 1994. "Canadian Ethnic Anthologies: Representations of Ethnicity." *ARIEL* 25 (4): 11–52.
Keefer, Janice Kulyk. 1986. *The Paris-Napoli Express*. Ottawa: Oberon.
———. 1987a. *Transfigurations*. Charlottetown: Ragweed Press.
———. 1987b. *Under Eastern Eyes: A Critical Reading of Maritime Fiction*. Toronto: University of Toronto Press.
———. 1990. *Travelling Ladies*. Toronto: Random House.
Kennedy, Gerald J. 1995. *Modern American Short Story Sequences: Composite Fictions and Fictive Communities*. Cambridge: Cambridge University Press.
Kimbel, Ellen. 1984. "The American Short Story: 1900–1920." In *The American Short Story 1900–1945*, ed. Philip Stevick, 33–69. New York: Twayne.
King, Thomas. 1987. "Introduction." *Canadian Fiction Magazine* 20: 4–10.
———. 1990. "Godzilla vs. Post-Colonial." *World Literature Written in English* 30 (2): 10–16.
———. 1993. *One Good Story, That One*. Toronto: HarperCollins.
———. 1993. "A Coyote Columbus Story." *One Good Story, That One*, 119–27. Toronto: HarperCollins. First published 1992.
———. 1993. "One Good Story, That One." *One Good Story, That One*, 1–10. Toronto: HarperCollins. First published 1988.
———. 2005. *A Short History of Indians in Canada*. Toronto: HarperCollins.
———. 2005. "A Short History of Indians in Canada." *A Short History of Indians in Canada*, 1–4. Toronto: HarperCollins.
———. 2005. "The Closer You Get to Canada, the More Things Will Eat Your Horses." *A Short History of Indians in Canada*, 94–106. Toronto: HarperCollins. First published 1989.
———. 2005. "Domestic Furies." *A Short History of Indians in Canada*, 178–89. Toronto: HarperCollins.

Works Cited

Knister, Raymond, ed. 1971. *Canadian Short Stories*. Toronto: Macmillan of Canada. First published 1928.

―――. 1971a. "The Canadian Short Story." Introduction to *Canadian Short Stories*, xi–xix. Freeport, NY: Books for Libraries Press. First published 1928.

―――. 1972. *Selected Stories of Raymond Knister*, edited and introduced by Michael Gnarowski. Ottawa: University of Ottawa Press.

―――. 1975a. "Canadian Literati." *Journal of Canadian Fiction* 4 (2): 160–68.

―――. 1975b. "Democracy and the Short Story." *Journal of Canadian Fiction* 4 (2): 146–48. (Written in 1920.)

―――. 1975c. *Raymond Knister: Poems, Stories and Essays*, ed. David Arnason. Montreal: Bellrock.

―――. 1976a. *The First Day of Spring: Stories and Other Prose*, selected and introduced by Peter Stevens. Toronto: University of Toronto Press.

―――. 1976b. "The Canadian Short Story." *The First Day of Spring: Stories and Other Prose*, selected and introduced by Peter Stevens, 388–92. Toronto: University of Toronto Press. First published 1923.

―――. 1976c. "The First Day of Spring." In *The First Day of Spring: Stories and Other Prose*, selected and introduced by Peter Stevens, 3–8. Toronto: University of Toronto Press. (Written in 1924–1925.)

Korkka, Janne. 2002. "Resisting Cultural Domination: Thomas King's Canadian Mosaic." *The Atlantic Literary Review* 3 (2): 143–54.

Kroetsch, Robert. 1989. "No Name Is My Name." *The Lovely Treachery of Words: Essays Selected and New*, 41–52. Toronto: Oxford University Press.

Kunow, Rüdiger. 2012. "Alter(n) und Globalisierung." In *Alter(n) in Literatur und Kultur der Gegenwart*, ed. Rudolf Freitag and Dirk Kretzschmar, 53–77. Würzburg: Königshausen and Neumann.

Kuttainen, Victoria. 2010. *Unsettling Stories: Settler Postcolonialism and the Short Story Composite*. Newcastle upon Tyne: Cambridge Scholars Publishing.

Lamonde, Yvan, Patricia Lockhart Fleming, and Fiona A. Black, eds. 2005. *History of the Book in Canada: 1840–1918*. Vol. II. Toronto: University of Toronto Press.

Laurence, Margaret. 1962. "A Canadian Classic" (review of W. O. Mitchell, *Jake and the Kid*). *Canadian Literature* 11: 68–70.

―――. 1963. *The Tomorrow-Tamer*. Toronto: McClelland and Stewart.

―――. 1970. *A Bird in the House*. New York: Knopf.

Leacock, Stephen. 1996. *Sunshine Sketches of a Little Town*. Toronto: McClelland and Stewart. First published 1912.

Lee, Sky. 1985. "Broken Teeth." In *Vancouver Short Stories*, ed. Carole Gerson, 144–49. Vancouver: University of British Columbia Press. First published 1981.

Legge, Valerie. 1992. "Sheila Watson's 'Antigone': Anguished Rituals and Public Disturbances." *Studies in Canadian Literature* 17 (2): 28–46.

Leung, Marlene. 2013. "Alice Munro Wins Nobel Prize in Literature: A Master of the Short Story." *CTV News*, October 10. http://www.ctvnews.ca/entertainment/alice-munro-wins-nobel-prize-in-literature-a-master-of-the-short-story.1.1491581.

Levine, Norman. 2000. *By a Frozen River: The Short Stories of Norman Levine*. Toronto: Key Porter Books.

Livesay, Dorothy. 1974. "Knister's Stories: Review of *Selected Stories* of Raymond Knister." *Canadian Literature* 62: 79–83.

―――. 1977. *Right Hand Left Hand*. Erin, ON: Press Porcepic.

Lodge, David. 1980. "Analysis and Interpretation of the Realist Text: A Pluralistic Approach to Ernest Hemingway's 'Cat in the Rain.'" *Poetics Today* 1 (4): 5–22.

―――. 1997. "The Novelist Today: Still at the Crossroads?" *The Practice of Writing*, 3–19. Auckland: Penguin.

Lopate, Phillip. 2016. "Michael Kinsley's *Old Age: A Beginner's Guide*." *The New York Times*, April 24. [Book review.]

Lorre, Christine. 2002. "Ordinary Tragedies in Madeleine Thien's 'A Map of the City.'" *Journal of the Short Story in English* 38: 87–101.
Lotman, Jurij M. 1972. *Die Struktur literarischer Texte*. Trans. Rolf-Dietrich Keil. Munich: Fink.
Lu, Duanfang. 2000. "The Changing Landscape of Hybridity: A Reading of Ethnic Identity and Urban Form in Vancouver." *Traditional Dwellings and Settlements Review* 11 (1): 19–28.
Lucas, Alec. 1958. "Introduction." In *The Last Barrier and Other Stories*, ed. Charles G. D. Roberts, v–x. Toronto: McClelland and Stewart.
Lundén, Rolf. 1999. *The United Stories of America: Studies in the Short Story Composite*. Amsterdam: Rodopi.
Lutz, Hartmut. 1991. "Thomas King." *Contemporary Challenges: Conversations with Canadian Native Authors*, 107–16. Saskatoon: Fifth House.
———. 2002. *Approaches: Essays in Native North American Studies and Literatures*. Augsburg: Wißner.
Lynch, Gerald. 2001. *The One and the Many: English-Canadian Short Story Cycles*. Toronto: University of Toronto Press.
———. 2007. "Mariposa Medicine: Thomas King's *Medicine River* and the Canadian Short Story Cycle." In *Tropes and Territories: Short Fiction, Postcolonial Readings, Canadian Writings in Context*, ed. Marta Dvořák and William H. New, 214–30. Montreal: McGill-Queen's University Press.
MacLaren, I. S., and C. Potvin, eds. 1989. *Questions of Funding, Publishing and Distribution/Questions d'édition et de diffusion*. Edmonton, AB: Research Institute for Comparative Literature, University of Alberta.
Mann, Susan Garland. 1989. *The Short Story Cycle: A Genre Companion and Reference Guide*. New York: Greenwood.
Manning, Gerald F. 1993. "Loss and Renewal in Old Age: Some Literary Models." *Canadian Journal on Aging/La Revue canadienne du vieillissement* 12 (4): 469–84.
Maracle, Lee. 1990. *Bobbie Lee: Indian Rebel*. Toronto: Women's Press.
———. 1990. *Sojourner's Truth and Other Stories*. Vancouver: Press Gang Publishers.
———. 2005. "Polka Partners, Uptown Indians and White Folks." In *The Vancouver Stories: West Coast Fiction from Canada's Best Writers*, ed. Derek Fairbridge, 179–201. Vancouver: Raincoast. First published 1999.
Marcus, Mordecai. 1960–61. "What Is an Initiation Story?" *Journal of Aesthetics and Art Criticism* 19 (2): 221–28.
Marshall, Joyce. 1975. *A Private Place*. Ottawa: Oberon.
———. 1993. *Any Time at All and Other Stories*. Toronto: McClelland and Stewart.
———. 1993. "The Heights." *Any Time at All and Other Stories*, 34–55. Toronto: McClelland and Stewart.
———. 1995. *Blood and Bone/En chair et en os*. Oakville, ON: Mosaic Press. (bilingual edition)
Matthews, Brander. 1994. "The Philosophy of the Short Story." In *The New Short Story Theories*, ed. Charles E. May, 73–80. Athens: Ohio University Press. First published 1885.
McCulloch, Thomas. 1862. *Letters of Mephibosheth Stepsure*. Repr. from the *Acadian Recorder* of the years 1821 and 1822. Halifax, Nova Scotia: H. W. Blackadar.
McGrath, Charles. 2013. "Alice Munro Puts Down Her Pen to Let the World In." *The New York Times* (July 1).
MacLeod, Alistair. 1976. *The Lost Salt Gift of Blood*. Toronto: McClelland and Stewart.
———. 1986. *As Birds Bring Forth the Sun and Other Stories*. Toronto: McClelland and Stewart.
McMullen, Lorraine, and Sandra Campbell, eds. 1993. *Pioneering Women: Short Stories by Canadian Women. Beginnings to 1880*. Ottawa: University of Ottawa Press.
Melville, Herman. 1856. *The Piazza Tales*. New York: Dix and Edwards.
Menasse, Eva. 2013. "So leicht, als wäre es nichts: Die Erzählungen der Literaturnobel-

preisträgerin Alice Munro haben eine Form, die Schriftsteller bewundern." *Die Zeit* 43 (October 17).
Metcalf, John. 1970. *The Lady Who Sold Furniture*. Toronto: Clarke, Irwin.
____, ed. 1970. *Sixteen by Twelve: Short Stories by Canadian Writers*. Toronto: McGraw-Hill Canada.
____. 1972a. "Soaping a Meditative Foot (Notes for a Young Writer)." In *The Narrative Voice: Short Stories and Reflections by Canadian Authors*, ed. John Metcalf, 154–59. Toronto: McGraw-Hill Ryerson.
____. 1972b. "A Conversation with Alice Munro." *Canadian Fiction Magazine*: 54–62.
____. 1975. *The Teeth of My Father*. Ottawa: Oberon.
____. 1982a. *Kicking Against the Pricks*. Downsview, ON: ECW Press.
____, ed. 1982b. *Making It New: Contemporary Canadian Stories*. Toronto: Methuen.
____. 1982c. *Selected Stories*. Toronto: McClelland and Stewart.
____. 1982d. "Gentle as Flowers Make the Stones." *Selected Stories*, 229–49. Toronto: McClelland and Stewart. First published 1975.
____. 1982e. "The Strange Aberration of Mr. Ken Smythe." *Selected Stories*, 161–73. Toronto: McClelland and Stewart. First published 1973.
____. 1986. *Adult Entertainment*. Toronto: Macmillan of Canada.
____. 1986. *The Bumper Book*. Toronto: ECW Press.
____. 1993. *Shooting the Stars*. Erin Mills, ON: Porcupine's Quill Press.
____. 1994. *Freedom from Culture: Selected Essays 1982–92*. Toronto: ECW Press.
____. 2011. *Going Down Slow*. Windsor, ON: Biblioasis. First published 1972.
Mistry, Rohinton. 1987. *Tales from Firozsha Baag*. Markham, ON: Penguin.
Mitchell, W. O. 1961. *Jake and the Kid*. Toronto: Macmillan of Canada.
____. 1989. *According to Jake and the Kid: A Collection of New Stories*. Toronto: McClelland and Stewart.
Moodie, Susanna. 1970. *Roughing It in the Bush*. Upper Saddle River, NJ: Literature House. First published 1852.
Morano, Michele. 2003. "Facts and Fancy: The 'Nonfiction Short Story.'" In *The Postmodern Short Story: Forms and Issues*, ed. Farhat Iftekharrudin, Joseph Boyden, Mary Rohrberger, and Jaie Claudet, 35–46. Westport, CT: Praeger.
Morley, Patricia. 1978. *Morley Callaghan*. Toronto: McClelland and Stewart.
Morris, Paul. 2007. "Ankunft in Toronto: Zeitgenössische kanadische Literatur und die Repräsentation der Identität von MigrantInnen." In *Montréal–Toronto: Stadtkultur und Migration in Literatur, Film und Musik*, ed. Verena Berger, Fritz Peter Kirsch, and Daniel Winkler, 87–98. Berlin: Weidler.
Moss, Laura. 2006. "Margaret Atwood: Branding an Icon Abroad." In *Margaret Atwood: The Open Eye*, ed. John Moss and Toby Kozakewich, 19–33. Ottawa: University of Ottawa Press.
Munro, Alice. 1968. *Dance of the Happy Shades*. Toronto: McGraw-Hill Ryerson.
____. 1968. "Boys and Girls." *Dance of the Happy Shades*, 111–27. Toronto: McGraw-Hill Ryerson.
____. 1968. "The Office." *Dance of the Happy Shades*, 59–74. Toronto: McGraw-Hill Ryerson.
____. 1971. *Lives of Girls and Women*. Harmondsworth: Penguin, 1982.
____. 1971. "Epilogue: The Photographer." *Lives of Girls and Women*, 239–50. Harmondsworth: Penguin, 1982.
____. 1971. "The Flats Road." *Lives of Girls and Women*, 1–27. Harmondsworth: Penguin, 1982.
____. 1974. *Something I've Been Meaning to Tell You*. Toronto: McGraw-Hill Ryerson.
____. 1974. "The Ottawa Valley." *Something I've Been Meaning to Tell You*, 182–97. Toronto: McGraw-Hill Ryerson.
____. 1978. *Who Do You Think You Are?* Toronto: Macmillan of Canada. [The edition used is the Penguin edition of 1980 under the title *The Beggar Maid*, see below.]

_____. 1978. "Simon's Luck." *Who Do You Think You Are*, 156–77. Toronto: Macmillan of Canada [The edition used is the Penguin edition of 1980 under the title *The Beggar Maid*, see below.]
_____. 1980. *The Beggar Maid: Stories of Flo and Rose*. Harmondsworth: Penguin. First published 1979. [Previously published as *Who Do You Think You Are?* (1978), see above.]
_____. 1982. *The Moons of Jupiter*. Toronto: Macmillan of Canada.
_____. 1982. "Dulse." *The Moons of Jupiter*, 36–59. Toronto: Macmillan of Canada. First published 1978.
_____. 1986. *The Progress of Love*. Toronto: McClelland and Stewart.
_____. 1986. "Miles City, Montana." *The Progress of Love*, 84–105. Toronto: McClelland and Stewart. First published 1985.
_____. 1990. *Friend of My Youth*. Toronto: McClelland and Stewart.
_____. 1993. "Author's Commentary on 'An Ounce of Cure' and 'Boys and Girls.'" In *How Stories Mean*, ed. John Metcalf and J. R. (Tim) Struthers, 185–87. Erin, ON: Porcupine's Quill Press. First published 1970.
_____. 1993. "On Writing 'The Office.'" In *How Stories Mean*, ed. John Metcalf and J. R. (Tim) Struthers, 192–94. Erin, ON: Porcupine's Quill Press.
_____. 1994. *Open Secrets*. Toronto: McClelland and Stewart.
_____. 1996. *Selected Stories*. Toronto: McClelland and Stewart.
_____. 1998. *The Love of a Good Woman*. Toronto: McClelland and Stewart.
_____. 2001. *Hateship, Friendship, Courtship, Loveship, Marriage*. Toronto: McClelland and Stewart.
_____. 2004. *Runaway*. Toronto: McClelland and Stewart.
_____. 2006. *The View from Castle Rock*. Toronto: McClelland and Stewart.
_____. 2009. *Too Much Happiness*. Toronto: McClelland and Stewart.
_____. 2009. "Fiction." *Too Much Happiness*, 32–61. Toronto: McClelland and Stewart. First published 2007.
_____. 2012. *Dear Life*. London: Chatto and Windus.
_____. 2012. "Dear Life." *Dear Life*, 299–319. London: Chatto and Windus. First published 2011.
_____. 2012. "In Sight of the Lake." *Dear Life*, 217–32. London: Chatto and Windus.
Nagel, James. 2001. *The Contemporary American Short-Story Cycle: The Ethnic Resonance of Genre*. Baton Rouge: Louisiana State University Press.
Neuman, Shirley. 1982. "Sheila Watson." In *Profiles in Canadian Literature*, ed. Jeffrey M. Heath. Vol. 4, 45–52. Toronto: Dundurn.
New, William H. 1987. *Dreams of Speech and Violence: The Art of the Short Story in Canada and New Zealand*. Toronto: University of Toronto Press.
_____. 1998. *Borderlands: How We Talk about Canada*. Vancouver: UBC Press.
Nicol, Heather. 2006. "The Canada-U.S. Border after September 11th: The Politics of Risk Constructed." *Journal of Borderlands Studies* 21 (1): 47–68.
Nischik, Reingard M. 1987. "The Short Story in Canada: Metcalf and Others Making It New." *Die Neueren Sprachen* 86 (3–4): 232–46.
_____. 1988. "Contrastive Structures in John Metcalf's Artist Stories." *Critique* 29 (3): 163–78.
_____. 1991. *Mentalstilistik: Ein Beitrag zu Stiltheorie und Narrativik—Dargestellt am Erzählwerk Margaret Atwoods*. Tübingen: Narr.
_____, ed. 2007. *The Canadian Short Story: Interpretations*. Rochester, NY: Camden House.
_____, ed. 2008a. *History of Literature in Canada: English-Canadian and French-Canadian*. Rochester, NY: Camden House.
_____. 2008b. "Introduction: Writing a History of Literature in Canada." In *History of Literature in Canada: English-Canadian and French-Canadian*, ed. Reingard M. Nischik, 1–24. Rochester, NY: Camden House.
_____. 2009. *Engendering Genre: The Works of Margaret Atwood*. Ottawa: University of Ottawa Press.

———, ed. 2014. *The Palgrave Handbook of Comparative North American Literature*. New York: Palgrave Macmillan.
———. 2016. *Comparative North American Studies: Transnational Approaches to American and Canadian Literature and Culture*. New York: Palgrave Macmillan.
———, and Caroline Rosenthal. 2002. "Einleitung." In *Schwellentexte der Weltliteratur*, ed. Reingard M. Nischik and Caroline Rosenthal, 9–31. Konstanz: UVK Universitätsverlag Konstanz.
Norris, Ken. 1984. *The Little Magazine in Canada 1925–80: Its Role in the Development of Modernism and Post-Modernism in Canadian Poetry*. Toronto: ECW Press.
Nowlan, Alden. 1968. *Miracle at Indian River*. Toronto: Clarke, Irwin.
———. 1984. *Will Ye Let the Mummers In? Stories*. Toronto: Irwin Publishing.
Ong, Walter J. 1982. *Orality and Literacy*. London: Methuen.
Orlovsky, Michael. 2003. "Historiografiction: The Fictionalization of History in the Short Story." In *The Postmodern Short Story: Forms and Issues*, ed. Farhat Iftekharrudin, Joseph Boyden, Mary Rohrberger, and Jaie Claudet, 47–62. Westport, CT: Praeger.
Orr, Katherine. 2015. "Liminality, Metaphoric Experience, and the Short-Story Form: Alice Munro's 'Wenlock Edge.'" In *Liminality and the Short Story: Boundary Crossings in American, Canadian, and British Writing*, ed. Jochen Achilles and Ina Bergmann, 251–62. New York: Routledge.
Padolsky, Enoch. 1997. "Cultural Diversity and Canadian Literature: A Pluralistic Approach to Majority and Minority Writing in Canada." In *New Contexts of Canadian Criticism*, ed. Ajay Heble, Donna Palmateer Pennee, and J. R. (Tim) Struthers, 24–42. Peterborough, ON: Broadview.
Palmer, Howard. 1994. "Reluctant Hosts: Anglo-Canadian Views of Multiculturalism in the Twentieth Century." *Immigration in Canada: Historical Perspectives*, ed. Gerald Tulchinsky, 297–333. Toronto: Longman.
Papinchak, Robert Allen. 1992. *Sherwood Anderson: A Study of the Short Fiction*. New York: Twayne.
Parker, George L. 2005. "English-Canadian Publishers and the Struggle for Copyright." In *History of the Book in Canada: 1840–1918*, ed. Yvan Lamonde, Patricia Lockhart Fleming, and Fiona A. Black. Vol. II, 148–59. Toronto: University of Toronto Press.
Penn, Arthur, dir. 1976. *The Missouri Breaks*. United Artists Corporation. Twentieth Century Fox Home Entertainment, 2006.
Pijoan, Teresa. 2005. *American Indian Creation Myths*. Santa Fe, NM: Sunstone.
Pratt, Mary Louise. 1991. "Arts of the Contact Zone." *Profession*: 33–40.
Rabb, Jane M., ed. 1995. *Literature and Photography: Interactions, 1840–1990: A Critical Anthology*. Albuquerque: University of New Mexico Press.
Rao, Eleonora. 2009. "'It's a Howling Wilderness': Forests and Mazes in Margaret Atwood's *The Tent*." *Cuadernos de Literatura Inglesa y Norteamericana* 12 (1–2): 61–67.
Resnick, Mike. 2012. *Resnick on the Loose*. Rockville, MD: Wildside.
Rich, Adrienne. 1979. "When We Dead Awaken: Writing as Re-Vision (1971)." *On Lies, Secrets, and Silence: Selected Prose 1966–1978*, 33–49. New York: Norton.
Richards, David Adams. 1978. *Dancers at Night*. Ottawa: Oberon.
Richler, Mordecai. 1969. *The Street*. Toronto: McClelland and Stewart.
Ricou, Laurence. 1973. *Vertical Man, Horizontal World: Man and Landscape in Canadian Prairie Fiction*. Vancouver: University of British Columbia Press.
Roberts, Charles G. D. 1903. *Earth's Enigmas: A Book of Animal and Nature Life*. Boston: Page. First published 1896.
Rollins, Douglas. 1985. "John Metcalf (1938–)." In *Canadian Writers and Their Works*, ed. Robert Lecker, Jack David, and Ellen Quigley, 155–211. Fiction Series, vol. 7. Toronto: ECW Press.
Rooke, Constance. 1986. "Fear of the Open Heart." In *A Mazing Space: Writing Canadian Women Writing*, ed. Shirley Neuman and Smaro Kamboureli, 256–69. Edmonton: Longspoon/NeWest.

_____. 1990. "Interview with Tom King." *World Literature Written in English* 30 (2): 62–76.

_____. 1992. "Old Age in Contemporary Fiction: A New Paradigm of Hope." In *Handbook of the Humanities and Aging*, ed. Thomas R. Cole, David D. Van Tassel, and Robert Kastenbaum, 241–57. New York: Springer Publishing Company.

Rosenthal, Caroline. 2008. "English-Canadian Literary Theory and Literary Criticism." In *History of Literature in Canada: English-Canadian and French-Canadian*, ed. Reingard M. Nischik, 291–309. Rochester, NY: Camden House.

_____. 2011. *New York and Toronto Novels after Postmodernism: Explorations of the Urban*. Rochester, NY: Camden House.

Ross, Sinclair. 1968. *The Lamp at Noon and Other Stories*. Toronto: McClelland and Stuart.

_____. 1982. *The Race and Other Stories*. Ottawa: University of Ottawa Press.

Rule, Jane. 1975. *Theme for Diverse Instruments*. Vancouver: Talonbooks.

_____. 1981. *Outlander: Short Stories and Essays*. Tallahassee, FL: Naid Press.

_____. 1985. *Inland Passage and Other Stories*. Tallahassee, FL: Naid Press.

_____. 1985. "Slogans." *Inland Passage and Other Stories*, 181–91. Tallahassee, FL: Naid Press.

Rutherford, Anna. 1992. "The Essential Heterogeneity of Being." *From Commonwealth to Postcolonial*, ed. Anna Rutherford, iii–ix. Sydney: Dangaroo.

Sadowski-Smith, Claudia. 2008. *Border Fictions: Globalization, Empire, and Writing at the Boundaries of the United States*. Charlottesville: University of Virginia Press.

_____. 2014. "The Literatures of the Mexico-US and Canada-US Borders." In *The Palgrave Handbook of Comparative North American Literature*, ed. Reingard M. Nischik, 185–97. New York: Palgrave Macmillan.

Schaeffer, Jean-Marie. 2009. "Fictional vs. Factual Narration." In *Handbook of Narratology*, ed. Peter Hühn, John Pier, Wolf Schmid, and Jörg Schönert, 98–114. Berlin: de Gruyter.

Scobie, Stephen. 1985. "Sheila Watson." In *Canadian Writers and Their Works*, ed. Robert Lecker, Jack David, and Ellen Quigley. Fiction Series, vol. 7, 259–312. Toronto: ECW Press.

Scofield, 2006. *The Cambridge Introduction to the American Short Story*. Cambridge: Cambridge University Press.

Scott, Duncan Campbell. 1896. *In the Village of Viger*. Boston: Copeland and Day.

Shackleton, Mark. 2003. "The Trickster Figure in Native North American Writing: From Traditional Storytelling to the Written Word." In *Connections: Non-Native Responses to Native Canadian Literature*, ed. Hartmut Lutz and Coomi S. Vevaina, 109–28. New Delhi: Creative.

_____. 2012. "'Have I Got Stories—' and 'Coyote Was There': Thomas King's Use of Trickster Figures and the Transformation of Traditional Materials." In *Thomas King: Works and Impact*, ed. Eva Gruber, 184–98. Rochester, NY: Camden House.

Shields, Carol. 1985. *Various Miracles*. Toronto: Stoddart.

_____. 1989. *The Orange Fish*. Toronto: Random House.

_____. 2000. *Dressing Up for the Carneval*. Toronto: Random House.

Simal, Begoña. 2014. "Memory Matters: Alice Munro's Narrative Handling of Alzheimer's in 'The Bear Came Over the Mountain' and 'In Sight of the Lake.'" *Miscelánea: A Journal of English and American Studies* 50: 61–78.

Small, Judy Jo. 1994. *A Reader's Guide to the Short Stories of Sherwood Anderson*. New York: G. K. Hall.

Smith, Ray. 1969. "Cape Breton Is the Thought-Control Centre of Canada." *Cape Breton Is the Thought-Control Centre of Canada*, 19–35. Toronto: Anansi.

_____. 1974. *Lord Nelson Tavern*. Toronto: McClelland and Stewart.

Sohngen, Mary. 1977. "The Experience of Old Age as Depicted in Contemporary Novels." *The Gerontologist* 17: 70–78.

Soja, Edward W. 1996. *Thirdspace: Journeys to Los Angeles and Other Real-and-Imagined Places*. Oxford: Blackwell.

Spettigue, Douglas O. 1972. "The Grove Enigma Resolved." *Queen's Quarterly* 79: 1–2.

Squamish Nation. "About Us—Our Land." www.squamish.net/about-us/our-land. Accessed July 20, 2016.
Stanzel, Franz K. 1990. "Textual Power in (Short) Short Story and Poem." In *Modes of Narrative: Approaches to American, Canadian and British Fiction*, ed. Reingard M. Nischik and Barbara Korte, 20–30. Würzburg: Königshausen and Neumann.
Struthers, John Russell. 1982. *Intersecting Orbits: A Study of Selected Story Cycles by Hugh Hood, Jack Hodgins, Clark Blaise, and Alice Munro, in Their Literary Contexts*. Thesis. The University of Western Ontario.
———. 1983. "The Real Material: An Interview with Alice Munro." In *Probable Fictions: Alice Munro's Narrative Acts*, ed. L. K. Mackendrick, 5–36. Downsview, ON: ECW Press. First published 1981.
———. 1985. *The Montreal Storytellers: Memoirs, Photographs, Critical Essays*. Montreal: Véhicule Press.
Sullivan, Rosemary. 1998. *The Red Shoes: Margaret Atwood Starting Out*. Toronto: Harper Flamingo.
Thacker, Robert. 1988. "'So Shocking a Verdict in Real Life': Autobiography in Alice Munro's Stories." In *Reflections: Autobiography and Canadian Literature*, ed. K. P. Stich, 153–61. Ottawa: University of Ottawa Press.
———. 1994. "Alice Munro and the Anxiety of American Influence." In *Context North America: Canadian/U.S. Literary Relations*, ed. Camille R. La Bossière, 133–44. Ottawa: University of Ottawa Press.
———. 2001. *Alice Munro: Writing Her Lives: A Biography*. Toronto: McClelland and Stewart. First published 2005.
Thien, Madeleine. 2005. "A Map of the City." In *The Vancouver Stories: West Coast Fiction from Canada's Best Writers*, ed. Derek Fairbridge, 307–30. Vancouver: Raincoast. First published 2001.
Thomas, Audrey. 1967. *Ten Green Bottles*. Indianapolis: Bobbs-Merrill Company.
———. 1967. "If One Green Bottle." *Ten Green Bottles*, 1–13. Indianapolis: Bobbs-Merrill Company. First published 1965.
———. 1977. *Ladies and Escorts*. Ottawa: Oberon.
———. 1981. *Real Mothers*. Vancouver: Talon Press.
———. 1981. *Two in the Bush and Other Stories*. Toronto: McClelland and Stewart.
———. 1986. *Goodbye, Harold, Good Luck*. Toronto: Viking.
———. 1986. "The Man with Clam Eyes." *Goodbye, Harold, Good Luck*, 15–23. Toronto: Viking.
———. 2001. *The Path of Totality: New and Selected Stories*. Toronto: Penguin.
———. 2001. "Salon des Refusés." *The Path of Totality: New and Selected Stories*, 159–73. Toronto: Penguin. First published 1967.
Thomas, Joan. 1999. "Introduction." In *Turn of the Story: Canadian Short Fiction on the Eve of the Millenium*, ed. Joan Thomas and Heidi Harms, vii–xv. Toronto: Anansi.
Thomassen, Bjørn. 2015. "Thinking with Liminality: To the Boundaries of an Anthropological Concept." In *Breaking Boundaries: Varieties of Liminality*, ed. Agnes Horvath, Bjørn Thomassen, and Harald Wydra, 39–58. New York: Berghahn.
Tieck, Ludwig. 1966. *Franz Sternbalds Wanderungen: Eine altdeutsche Geschichte (1798)*. Berlin: de Gruyter.
Tilden, Norma. 2004. "Nothing Quite Your Own: Reflections on Creative Nonfiction." *Women's Studies* 33: 707–18.
Trehearne, Brian. 1989. *Aestheticism and the Canadian Modernists: Aspects of a Poetic Influence*. Montreal: McGill-Queen's University Press.
Traill, Catharine Parr. 1989. *The Backwoods of Canada*. Toronto: McClelland and Stewart. First published 1836.
Truchan-Tataryn, Maria, and Susan Gingell. 2006. "Dances with Coyote: Narrative Voices in Thomas King's *One Good Story, That One*." *Postcolonial Text* 2 (3): 1–23.
Turcotte, Gerry. 2003. "Re/marking on History, or, Playing Basketball with Godzilla: Thomas King's Monstrous Post-Colonial Gesture." In *Connections: Non-Native Responses to*

Native Canadian Literature, ed. Hartmut Lutz and Coomi S. Vevaina, 205–35. New Delhi: Creative.
Turner, Victor. 1969. *The Ritual Process: Structure and Anti-Structure*. London: Routledge and Kegan Paul.
_____. 1982. *From Ritual to Theatre: The Human Seriousness of Play*. New York: PAJ Publications.
Tyrer, Pat. 2009. "Underground Railroad." In *American Countercultures: An Encyclopedia of Nonconformists, Alternative Lifestyles, and Radical Ideas in U.S. History*, ed. Gina Misiroglu. Vol. III, 726–28. Armonk, NY: Sharpe.
Valgardson, W. D. 1973. *Bloodflowers: Ten Stories*. Ottawa: Oberon.
_____. 1990. *What Can't Be Changed Shouldn't Be Mourned: Short Stories*. Vancouver: Douglas and McIntyre.
_____. 1999. *The Divorced Kids Club and Other Stories*. Toronto: Douglas and McIntyre.
Vanderhaeghe, Guy. 1982. *Man Descending: Selected Stories*. Toronto: Macmillan of Canada.
_____. 1983. *The Trouble with Heroes: And Other Stories*. Ottawa: Borealis Press.
_____. 1992. *Things As They Are? Short Stories*. Toronto: McClelland and Stewart.
Van Gennep, Arnold. 1909. *Les rites de passage*. Paris: Emile Nourry.
_____. 1977. *The Rites of Passage*. London: Routledge and Kegan Paul. Originally published 1909 in French, first translated into English 1960.
Ventura, Heliane. 1992. "Alice Munro's 'Boys and Girls': Mapping out Boundaries." *Commonwealth Essays and Studies* 15: 80–87.
Vizenor, Gerald. 1993. "Trickster Discourse: Comic and Tragic Themes in Native American Literature." In *Buried Roots and Indestructible Seeds: The Survival of American Indian Life in Story, History, and Spirit*, ed. Mark A. Lindquist and Martin Zanger, 67–83. Madison: University of Wisconsin Press.
Von Flotow, Luise, and Brita Oeding. 2007. "The 'Other Women': Canadian Women Writers Blazing a Trail into Germany." In *Translating Canada: Charting the Institutions and Influences of Cultural Transfer: Canadian Writing in German/y*, ed. Luise von Flotow and Reingard M. Nischik, 79–92. Ottawa: University of Ottawa Press.
Waddington, Miriam. 1982. *Summer at Lonely Beach and Other Stories*. Oakville, ON: Mosaic.
_____. 1982. "I'm Lonesome for Harrisburg." *Summer at Lonely Beach and Other Stories*, 85–86. Oakville, ON: Mosaic.
Wagner, Linda W. 1980. "Sherwood, Stein, the Sentence, and Grape Sugar and Oranges." *American Modern: Essays in Fiction and Poetry*, 31–41. Port Washington, NY: Kennikat Press.
Wahl, Greg. 1997. "An Interview with Clark Blaise." In *Speaking of the Short Story: Interviews with Contemporary Writers*, ed. Farhat Iftekharuddin, Mary Rohrberger, and Maurice Lee, 45–56. Jackson: University Press of Mississippi.
Walton, Priscilla. 1996. "It Is Indeed, 'One Good Story, That One': Thomas King's Parodic Treatment of Genesis." In *"And the Birds Began to Sing": Religion and Literature in Post-Colonial Cultures*, ed. Jamie S. Scott, 47–55. Amsterdam: Rodopi.
Washington, Kate. 2006. "Review of *The Tent*." *The San Francisco Chronicle* (January 22).
Watson, Sheila. 1984. *Five Stories*. Toronto: Coach House Press.
Weaver, Robert. 1958. "A Talk with Morley Callaghan." *The Tamarack Review* 7: 3–29.
_____. 1960. "Introduction." In *Canadian Short Stories*, selected by Robert Weaver, ix–xiii. Toronto: Oxford University Press.
Weber, Ronald. 1980. *The Literature of Fact: Literary Nonfiction in American Writing*. Athens: Ohio University Press.
Wesley, Marilyn C. 1994. "Love's Journey in *Crossing the Border*." In *Joyce Carol Oates: A Study of the Short Fiction*, ed. Greg Johnson, 174–80. New York: Twayne.
Wiebe, Rudy. 1974. *Where Is the Voice Coming From?* Toronto: McClelland and Stewart.
_____. 1974. "Where Is the Voice Coming From?" *Where Is the Voice Coming From?*, 135–43. Toronto: McClelland and Stewart.
_____. 1974. "The Naming of Albert Johnson." *Where Is the Voice Coming From?*, 145–55. Toronto: McClelland and Stewart.

———. 1982. *The Angel of the Tar Sands and Other Stories*. Toronto: McClelland and Stewart.
———. 1995. *River of Stones: Fictions and Memories*. Toronto: Vintage Canada.
Wilke, Gundula. 2003. "Look Twice: Thomas King's *Coyote Columbus Stories*." In *Connections: Non-Native Responses to Native Canadian Literature*, ed. Hartmut Lutz and Coomi S. Vevaina, 236–48. New Delhi: Creative.
Wilson, Ethel. 1990. *Mrs. Golightly and Other Stories*. Toronto: McClelland and Stewart. First published 1961.
———. 1990. "On Nimpish Lake." *Mrs. Golightly and Other Stories*, 36–40. Toronto: McClelland and Stewart. First published 1942.
Wilson, Milton. 1975. "Callaghan's Caviare." In *Morley Callaghan*, ed. Brandon Conron, 79–83. Toronto: McGraw-Hill. First published 1962.
Wilson, Sharon R. 2003. "Fiction Flashes: Genre and Intertexts in *Good Bones*." In *Margaret Atwood's Textual Assassinations: Recent Poetry and Fiction*, ed. Sharon Wilson, 18–41. Columbus: Ohio State University Press.
Winkler, Mary G. 1992. "Walking to the Stars." In *Handbook of the Humanities and Aging*, ed. Thomas R. Cole, David D. Van Tassel, and Robert Kastenbaum, 258–84. New York: Springer Publishing Company.
Wolf, Doris. 2012. "'All My Relations': Thomas King's Coyote Tetralogy for Kids." In *Thomas King: Works and Impact*, ed. Eva Gruber, 98–109. Rochester, NY: Camden House.
Wolf, Margery. 1985. *Revolution Postponed: Women in Contemporary China*. Stanford: Stanford University Press.
Woodcock, George. 1980. *George Woodcock's Introduction to Canadian Fiction*. Toronto: ECW Press.
———. 1993. *Moral Predicament: Morley Callaghan's* More Joy in Heaven. Toronto: ECW Press.
Woodward, Kathleen. 2012. "Assisted Living: Aging, Old Age, Memory Aesthetics." *Occasion: Interdisciplinary Studies in the Humanities* 4. http://occasion.stanford.edu/node/104. Accessed April 4, 2016.
Woolf, Virginia. 2001. *A Room of One's Own*. Peterborough, ON: Broadview. First published 1929.
Wyatt-Brown, Anne M. 1992. "Literary Gerontology Comes of Age." In *Handbook of the Humanities and Aging*, ed. Thomas R. Cole, David D. Van Tassel, and Robert Kastenbaum, 331–51. New York: Springer Publishing Company.
———. 1993. "Introduction: Aging, Gender, and Creativity." In *Aging and Gender in Literature: Studies in Creativity*, ed. Anne M. Wyatt-Brown and Janice Rossen, 1–15. Charlottesville: University Press of Virginia.
Wyile, Herb. 1999. "'Trust Tonto': Thomas King's Subversive Fictions and the Politics of Cultural Literacy." *Canadian Literature* 161/162: 105–24.
York, Lorraine M. 1988. *The Other Side of Dailiness: Photography in the Works of Alice Munro, Timothy Findley, Michael Ondaatje, and Margaret Laurence*. Toronto: ECW Press.
Zipp, Yvonne. 2006. "Review of *The Tent*." *The Christian Science Monitor* (January 17).

Index

"Absence" 67
Acadian Recorder 4
"Acceptance of Their Ways" 58
According to Jake and the Kid: A Collection of New Stories 60
Achilles, Jochen 120–21, 129
adaptation 113, 204
Adderson, Caroline 70
Adult Entertainment 52, 221n2
adventure tale *see* tale
The Adventures of Huckleberry Finn 34
An Aesthetic Underground 52
Africa 61, 66, 122
African American literature 3
After All: The Collected Stories V 54
Agassiz Stories/A Novel in Series (American edition) 67
age/aging 10, 55, 64, 66, 76, 114, 116, 118–34, 168, 205–7, 216ch8n4, 216n5, 216n6; Age Studies 10, 118, 121, 123; ageism/new ageism 122–24, 137–39; *see also* caring home
"The Age of Lead" 59
Albania 75
"The Albanian Virgin" 56
alienation 25, 109, 207
allegory 12, 26, 27, 54, 89, 180, 186–87
Allen, Paula Gunn 191
allusion 16, 17, 25, 26, 212n19
ambiguity 17, 19, 26, 38, 77, 78, 119, 125, 140, 212n19
ambivalence 113, 142, 144, 151, 157, 184, 201, 206, 207
American Dream *see* national myth
American literature 36, 40, 85, 87, 96, 122, 213n33; *see also* North American literature
American Renaissance 1, 28, 46
American Revolution 139
American short fiction *see* short fiction: American short fiction

American short story *see* short story: American short story
American writers 1, 6, 18, 29, 38, 45–47, 143
Americanization 16, 32
"And the Four Animals" 26, 27
Anderson, Sherwood 6, 28, 29–35, 37, 38, 45, 85, 89, 211ch2n4, 212n8, 212n9, 212n17, 212n18, 213n30, 213n33; "Death in the Woods" 31, 34; *Death in the Woods* 30, 31; "The Egg" 31; *Horses and Men* 30, 31; "I Want to Know Why" 6, 31, 33–35; "The Man Who Became a Woman" 31; "The Rabbit-pen" 212n9; *A Story Teller's Story* 30; *The Triumph of the Egg* 30, 31, 33; *Winesburg, Ohio* 29, 30, 31, 85, 89; *The Writer's Book* 30, 212n8
anecdote 3, 4, 87, 88, 89, 102–3; *see also* short story: precursors/roots
"The Angel of the Tar Sands" 61
The Angel of the Tar Sands and Other Stories 61
anglophone *see* English language/English
animal story 4–5, 34
animalization 207
"The Animals Reject Their Names and Things Return to Their Origins" 204
Annals of a Sportsman 211n5
anthropology 118, 119, 120, 193–94
anti–Americanism 55
anti–intellectualism 24
"Antigone" 27
antirealism *see* realism
Any Day But This 68
Any Time at All and Other Stories 25
"Apples" 69
approaches 2–3, 8, 9, 10, 85–94, 95–105; comparative 2, 6, 10, 28–47, 85, 189–202; didactic 2; gender-based 9, 95–105, 106–

243

17, 165–75; generic/subgeneric 2, 85–94, 95–105, 176–88; historical 2, 15–27, 28–47, 48–70, 71–84, 85–88, 95; literary-sociological 2, 85–88, 118–34; narratological 2, 203–10; regional 2, 135–49, 150–64
"Aquarius" 66
Arnason, David 51
Around the Mountain: Scenes from Montreal Life 54
"Art" 69
"The Art of Cooking and Serving" 114–16
The Art of Cooking and Serving 115
artist novel 92, 95–96
artist novella *see* artist novel
artist story 11–12, 52, 60, 64, 76, 77, 95–105, 109, 132, 169–70, 176–88, 205–7, 218n12, 221n4; artist-audience relationship *see* reader/readership/audience; artist figure 3, 9, 12, 60, 64, 95–105, 176, 179–80, 187, 205–9; Canadian 2, 9, 95–105, 176, 180
"As Birds Bring Forth the Sun" 63
As Birds Bring Forth the Sun and Other Stories 63
As for Me and My House 20
"Assomons les pauvres" 110
Atlantic Monthly 38, 65
The Atlantic Review 51
Atwood, Margaret 1, 2, 3, 7, 9, 10, 12–13, 47, 49, 51, 55–59, 60, 64, 69, 72, 96, 101–5, 106–17, 118, 130–31, 32, 166, 168, 191, 192, 203–9, 215ch6n4; "The Age of Lead" 59; "The Animals Reject Their Names and Things Return to Their Origins" 204; "The Art of Cooking and Serving" 114–16; "The Bad News" 110, 114, 130, 132; "A Beggar" 110; "Betty" 114; "Bluebeard's Egg" 59; *Bluebeard's Egg* 58, 59, 101, 105, 107 108–9, 114, 215ch6n4; "Bottle" 204; "The Boys at the Lab" 114; "Bring Back Mom: An Invocation" 204; *Cat's Eye* 96, 109; "Chicken Little Goes Too Far" 204; "Dancing Girls" 58; *Dancing Girls* 58–59, 105, 107, 114; "Death by Landscape" 59, 109, 112, 114, 215ch6n5, 223n17; "Encouraging the Young" 13, 205–6; "The Entities" 117; "Gateway" 223n6; "Gertrude Talks Back" 59, 112; "Giving Birth" 58; *Good Bones* 59, 107, 110, 111, 112, 116, 203; "The Grave of the Famous Poet" 58; "Hair Jewellery" 58; "Hairball" 59, 109; "Happy Endings" 204; "The Headless Horseman" 114; "Horatio's Version" 12, 204; "Hurricane Hazel" 114; "Iconography" 59, 110; "Instructions for the Third Eye" 116; "It's Not Easy Being Half-Divine" 204; "King Log in Exile" 204; "The Labrador Fiasco" 114; *Lady Oracle* 96; "Let Us Now Praise Stupid Women" 110; "Liking Men" 59, 111–12; "The Little Red Hen Tells All" 59, 112; "Lives of the Poets" 58, 105; "Loulou; or, The Domestic Life of Language" 105, 109; "Making a Man" 59, 111, 112; "The Man from Mars" 58, 108; "Men at Sea" 59, 110, 112; *Moral Disorder* 58, 107, 114–17, 130, 204, 215ch6n5; *Murder in the Dark: Short Fictions and Prose Poems* 59, 107, 110, 111, 116, 203, 204, 209, 223n1; "My Last Duchess" 114, 215ch6n5; *Negotiating with the Dead: A Writer on Writing* 104; *The New Oxford Book of Canadian Short Stories in English* 49; "Nightingale" 204; "No More Photos" 205; "Our Cat Enters Heaven" 204; *The Oxford Book of Canadian Short Stories in English* 49; "Polarities" 58; "Resources of the Ikarians" 204; "The Resplendent Quetzal" 58; "Salome Was a Dancer" 204; "Significant Moments in the Life of My Mother" 9, 101–5, 109; *Stone Mattress* 107; *Survival* 116; "Take Charge" 204; "The Tent" 13, 110, 207–8, 223n6; *The Tent* 2, 3, 12, 107, 203–9; "Thylacine Ragout" 223ch14n9; "A Travel Piece" 58; "Two-Headed Poems" 107; "Uglypuss" 59; "Uncles" 109, 114; "Under Glass" 58; "Unearthing Suite" 109, 215ch6n4; "Voice" 13, 206–7, 209; "The War in the Bathroom" 59; "Weight" 110, 215ch6n5; "Wilderness Tips" 59; *Wilderness Tips* 58, 59, 107, 109, 114, 215ch6n5; "Winter's Tales" 205, 223n6; "Women's Novels" 59; "Worship" 59, 110
"Au lecteur" 110
Australia 75
auto/biographical elements 34, 53, 60, 63, 65, 74, 76, 83, 97, 98, 101, 103, 104, 114, 130, 140, 154, 167, 168, 169, 173, 205, 206–7, 217n11, 218n11, 218n12, 220n5, 221ch11n6, 223n17
Away from Her (film) 216n8
The Axe's Edge 68

The Backwoods of Canada 87
"Bad Men Who Love Jesus" 193
"The Bad News" 110, 114, 130, 132
Baker, Carlos 40, 41
The Barclay Family Theatre 62, 90
Baudelaire, Charles 9, 59, 110–12; "Assomons les pauvres" 110; "Au lecteur"

110; "Le chat" 110; "Un cheval de race" 110; *Les fleurs du mal* 110, 112; "Un hémisphère dans une chevelure" 110; "L'homme et la mer" 59, 110, 112; "Le serpent qui danse" 110; *Le spleen de Paris* 110
Bear 64
"The Bear Came Over the Mountain" 56, 132, 216n8, 216n9
"A Beggar" 110
Benjamin, Walter 218n10
Bennett, Bill 159
Bergmann, Ina 120
"Bertha" 68
Best (American) Short Stories 20, 38
Best American Stories 63
Best Canadian Short Stories 50
Best Canadian Stories 50, 178
"Betty" 114
Bible 12, 26, 191, 192–94
Bierce, Ambrose 18, 29
bildungsroman 61, 92, 95
A Bird in the House 7, 60–61, 64, 65, 90
"The Birds" 23
Birdsell, Sandra 7, 67, 69; *Agassiz Stories/A Novel in Series* (American edition) 67; "Flowers for Weddings and Funerals" 67; "Judgement" 67; "Keepsakes" 67; *Ladies of the House* 67; "The Man from Mars" 67; "Night Travellers" 67; *Night Travellers* 67; *The Two-Headed Calf* 67
Bissoondath, Neil 7, 68; *Digging Up the Mountains* 68; *On the Eve of Uncertain Tomorrows* 68
Blaise, Clark 7, 51, 52–53, 60, 178; "A Class of New Canadians" 53; "Eyes" 54; "Going to India" 54; "How I Became a Jew" 54; "Identity" 54; "I'm Dreaming of Rocket Richard" 54; *Man and His World* 53; *Montreal Stories* 53; "North" 54; "A North American Education" 53, 54; *A North American Education* 53, 54; "Notes Beyond a History" 54; *Pittsburgh Stories* 53; *Resident Alien* 53, 54; *The Selected Stories of Clark Blaise* 53; *Southern Stories* 53; *Tribal Justice* 54; *World Body* 53
Blood and Bone/En chair et en os (bilingual edition) 25, 26
"Bloodflowers" 68
Bloodflowers: Ten Stories 68
"Bluebeard's Egg" 59
Bluebeard's Egg 58, 59, 101, 105, 107 108–9, 114, 215ch6n4
"The Boat" 18, 63

Bobbi Lee: Indian Rebel 219n12
Boccaccio, Giovanni 85; *Decamerone* 85
Bonheim, Helmut 50–51
Boni & Liveright 36, 213n22
book series *see* short story: book series
border 10, 135–37, 139, 140, 143–49, 203, 209, 218n10, 219n18; borderland 135; borderline 135, 137, 140, 143, 149, 152, 157, 162, 196, 207, 208, 218n10; Canada-U.S. 10, 131, 135–37, 139–40, 143–46, 149, 218n14; crossing 10, 131–32, 135–37, 139–41, 143, 145–49, 151–52, 218n14; guard 139, 145–49, 218n15; narrative 2, 10, 135, 137, 139, 140, 147, 149m, 218n18; region 120, 135, 139, 140, 143, 218n10; studies 135
"The Border Crossing" 145
"Borders" 67, 135, 137, 148, 149, 196, 218n15
"Bottle" 204
The Boundaries of Genre 223n1
Bovenschen, Silvia 216ch8n3
Bowering, George 7, 27, 69; "Apples" 69; *Flycatcher* 69; *A Place to Die* 69; "A Short Story" 69
Bowman, Louise Morey 213n36
"Boys and Girls" 11, 55, 74, 165, 168–75
Boys and Girls (film) 212n11
"The Boys at the Lab" 114
Brand, Dionne 7, 68, 96; "Photograph" 68; "Sans Souci" 68; *Sans Souci and Other Stories* 68
Brantford (Ontario) 152
"Bring Back Mom: An Invocation" 204
British Columbia 22, 74, 144, 153, 158
British literature 59, 85, 87, 88, 89
British short fiction *see* short fiction: British short fiction
"Broken Teeth" 158–59, 162
"Brother and Sister" 65
Buller, Cecil 213n36
The Bumper Book 52
Burns, Robert 181
"Burnt Norton" 214n7, 215n9
Butler, Judith 9, 107, 175
Butler, Robert 122
By a Frozen River: The Short Stories of Norman Levine 49

Cabbagetown 24
Café Le Dog 69
"Cages" 62
California 145, 147
Callaghan, Morley 1, 5, 6, 18–20, 22, 24, 28, 35–39, 42–45, 46, 47, 48, 176, 212n13, 213n24, 213n26, 213n27, 213n30, 213n32,

213n33; *The Complete Stories of Morley Callaghan* 213n23; "A Girl with Ambition" 19, 36; *The Lost and Found Stories of Morley Callaghan* 19, 213n23; *The Morley Callaghan Reader* 213n23; *Morley Callaghan's Stories* 19, 36, 213n23; *A Native Argosy* 19, 36, 213n23; *The New Yorker Stories* 213n23; *Now That April's Here and Other Stories* 19, 213n23; "The Shining Red Apple" 6, 39, 42–45; *Strange Fugitive* 37; "That Summer in Paris" 37; *That Summer in Paris* 36, 38–39, 45
Campbell, Sandra 3, 211ch2n3
Canada 2, 4, 7–8, 10, 16, 24, 25, 26, 29, 31–32, 38, 45–47, 48–53, 55, 58–62, 68, 71–73, 84, 85, 86–91, 95, 135–39, 141–42, 148–49, 165, 169; English 23, 50; French 211n2
Canada Council 49, 178
Canadian Authors Association's Jubilee Award for Short Stories 166, 214n4
Canadian Broadcasting Corporation (CBC) 49, 60, 179; CBC Radio 25, 49, 60, 176
Canadian dream *see* national myth
Canadian Fiction Magazine 50
The Canadian Forum 31
Canadian Home Journal 24
Canadian literature 6, 8–9, 16, 23, 26, 31–32, 39, 47, 48–51, 58, 59, 63–64, 65, 68, 72, 85–88, 90, 94, 96–97, 110, 177–78, 180, 188, 201, 219n6, 220n19; Canadian and Québécois literature 211; contemporary literature 27, 58, 59; *see also* North American literature
Canadian Mosaic 53, 59, 152
Canadian Renaissance 6, 48, 55, 177, 187
Canadian short fiction *see* short fiction: Canadian short fiction
Canadian Short Stories 16, 32, 212n13
Canadian short story *see* short story: Canadian short story
"The Canadian Short Story" 32
Canadian-U.S. relations 87, 135–37, 141–42, 144–45
canon 3, 15, 29, 32, 70, 96, 111, 118, 162, 178, 211ch2n3
The Canterbury Tales 85
Cape Breton 63
"Cape Breton Is the Thought Control Centre of Canada" 55
capitalism 113
caricature 191
caring home 120, 122, 127–30, 132; *see also* age/aging; liminality: liminal location
carpe diem 131
Carr, Emily 11, 153–55, 157, 162; *Klee Wyck* 154; "Sophie" 154, 157, 162
Carried Away 166
cartoon 108
Carver, Raymond 29, 201
Casgrain, Abbé Henri-Raymond 211n2
"Cat in the Rain" 6, 39–45
Cather, Willa 29, 98, 211ch2n2
Cat's Eye 96, 109
CBC Anthology 49, 74
"Le chat" 110
Chatelaine 24, 31, 74
Chaucer, Geoffrey 85; *The Canterbury Tales* 85
"Chemistry" 66
Cheney, Harriet Vaughan 3, 211ch2n3
Chesnutt, Charles W. 3
"Un cheval de race" 110
"Chicken Little Goes Too Far" 204
China 151, 197
Chinese Canadians 150–51, 158–62; writers 10, 150–52, 157–58, 189; *see also* Chinese Canadian short fiction
Choosing His Coffin: The Best Stories of Austin Clarke 68
"Circus in Town" 21
citizenship 146–47
city *see* setting
Clarke, Austin 7, 60, 68, 69; *Choosing His Coffin: The Best Stories of Austin Clarke* 68
class 19, 23, 66, 67, 123, 157
"A Class of New Canadians" 53
Clinton (Ontario) 74, 220n4
The Clockmaker; or, The Sayings and Doings of Samuel Slick of Slickville 4, 87, 89
"The Closer You Get to Canada, the More Things Will Eat Your Horses" 137–39, 147, 217n3, 217n4, 217n5, 217n6, 217n8
"The Closing Down of Summer" 63
Coach House Press 48
Cohen, Matt 7, 69; *Café Le Dog* 69; *Columbus and the Fat Lady* 69; "Keeping Fit" 69; *Lives of the Mind Slaves: Selected Stories* 69; "The Sins of Tomas Benares" 69
Collected Poems 214n7, 215n9
Collected Poems of Raymond Knister 212n11
Collected Stories: 1955–2010 61
collection *see* short prose collection, short story collection
colonialism 8, 137, 153, 174, 194, 197
Columbus, Christopher 196–97

Index

Columbus and the Fat Lady 69
comedy/comic element 9, 12, 22, 23, 59, 111
comic strip 203
coming-of-age novel 92
commercialization 16, 32
Commonwealth Writers' Prize 73, 166
The Complete Short Stories of Ernest Hemingway 213n22
The Complete Stories of Morley Callaghan 213n23
"Condolence Visit" 68
Confederation of Canada 3, 46, 86, 89
"The Confession Tree" 64
Connor, Ralph 21
Contact Publishing 36, 213n22
continentalism 46
Cooper, James Fenimore 86
copyright 86
"Cornet at Night" 21
cosmopolitanism, rooted 53, 59–60, 163
Cost of Living 57
Coupland, Douglas 152
Coyote *see* trickster figure
"Coyote and the Enemy Aliens" 196
"A Coyote Columbus Story" 196, 223n15
Crane, Stephen 18, 29
Crawford, Isabella Valancy 1, 4, 15, 211n3; "Extradited" 211n3
creation story *see* myth/mythology
Cree 62
crime story 17, 21
criticism 33, 57, 177, 195; cultural 31, 49, 177–78, 203; literary 1, 2, 8, 13, 18, 23, 24, 25, 26, 29, 31, 33, 39, 41, 45, 49, 52, 54, 55, 57, 66, 68, 91, 123, 166, 177–78, 203; short fiction 177; thematic 52, 177
"Crossing the Border" 148
crossover fiction 7, 69
culture 68, 85, 86–87, 122, 154–57, 161, 182, 193, 195–96, 202; Canadian 52, 54, 72, 86–87, 176–77, 187; Chinese 158–59, 220n16;

Dahlie, Hallvard 221n8
Dance of the Happy Shades 55, 56, 73, 74, 75, 100, 165, 168, 169, 173, 175
Dancers at Night 63
"Dancing Girls" 58
Dancing Girls 58–59, 105, 107, 114
Dark Glasses 54
Darwin, Charles 4
Daudet, Alphonse 85; *Lettres de mon moulin* 85
"A Day with Pegasus" 21
Dean, Misao 15, 211n3

"Dear Life" 56, 75, 76
Dear Life 56, 75, 77, 127, 166, 168
death 16, 21, 42, 118, 121, 127, 128, 129, 130–34, 159, 168, 209
"Death by Landscape" 59, 109, 112, 114, 215ch6n5
Death Goes Better with Coca-Cola 69
"Death in the Woods" 31, 34
Death in the Woods 30, 31
"Death of an Artist" 66
de Beauvoir, Simone 123; *Old Age/La Vieillesse* 123
Decamerone 85
Le Déjeuner sur l'herbe 129
de la Roche, Mazo 212ch2n13
DelConte, Matt 208
Delville, Michel 9, 107, 204
dementia 122, 127–30, 132, 133, 216n8, 216n9; *see also* age/aging
"Democracy and the Short Story" 15
Deneuve, Catherine 125
Denison, Merrill 212ch2n13
Derrida, Jacques 11, 172
Desert Hearts (film based on Rule novel) 64
Desert of the Heart 64
detective story 4
developmental novel 95
diaspora 11, 68
dichotomy 8, 109, 155, 160, 170, 224n10
didactic narrative 19, 61, 87, 112, 116, 180, 184
Digging Up the Mountains 68
The Diviners 96
The Divorced Kids Club: And Other Stories 68
"Do Seek Their Meat from God" 4
"The Dog I Wish I Had, I Would Call It Helen" 200
"Domestic Furies" 200, 201
draft dodgers *see* war
drama 12, 59, 110, 113, 203, 204
dream/dreaming 10, 66, 126–28, 130, 132, 139, 143; *see also* nightmare
Dreiser, Theodore 24, 29
Dressing Up for the Carnival 66–67
"Drummer" 62
Dubliners 85
"Dulse" 9, 55, 56, 77, 97–100, 105
Duncan, Norman 212ch2n13
Duncan, Sara Jeannette 5, 18, 214ch2n37; *The Pool in the Desert* 5
dystopia 137–39

"Early Morning Rabbits" 52, 179
Earth's Enigmas 4

Eastern Canada 7, 54, 60
"Edith-Esther" 66
editorial 3; *see also* short story: precursors/roots
"The Egg" 31
Eíbl, Doris ix
"Elaine" 16, 17, 31, 212*ch*2*n*19
Eliot, T.S. 16, 31, 40, 42, 45–46, 77, 94, 214*n*7, 215*n*9; "Burnt Norton" 214*n*7, 215*n*9; *Collected Poems* 214*n*7, 215*n*9; "Hamlet and His Problems" 31; "Tradition and the Individual Talent" 16, 31
ellipsis 16, 17, 212*n*19
emigration *see* migration
"Encouraging the Young" 13, 205–6
"The End of Summer" 65
The End of the World and Other Stories 57
Engel, Marian 7, 64, 69; *Bear* 64; "The Confession Tree" 64; *Inside the Easter Egg* 64; "The Tattooed Woman" 64; *The Tattooed Woman* 64
Engendering Genre: The Works of Margaret Atwood 106, 203
England 57, 89, 169, 177
English language/English ix, 47, 49–50, 56, 95, 153, 160, 182, 190, 199, 223*n*10
English literature *see* British literature
"The Entities" 117
"Epilogue: The Photographer" 56, 77, 93
epiphany 16, 20, 22, 38, 56, 80, 99, 142, 168
Erber, Joan T. 121, 122, 123
ersatz images 25
essay 3, 89, 120, 203, 204, 205, 206, 208, 209; *see also* short story: precursors/roots
essay-fiction 9, 12, 107, 110, 113, 205–9
ethnicity 2–3, 10, 12, 50, 67, 108, 150–57, 161, 162–63, 189, 219*n*6, 220*n*19
euphemism 128
Europe 19, 23, 45–46, 57, 86, 122, 137, 153, 196, 197
Even-Zohar, Itamar 97; *see also* polysystem theory
evolutionary theory 4
exile 57
Exile 213*n*23
existentialism 18
expatriation 33, 46, 56
EXPO '67 54
"The Extra Man" 18
"Extradited" 211*n*3
"Eyes" 54

Faber and Faber 215*n*9
fable 113, 204
Fairbridge, Derek 152; *The Vancouver Stories: West Coast Fiction from Canada's Best Writers* 152
fairy tale *see* tale
Family Furnishings: Selected Stories 166
family story 12, 16, 21, 55, 60, 62–63, 66, 102–5, 109, 114–16, 143–45, 158–62, 191, 200–1, 215*ch*6*n*2, 221*ch*11*n*6, 221*n*9
fantastic story 12, 192, 198
fantastic style 50, 62, 64, 190, 192, 198
farm story 16–17
"The Fate of Mrs. Lucier" 16, 31
Faulkner, William 29, 215*ch*5*n*9
feminism 11, 97, 167–69, 173
"Fiction" 8, 56, 79–84
fictional essay *see* essay-fiction
The Fifth Column and the First Forty-Nine Stories 213*n*22
Findley, Timothy 65
"The First Day of Spring" 6, 16, 33–35, 212*n*19
First Nations 11, 25, 61, 150, 153–57, 162, 220*n*15; writers 2–3, 10–12, 150, 152, 153, 162, 189; *see also* indigeneity; short fiction: First Nations short fiction; short story: Canadian, First Nations short story
"Fits" 56
Fitzgerald, Scott F. 20, 31, 36–38, 45
Five Stories 26, 27
flashback 121
"The Flats Road" 214*n*8, 220*n*2
Fleming, May Agnes 3, 211*ch*2*n*3
Les fleurs du mal 110, 112
"Flitting Behaviour" 66
"Flowers for Weddings and Funerals" 67
"The Flowers That Killed Him" 21
Fludernik, Monika 223*n*5, 223*n*7
Flycatcher 69
"Flying a Red Kite" 54
Flying a Red Kite: Stories 54, 176, 215*ch*6*n*2
"Fog" 22
folk tale *see* tale
Forde Abroad: A Novella 52
formula story/formulaic style 4, 16, 24
Foucault, Michel 129
Four Stories (early version of *Five Stories*) 26
France 18, 87, 110–11, 125–26, 129, 130–31, 169
Franz Sternbalds Wanderungen 215*ch*6*n*1
Fraser, Raymond 7, 51, 178
Das Fräulein von Scuderi 96
Freedom from Culture: Selected Essays 52
Freud, Sigmund 26
"Friend of My Youth" 74, 168
Friend of My Youth 74, 166, 167, 168

"From the Fifteenth District" 58
From the Fifteenth District 57, 58
frontier 22
The Fruit Man, the Meat Man and the Manager 54
Frye, Northrop 86

Gadpaille, Michelle 2, 3, 4, 211*n*3, 223*n*1
Gallant, Mavis 7, 10, 51, 55–59, 69, 96, 118, 125–26, 127, 134, 179; "Acceptance of Their Ways" 58; *Cost of Living* 57; *The End of the World and Other Stories* 57; "From the Fifteenth District" 58; *From the Fifteenth District* 57, 58; *Home Truths: Selected Canadian Stories* 57, 58; "The Ice Wagon Going Down the Street" 58; "In Transit" 58, 125, 134; "In Youth Is Pleasure" 58; "The Latehomecomer" 58; "Madeline's Birthday" 57; "The Moslem Wife" 58; "My Heart Is Broken" 58; *My Heart Is Broken* 57, 58; *The Other Paris* 57; *Overhead in a Balloon: Stories of Paris* 57; "The Pegnitz Junction" 58; *The Pegnitz Junction* 57; *The Selected Stories of Mavis Gallant* 58; "Virus X" 58
"The Garden Court Motor Hotel" 193
Garner, Hugh 22, 24–25, 48; *Cabbagetown* 24; *Hugh Garner's Best Stories* 24; "The Legs of the Lame" 24; *The Legs of the Lame* 24; *Men and Women* 24; *One Damn Thing After Another* 24; "One-Two-Three Little Indians" 24, 25; *Violation of the Virgins* 24; "The Yellow Sweater" 24; *The Yellow Sweater* 24
"Gateway" 223*n*6
gay rights movement 64
gender/gender relations 2, 3, 9, 11, 21, 50, 55, 59, 60, 64, 65, 66, 72, 74, 76, 92, 95–105, 106–17, 123, 158–59, 165–75, 195, 212*n*15; *see also* approaches: gender-based approach; men/male; misogyny; women/female
General Ludd 180
genre 1–13, 15, 19, 20, 24, 27, 28–29, 39, 47, 48–51, 55, 57, 58, 69, 71–72, 77–78, 84, 85, 88–91, 94, 95–96, 106–7, 110, 118, 120–21, 124, 166–67, 179, 180, 190, 197, 203–4, 209; crossing 3, 9, 11–13, 91, 107, 203, 209; subgenre 4, 9, 95, 97, 107, 176, 203, 209; theory 85, 107, 203–4
"Gentle as Flowers Make the Stones" 52, 179, 215*ch*6*n*2
German classicism 95
German literature 95–96
Germany 23, 57, 87, 91, 95–97, 182–87

Gerson, Carole 152; *Vancouver Short Stories* 152
"Gertrude Talks Back" 59, 112
"Getting to Williamstown" 54
Gibbins, Roger 135
Gibert, Teresa 189, 190–91, 200, 223*n*10, 223*n*13
Gibson, Douglas 72
Giller Prize 51, 73, 166
"Girl in Gingham" 52, 221*n*2
"A Girl with Ambition" 19, 36
"Giving Birth" 58
Godard, Barbara 27
Godfrey, Dave 7, 69; *Death Goes Better with Coca-Cola* 69; "A New Year's Morning on Bloor Street" 69; "River Two Blind Jacks" 69
"Godman's Master" 61
"Godzilla vs. Post-Colonial" 190, 192
Goetsch, Paul 45
Going Down Slow 180
"Going Out as a Ghost" 54
"Going to India" 54
Goldman, Marlene 212*n*14, 212*n*15, 221*ch*11*n*7, 221*n*8
Good Bones 59, 107, 110, 111, 112, 116, 203
Goodbye Harold, Good Luck 66
Gordimer, Nadine 92
Gough, Laurie 10, 145–48; "The Border Crossing" 145
"A Gourdful of Glory" 61
Governor General's Award for Fiction 2, 51, 56, 57, 62, 73, 154, 165, 166
Govier, Katherine 7, 67
graphic novel 203
"The Grave of the Famous Poet" 58
Great Britain 8, 73, 86–87, 89, 91, 119, 151, 153
Great Depression 6, 20, 21, 36, 43, 44, 140
Greve, Felix Paul *see* Grove, Frederick Philip
Grove, Frederick Philip 5–6, 17–20, 23, 48, 60, 214*n*37; "The Boat" 18; "The Extra Man" 18; "In Search of Acirema" 18; *Lazybones* 18; "Lost" (earlier version of "Snow") 17; "The Sale" 18; "Saturday Night at the Crossroads" 18; "Snow" 17–18; *Tales from the Margin: Selected Stories of Frederick Philip Grove* 17, 18
Gruber, Eva 135, 139, 148, 196, 198, 199, 218*n*15, 222*n*1, 222*n*5, 223*n*11
Der grüne Heinrich 95
The Guest House and Other Stories 68
Gulette, Margaret 122
Gunnars, Kristjana 7, 68; *Any Day But*

This 68; *The Axe's Edge* 68; *The Guest House and Other Stories* 68

"Hackman's Night" 17
"Hair Jewellery" 58
"Hairball" 59, 109
Hale, Katherine 213ch2n36
Hale, Sarah Josepha 89; *Sketches of American Character* 89
Haliburton, Thomas Chandler 4, 87, 88, 89; *The Clockmaker; or, The Sayings and Doings of Samuel Slick of Slickville* 4, 87, 89
Hamlet 12, 59, 204
"Hamlet and His Problems" 31
Hancock, Geoff 50, 166, 176; *Illusion One/Illusion Two: Fables, Fantasies and Metafiction* 50; *Invisible Fictions* 50; *Moving Off the Map: From "Story" to "Fiction"* 50
"Haply the Soul of My Grandmother" 22
"Happy Endings" 204
Harcourt, Joan 180; *73: New Canadian Stories* 180
Harper's Bazaar 52, 180, 212n9
Harrison, Susan Frances 1, 4, 15
Harte, Bret 18
Hateship, Friendship, Courtship, Loveship, Marriage 56, 132, 166
Hawthorne, Nathaniel 1, 29
"The Headless Horseman" 114
Heble, Ajay 11, 172
"The Heights" 25
Heine, Heinrich 186, 222n10
Helwig, David 180; *73: New Canadian Stories* 180
Hemingway, Ernest 6, 19–20, 24, 28, 29, 31, 35–45, 176, 212n10, 213n22, 213n24, 213n27, 213n32; "Cat in the Rain" 6, 39–45; *The Complete Short Stories of Ernest Hemingway* 213n22; *The Fifth Column and the First Forty-Nine Stories* 213n22; "Hills Like White Elephants" 39; *in our time* 36, 212n21, 213n22; *In Our Time* 36, 212n21, 213n22; *Men Without Women* 39, 213n22; *A Moveable Feast* 213n27; *The Nick Adams Stories* 213n22; "The Revolutionist" 212n21; *Three Stories & Ten Poems* 36, 213n22; "A Very Short Story" 212n21; *Winners Take Nothing* 213n22
"Un hémisphère dans une chevelure" 110
Henry, O. 29
heterotopia 129; *see also* Foucault, Michel
Highway, Tomson 192
"Hills Like White Elephants" 39

historiography 153
history 59, 61–62, 68, 130–31, 139, 153, 157, 191, 192, 197–98, 202; (re-)writing 12, 61–62, 195–96
Hitting the Charts: Selected Stories 69
Hodgins, Jack 7, 62–63, 69, 90; *The Barclay Family Theatre* 62, 90; *Spit Delaney's Island* 62, 90
Hoffmann, E.T.A. 96; *Das Fräulein von Scuderi* 96
Hollywood 156
Home Truths: Selected Canadian Stories 57, 58
"L'homme et la mer" 59, 110, 112
homosexuality 65; homoeroticism 65; homophobia 65; *see also* gay rights movement; gender/gender relations
Hood, Hugh 7, 51, 54, 69, 176, 178, 215ch6n2; *After All: The Collected Stories V* 54; *Around the Mountain: Scenes from Montreal Life* 54; *Dark Glasses* 54; "Flying a Red Kite" 54; *Flying a Red Kite: Stories* 54, 176, 215ch6n2; *The Fruit Man, The Meat Man and the Manager* 54; "Getting to Williamstown" 54; "Going Out as a Ghost" 54; *The New Age/Le nouveau siècle* 54; "Three Halves of a House" 54; "Where the Myth Touches Us" 215ch6n2
"Horatio's Version" 12, 204
horror 23
Horses and Men 30, 31
House of Anansi Press 48
"How Corporal Colin Sterling Saved Blossom, Alberta, and Most of the Rest of the World as Well" 198
"How I Became a Jew" 54
Howells, Coral Ann 78, 165, 167–68, 214n6, 214n10, 220n4
Howells, William Dean 5
Huggan, Isabel 7, 67
Hugh Garner's Best Stories 24
humanities 119, 123
humor/humorous tradition 4, 12, 18, 58, 59, 60, 67, 97, 112, 116, 191, 192, 194, 201, 202
"Hurricane Hazel" 114
"Hurry, Hurry" 22, 23
Hutcheon, Linda 204
hybridization 13, 91, 94, 110, 113, 120, 191, 196, 198, 204–5, 209
hyperrealism *see* realism

"I Want to Know Why" 6, 31, 33–35
"The Ice Wagon Going Down the Street" 58

Index

iceberg theory 37, 42
iconography 6, 153, 160, 161
"Iconography" 59, 110
"Identity" 54
identity 25, 59, 116, 119, 122, 125, 149, 162–63, 169–71, 193; collective 163; ethnic 150; formation 161–63; national 38, 55, 59, 152, 220n20 (*see also* nationalism/national perspective); urban *see* urbanism
"If One Green Bottle" 65
"Ilk" 67
Illusion One/Illusion Two: Fables, Fantasies and Metafiction 50
"I'm Dreaming of Rocket Richard" 54
"I'm Lonesome for Harrisburg" 140–43, 147
image (of Canada, of the U.S.)/imagology 10, 53, 141, 148
imagery 26, 32, 112, 133, 161
imagism 16, 20, 38, 179
immigration *see* migration
in medias res 18, 25, 35
in our time 36, 212n21, 213n22
In Our Time 36, 212n21, 213n22
"In Search of Acirema" 18
"In Sight of the Lake" 127
In the Village of Viger 4, 5, 88, 89, 212n13, 214n37
"In Transit" 58, 125, 134
"In Youth Is Pleasure" 58
independence (political) 46, 61, 86
India 68
indigeneity 7, 25, 62, 137–38, 150–51, 153–57, 191–94, 196–97, 199–202, 211, 219n13; writers 190, 192, 202; *see also* First Nations
Indonesia 160
industrialism 140, 142
Ingram, Forrest 88
initiation 10–11, 16, 21, 33, 34, 92, 170–74, 180; novel 92; story 33, 34, 92, 115, 121; *see also* epiphany
"Initram" 66
Inland Passage and Other Stories 65, 132
"Inland Passage" 65
"Innocent Man" 17
Inside the Easter Egg 64
"Instructions for the Third Eye" 116
interculturalism *see* themes: intercultural themes
internationalism 6, 19, 35, 38, 46, 89
Internet 145
intertextuality 6, 9, 26, 59, 66, 110–12, 191
interview 176–77, 192
interzone 204

Inuit 61
inversion poetics/inversion techniques 111–12, 116, 216ch7n4
Invisible Fictions 50
irony 4, 18, 19, 23, 67, 80, 103, 108, 111–13, 129, 137, 144, 183, 185, 191, 198, 205, 219n13
Irving, Washington 28, 89; *The Sketch Book of Geoffrey Crayon, Gent.* 89
Island: The Collected Stories 63
isotope 138
"It's Not Easy Being Half-Divine" 204

Jake and the Kid 60
James, Henry 5, 29, 96; "The Real Thing" 96
Jean, Michaëlle 163
Jelinek, Elfriede 97
"Joe the Painter and the Deer Island Massacre" 196
Johnson, Pauline 11, 151, 152–53, 157, 160, 162; *Legends of Vancouver* 152; "The Two Sisters" 153, 157, 162
journal 19, 20, 36, 38; *see also* magazine/literary magazine
journalism 3, 57, 112; style 20, 38, 54
journey *see* travel
"Joy" 65
Joyce, James 26, 42, 52, 56, 85, 168, 212n10, 213n27; *Dubliners* 85; *Ulysses* 42
"Judgement" 67
"Jug and Bottle" 21
Jung, Carl Gustav 26
juxtaposition 112, 185, 191

"Kat" 26
Keefer, Janice Kulyk 7, 63, 68; *The Paris-Napoli Express* 68; *Transfigurations* 68; *Travelling Ladies* 68
"Keeping Fit" 69
"Keepsakes" 67
Keller, Gottfried 95; *Der grüne Heinrich* 95
Kermode, Frank 55
"Keys and Watercress" 52, 179, 215ch6n2
Kicking Against the Pricks 52
King, Thomas 3, 7, 10, 12, 67, 118, 135, 137–39, 141, 147–49, 189–202, 217n1, 222n3; "Bad Men Who Love Jesus" 193; "Borders" 67, 135, 137, 148, 149, 196, 218n15; "The Closer You Get to Canada, the More Things Will Eat Your Horses" 137–39, 147, 217n3, 217n4, 217n5, 217n6, 217n8; "Coyote and the Enemy Aliens" 196; "A Coyote Columbus Story" 196, 223n15; "The Dog I Wish I Had, I

Would Call It Helen" 200; "Domestic Furies" 200, 201; "The Garden Court Motor Hotel" 193; "Godzilla vs. Post-Colonial" 190, 192; "How Corporal Colin Sterling Saved Blossom, Alberta, and Most of the Rest of the World as Well" 198; "Joe the Painter and the Deer Island Massacre" 196; "Little Bombs" 198; "Looking for Home: Chapter One" 222*n*1; "Magpies" 200; *Medicine River* 189; "Not Counting the Indian, There Were Six" 200-1; "The One About Coyote Going West" 193, 196; "One Good Story, That One" 67, 193, 195-96; *One Good Story, That One* 67, 137, 189, 193, 196, 198, 200; "Prairie Time" 222*n*1; "Rendezvous" 198; "A Seat in the Garden" 198; "A Short History of Indians in Canada" 198-99; *A Short History of Indians in Canada* 137, 189, 193, 196, 200-1; "Simple Sufferings" 222*n*1; "States to Avoid" 200; "Totem" 198; "Trap Lines" 200; *Truth and Bright Water* 135
"King Log in Exile" 204
Kinsley, Michael 123; *Old Age: A Beginner's Guide* 123
Klee Wyck 154
Knister, Raymond 1, 5, 6, 15-20, 23, 28, 29, 31-34, 35, 36, 38-39, 45, 47, 48, 51, 212*n*10, 212*n*19, 213*n*26; *Canadian Short Stories* 16, 32, 212*n*13; "The Canadian Short Story" 32; *Collected Poems of Raymond Knister* 212*n*11; "Democracy and the Short Story" 15; "Elaine" 16, 17, 31, 212*ch*2*n*19; "The Fate of Mrs. Lucier" 16, 31; "The First Day of Spring" 6, 16, 33-35, 212*n*19; "Hackman's Night" 17; "Innocent Man" 17; "The Loading" 16-17, 31; "Mist-Green Oats" 16, 31; "The One Thing" 31; "The Strawstack" 16, 31
Kroetsch, Robert 50
Kunow, Rüdiger 122
Kureishi, Hanif 220*n*15; *My Beautiful Launderette* 220*n*15

"The Labrador Fiasco" 114
Ladies and Escorts 66
Ladies of the House 67
Lady Oracle 96
"The Lady Who Sold Furniture" 52, 221*n*2
The Lady Who Sold Furniture 52, 179
Lake Huron (Ontario) 74, 143, 145, 165, 220*n*4
Lakehead Review 49
The Lamp at Noon 20, 21, 22

land 153, 155
landscape 18, 21, 63, 65, 144
"The Latehomecomer" 58
Laurence, Margaret 7, 18, 23, 60-61, 64-66, 69, 90, 96; *A Bird in the House* 7, 60-61, 64, 65, 90; *The Diviners* 96; "Godman's Master" 61; "A Gourdful of Glory" 61; "The Rain Child" 61; "The Tomorrow-Tamer" 61; *The Tomorrow-Tamer* 61
"Lazybones" 18
Leacock, Stephen 4, 87, 88, 90, 212*n*13; *Sunshine Sketches of a Little Town* 88, 90
Lee, Sky 11, 158-59, 162; "Broken Teeth" 158-59, 162
Legends of Vancouver 152
"The Legs of the Lame" 24
The Legs of the Lame 24
Leprohon, Rosanna 4
"Let Us Now Praise Stupid Women" 110
letter to the editor 8, 87
Letters of Mephibosheth Stepsure 4, 87
Lettres de mon moulin 85
Levine, Norman 49; *By a Frozen River: The Short Stories of Norman Levine* 49; "We All Begin in a Little Magazine" 49
"Lichen" 77
"Liking Men" 59, 111-12
"Lilian" 65
liminality 9-10, 118-34, 135, 140-43, 149, 197, 216*ch*8*n*2, 218*n*9, 218*n*10; experience 119-20, 121, 125; location 9, 10, 118, 120, 129, 132; period 10, 118-20, 124, 130; phase 119, 218*n*9; space 10, 22, 66, 124, 125, 127, 129, 131, 135, 140, 149, 196, 218*n*9; state 9-10, 115, 118, 120, 124, 125-26, 127, 132, 135, 140, 149; liminoid 119-20, 125, 127, 132
The Literary Garland 87-88, 89
literary gerontology 123, 124; see also age/aging
"Literary Gerontology Comes of Age" 124
literary history 15-27, 28-47, 48-70, 71-84, 85-87, 94
literary market 8, 19, 20, 23, 29, 38-39, 46-47, 48, 86, 88, 91, 97, 178
literary period 95
literary sociology 85, 86, 94
literary studies 72, 73, 177
literary theory 2
"Little Bombs" 198
little magazine 30, 49, 211*ch*2*n*2
"The Little Red Hen Tells All" 59, 112
The Little Review 30
Lives of Girls and Women 8, 55, 56, 74, 77,

78, 90, 91–94, 165, 166, 175, 214n8, 214n10, 220n5, 221ch11n6
Lives of the Mind Slaves: Selected Stories 69
"Lives of the Poets" 58, 105
Livesay, Dorothy 23, 46
"The Loading" 16–17, 31
local-color fiction/story 3–4, 21, 60, 63, 65, 88–90, 165
Lodge, David 7, 39, 69
London, Jack 18
London (Ontario) 74, 75, 165
London (UK) 46, 86, 181
"Looking for Home: Chapter One" 222n1
Lopate, Phillip 123
Lord Nelson Tavern 55
"Lost" (earlier version of "Snow") 17
The Lost and Found Stories of Morley Callaghan 19, 213n23
lost generation 45
"The Lost Salt Gift of Blood" 63
The Lost Salt Gift of Blood 63
Lotman, Jurij M. 221n1, 221n7
"Loulou; or, The Domestic Life of Language" 105, 109
The Love of a Good Woman 73, 166, 168, 214n3, 214n5
"Love So Fleeting, Love So Fine" 66
Lucas, Alec 5
Lukács, Georg 94, 215ch5n10; *Die Theorie des Romans* 215n10
Lying Under the Apple Tree 166
Lynch, Gerald 189
Lyon, Annabel 70

MacLean's Magazine 31
MacLeod, Alistair 7, 51, 63; "As Birds Bring Forth the Sun" 63; *As Birds Bring Forth the Sun and Other Stories* 63; "The Boat" 63; "The Closing Down of Summer" 63; *Island: The Collected Stories* 63; "The Lost Salt Gift of Blood" 63; *The Lost Salt Gift of Blood* 63; *No Great Mischief* 63; "The Road to Rankin's Point" 63; "Vision" 63
Macmillan 19, 36, 213n23
"Madeline's Birthday" 57
magazine/literary magazine 3, 8, 16, 20, 24, 29–32, 47, 48–49, 51, 86–88, 211ch2n2; *Atlantic Monthly* 38, 65; *The Atlantic Review* 51; *Canadian Fiction Magazine* 50; *The Canadian Forum* 31; *Canadian Home Journal* 24; *Chatelaine* 24, 31, 74; *Harper's Bazaar* 52, 180, 212n9; *Lakehead Review* 49; *The Literary Garland* 87–88, 89; *The Little Review* 30; *MacLean's Magazine* 31; *Malahat Review* 49; *Masses* 30; *The Midland* 31, 33, 212n10; *National Home Monthly* 24; *The New Brunswick Religious and Literary Repository* 87; *The New Yorker* 1, 19, 38, 42, 49, 51, 56–57, 75, 166, 214n5; *The Nova Scotian* 87; *Paris Review* 213n27; *Province Magazine* 152; *Queen's Quarterly* 20; *Saturday Night* 45, 51; *Scribner's Magazine* 19, 36, 38; *The Seven Arts* 30; *The Smart Set* 33, 213n33; *Stewart's Quarterly* 90; *Tamarack Review* 74; *This Quarter* 19, 31, 36, 212n10; *Time Magazine* 56; *University of Windsor Review* 49; *Wascana Review* 49; *Winnipeg Tribune Magazine* 17
magic realism *see* realism
"Magpies" 200
Mahler, Gustav 82
"Making a Man" 59, 111, 112
Making It New: Contemporary Canadian Stories 49–50, 178
Malahat Review 49
Man and His World 53
Man Booker International Prize 73
"Man Descending" 62
Man Descending: Selected Stories 62
"The Man from Mars" 58, 67, 108
"The Man Who Became a Woman" 31
"The Man with Clam Eyes" 66
Manet, Édouard 129; *Le Déjeuner sur l'herbe* 129
Mann, Thomas 96; *Tonio Kröger* 96
Manning, Gerald F. 122
Mansfield, Katherine 23
Manson, Charles 110, 139
map/mapping 141, 159–62, 163
"A Map of the City" 159–62
Maracle, Lee 7, 11, 67–68, 151, 152, 154, 157, 160, 162–63, 219n12, 220n15; "Bertha" 68; *Bobbi Lee: Indian Rebel* 219n12; "Polka Partners, Uptown Indians and White Folks" 68, 154–57, 162; *Sojourner's Truth* 68; "Yin Chin" 68
Marcus, Mordecai 33
maritime *see* setting
maritime fiction 7, 63
Marriott, Anne 213n36
Marshall, Joyce 6, 25–26, 27; *Any Time at All and Other Stories* 25; *Blood and Bone/En chair et en os* (bilingual edition) 25, 26; "The Heights" 25; "Kat" 26; "The Old Woman" 25; *A Private Place* 25
Masses 30
"Material" 56

254   Index

"A Matter of Balance" 68
Matthews, Brander 3, 13, 209, 224n11
Maugham, W. Somerset 24
McCullers, Carson 76
McCulloch, Thomas 4, 87; *Letters of Mephibosheth Stepsure* 4, 87
McMullen, Lorraine 3, 211ch2n3
Medicine River 189
Melville, Herman 1, 29, 89; *The Piazza Tales* 89
memory 125, 127, 130, 132, 142–43, 158; collective 124; space 143
Men and Women 24
"Men at Sea" 59, 110, 112
men/male 16, 21, 33, 111–12, 116, 170–75; masculinity 9, 65, 211n3; perspective 16, 21, 33, 53, 62; writers 7, 55, 62–63, 72, 76, 96, 97, 111; *see also* female perspective; gender relations; women/female
Men Without Women 39, 213n22
Menasse, Eva 71
Mennonite 61, 67
metafiction 7, 9, 62, 66, 69, 77, 78, 83, 84, 93, 103–4, 175
metanarrative 191, 196
metaphor 13, 125, 130, 133–34, 140, 205, 206–8
"The Metaphor Is Dead—Pass It On" 67
metapoetry 58, 77, 97, 205
Metcalf, John 2, 7, 11–12, 49–50, 51–53, 91, 96, 176–88, 215ch6n2; *Adult Entertainment* 52, 221n2; *An Aesthetic Underground* 52; *Best Canadian Short Stories* 50; *Best Canadian Stories* 50, 178; *The Bumper Book* 52; "Early Morning Rabbits" 52, 179; *Forde Abroad: A Novella* 52; *Freedom from Culture: Selected Essays* 52; *General Ludd* 180; "Gentle as Flowers Make the Stones" 52, 179, 215ch6n2; "Girl in Gingham" 52, 221n2; *Going Down Slow* 180; "Keys and Watercress" 52, 179, 215ch6n2; *Kicking Against the Pricks* 52; "The Lady Who Sold Furniture" 52, 221n2; *The Lady Who Sold Furniture* 52, 179; *Making It New: Contemporary Canadian Stories* 49–50, 178; *New Canadian Stories* 50, 178; "Polly Ongle" 52, 221n2; "Private Parts: A Memoir" 52, 221n2; *Selected Stories* 52, 179, 215ch6n2, 221n4; *Shooting the Stars* 179, 221n2, 221ch12n5; *Sixteen by Twelve: Short Stories by Canadian Writers* 49, 178; *Standing Stones: The Best Stories of John Metcalf* 52, 179; "The Strange Aberration of Mr. Ken Smythe" 11, 52, 176, 179–88, 215ch6n2; "The Teeth of My Father" 52, 179; *The Teeth of My Father* 52, 180, 221n4; "Travelling Northward" 52, 221n2; "The Years in Exile" 52, 179
methodology *see* approaches
Métis 61, 67, 154; *see also* First Nations
The Midland 31, 33, 212n10
migration 68, 147; emigration 57, 147, 159; immigration 53, 57, 67–68, 87, 89, 108, 150–51, 158–63, 215ch6n2
"Miles City, Montana" 135, 143–45, 149
"Milk Bread Beer Ice" 66
miniature story 55
minorities 61, 67, 151, 162, 219n6, 220n19; writing 67–68, 151–52, 162, 219n6, 220n19
Miracle at Indian River 63
mise-en-abyme 103, 170
misogyny 9, 110–12; *see also* gender/gender relations; men/male; women/female
"Miss Foote" 132
The Missouri Breaks (film) 217n8
"Mist-Green Oats" 16, 31
Mistry, Rohinton 7, 68, 69, 215ch6n2; "Condolence Visit" 68; "Swimming Lessons" 68, 215ch6n2; *Tales from Firozsha Baag* 68, 215ch6n2
Mitchell, W.O. 18, 60, 69; *According to Jake and the Kid: A Collection of New Stories* 60; *Jake and the Kid* 60; *Who Has Seen the Wind* 60
modernism 2, 3, 5, 6, 18, 28, 32, 45–46, 68–70, 150; American 6, 28, 29, 46 (*see also* short story: modernist American short story); Canadian 6, 15, 26, 28, 29, 31–32, 39, 46, 48, 50, 71, 213n35 (*see also* short story: modernist Canadian short story); European 29; modernist style 5–6, 16, 17, 19, 20, 21, 25, 26, 27, 29, 34, 35, 38, 42, 50, 52, 179, 182; realist-modernist tradition *see* realism: realist-modernist tradition
modernity 15, 18, 25, 27, 34, 88
montage 59, 77, 114, 129, 168
Montreal 19, 24, 25, 38, 51, 53–54, 60, 177–78
Montreal Star 90
Montreal Stories 53
Montreal Story Tellers Fiction Performance Group 7, 51–55, 60, 178; *see also* Blaise, Clark; Fraser, Raymond; Hood, Hugh; Metcalf, John; Smith, Ray
Moodie, Susanna 3, 87, 89, 211ch2n3; *Roughing It in the Bush* 87
"The Moons of Jupiter" 55, 221ch11n6
The Moons of Jupiter 55, 56, 72, 77, 78, 91, 97, 166, 168, 221ch11n6

Moral Disorder 58, 107, 114–17, 130, 204, 215*ch*6*n*5
Mörike, Eduard 96; *Mozart auf der Reise nach Prag* 96
Morley, Patricia 45
The Morley Callaghan Reader 213*n*23
Morley Callaghan's Stories 19, 36, 213*n*23
Morson, Gary Saul 223*n*1; *The Boundaries of Genre* 223*n*1
"The Moslem Wife" 58
Moss, Laura 149
motif 3, 5, 6, 9, 10, 33, 34, 39, 58, 76, 80, 88, 98, 125, 149, 178, 180, 200, 208
A Moveable Feast 213*n*27
Moving Off the Map: From "Story" to "Fiction" 50
Mozart auf der Reise nach Prag 96
Mrs. Golightly and Other Stories 22, 23
"Mrs. Golightly and the First Convention" 23
"Mrs. Turner Cutting the Grass" 67
Muir, Edwin 23
Mukherjee, Bharati 53
multiculturalism 7, 53, 57, 58, 59, 67–68, 108, 150, 152, 157, 162, 189, 220*n*19; melting-pot model 162, 220*n*20
Munro, Alice 1, 2, 7–8, 9, 10, 11, 23, 47, 51, 55–56, 57, 58, 59, 69, 71–84, 85, 90–94, 96, 97–101, 105, 118, 127, 132, 135, 143–45, 149, 165–75, 179, 180, 212*n*13, 214*n*3, 214*n*9, 215*ch*5*n*3, 215*ch*5*n*4, 215*n*7, 215*ch*6*n*3, 220*n*3, 220*n*5; "The Albanian Virgin" 56; *Away from Her* (film based on Munro story) 216*n*8; "The Bear Came Over the Mountain" 56, 132, 216*n*8, 216*n*9; "Boys and Girls" 11, 55, 74, 165, 168–75; *Boys and Girls* (film based on Munro story) 212*n*11; *Carried Away* 166; *Dance of the Happy Shades* 55, 56, 73, 74, 75, 100, 165, 168, 169, 173, 175; "Dear Life" 56, 75, 76; *Dear Life* 56, 75, 77, 127, 166, 168; "Dulse" 9, 55, 56, 77, 97–100, 105; "Epilogue: The Photographer" 56, 77, 93; *Family Furnishings: Selected Fiction* 166; "Fiction" 8, 56, 79–84; "Fits" 56; "The Flats Road" 214*n*8, 220*n*2; "Friend of My Youth" 74, 168; *Friend of My Youth* 74, 166, 167, 168; *Hateship, Friendship, Courtship, Loveship, Marriage* 56, 132, 166; "In Sight of the Lake" 127; "Lichen" 77; *Lives of Girls and Women* 8, 55, 56, 74, 77, 78, 90, 91–94, 165, 166, 175, 214*n*8, 214*n*10, 220*n*5, 221*ch*11*n*6; *The Love of a Good Woman* 73, 166, 168, 214*n*3, 214*n*5; *Lying Under the Apple Tree* 166; "Material" 56; "Miles City, Montana" 135, 143–45, 149; "The Moons of Jupiter" 55, 221*ch*11*n*6; *The Moons of Jupiter* 55, 56, 72, 77, 78, 91, 97, 166, 168, 221*ch*11*n*6; *New Selected Stories* 166; *No Love Lost* 166; "The Office" 9, 55, 74, 100–1, 105; *Open Secrets* 56, 166; "The Ottawa Valley" 55, 74, 77, 220*n*3; "The Peace of Utrecht" 55, 74, 168, 217*n*10; *The Progress of Love* 56, 73, 77, 143, 166, 215*n*11; *Runaway* 73, 166; *Selected Stories* 166, 214*n*10; "Simon's Luck" 56, 79; *Something I've Been Meaning to Tell You* 55, 56, 74, 78, 166; "Spelling" 217*n*10; *Too Much Happiness* 56, 79, 166, 214*n*3; *The View from Castle Rock* 166; *Vintage Munro* 166; "Walker Brothers Cowboy" 75; "What Is Remembered" 132; "White Dump" 56; *Who Do You Think You Are?/The Beggar Maid: Stories of Flo and Rose* (American and British edition) 55, 56, 73, 74, 78, 79, 91, 93, 94, 166, 214*n*3, 214*n*9, 220*n*1
Murder in the Dark: Short Fictions and Prose Poems 59, 107, 110, 111, 116, 203, 204, 209, 223*n*1
Murtha, Thomas 212*n*13
music 182–87
musical 182; *Oklahoma* 182; *The Sound of Music* 182
My Beautiful Launderette 220*n*15
"My Father's House" 65
"My Heart Is Broken" 58
My Heart Is Broken 57, 58
"My Last Duchess" 114, 215*ch*6*n*5
mythology 26, 113, 147, 191–93, 195–96, 202, 204, 223*n*14; ancient 26, 27; biblical creation 112, 192–94, 197, 222*n*4; creation story 12, 192–93; indigenous 152–54, 191, 193–94, 222*n*4; European 26, 197; motherhood 115; *see also* national myth

NAFTA *see* North American Free Trade Agreement
Nagel, James 85
"The Naming of Albert Johnson" 62
narrative perspective 5, 11, 16, 17, 21, 25, 33, 35, 52, 53, 54, 55, 56, 60–61, 62, 63, 65, 77, 81, 127, 140–42, 154, 157, 169, 172, 181–82, 191–96, 198–200, 201, 205–8
narrative technique 9, 12–13, 16, 17, 18, 19, 20, 21, 23, 26, 33, 34–35, 38, 39–41, 44–45, 52, 54, 55, 56, 57–58, 59, 62, 63, 65, 78, 80–81, 97, 105, 113, 114, 121, 125, 127–28, 129, 131, 132–33, 161, 167, 168, 169, 175, 177, 181, 186, 190–92, 193–94, 196, 201, 205–9

nation/nation-state 89, 136, 137, 140
National Film Board of Canada 212*n*11
National Home Monthly 24
national literature 8, 15, 46, 48, 51, 52, 85, 149
national myth 148-49; American Dream 143, 146-47; Canadian Dream 58, 139, 148, 160; Canadian myths 59, 86; First Nations/Native myths 195, 199, 200, 202
nationalism/national perspective 52, 143-45, 148, 178, 183-85
A Native Argosy 19, 36, 213*n*23
Native Canadian *see* First Nations
Native discourse 195, 197
Native folklore 200
naturalism 3, 4-5, 17-18, 19, 29
nature 16, 17-18, 21, 22-23, 25, 63, 86, 100, 133, 137-38, 153, 155, 157, 169, 174
Negotiating with the Dead: A Writer on Writing 104
neorealism *see* realism
Neuman, Shirley 27
New, William H. 91, 135
The New Age/Le nouveau siècle 54
New Brunswick 98, 99
The New Brunswick Religious and Literary Repository 87
New Canadian Stories 50, 178
The New Oxford Book of Canadian Short Stories in English 49
New Selected Stories 166
New World 61
"A New Year's Morning on Bloor Street" 69
New York City 19, 20, 38, 86
New York Herald Tribune 37
The New York Times 75, 123
The New York Times Book Review 215*ch*5*n*5
The New Yorker 1, 19, 38, 42, 49, 51, 56-57, 75, 166, 214*n*5
The New Yorker Stories 213*n*23
newspaper 8, 32, 86-88, 130; *Acadian Recorder* 4; *Montreal Star* 90; *New York Herald Tribune* 37; *The New York Times Book Review* 215*ch*5*n*5; *The New York Times* 75, 123; *The Novascotian* 4; *The Saturday Evening Post* 51; *Toronto Daily Star* 20; *Toronto Star* 36; *Toronto Star Weekly* 31; *The Vancouver Sun* 73
The Nick Adams Stories 213*n*22
"Night Travellers" 67
Night Travellers 67
"Nightingale" 204
nightmare 10, 127-28, 143; *see also* dream/dreaming

9/11 10, 135-36, 143, 146, 148, 218*n*14, 218*n*18
Nischik, Reingard M. ix, 1, 2, 8, 10, 47, 49, 135, 137, 141, 147, 148, 178, 180, 203, 218*n*10; *Engendering Genre: The Works of Margaret Atwood* 106, 203
No Great Mischief 63
No Love Lost 166
"No More Photos" 205
"No Other Way" 22
Nobel Prize in Literature 1-2, 7-8, 36, 51, 55, 71-73, 84, 90, 91, 127, 166, 167, 214*n*3
nonrealism *see* realism
Norris, Ken 29, 213*n*35
"North" 54
North America 57, 136, 143-44, 147, 149, 173, 192-93, 198, 201
"A North American Education" 53, 54
A North American Education 53, 54
North American Free Trade Agreement (NAFTA) 136
North American literature 6, 12, 36, 85, 96, 131, 173, 201; *see also* American literature; Canadian literature
"Not Counting the Indian, There Were Six" 200-1
"Notes Beyond a History" 54
The Nova Scotian 87
The Novascotian 4
novel 2, 8, 11, 69, 72, 74, 78, 84, 85, 88-94, 95, 120, 121, 135, 166, 214*n*10, 215*ch*5*n*3, 215*ch*5*n*3, 215*ch*5*n*5, 215*n*7
novella 52, 179, 180
Now That April's Here and Other Stories 19, 213*n*23
Nowlan, Alden 7, 63; *Miracle at Indian River* 63; *Will Ye Let the Mummers In?* 63

Oates, Joyce Carol 148; "Crossing the Border" 148
Oberon Press 48
objective correlative 16, 20, 37-44
O'Connor, Flannery 29, 76
Oeding, Brita 97
"The Office" 9, 55, 74, 100-1, 105
Oklahoma 182
Old Age: A Beginner's Guide 123
Old Age/La Vieillesse 123
"The Old Woman" 25
"On Nimpish Lake" 22
On the Eve of Uncertain Tomorrows 68
Ondaatje, Michael 72
"The One About Coyote Going West" 193, 196
One Damn Thing After Another 24

"One Good Story, That One" 67, 193, 195–96
One Good Story, That One 67, 137, 189, 193, 196, 198, 200
"The One Thing" 31
"One-Two-Three Little Indians" 24, 25
"One's a Heifer" 21
Ong, Walter J. 190; *Orality and Literacy* 190
onomatopoeia 132, 200
Ontario 16, 19, 33, 60, 74, 75–76, 79, 90, 92, 141–42, 143–45, 165, 167, 220*n*4
Ontario Trillium Book Award 73, 166
open ending 40, 78, 167
Open Secrets 56, 166
oral tradition 12, 60, 113, 189, 190–91, 193, 200, 223*n*13
Orality and Literacy 190
"The Orange Fish" 66
The Orange Fish 66
Orr, Katherine 120–21
the Oscar 212*n*11
The Other 64, 65, 108, 193, 199, 212*n*14
The Other Paris 57
Ottawa 60, 178
"The Ottawa Valley" 55, 74, 77, 220*n*3
"Our Cat Enters Heaven" 204
"Our Men and Women" 67
"Out in the Midday Sun" 66
"Outlander" 65
Outlander: Short Stories and Essays 65
"The Outlaw" 21, 22
Overhead in a Balloon: Stories of Paris 57
The Oxford Book of Canadian Short Stories in English 49
Oxford University Press 49

parable 13, 19, 27, 113, 138, 189, 192, 198, 204, 205, 208
"Pardon" 67
Paris 19, 20, 36–38, 46, 56–57
The Paris-Napoli Express 68
Paris Review 213*n*27
Parisian Salon de Refusés 129
Parker, Gilbert 4, 212*n*13
parody 67, 112–13, 185, 191, 192–95
passenger 119
pastoralism 153
Path of Totality 132
patriotism 148
"The Peace of Utrecht" 55, 74, 168, 217*n*10
"The Pegnitz Junction" 58
The Pegnitz Junction 57
PEN Malamud Award for Excellence in Short Fiction 166, 214*n*4
Penguin 72, 91

periodicals *see* magazine/literary magazine
personification 207
philosophy 54
"Photograph" 68
photography 90, 93, 215*n*8
The Piazza Tales 89
Pickthall, Margery L. C. 212*n*13
pioneer 3, 18, 86, 211*ch*2*n*3
Pittsburgh Stories 53
A Place to Die 69
playwright 60
plot story 16, 19, 30
Poe, Edgar Allan 1, 4, 29, 88, 89, 224*n*11
poetry 31, 51, 58, 110–11, 113, 120, 178, 203, 204, 205, 208
The Poison Plot 30
"Polarities" 58
politics/political sciences 52, 112, 114, 119, 137, 139, 149, 187, 202
"Polka Partners, Uptown Indians and White Folks" 68, 154–57, 162
"Polly Ongle" 52, 221*n*2
polysystem theory 97
The Pool in the Desert 5
Porcupine's Quill Press 53
postcolonialism 46, 55, 72, 88, 153, 169
postmodernism 46, 50, 54, 66, 68–70, 110, 175, 178–79, 190, 213*n*35; style 6, 7, 26, 27, 50, 52, 61, 64, 66, 69, 107, 168, 173, 190, 203, 215*n*11
postrealism *see* realism
poststructuralism 215*n*11, 224*n*10
Pound, Ezra 45–46, 212*n*10, 213*n*27
prairie 5–6, 17–18, 20–21, 50, 60–62, 67; fiction 5, 7, 21; realism *see* realism: prairie realism; story 5–6, 17–18, 20–21, 60–62; writer 17–18, 20–21, 60, 62
"Prairie Time" 222*n*1
premodernism 2, 15, 29
"The Princess, the Boeing, and the Hot Pastrami Sandwich" 54–55
"Private Parts: A Memoir" 52, 221*n*2
A Private Place 25
prize/literary prize 1–2, 51, 72–73, 91, 165–66, 179; Canadian Authors Association's Jubilee Award for Short Stories 166, 214*n*4; Commonwealth Writers' Prize 73, 166; Giller Prize 51, 73, 166; Governor General's Award for Fiction 2, 51, 56, 57, 62, 73, 154, 165, 166; Man Booker International Prize 73; Nobel Prize in Literature 1–2, 7–8, 36, 51, 55, 71–73, 84, 90, 91, 127, 166, 167, 214*n*3; Ontario Trillium Book Award 73, 166; the Oscar 212*n*11; PEN Malamud Award for Excel-

lence in Short Fiction 166, 214*n*4; Stephen Leacock Award for Humour 60; U.S. National Book Critics Circle Award 73, 166; W.H. Smith Award in England 166
The Progress of Love 56, 73, 77, 143, 166, 215*n*11
prose poetry/prose poem 9, 12, 26, 58, 106–7, 110–11, 203, 205, 207–9
Province Magazine 152
public reading 51, 73
publisher/publishing industry 3, 6–7, 8, 16, 19, 20, 29, 31, 32, 36, 38, 46, 47, 48, 75, 86, 87, 88, 90, 91, 162, 166, 214*ch*5*n*2; Boni & Liveright 36, 213*n*22; Coach House Press 48; Contact Publishing 36, 213*n*22; Exile 213*n*23; Faber and Faber 215*n*9; House of Anansi Press 48; Macmillan 19, 36, 213*n*23; Oberon Press 48; Oxford University Press 49; Penguin 72, 91; Porcupine's Quill Press 53; Random House 213*n*23; Scribner 19, 36, 37, 213*n*22, 213*n*23; Talonbooks 48; Three Mountains Press 36, 213*n*22
"Puzzle" 65, 132

Quebec ix, 5, 24, 25, 90, 220*n*19
Queen's Quarterly 20

"The Rabbit-pen" 212*n*9
race 123, 150
"The Race" 22
The Race 21, 22
racism 25, 122, 184–85, 211*n*3, 220*n*15
radio 25, 49, 60, 74
"The Rain Child" 61
Random House 213*n*23
"Rapunzel" 66
Real Mothers 66
"The Real Thing" 96
reader/readership/audience 1, 4, 10, 24, 39, 49, 50, 51, 54, 56, 60, 73, 74, 86, 89, 91, 96, 102, 166, 167, 176, 177, 178, 180, 181, 186–88, 190, 198, 202, 203, 207–8
realism 3–5, 6, 12, 16–19, 29, 54, 63, 64, 68–70, 190, 198, 200, 214*n*37; American 24; antirealism 50, 69; hyperrealism 7, 67, 69; magic 12, 190, 192, 198; neorealism 6, 50, 68–70; nonrealism 7; postrealism 50; prairie 6, 17–18, 50, 60, 61; psychological 18, 58, 201; realist-modernist tradition 7, 49, 50, 66, 69, 179; social 18, 24; super-realism 54; surrealism 7, 12, 64, 69, 192, 198, 200, 209
region/regionalism 3, 7, 8, 16–18, 32–33, 50, 59–63, 65, 75–76, 78, 86, 88, 89, 90, 92, 165, 167

religion 54, 92
"Rendezvous" 198
Resident Alien 53, 54
"Resources of the Ikarians" 204
"The Resplendent Quetzal" 58
"Reunion" 62
"The Revolutionist" 212*n*21
rewriting/reconstruction 110, 113, 172, 196, 204
Rich, Adrienne 172
Richards, David Adams 7, 63; *Dancers at Night* 63
Richler, Mordecai 69; *The Street* 69
Ricou, Laurence 21
rites of passage 118–19, 120, 216*ch*8*n*1, 218*n*9; *see also* liminality; van Gennep, Arnold
The Rites of Passage/Les rites de passage (French original) 118–19, 218*n*9
ritual 110, 118–20, 125, 137, 200
River of Stones: Fictions and Memories 61
"River Two Blind Jacks" 69
"The Road to Rankin's Point" 63
Roberts, Charles G. D. 1, 4–5, 15, 211*n*3, 212*n*13; "Do Seek Their Meat from God" 4; *Earth's Enigmas* 4
Robinson, Eden 151
roman-fleuve 54
romanticism 89, 92; German 95; postromanticism 18
Rooke, Constance 57, 121, 123, 124, 129, 189, 198, 202, 222*n*3
Rooke, Leon 7, 69; "Art" 69; *Hitting the Charts: Selected Stories* 69; "Wintering in Victoria" 69; "The Woman Who Talked to Horses" 69
A Room of One's Own 100
Rosenthal, Caroline 38, 177, 218*n*10
Ross, Sinclair 5–6, 18, 20–22, 47, 50, 60; *As for Me and My House* 20; "Circus in Town" 21; "Cornet at Night" 21; "A Day with Pegasus" 21; "The Flowers That Killed Him" 21; "Jug and Bottle" 21; *The Lamp at Noon* 20, 21, 22; "No Other Way" 22; "One's a Heifer" 21; "The Outlaw" 21, 22; "The Race" 22; *The Race* 21, 22; "The Runaway" 21; "Saturday Night" 21, 22; "Spike" 21
Roughing It in the Bush 87
Rule, Jane 7, 60, 64–65, 96, 118, 132; "Brother and Sister" 65; *Desert Hearts* (film based on Rule novel) 64; *Desert of the Heart* 64; "The End of Summer" 65; "Inland Passage" 65; *Inland Passage and Other Stories* 65, 132; "Joy" 65; "Lilian" 65; "My Father's House" 65; "Outlander"

65; *Outlander: Short Stories and Essays* 65; "Puzzle" 65, 132; "Slogans" 65; *Theme for Diverse Instruments* 65
Runaway 73, 166
"The Runaway" 21
rural *see* setting
Rushdie, Salman 220*n*15

"The Sale" 18
Salinger, J. D. 29, 35
"Salome Was a Dancer" 204
"Salon des Refusés" 66, 129–30, 132–33
"Sans Souci" 68
Sans Souci and Other Stories 68
sarcasm 194, 198–99
satire 12, 52, 58, 67, 87, 137, 147, 180, 186, 189, 191
The Saturday Evening Post 51
Saturday Night see magazine/literary magazine
"Saturday Night" 21, 22
Saturday Night 45, 51
"Saturday Night at the Crossroads" 18
"A Scarf" 67
Schaeffer, Jean-Marie 208–9, 224*n*10
Schoemperlen, Diane 7, 51, 67
Scobie, Stephen 27
Scotland 75, 181–87
Scott, Duncan Campbell 4, 5, 18, 88, 89, 212*n*13, 214*n*37; *In the Village of Viger* 4, 5, 88, 89, 212*n*13, 214*n*37
screenwriter/screenwriting 60
Scribner 19, 36, 37, 213*n*22, 213*n*23
Scribner's Magazine 19, 36, 38
"A Seat in the Garden" 198
Second Wave of the women's movement *see* feminism
Selected Stories 52, 166, 179, 214*n*10, 215*ch*6*n*2, 221*n*4
The Selected Stories of Clark Blaise 53
The Selected Stories of Mavis Gallant 58
sentimentalism 20–21, 24, 60; fiction 3, 4
"Le serpent qui danse" 110
Seton, Ernest Thompson 1, 4, 5, 15
setting 5, 6, 11, 16, 18, 19, 20, 22–23, 24, 32, 33, 38, 39–40, 57, 59, 60, 63, 75–76, 79, 88, 90, 119, 121, 125, 127, 128, 131, 140–42, 154–57, 159–61, 167–69, 178, 180; city 5, 6, 7, 10–11, 18, 19, 21, 22, 23, 24, 25, 32, 60, 125–26, 140–44, 145, 150–57, 159–63, 198–99 (*see also* urbanism); international 75, 167, 180; maritime 60, 63, 87; rural 11, 19, 22, 32, 55, 59–60, 63, 90, 92, 142, 144, 153, 160, 167–69, 173; small town 11, 19, 32, 55, 60–61, 75, 87, 90, 127–28, 155, 167–69

The Seven Arts 30
73: New Canadian Stories 180
sexism 101, 122, 170–75, 183–85; *see also* gender/gender relations, misogyny
Shakespeare, William 26, 59, 112; *Hamlet* 12, 59, 204
Shields, Carol 7, 64, 65, 66–67, 105, 118; "Absence" 67; "Chemistry" 66; "Death of an Artist" 66; *Dressing Up for the Carnival* 66–67; "Edith-Esther" 66; "Flitting Behaviour" 66; "Ilk" 67; "Love So Fleeting, Love So Fine" 66; "The Metaphor Is Dead—Pass It On" 67; "Milk Bread Beer Ice" 66; "Mrs. Turner Cutting the Grass" 67; "The Orange Fish" 66; *The Orange Fish* 66; "Our Men and Women" 67; "Pardon" 67; "A Scarf" 67; "Soup du Jour" 66; *The Stone Diaries* 66; *Swann: A Mystery* 66; "Various Miracles" 67; *Various Miracles* 66, 67
"The Shining Red Apple" 6, 39, 42–45
Shooting the Stars 179, 221*n*2, 221*ch*12*n*5
short fiction 8, 9, 10, 12, 16, 30, 203, 204; American 3; British 3; Canadian 1, 2–5, 7, 12, 15, 51, 52, 64, 86, 88, 96, 150, 176–78, 188, 189; Chinese Canadian 2, 10; definition 3; First Nations 2, 10, 67, 151; French Canadian 3, 50, 211*n*1, 211*n*2; postmodernist 50; Vancouver 10–11, 150, 152 (*see also* Vancouver fiction)
short fictions 9, 12, 106–7, 113, 203
"A Short History of Indians in Canada" 198–99
A Short History of Indians in Canada 137, 189, 193, 196, 200–1
short prose 4, 9, 11, 12, 88–89, 106, 190, 203, 209, 211*ch*2*n*3; *see also* short story: precursors/roots
short prose collection 2, 59, 203, 207
short story 2–4, 6, 7, 8, 10, 13, 28–30, 49, 51, 71–73, 77–78, 84, 88–89, 91–93, 110, 120–21, 124, 135, 178, 180, 204, 211*ch*2*n*3, 214*n*10, 215*ch*5*n*3, 215*ch*5*n*4, 215*ch*5*n*5, 224*n*11; American 1, 2, 4, 5, 6, 7, 15–16, 18, 28–47, 51, 89, 136, 137; Canadian 1–13, 15–72, 86–88, 91, 118, 136–37, 157, 166, 176, 179, 214*n*37; definition 15; North American 12, 28, 47, 131, 136, 190; precursors/roots 3–5, 87–88, 89; short 39–42, 110, 140, 198, 204
"A Short Story" 69
short story anthology 2, 4, 6, 15, 16, 32, 48, 50, 162, 178
short story book series 50, 178
short story collection 2, 48, 50, 51, 85, 88, 91, 110, 215*ch*5*n*5

short story cycle 2, 4, 7, 8, 55, 69, 78, 85–94, 107, 114, 116, 130, 166, 189, 203, 204, 214*ch5n*1
short story esthetics 8, 10, 15, 30, 32, 56, 75, 77–78, 135, 167–68
short story theory 209
"Significant Moments in the Life of My Mother" 9, 101–5, 109
"Simon's Luck" 56, 79
Simple Recipes 159
"Simple Sufferings" 222*n*1
"The Sins of Tomas Benares" 69
Sixteen by Twelve: Short Stories by Canadian Writers 49, 178
sketch 3, 4, 61, 87, 88, 89, 90, 211*ch2n*3; *see also* short story: precursors/roots
The Sketch Book of Geoffrey Crayon, Gent. 89
Sketches of American Character 89
slapstick 191, 198
slavery 139
slice-of-life story 121, 167
"Slogans" 65
small town *see* setting
Smart, Elizabeth 213*n*36
The Smart Set 33, 213*n*33
Smith, Ray 7, 51, 54–55, 69, 178; "Cape Breton Is the Thought Control Centre of Canada" 55; *Lord Nelson Tavern* 55; "The Princess, the Boeing, and the Hot Pastrami Sandwich" 54–55
"Snow" 17–18
social critique 3, 211*ch2n*3
social realism *see* realism
social sciences 119
Sohngen, Mary 123
Soja, Edward W. 140
Sojourner's Truth 68
Something I've Been Meaning to Tell You 55, 56, 74, 78, 166
"Sophie" 154, 157, 162
The Sound of Music 182
"Soup du Jour" 66
South, the American 31, 33, 76
South, the Canadian *see* setting
Southern Stories 53
space 10, 22, 26, 66, 78, 81, 100–1, 120, 125, 131–32, 100–1, 140, 143, 149, 151–52, 154–55, 157, 163, 170, 173, 181–82, 186, 221*ch12n*7, 222*n*12
"Spelling" 217*n*10
Spettigue, Douglas O. 17
"Spike" 21
Spit Delaney's Island 62, 90
Le spleen de Paris 110
Splint, Sarah Field 115; *The Art of Cooking and Serving* 115

A Sportsman's Sketches 85
Standing Stones: The Best Stories of John Metcalf 52, 179
The Starry Night 133
state-of-mind story 16
"States to Avoid" 200
Stefan, Verena 97
Stein, Gertrude 26, 29, 41, 45–46, 213*n*27
Stephen Leacock Award for Humour 60
stereotype 23, 111–13, 122–23, 141, 147–48, 172, 173, 186–87, 191, 220*n*15
Stevens, Peter 33
Stewart's Quarterly 90
The Stone Diaries 66
Stone Mattress 107
A Story Teller's Story 30
storytelling 102–5, 189–91, 200, 202, 222*n*6; indigenous/Native 189–91, 193–96
"The Strange Aberration of Mr. Ken Smythe" 11, 52, 176, 179–88, 215*ch6n*2
Strange Fugitive 37
"The Strawstack" 16, 31
stream of consciousness 52, 65
The Street 69
The Strickland Sisters *see* Traill, Catharine Parr; Moodie, Susanna
Struck, Karin 97
structure 3, 4, 10, 16, 35, 59, 63, 69, 78, 90–93, 103, 120, 121, 127, 129, 130, 157, 167, 168, 170, 180, 182, 189
Struthers, John Russell 51, 76, 85, 91, 166, 178
Stuewe, Paul 24
style/language 3, 5, 12, 13, 16–17, 18, 19–20, 23, 25–26, 34, 37–38, 41–42, 43, 45, 56, 57–58, 59, 62, 66, 78, 80, 97, 99, 103, 116, 127, 130, 176, 177–80, 181, 182, 184, 189, 190, 192, 196, 199, 200, 201–2, 204–9, 212*n*19
The Style of Innocence 213*n*32
subgenre *see* genre
subsidy 49, 52, 86
subversion 111–12, 116
Summer at Lonely Beach 140
Sunshine Sketches of a Little Town 88, 90
surrealism *see* realism
Survival 116
Sutherland, Fraser 213*n*32; *The Style of Innocence* 213*n*32
Swann: A Mystery 66
"Swimming Lessons" 68, 215*ch6n*2
symbolism 13, 16, 18, 19, 21, 22, 25, 26, 34, 39–42, 100, 101, 102–3, 126, 128, 141–42, 153, 160, 161, 171, 173, 174, 179, 181–82, 186, 199, 205, 209; spatial 39–40, 161; temporal 40, 161

Index

"Take Charge" 204
tale 113, 216ch7n2; adventure 4; fairy 113, 194, 205; folk 89, 113 (*see also* short story: precursors/roots); tall 3, 60
Tales from Firozsha Baag 68, 215ch6n2
Tales from the Margin: Selected Stories of Frederick Philip Grove 17, 18
tall tale *see* tale
Talonbooks 48
Tamarack Review 74
"The Tattooed Woman" 64
The Tattooed Woman 64
"The Teeth of My Father" 52, 179
The Teeth of My Father 52, 180, 221n4
television 60
Ten Green Bottles 65, 66
"The Tent" 13, 110, 207–8, 223n6
The Tent 2, 3, 12, 107, 203–9
terra incognita 89
Thacker, Robert 168, 173
"That Summer in Paris" 37
That Summer in Paris 36, 38–39, 45
theme 5, 9, 10, 17, 20, 23, 24, 33, 34, 57, 58, 59, 61, 76, 96, 105, 107, 109, 111, 120, 121, 135–36, 150, 167, 168, 177, 178, 179, 191–93, 200–1
Theme for Diverse Instruments 65
Die Theorie des Romans 215n10
Thien, Madeleine 11, 70, 159, 162–63; "A Map of the City" 159–62; *Simple Recipes* 159
"Things As They Are?" 215ch6n2
Things As They Are? Short Stories 62, 215ch6n2
This Quarter 19, 31, 36, 212n10
Thomas, Audrey 7, 10, 60, 64, 65–66, 69, 96, 118, 129, 132–33; "Aquarius" 66; *Goodbye Harold, Good Luck* 66; "If One Green Bottle" 65; "Initram" 66; *Ladies and Escorts* 66; "The Man with Clam Eyes" 66; "Miss Foote" 132; "Out in the Midday Sun" 66; *Path of Totality* 132; "Rapunzel" 66; *Real Mothers* 66; "Salon des Refusés" 66, 129–30, 132–33; *Ten Green Bottles* 65, 66; "Two in the Bush" 66; *Two in the Bush* 66; "Xanadu" 66
Thomassen, Bjørn 119–20, 216ch8n1, 216ch8n2
Thomson, Edward William 4, 211n3, 212n13
"Three Halves of a House" 54
Three Mountains Press 36, 213n22
Three Stories & Ten Poems 36, 213n22
threshold *see* liminality
"Thylacine Ragout" 223ch14n9
Tieck, Ludwig 95, 215ch6n1; *Franz Sternbalds Wanderungen* 215ch6n1

"Till Death Us Do Part" 22
time 57, 120, 125, 131, 132, 143
Time Magazine 56
"The Tomorrow-Tamer" 61
The Tomorrow-Tamer 61
Tonio Kröger 96
Too Much Happiness 56, 79, 166, 214n3
Toronto 19, 24, 25, 38, 45, 54, 59, 60, 97, 140–42, 198
Toronto Daily Star 20
Toronto Star 36
Toronto Star Weekly 31
"Totem" 198
"Tradition and the Individual Talent" 16, 31
tragedy/tragic element 12; Greek 27
tragicomic element 199, 201
Traill, Catharine Parr 3, 87, 89, 211ch2n3; *The Backwoods of Canada* 87
transcendentalism 54
transculturalism 57, 68, 108, 151, 152
Transfigurations 68
translation 4, 73, 86, 87, 97
transnationalism 149, 218n18
"Trap Lines" 200
trauma 148, 158–59
travel 58, 118, 120, 125–26, 129, 130, 132–34, 140–42, 143–49, 180–81; literature 145, 147, 218n17
"A Travel Piece" 58
Travelling Ladies 68
"Travelling Northward" 52, 221n2
Tribal Justice 54
trickster figure 193, 195–97, 202; indigenous 193–98, 223n11
trickster story 12, 192, 195–96
The Triumph of the Egg 30, 31, 33
The Trouble with Heroes: And Other Stories 62
Trudeau, Pierre Elliott 159
Truth and Bright Water 135
Turgenev, Ivan 29, 85, 211n5; *Annals of a Sportsman* 211n5; *A Sportsman's Sketches* 85
Turner, Victor 10, 118–20, 124, 149
Twain, Mark 3, 18, 29, 34, 87; *The Adventures of Huckleberry Finn* 34
The Two-Headed Calf 67
"Two-Headed Poems" 107
"Two in the Bush" 66
Two in the Bush 66
"The Two Sisters" 153, 157, 162

"Uglypuss" 59
Ulysses 42
"Uncles" 109, 114

"Under Glass" 58
Underground Railroad 139; *see also* slavery
"Unearthing Suite" 109, 215*ch*6*n*4
United Nations Declaration of Human Rights 219*n*2
U.S.-Canadian relations *see* Canadian-U.S. relations
U.S. National Book Critics Circle Award 73, 166
United States of America 8, 10, 17, 19, 22–23, 28–29, 31, 32, 36, 38–47, 50, 53, 55, 58, 59, 73, 75, 86, 87, 89, 91, 125–26, 136–39, 141–45, 148–49, 187, 196–97
University of Windsor Review 49
urbanism 6, 22, 142, 151–52, 155, 163, 220*n*20; *see also* setting: city
Urquhart, Jane 96

Valgardson, W. D. 7, 51, 68; "Bloodflowers" 68; *Bloodflowers: Ten Stories* 68; *The Divorced Kids Club: And Other Stories* 68; "A Matter of Balance" 68; *What Can't Be Changed Shouldn't Be Mourned: Short Stories* 68
Vancouver 6, 10–11, 22, 60, 66, 74, 81, 143, 150–62, 219*n*1; Chinatown 150–52, 159; *see also* cultural location
Vancouver fiction 151–53, 157, 162
Vancouver Island 62, 64, 74, 90; Victoria (British Columbia) 74, 153–54
Vancouver Short Stories 152
The Vancouver Stories: West Coast Fiction from Canada's Best Writers 152
The Vancouver Sun 73
Vanderhaeghe, Guy 7, 51, 60, 62, 215*ch*6*n*2; "Cages" 62; "Drummer" 62; "Man Descending" 62; *Man Descending: Selected Stories* 62; "Reunion" 62; "Things As They Are?" 215*ch*6*n*2; *Things As They Are? Short Stories* 62, 215*ch*6*n*2; *The Trouble with Heroes: And Other Stories* 62; "The Watcher" 62
van Gennep, Arnold 10, 118–20, 216*ch*8*n*1, 218*n*9; *The Rites of Passage/Les rites de passage* (French original) 118–19, 218*n*9
van Gogh, Vincent 133; *The Starry Night* 133
"Various Miracles" 67
Various Miracles 66, 67
Ventura, Heliane 221*n*6, 212*n*12
"A Very Short Story" 212*n*21
Victorianism 50
Vietnam War 108, 135, 139
The View from Castle Rock 166
Vintage Munro 166

Violation of the Virgins 24
violence 137–39, 148, 187, 217*n*4
"Virus X" 58
"Vision" 63
Vizenor, Gerald 202
"Voice" 13, 206–7, 209
voice piece 190, 199–200
von Flotow, Luise 97
von Goethe, Johann Wolfgang 95, 105, 215*ch*6*n*6; *Wilhelm Meisters Lehrjahre* 95, 105, 215*ch*6*n*6; *Wilhelm Meisters Wanderjahre* 95

Waddington, Miriam 10, 140, 142–43, 147; "I'm Lonesome for Harrisburg" 140–43, 147; *Summer at Lonely Beach* 140
"Walker Brothers Cowboy" 75
Walton, Priscilla 222*n*6, 222*ch*13*n*8
war 111, 139, 185; draft dodgers 139; Vietnam War 108, 135, 139; World War I 40; World War II 39, 57, 96, 123, 140, 185, 187, 219*n*2, 220*n*20
"The War in the Bathroom" 59
Wascana Review 49
"The Watcher" 62
Watson, Sheila 6, 26–27; "And the Four Animals" 26, 27; "Antigone" 27; *Five Stories* 26, 27; *Four Stories* (early version of *Five Stories*) 26
"We All Begin in a Little Magazine" 49
"We Have to Sit Opposite" 22, 23
Weaver, Robert 7, 49, 50, 52, 74; *CBC Anthology* 49, 74
"Weight" 110, 215*ch*6*n*5
Welty, Eudora 29, 76
Western Canada 6, 7, 22, 60, 61, 62, 65, 74, 75, 79–81, 90, 167
Western discourse 153, 191
Western societies 119–20, 121–23
W.H. Smith Award in England 166
Wharton, Edith 29
What Can't Be Changed Shouldn't Be Mourned: Short Stories 68
"What Is Remembered" 132
"Where Is the Voice Coming From?" 61–62
Where Is the Voice Coming From? 61
"Where the Myth Touches Us" 215*ch*6*n*2
"White Dump" 56
Who Do You Think You Are?/The Beggar Maid: Stories of Flo and Rose (American and British edition) 55, 56, 73, 74, 78, 79, 91, 93, 94, 166, 214*n*3, 214*n*9, 220*n*1
Who Has Seen the Wind 60
Widdowson, H.G. 205
Wiebe, Rudy 7, 18, 60, 61–62, 69; "The

Angel of the Tar Sands" 61; *The Angel of the Tar Sands and Other Stories* 61; *Collected Stories: 1955–2010* 61; "The Naming of Albert Johnson" 62; *River of Stones: Fictions and Memories* 61; "Where Is the Voice Coming From?" 61–62; *Where Is the Voice Coming From?* 61

wilderness 208; Canadian 4–5, 25, 59, 86, 109

"Wilderness Tips" 59

Wilderness Tips 58, 59, 107, 109, 114, 215ch6n5

Wilhelm Meisters Lehrjahre 95, 105, 215ch6n6

Wilhelm Meisters Wanderjahre 95

Will Ye Let the Mummers In? 63

Williams, William Carlos 37, 179

Wilson, Ethel 6, 22–23, 27; "The Birds" 23; "Fog" 22; "Haply the Soul of My Grandmother" 22; "Hurry, Hurry" 22, 23; *Mrs. Golightly and Other Stories* 22, 23; "Mrs. Golightly and the First Convention" 23; "On Nimpish Lake" 22; "Till Death Us Do Part" 22; "We Have to Sit Opposite" 22, 23; "The Window" 22

Wilson, Milton 19

Wilson, Sharon R. 203

"The Window" 22

Winesburg, Ohio 29, 30, 31, 85, 89

Wingham (Ontario) 74, 165, 169, 220n4, 221ch11n6

Winners Take Nothing 213n22

Winnipeg 67

Winnipeg Tribune Magazine 17

"Wintering in Victoria" 69

"Winter's Tales" 205, 223n6

"The Woman Who Talked to Horses" 69

women/female 11, 21, 42, 61, 64, 96–105, 109–14, 116, 159, 170–75; perspective 11, 17, 25, 42, 55, 64–67, 76, 96–105, 100–3, 167–75; tradition 9, 101, 103–5; writer 3, 6–7, 9, 23, 27, 46, 55–59, 63–67, 72, 76, 96–97, 100–5, 111, 211ch2n3; *see also* gender/gender relations; men/male; misogyny

Women's Liberation movement *see* feminism

women's magazine 9, 59, 112

"Women's Novels" 59

Woodcock, George 38–39

Woodward, Kathleen 123

Woolf, Virginia 23, 100; *A Room of One's Own* 100

World Body 53

world literature 4, 9, 23, 36, 59, 75, 85, 96, 112

World War I 40

World War II 39, 57, 96, 123, 140, 185, 187, 219n2, 220n20

"Worship" 59, 110

The Writer's Book 30, 212n8

writer's writer 56, 73, 168, 179, 214ch4n2

Wyatt-Brown, Anne M. 123, 124; "Literary Gerontology Comes of Age" 124

Wyile, Herb 10, 149

"Xanadu" 66

"The Years in Exile" 52, 179

"The Yellow Sweater" 24

The Yellow Sweater 24

"Yin Chin" 68

www.ingramcontent.com/pod-product-compliance
Lightning Source LLC
Chambersburg PA
CBHW051213300426
44116CB00006B/559